The Lutheran Church Past and Present

Edited by Vilmos Vajta

AUGSBURG PUBLISHING HOUSE
Minneapolis, Minnesota

The Lutheran Church - Past and Present

Copyright (c) 1977 Augsburg Publishing House

Library of Congress Catalog Card No. 76-46120

International Standard Book No. 0-8066-1573-7

Scripture quotations unless otherwise noted are from the Revised
Standard Version of the Bible, copyright 1946, 1952, and 1971 by
the Division of Christian Education of the National Council of
Churches.

Title of original German version:

Die Evangelisch-Lutherische Kirche - Vergangenheit und Gegenwart

Evangelisches Verlagswerk, Stuttgart 1976.

Manufactured in the United States of America

CONTENTS

ABBREVIATIONS

AELC	Association of Evangelical Lutheran Churches (USA)
ALC	The American Lutheran Church (USA)
Apol.	Apology of the Augsburg Confession (see: BC)
BEK	Bund Evangelischer Kirchen (GDR)
BC	*The Book of Concord*. The Confession of the Evangelical Lutheran Church. Trans. and ed. by Th.G. Tappert, Philadelphia: Fortress, 1959.
CA	Confessio Augustana (Augsburg Confession) (see: BC)
CLC	Canadian Lutheran Council
DDR	Deutsche Demokratische Republik (also: GDR)
EKD	Evangelische Kirche Deutschlands
EKU	Evangelische Kirche der Union
ELCC	Evangelical Lutheran Church of Canada
Ep	Epitome of the Formula of Concord (see: BC)
FC	Formula of Concord (see: BC)
FRG	Federal Republic of Germany (Bundesrepublik Deutschland)
LCA	Lutheran Church of America
LCUSA	Lutheran Council in the USA
LC-MS	Lutheran Church - Missouri Synod
Lg Cat	The Large Catechism of M. Luther (see: BC)
LR	*Lutherische Rundschau*
Luth W	*Lutheran World* - Publication of the LWF
LW	*Luther's Works*. American Edition. Philadelphia - St. Louis
LWC	Lutheran World Convention
LWF	The Lutheran World Federation
NLC	National Lutheran Council (USA)
SELC	Synod of Evangelical Lutheran Churches
Sm Art	Smalkald Articles (see: BC)
Sm Cat	The Small Catechism of M. Luther (see: BC)
Sol Decl	Solid Declaration of Formula of Concord (see: BC)
Tappert	see: BC
Tract.	*Treatise on the Power and Primacy of the Pope* (see: BC)
VELK	Vereinigte Evangelisch-Lutherische Kirche (in der/DDR)
VELKD	Vereinigte Evangelisch/Lutherische Kirche (in der BRD)
WA	Weimar Edition of M. Luther's Works
WA-Br	Weimar Edition - Letters of M. Luther
WA-T	Weimar Edition - Table-talks of M. Luther

PREFACE

This book is a presentation of the world-wide Lutheran
church. Theologians and church leaders describe the past and
present situation of their own church using historical and
theological analyses and portray her specific task which has been
handed down from the Reformation. Such an undertaking carries
with it a certain risk. First of all, in such a limited space
only a selection of relevant problems can be dealt with. The
authors and the editor hope, however, that they have made a
representative choice with regard to subject which will satisfy
both the expert on the Lutheran church as well as those readers
who are not of the Lutheran tradition. There is however, perhaps
a risk in the fact that no "outside" opinion is expressed in this
book. It might be asked whether we know ourselves sufficiently
and whether unconscious characteristics, which certainly belong
to the phenomenon of Lutheranism, as they do to any other church,
might not be brought more appropriately to memory by those outside of the Lutheran tradition.

Nevertheless, risky as our task may be, we are of the
opinion that for the Lutheran church as also for the Church of
Jesus Christ as a whole it is of decisive importance at present
how a church sees herself or at least how she would like to be
understood. For this reason the identity of our church has been
chosen as a study project by the Institute for Ecumenical Research
in Strasbourg (France). The plan for this book was worked out by
common effort of the research staff. It is in this framework that
this book seeks to fulfil its function. It is an aid to finding
our own identity and attempts to clarify the question of which
task is alloted to this identity within Christianity as a whole:
does the "Lutheran voice" hold a special *charisma* in ecumenism?
How has our church made use of this opportunity? How can her
genuine call for the edification of the Church of Jesus Christ be
made loud again in the midst of the present conditions in a changing

world? We have not tried to draw a veil over the fact that such questions include problems which need honest re-examination. Consequently, our aim is not a book on Lutheran self-justification but rather a searching of conscience in the present historical hour, so that we become able to represent the witness of Jesus Christ and to carry out the task our Lord has given us.

This book takes three approaches in investigating these problems. The historical origin of the Reformation and the different types of European Lutheranism in the 16th century are portrayed. (Part One). From the Reformation until the present time the identity of the Lutheran church is examined on the basis of fundamental theological themes (Part Two). Finally the problems of today are portrayed in some geographically oriented case-studies (Part Three). The editor has made an attempt to indicate the basic themes of the contributions by giving introductory comments on the three parts, thus bringing the readers' attention to the general perspective of the book. A connection between the different essays as well as between the readers and the individual authors could thereby be furthered.

We owe thanks to the Augsburg Publishing House for their interest which makes the publication of an American edition of this book possible. Twenty years ago they published the book "Lutheran Churches of the World", edited by Carl E. Lund-Quist under the auspices of the Lutheran World Federation. The occasion was its Fourth World Assembly in Minneapolis, Minn. 1957. This present book itself is appearing in the year of the Sixth World Assembly of the LWF which is scheduled for Dar-Es-Salaam (Tanzania). Though it be in another form compared to twenty years ago, this enquiry into the mission and loyalty of our churches should aid the discovery of our identity in a new world.

Institute for Ecumenical Research
Strasbourg, France
October 1976

                                        The Editor

PART ONE:

FROM REFORM MOVEMENT TO

THE EMERGENCE OF THE LUTHERAN CHURCH

The existence of the Lutheran church is in no way to be taken for granted. As a historical development it can only be explained as one which was forced by diverse factors - not all of them theological! The theological incentive of the Reformation was not enough to create a church. For the Reformation is primarily to be understood as a call inside the one and indivisible church, as a call for her theological and pastoral renewal. The division of the church is no basic Reformation principle, but an unavoidable necessity. Thus the entanglement of the church at that time with European politics played an essential role. Therefore the theological quarrel in the Reformation period was by necessity a decision about the relationship of the church to the secular power. Only in this way could a confrontation between two different conceptions, which basically intended to be theologically motivated, come about on the political (and military) battle field. The task of the historically oriented contributions in the first part of this book is to investigate the whole complex nature of this development.

The introductory essay (Chapter 1) portrays Martin Luther's original call for the reformation of the church. Here it becomes evident that Luther's new theological motivations can in no way be explained as being a consequence of his personality. The response to his call proves the contrary. Through the interference of Rome, and those bound to her politically, not only were the universities and the regional churches shaken to their foundations, but so also was the political balance of power in the empire. The theological-ecclesiastical quarrel brought not only canonical

proceedings but also a call to appear before the emperor and the
secular princes. The religious question was brought before the
diet. Divided sympathies for or against the Reformation accompanied the proclamation of the Gospel in its new reforming impetus.

Since these factors of political power could not lead to
a decision, the result of the theological division was a corresponding political division in the empire. It was only on the
basis of these facts that the cause of the Reformation was by
necessity forced to become institutionalized because of the
existing inner drive to create a church. The following essay
(Chapter 2) demonstrates that at first it resulted in a largely
provisional side-by-side arrangement of theological-ecclesiastical
tendencies, which even brought with them territorial division.
It was only possible for a "Lutheran church" to emerge as an
institution when the authority of Rome and her bishops could no
longer be accepted. This situation immediately put the problem
of the relationship to the secular authority in a new way. The
gap left by the cessation of papal and imperial authority was
filled by the quarrel between the reformers with their individual
princes, which came to a head particularly over the question of
powers of visitation.

Through the investigations of the historical development
in different areas by the essays in this book it should become
clear to the reader in what diverse ways the forced emergence of
the church in the Reformation took place. Two areas, in addition
to the neutralized political powers in the German Empire, are of
particular significance for Lutheranism. First, attention is
focused on the Scandinavian countries (Chapter 3). Here, the
transition of the medieval church to the Reformation happened in
the way originally intended. The motivations of the reformers
were supported here by a strong royal power which found independence from Rome a political advantage and which was sympathetic
to the religious renewal of the people through the efficacy of
the national reformers. Of course, the transition to the Reformation did not take place here without opposition first from the
Catholics and later from the Calvinists. However the forces of
the Scandinavian Reformation were strong enough to survive those
conflicts as well as those with the political authorities.

Things developed differently in those European countries
where the authorities were Catholic. Thus the Latin peoples have
remained alien to the Lutheran Reformation not only because the
"Germanic spirit" might not have been appropriate for them. The
union between the papal and the respective secular powers resulted

in severe persecutions which repressed the call to the Reformation.
In spite of this a Lutheran church did come into being (especially
in the East European countries) though it was a struggle
involving great sacrifice.   Chapter 4 shows impressively that this
has a decisive significance for the self-understanding of these
Lutheran minority churches up to the present day.   This historical
background is a disadvantage for both partners in the ecumenical
dialogue.   In the Reformation period the Lutheran minorities
had already placed much hope on the help of the newly-evangelical
countries.   Through the action of the Swedish king, Gustav-Adolf
II, in support of religious freedom, Reformation tendencies were
supported in the Thirty Years War.   At that time this resulted in
a freedom gradually achieved and in an independent existence.
Today the result has led to the present political engagement of
the Protestants for human rights.

In the following essays the way from the call to the
Reformation of the church to the emergence of independent Lutheran
churches is shown.   The essays intend not only to portray the
historical events but to bring attention, as it were, to the fact
that the "Structure of Lutheranism" (W. Elert) in its respective
historical context has created decisive differences.   In the
emergence of the Lutheran church this context can be characterized
as national and political.   In its country of origin, the existence
of the Reformation was safe-guarded by religious balance and
confessional tolerance.   In the north of Europe the type of unified
national church has developed, whereas in Central and Eastern
Europe it took the form of a confessing minority church.

CHAPTER 1

BERNHARD LOHSE

THE CALL FOR
THE REFORMATION OF THE CHURCH

Reform and Reformation

The Reformation of the sixteenth century led to the
division - not yet overcome today - of the western church as well
as to the formation of different confessional churches. This
division however was not Luther's original intention. What
Luther wanted was the reformation of the whole church according
to the New Testament. Luther's Catholic opponents also did not
desire a division of the one church. Rather both sides took for
granted that the church in its essence can only be one. The
question could only be if the church, the way it was, had become
unfaithful to its true essence; but the struggle for the true as
against the false church was something different than the attempt
to reunite divided churches.

Actually, the idea of the one church was an ideal that
was never quite reached in reality. There were divisions in all
periods. Many of the small groups that separated from the main
church in early times would be called denominations today. The
Middle Ages brought the schism between the western and eastern
church which we still have today. But even in the west the unity
of the church could only be preserved against movements like the
Cathari, Albigensians and Waldensians by the use of great force.
Already against the movement started by Wycliffe (d. 1384), Rome
could no longer entirely enforce its will. The Hussites in

particular, in spite of the execution of their leader Hus (1415),
were able to hold their own. They were even able to gain a
certain amount of recognition by the church in the "Compactata"
of 1433. In any case, they gave the west the first example of
a church independent from Rome.

These "heretical" movements would have never arisen if
there had not been such a great decline of the church and theology
in many areas since the high Middle Ages. Excesses in the worship
of saints or in the practice of indulgences, especially in
indulgences for the dead, and numerous abuses in the assignment
of church offices were rather the result than the cause of this
decline. Many of these deeper causes could only have been
corrected by the church itself with great difficulty. That is
especially true of papal power politics and the development of
the church-state into a territory which differed from other
countries only through the claim of primacy made by its papal
ruler. To change these conditions a shift in the balance of the
European powers would have been necessary, which only could
become possible on the basis of the Reformation.

But precisely the difficulty in overcoming these widespread abuses within the church was the reason that the criticism
of the church's decline and the many reform movements grew more
radical. The reform councils of the fifteenth century were able
to overcome the papal schisms. They decided at the same time
however that the council stands over the pope. The tensions
between the pope and the council as they arose in the fifteenth
century caused the popes in the sixteenth century to resist a
reform council for a long time. Limited movements like the reform
of the orders had more success, however only in certain areas.
Last but not least, the *Devotio moderna* with its quiet and deep
piety led to an inner spirituality. But the "reform from top to
bottom" (*in capite et membris*) demanded by many could not come
from these movements.

Many of these later medieval reform movements were important for Luther and perhaps even more for the Reformation movement
he began, in so far as they prepared the ground for a reform.
Nevertheless, Luther's call for the reformation of the church was
basically different from the criticism of abuses and from the
reform movements in the period before him. What Luther attacked
were not primarily abuses in certain areas of the life of the
church, but the decline in its theology and preaching. To be
sure, already the young Luther also criticized the signs of decay,
for example in monasticism. Far more important however was the

criticism Luther directed against the false striving for security
or self-righteousness. It was this basic rejection of self-
righteousness that made his criticism of individual abuses so
powerful and effective. The call for the reformation of the
church, which Luther brought before the public in 1517, is thus
the result of a new theology and only understandable as such.

The New Theological Starting Point of the Young Luther

The early Luther did not yet have a complete new theology,
but he worked it out step by step mainly in the preparation of
his lectures. These lectures, which Luther held on the Psalms
1513 to 1515, on Romans 1515-16, on Galatians 1516-17 and on
Hebrews 1517-18 reveal in many respects the development of his
theology.

First of all, Luther wrestled with an unusual intensity
with the meaning of Scripture. In the lectures on the Psalms, he
worked especially on the Christological and the so-called
tropological interpretation. As far as the former is concerned,
the Christological interpretation of the Psalms as such was
nothing new. New and unprecedented however was the fact that
Luther not only related the royal attributes such as "Son" or
"King" to Christ, but also the statements about suffering and
God-forsakenness. With the help of the tropological interpretation,
which had long served the "application", Luther applied Scripture
radically to the individual and the church. That led to his
strict understanding of God's Word as a judgment that man has to
accept in humility and faith; when man accepts God's judgment, he
receives the divine righteousness. The severe message of judgment
was soon to become the basic theme of the call for reformation.

In the lecture on Romans Luther further developed his
understanding of righteousness, justification and faith. From the
very beginning he said that righteousness is always "foreign",
"reckoned to" us. Here for the first time the idea is found that
the believer is "sinner and just at the same time". Sinner, in
so far as he looks at himself, just however in so far as he hopes
in the fulfillment of the divine promise. This new understanding
of righteousness and justification led in the following lectures
to a gradual reshaping of many of the church's doctrines.

The Reformation Break-Through

It is a matter of debate when Luther made his Reformation discovery. Some scholars date it 1518; the year 1514 however is more probable. This discovery was important for Luther personally as well as for his whole understanding of Scripture. We know that Luther entered a monastery in 1505 because he was anxious about the salvation of his soul. Actually the question of how he could find a gracious God had plagued him constantly. His fear and uncertainty were intensified by the question of whether he belonged to the damned. These doubts were basically caused by the fact that late medieval theology taught that man was able to love God above all things and keep his commandments, and that Luther conscientiously sought to live according to these teachings. By honest self-examination Luther had to recognize however that at best man can only attain the outward "appearance" of good works, but cannot fulfill the real meaning of the commandments. Thus there could be no final certainty of salvation for Luther. We are not justified however in seeing Luther as unusually scrupulous. And the attempts to interpret his doubts as arising from a conflict with his father or as the search for his own identity are not sufficiently documented in the sources.

Theologically Luther's Reformation discovery says that God's righteousness is not judging, but righteousness is a gift through which God justifies us. This righteousness cannot be earned by man in any way, but man can receive it only by faith. This is the way Luther understood Romans 1:17 which before had been a stumbling block for him. Thus the Reformation discovery was at the same time both exegetical and existential, but neither of these aspects can be emphasized to the exclusion of the other. Although a psychoanalytical interpretation hardly does justice to the real nature of Luther's doubts, Luther and the Reformation he shaped were unique in the fact that they understood the Word of God above all as comfort in the midst of doubt.

The Beginning of the Conflict with Rome

In 1512 Luther became a professor of theology in Wittenberg. In accordance with his doctoral oath he bore responsibility for the teaching and proclamation of the church. Besides his lectures, he always preached; in addition to that for a long period he held and conscientiously discharged different offices in his

order. But it was through academic disputations that he had his
most important and far-reaching influence. At that time such
disputations were every day occurrences at the university. In
his disputations however Luther occasionally took up questions of
eminent theological significance. Especially important was the
Disputation Against Scholastic Theology on September 4, 1517 in
which he flatly rejected the "Pelagians" of his time and also
criticized the influence of Aristotelian philosophy on theology.
It is significant that Luther, at the end of these theses,
emphasized that he had not said anything that did not agree with
the Catholic church and the teachings of the church (LW 31, p. 16).

Of far greater impact however were the *Ninety-five theses -*
or *Disputation on the power and efficacy of indulgences* which
Luther sent his church superior Archbishop Albert of Mainz on
October 31, 1517. Luther probably also nailed these theses on
the door of the Castle Church in Wittenberg. In any case, because
he also sent them to many friends, these theses became very widely
known in a short time. A voice was heard in them which had not
been heard before. What was new in the 95 Theses was not so much
this or that idea which appeared here for the first time, but
rather that the 95 Theses constituted a single call to the church
to repent.

True, Luther first of all attacked indulgences. He did
not yet reject indulgences outright, but limited them to the
temporal penalties imposed by the church. He rejected the church's
claim that indulgences had an effect on purgatory. Above all
Luther rejected the false trust in indulgences. The meaning of
repentance was also new in these theses: Luther understood
repentance not as a sacrament, but as the basic stance of the
believer. The first thesis read: "When our Lord and Master Jesus
Christ said, 'Repent' he willed the entire life of believers to be
one of repentance." (LW 31, 25, thesis no. 1). Repentance here
is not only an inward attitude, but is always also expressed in
"various outward mortifications of the flesh" (LW 31, 25, thesis
no. 3).

The 95 Theses also indirectly contained a new understanding
of the spiritual office. The pope, Luther said, can forgive sin
only in the sense that he announces and confirms that God has
already forgiven it (LW 31, 26, thesis no. 6). He emphasized the
duty of bishops and pastors to prohibit the false preaching of
indulgences. Far more important was the preaching of the Gospel:
"The true treasure of the Church is the most holy Gospel of the
glory and grace of God." (LW 31, 31, thesis no. 62).

The views that Luther put forth in the 95 Theses could not
at all be called uncatholic. Nevertheless, it was generally felt
that what they implied was more than what they said. It is
therefore understandable that many theologians who were true to
Rome sharply attacked Luther and accused him of heresy; the most
important of them was Johannes von Eck. But in so doing they
rejected the critical demands of the New Testament upon the church
of their time and self-righteously defended its authority. Luther
was soon charged with heresy; ecclesiastical proceedings against
him were started. Dangerous for Luther was the fact that he was
seen as renewing earlier heresies, above all those of Johann Hus.

In his *Resolutions Concerning the Virtue of Indulgences*
(1518) Luther explained in more detail much of what was only
touched on in the theses themselves. Here it became clear that
his real concern was nothing more and nothing less than the
authority of Christ. Christ is as it were "a divine lawgiver"
(LW 31, thesis no. 88). That means that his word alone, not that
of the pope, must be authoritative in the church (LW 31, 103).
And this must be understood as the basis on which Luther here
for the first time calls for a reformation of the church:

> The church needs a Reformation which is not
> the work of one man, namely, the pope, or of many
> men, namely the cardinals, both of which the most
> recent council has demonstrated, but it is the
> work of the whole world, indeed it is the work of
> God alone. However, only God who has created time
> knows the time for this reformation. In the mean-
> time we cannot deny such manifest wrongs. The
> power of the keys is abused and enslaved to greed
> and ambition. The raging abyss has received added
> impetus. We cannot stop it. (LW 31, 250).

Luther's Understanding of Reformation

Luther's call for a reformation of the church was not
limited either then or later to the demand that certain reforms
be introduced. Luther did not want to push through a program.
Instead he called for a reformation because the spiritual power
of the church had become weak and God's Word was hardly heard.
A reformation, which finally only God himself can bring about,
is therefore first of all judgment upon the unbelief and self-
righteousness of men. This reformation can only be carried out
when God's Word is once again proclaimed in the church.

This understanding of reformation is also decisive for
Luther's own self-understanding. Luther did not see himself as

a reformer as such. He did not claim to have received any special revelations. When he later on could occasionally say that he did not receive the Gospel from men, but directly from heaven through our Lord Jesus Christ so that he could indeed call himself a servant and an evangelist (LW 48, 390), he was not thinking in terms of some new revelation of the Spirit, but of the renewal of the final revelation of God in Jesus Christ. It is also characteristic when Luther repeatedly says that the "cause" was not his, but Jesus Christ's. On the whole, Luther also did not claim the title "prophet" for himself, although he did occasionally call himself the "Prophet to the Germans". Luther's self-understanding was thus oriented exclusively on the cause to which he gave himself and which he saw as God's own cause. For him then the Reformation had to do finally with the meaning of Scripture: Luther wanted to stand or fall with his appeal to Scripture.

Luther's principle of "Scripture alone" should not be misunderstood however in a biblicistic or fundamentalistic sense. Both in his controversies with Rome as well as with Zwingli, Luther did indeed appeal to certain biblical texts whose authority for him were beyond question. On the other hand however, Luther also criticized certain books of the canon; above all the epistle of James because of the "works righteousness" taught in it. But the contradiction between Luther's faithfulness to the letter and his criticism of Scripture is only apparent; for Scripture must finally be understood as pointing to and coming from Christ.

The "Theology of the Cross" and the "Theology of Glory"

Actually Luther only fully developed these ideas during the course of his controversy with Rome. But his Catholic opponents in their reply to the 95 Theses tried less to meet his criticism of indulgences than to point out its ecclesiological consequences. In their opinion, Luther questioned the authority of the pope and of the councils. The view which Luther formulated for the first time in the "Resolutions" (that it is not the sacrament that justifies, but faith in the sacrament) imperiled in their opinion the objectivity of the sacramental gift of salvation. Luther's opponents however were chiefly concerned with proving that Luther held heretical views that had been condemned long before. There was hardly any objective discussion of the basic issues in the period immediately following Luther's first public appearance; later on it was already too late for objective discussion because the positions had become far too rigid.

It must be said then that neither on the part of Rome nor in the leading circles of the German church and theology was there any real willingness to take Luther's call for a Reformation seriously. Such a willingness would have implied that the church did not consider itself in full possession of the truth. The church at least would have had to consider the possibility that in some ways it did not correspond to the New Testament.

That is the reason that although the 95 Theses caused a great stir the official leadership of the church did not react at all or only negatively. And at first, the canonical lawsuit against Luther proceeded very slowly because this "monk's squabble" in Germany was not taken seriously in Rome. In Germany however the theological controversy continued.

In the spring of 1518 in the *Heidelberg Disputation* Luther expressed his new theology in its most vigorous formulation. Here for the first time the concept "theology of the cross" was used and set over against a "theology of glory". The law of God, Luther said, cannot bring man to righteousness; how much less then his own works. On the other hand the best works of God, as insignificant as they may appear, are of eternal value. Following the fall of man, free will is a meaningless concept; when man does what he is able to do, he can only sin mortally.

> A theology of glory calls evil good and good evil. A theology of the cross calls the thing what it actually is. That wisdom which sees the invisible things of God in works as perceived by man is completely puffed up, blinded and hardened. The law brings the wrath of God, kills, reviles, accuses, judges and condemns everything that is not in Christ. Yet that wisdom is not of itself evil, nor is the law to be evaded, but without the theology of the cross man misuses the best in the worst manner. He is not righteous who does much, but he who, without work, believes much in Christ...The love of God does not find, but creates, that which is pleasing to it. The love of man comes into being through that which is pleasing to it. (LW 31, 40ff).

Labeling scholasticism a "theology of glory" as Luther does here cannot be accepted as a historical judgment. It does not at all do justice to the great scholastics above all Thomas Aquinas; in this general form it also does not apply to many late medieval theologians. Nevertheless, it is a prophetic judgment upon a theology which was unable to correct the many abuses in church and piety in the light of the New Testament; and it was also an adequate description of basic tendencies and aspects in the theology of the waning Middle Ages. To be sure, those attacked by Luther in this way were not at all willing to accept the strict

alternative between a theology of glory and a theology of the
cross.

It was all the more important then that the way in which
Luther disputed in Heidelberg made a very strong impression: it
was his first appearance before a larger public. Among the
students present where Martin Bucer and Johannes Brenz, who were
won at that time for Luther's cause. Later they worked as
reformers in Strassburg and in Württemberg.

The Canonical Process Against Luther

In the meantime the proceedings against Luther were
continuing in Rome. On August 7, 1518 Luther received a summons
to appear in Rome within 60 days to justify his teachings.
Sylvester Prierias who had prepared a theological opinion for the
pope that Luther received together with the summons, named the
authority of the church and of the pope as the most important
points of controversy. Had Luther gone to Rome at that time, he
would hardly have returned alive. Luther however at the advice
of lawyer friends, petitioned Elector Frederick the Wise of Saxony
to request that the hearing be moved to Germany.

Such a request at that time had good chances of being
accepted. For just then the Diet of Augsburg was debating the
question of a successor for the old Emperor Maximilian. The Roman
curia wanted above all to keep the future Charles V from being
emperor, for it feared the surrounding of the papal territory by
a Hapsburg empire. The majority of the Electors however wanted
to elect Charles. Thus Frederick who was against the election of
Charles became, for the time being, the pope's most important ally
in German politics; and the curia had to be very careful not to
offend him. It was then easy for Frederick to get Luther's
hearing before Cardinal Cajetan moved to Augsburg. In a brief
of August 23, 1518, the pope instructed Cajetan to summon Luther
as a notorious heretic. Should he recant, he was to be received
in mercy; otherwise however Luther was to be arrested and turned
over to Rome.

The hearing before Cajetan took place in October, 1518 in
Augsburg. Cajetan wanted to avoid a debate if possible and
demanded that Luther recant his errors, promise not to teach them
in the future and give assurance that he would not disturb the
peace of the church. Only when Luther wanted to know what his
errors were, Cajetan could no longer avoid answering him. The

discussion touched upon the concept of the "treasury of the church" which arises from the excess merits of Christ and the saints. Luther was not willing to listen to the views of the cardinal, but contradicted him sharply. He insisted that as long as he was not shown to be in error, he could not be forced to recant. After the hearing Luther appealed "From the Pope Badly Informed to the Pope to be Better Informed": he rejected his Roman judges as biased and demanded a hearing by learned papal commissioners at a safer place than Rome. The recantation which Cajetan had demanded, Luther once again refused.

Up to this point Luther had repeatedly emphasized that the doctrine of indulgences was not yet decided as far as the church was concerned and that as a doctor of theology he therefore had the right to debate it. Cajetan had noticed that the position of the curia in this point was weak. At his insistence and on the basis of an outline he provided, the pope quickly delivered what was lacking: in the decretal "Cum postquam" of November 9, 1518, Leo X declared that in indulgences the pope through his power of the keys can forgive punishment for sin out of the treasury of excess merits. This indulgence is granted to the living through absolution, to the dead through intercession. So now no one should be able to plead ignorance of the church's teaching about indulgences. This decretal however did not receive much attention.

Luther's Appeal for a Council

Luther for his part also became more aggressive: on November 28, 1518 he appealed in Wittenberg before a notary and witnesses to a council to be called without delay and properly constituted in the Holy Spirit. In it Luther followed the wording of the Appeal of the Sorbonne, which had also appealed to a council in March 1518 in a controversy concerning "Gallican Liberties".

Thus since the end of 1518, all those groups were occupied with Luther's cause which were instrumental in shaping his call for a reformation in the following decades, namely besides Luther and his followers, the secular authorities, then of course the curia and finally those reform elements in the church and in the world which no longer expected significant reform from the pope, but at the most from a council. Luther's cause was thus drawn into a plexus of different tendencies and goals and could no longer be finally decided either within the church or wholly outside it.

The further controversy was complicated last but not least by the fact that while Rome feared a new council, Charles V, who succeeded Maximilian in 1519, as a true son of the Catholic Church expected the necessary reforms only from a council. The reforms which many people hoped for were not, however, identical with the reformation which Luther sought.

The controversy went on. In the "Leipzig Debate" in the summer of 1519 Eck and Luther debated above all the authority of the pope and that of councils. Provoked by Eck, Luther said that both the pope and the councils could err; the Council of Constance had erred in its condemnation of Hus. In saying that, Luther had expressed an opinion that was clearly heretical. Actually he had only expressed a view which he had already held before: that the Bible is the only source of faith and teaching. Luther no longer accepted the highest teaching office of the church. We must consider that although the infallibility of the pope, which was defined at the first Vatican Council in 1870 was not then accepted by all, nobody questioned the infallibility of councils. Luther's statements in Leipzig therefore gained widest attention. The Universities of Cologne and Louvain demanded that his writings be burned. Duke George of Saxony, who had acted as host at Leipzig, became a bitter enemy of Luther. And other powerful opponents also joined together to fight the movement coming out of Wittenberg. On the other hand, after Leipzig Luther was seen by many as a national hero.

Luther's Three Primary Works

In addition to his lectures and sermons, Luther published – mostly after 1518 – a large number of German and Latin writings, in which he dealt with questions of doctrine and piety. Although these writings were widely read, the so-called three "primary works" of the Reformation from 1520 achieved the greatest importance, because in them Luther set forth clearly his demand for a reformation and now did develop a certain program of reforms. This program was not meant legalistically however.

The first of these writings, *To the Christian Nobility of the German Nation Concerning the Reform of the Christian Estate*, is dedicated to the emperor, in whom Luther at that time still set his hope. Above all, however, Luther wanted to call attention to the "distress and affliction that God may inspire someone with his

Spirit to lend a helping hand to this distressed and wretched
nation" (LW 44, 124). Luther warned though that "we must not
start something by trusting in great power or human reason, even
if all the power in the world were ours. For God cannot and will
not suffer that a good work begin by relying upon one's own power
and reason. He dashes such works to the ground" (LW 44, 125).

According to Luther, the "Romanists" have erected three
wals around themselves, with which they have prevented every
reformation and so brought all Christianity to a terrible fall.
The first wall they erected against the temporal power; any
pressure by it they evaded by saying that the temporal power had
no jurisdiction over them, but that the spiritual is above the
temporal power. The second wall they built to protect themselves
from attempts to "reprove" them out of the Scriptures. If that
happens they raise the objection that the interpretation of the
Scriptures belongs to no one but the pope. If they are finally
threatened with a council they have erected still a third wall in
saying that only a pope can call a council. So far, according to
Luther, no one has succeeded in overcoming these three walls.

Against the first wall Luther put his doctrine of the
general priesthood of all believers. This doctrine is not just
important for Luther in connection with his polemic against Rome.
It is rather already prepared in his lecture on Romans and already
taught in *A Treatise on the New Testament, That is the Holy Mass*
(1520). The doctrine received its full significance however first
in the polemic against the three "walls". On the basis of it,
Luther rejected the medieval division between a spiritual and a
temporal estate. "All Christians are truly of the spiritual
estate, and there is no difference among them except that of
office...for baptism, gospel, and faith alone make us spiritual
and a Christian people...we are all consecrated priests through
baptism...For whoever comes out of the water of baptism can boast
that he is already a consecrated priest, bishop, and pope
although of course it is not seemly that just anybody should exercise such office" (LW 44, 127-129). For Luther that brought the
first wall down.

The doctrine of the general priestood was, however, also
the decisive argument against the other two walls. If all are
baptised priests, then the pope is not the only one who has the
right to interpret Scripture, but then every Christian, if he has
a better understanding, has the basic right "to espouse the cause
of the faith...and to denounce every error" (LW 44, 136). But
then every Christian also has the right and duty if necessary to

see that a council is called together. Luther pointed to the fact
that the first ecumenical councils were called by the emperors
and said that in the present no one could bring about a council
better than the "temporal sword" because "they (the temporal
authorities) are also fellow-Christians, fellow-priests, fellow-
members of the spiritual estate, fellow-lords over all things"
(LW 44, 137). It was thus based on the doctrine of the general
priesthood that Luther appealed to the temporal authorities to
call for a reformation.

In the treatise *To the Christian Nobility*, Luther also
made many concrete proposals for reforms, which were not at all
utopian, but quite feasible. The pope should lay aside the
triple crown and be content with an ordinary bishop's crown. The
number of cardinals should be reduced. The exploitive financial
policies of the papal court should be reformed, for which Luther
gives examples. The pilgrimages to Rome should be stopped. The
number of orders should be reduced and the obligation to keep the
vows abolished. The numerous church festivals should be reduced.
Fasting should be a matter of individual choice. Indulgences
should be done away with altogether. Rome should reconcile the
Bohemians. Reforms should be carried out at the universities so
that the study of languages, mathematics and history were given
greater importance (LW 44, 202); on the other hand, Aristotelian
philosophy should no longer be taught as the philosophical basis.
In the economic realm, extravagance and traffic in annuities should
be controlled.

Luther did not understand these proposals as a legalistic
program. And yet this treatise shows how carefully he had dealt
with the various abuses as well as with possible reforms. Such
an extensive reform of church and state would only have been
possible if the emperor and a large majority of the German rulers
could have accepted this program. Without strong political
backing, only partial reforms in some territories could be expected.
Compared to some of the utopian reform ideas of Carlstadt not to
speak of those of Thomas Müntzer, Luther's proposals were all
realistic.

While Luther's treatise *To the Christian Nobility* demanded
the reform of the church and to some degree also of the state, his
treatise *On the Babylonian Captivity of the Church* was concerned
with doctrine, especially with the doctrine of the sacraments.
Although the sacraments were already very important in the life
of the early church, in the Middle Ages they were understood

almost exclusively as means of grace. By the Middle Ages seven
sacraments - baptism, confirmation, Eucharist, penance, extreme
unction, holy orders, marriage - had gained acceptance and were
officially recognized at the Council of Florence in 1439. Already
at the Fourth Lateran Council in 1215, the doctrine of
transubstantiation had become dogma; according to which in the
Lord's Supper the priest's words of consecration change the
substance of the bread and wine into the body and blood of Christ.
The whole life of the Christian was accompanied by the different
sacraments; in a sense grace could only be received in form of a
sacrament. The central sacrament was the Eucharist. It had
long been understood as a "sacrifice". That meant that the
unique sacrifice of Jesus Christ on the cross could be made present
again in the Eucharist through the sacrifice of the church. However in late medieval theology and even more so in folk piety
there was often a much cruder notion of the sacrifice since that
"sacrifice" was also offered for the sake of the dead. Because
of the superstitious fear of misuse, the laity in the high Middle
Ages more and more gave up the cup and the church had confirmed
this change by withholding the cup. It was taught however that
the consecrated host alone also contained the whole sacrament.
The real problem lay in the fact that in the development of the
doctrine of the sacraments, the church took less and less notice
of the New Testament teachings.

Luther had already developed a new doctrine of the
sacraments before 1520 and in his different sermons on the
sacrament he had made the idea of "communion" with Christ and all
the saints central. In 1520 then, prior to his three "primary
works", Luther in his *Treatise on the New Testament, That is the
Holy Mass* developed the doctrine of the Lord's Supper on the basis
of the words of institution for the first time. In the treatise
On the Babylonian Captivity of the Church Luther now sharply
attacked the Catholic doctrine of the sacraments. His critique
of the Catholic doctrine of the sacraments was made solely on
the basis of the New Testament. Luther composed this treatise not
in German but in Latin out of consideration for the common people:
such revolutionary thoughts were at first to be presented before
the scholars only.

Luther first of all denied that there were seven sacraments.
Instead he maintained that there were only three or two sacraments,
namely baptism, the Lord's Supper and perhaps also penance,
although here the "sign" added to the promise was lacking. It is
also important here that Luther no longer first defined the nature

of the sacrament and then on the basis of this developed the special characteristics of baptism and the Lord's Supper, but that he interpreted baptism and the Lord's Supper on the basis of their institution.

Luther then attacked the "Babylonian Captivity" of the Lord's Supper, which not only took away the cup but also forced upon the believer the dogma of transubstantiation. In regard to the cup Luther asked: what right had the church to change the form Christ instituted. In the doctrine of transubstantiation it was not the basic view of Christ's presence in the sacrament that Luther attacked, but rather the fact that such a teaching, which could never be more than a tentative explanation, was made dogma. Luther accepted the presence of Christ's body and blood, but rejected a transformation of the bread.

The most wicked for Luther was the third Babylonian Captivity of the Lord's Supper, namely that the Mass was seen as a good work and a sacrifice. This criticism of Luther's certainly did not do justice to the theology of the Mass of a man like Thomas Aquinas; but it was justified in regard to much late-medieval teaching. Luther was aware of the fact that in the Mass he had touched the heart of the Catholic church; if it was to be changed radically, then at the same time "it would be necessary to abolish most of the books now in vogue, and to alter almost the entire external form of the churches and introduce, or rather reintroduce, a totally different kind of ceremonies (LW 36, 36).

But Luther did not have revolutionary change in mind in either his treatise *To the Christian Nobility* or in *On the Babylonian Captivity*. To the contrary, Luther rejected the use of force and wanted only to "instruct men's consciences so that they may endure the Roman Tyranny, knowing well that they have been forcibly deprived of their rightful share in the sacrament (...) because of their own sin"(LW 36, 28). But it was hardly to be expected that his followers would accept such a position very long.

The third "basic work" - *The Freedom of a Christian* - served to develop a new ethic on the basis of the Reformation doctrine of justification. Luther reformulated here the Pauline understanding of Christian liberty in the words: "A Christian is a perfectly free lord of all, subject to none. A Christian is a perfectly dutiful servant of all, subject to all (LW 31, 344).

Excommunication and Outlawry

While Luther worked out his Reformation treatises, the canonical proceedings against him had been completed. On June 15, 1520 the bull of condemnation was published in Rome which demanded that Luther retract his heresies within sixty days. Forty-one statements drawn rather arbitrarily from Luther's writings were condemned in this bull. They had to do primarily with Luther's concept of sin, penance, repentance, confession or the bondage of the will. In addition it damned Luther's view that it was against the will of the Holy Spirit to burn heretics. The bull thus reaffirmed the traditional way of dealing with heretics. On December 10, 1520, Luther publicly burned this bull together with other books of canon law and scholastic doctrine. The final excommunication of Luther took place on January 3, 1521.

Already toward the end of 1520 efforts were made to invite Luther to the next Diet. After a long period of wavering and against the will of the papal nuncio Aleander, Luther was finally cited to the Diet of Worms. This fact alone shows that there were considerable political powers in Germany which were not willing simply to follow the excommunication of the pope with the outlawry of the empire. In Worms on April 18, 1521 Luther refused to retract his teachings unless convinced of error by the testimony of Scripture or by clear reason; he could not and would not act against his conscience. In the Edict of Worms, signed by the emperor on May 26, 1521 but back-dated to May 8, Luther was placed under the imperial ban mainly because of his "errors" in the pamphlet *On the Babylonian Captivity*; this ban also included his followers.

Now, however, it became apparent how wide-spread the Reformation movement already was. For the time being the Elector of Saxony, Frederick the Wise, had Luther brought to a safe place, namely the Wartburg Castle. Luther used the months of forced inactivity at the Wartburg mainly to translate the New Testament. It took him about eleven weeks. It was not the first German translation of the New Testament, but it was far superior to the earlier translations because Luther did not base it on the Latin *Vulgata*, but on the original Greek text and because he grasped and creatively expressed the meaning of the text on the basis of his new Reformation theology. In his work *On Monastic Vows*, Luther attacked those vows if they were used to earn merit or gain a rank superior to life in the secular world. This work led many monks and nuns to leave the monastery. In many parts of the

empire, Catholic church life practially ceased to exist. But
there was still no concept of what evangelical church life should
be like.

The Wittenberg Disturbances: Luther and Carlstadt

While Luther stayed at the Wartburg, the Reformation
movement continued. It now for the first time became evident that
in the Reformation different people had different goals. All
were united in their fight against Rome, but not in the question
of how reforms should be introduced. Especially in Wittenberg
there were many who did not want to stop at merely pointing out
the discrepancy between the Catholic church and the New Testament,
but wanted to carry out practical reforms. The Wittenberg
Augustinians along with Carlstadt, Luther's older faculty colleague,
began with changes in the Mass. On Christmas Day, 1521, Carlstadt
celebrated the first German Mass in which he dispensed both bread
and wine. He was also one of the main initiators of the "Ordinance
of the City of Wittenberg" which was adopted on January 24, 1522.
Saints' pictures were to be removed from the churches. The
"prophets" of Zwickau, who appeared in Wittenberg around the turn
of the year 1521/22 and demanded radical reforms on the basis of
revelations of the Spirit, made even Melanchthon waver and increased
the general confusion. The electoral government did not know if
and how it should intervene.

At the beginning of March 1522 Luther returned from the
Wartburg to Wittenberg against the advice of the elector. In
the *Invocavit* sermons from March 9 to 16, Luther dealt with the
situation. With gravity he reminded his Wittenbergers that we
are all marked by death and that no one can die for another;
therefore we must all know the main articles of faith which concern
every Christian. Luther did not criticize the reforms which had
been introduced as such, but rather the lack of patience and love
and consideration for the "weak". Also nothing should have been
done without the consent of "the authorities"; for then it would
have been clear "that it had come from God" (LW 51, 73).

The differences that arose here for the first time in the
evangelical movement were far-reaching indeed, even though there
was basic agreement about the reforms as such. Obedience to God's
law was the most important thing for Carlstadt, whereby the
guidance and interpretation of the Spirit actualized the law.
Carlstadt was prepared to proceed together with the town council

even without the elector.   Luther on the other hand viewed the
question of reforms under the perspective of Pauline freedom.
Therefore he could be very flexible in the matter of the timing
and scope of the reforms.   He was mainly interested in overcoming the false understanding of certain rites of the church in
terms of works righteousness.   Luther was also unwilling to
proceed without the consent of the government, although the
reasons for this position of his are not quite clear; to be sure
Luther had already appealed to the temporal leaders in the pamphlet
To the Christian Nobility.   The differences which first became
apparent in this time grew during the following years.   At the
same time however the different positions became better defined.

Luther developed the basic principles of his so-called
doctrine of the "two realms" in his pamphlet *Temporal Authority:
To What Extent it Should be Obeyed* (1523).   It is important in
connection with the discussion of that time that Luther made a
clear distinction between the spiritual and the temporal realms.
One reason for writing this pamphlet was the fact that in some
territories Luther's translation of the New Testament was
forbidden and the people were commanded to surrender the copies
they possessed.   In Luther's opinion such measures meant that
the princes interfered in the spiritual realm; they have as little
right to do that as bishops have to intervene in the temporal
realm.   Heresy is solely "a spiritual matter".   Heresy should be
met only with the Word.

The Diets and the Reformation Movement

There is no doubt that without the protection of the
temporal powers the Reformation movement would have been doomed
to failure.   The Edict of Worms could have provided the means of
stamping out the Reformation from the start.   The reason that this
did not happen was due not only to German particularism, but also
to the fact that Charles V was too preoccupied with long wars
with France and later also with the Turks to enforce the edict.
The Imperial Council of Regency that acted in his absence was too
weak to enforce its policies even if it should have come to an
agreement.   That is the reason the Diets of Nürnberg in 1522-23
and 1524 failed to decide the religious question.   Pope Adrian VI,
who during his short pontificate (1522-23) sincerely sought to
reform the curia, had a confession of guilt read at the Diet on
January 3, 1523:   prelates and priests, who were mainly responsible

for the abuses in the church, could only return to the right way
through repentance and humility. However this confession of
guilt came too late. Besides, Adrian's reform efforts never got
beyond the first attempts. Many in Germany supported a national
council instead, because they did not expect any change from the
curia. But neither the pope nor the emperor would agree to that.
Thus for the time being all attempts, even those of the Catholic
princes, to introduce reforms remained futile.

Although at first Luther found followers everywhere
because of the general desire for reform, later the differences
among the various movements became obvious. In 1522-23 there
was a revolt of the imperial knights whose outstanding leader
was Franz von Sickingen. The underlying cause of this uprising
was the fact that the age of knighthood was over. Many of the
knights were therefore concerned about the economic future and
had utopian national and religious expectations. Many had put
their hopes in Luther. Luther however never considered making
common cause with them.

The Peasants' Revolt: Thomas Müntzer and Luther

Of far greater consequences also for an understanding of
the call for reformation was the Peasants' Revolt 1524-25. The
peasant uprising had many causes. To be sure, an economic pinch
was felt by a great many peasants who in addition were plundered
by the impoverished lesser nobility. More important however was
the loss of many rights, that was caused by the far-reaching
economic changes which were evident in the flowering of the cities
as well as in the development of industry. In protest against
these changes, the peasants called for the reestablishment of the
ancient or divine right. It seemed to them that Luther's
Reformation understanding of the freedom of the Christian provided
the decisive argument against serfdom, which was still practiced
in some regions. And so especially many peasants put their hope
in the Reformation.

At the same time Thomas Müntzer appeared with his proclamation of a Spiritual Christianity. He was influenced by mysticism
and probably also by some of the ideas of Hus. For a while he
thought of himself as a follower of Luther, but since 1521
proclaimed his own spirit-theology. The opposition between Luther
and Müntzer came to a head in 1524. Müntzer argued that Luther
made it too easy for men in preaching a "honey sweet" Christ.

Man must rather experience the utter depts of temptation so that
a word can then arise out of the depths of the soul that proves
to be God's Word. Müntzer did not go along with Luther's distinction between the way man stands "before God" and "before the
world". For him a reformation of the church was only possible
together with a reformation of the world. Although Müntzer had
no concrete plans to offer, he demanded that the new Spirit-Church
should have immediate impact on political life.

The peasant uprising and the Spirit-Church which Müntzer
sought were actually two quite different movements. But when the
peasants revolted Müntzer joined their cause and in flaming words
called the peasants and miners in Thuringia to fight against the
princes. All power was to be given to the people. And the godless
were to be destroyed for they had no right to live. This should
lead to the "transformation of the world" and to the "invincible
future reformation". Müntzer thus no longer made a clear
distinction between the future rule of Christ and this situation
in which the elect govern.

Luther disassociated himself from both the rebellious
peasants and Thomas Müntzer and so further defined his understanding
of the reformation. Luther accused the peasants but also Müntzer
of breaking the first commandment in applying the word "Christian"
to their cause, for the term "Christian" cannot be used for a
secular program. Further, they wanted to be the judge in their
own matter. Finally, the fact that they were the first to use
force spoke against them. Luther argued that a Christian may
never use force unless ordered to do so by the authorities. The
Christian rather must be prepared to suffer. In this critique
Luther unfortunately failed to acknowledge the basically justified
demands of the peasants.

Luther especially charged Müntzer with confusing God's
kingdom and the temporal kingdom which falsified both the Law
as well as the Gospel. Finally for Luther, Müntzer was a false
prophet whose message was basically *hubris*. The stand Luther
took in the battle between the peasants and the authorities was
therefore at the same time a decision about the right or wrong of
Müntzer's prophecy. For the course of the Reformation the peasant's
uprising signaled the end of the Reformation as a popular movement:
the peasants were reduced to political and religious impotence.
In the cities however the Reformation movement continued to flourish
for some time. This meant for the carrying out of the Reformation
that even more than before it was dependent upon the support and
the co-operation of the authorities.

Humanism and Reformation

Finally there was also a break between humanism and the
Reformation. Here too had been common concerns, indeed to a great
degree. Already before the Reformation, humanism insisted that
one must always go back to the original texts and so in many
respects prepared the way for the Reformation understanding of
Scripture. In addition, many humanists criticized Scholastic
theology and here also prepared for the Reformation. Finally,
the humanists called for reforms which coincided in part with the
aims of the Reformation. Many humanists showed open sympathy
toward Luther; some, like Philip Melanchthon, joined the Reformation
movement. And yet there were also differences from the beginning
which were felt both by the leading humanists and by Luther.
Humanism was a movement limited to the cultured elite, who remained
aloof from the stormy inroads of the Reformation into all levels
of society. Furthermore, in spite of their criticism of the many
abuses of the church, many humanists wanted to avoid a break with
Rome. And also theologically there were fundamental differences
between the Reformation and the reform-catholicism of the humanists.

For a long time Erasmus, the leader of the humanist movement, remained noncommittal. Finally at the insistence of secular
and church leaders he decided against Luther. In 1524 his
pamphlet *On Free Will* appeared. Erasmus emphasized here against
Luther that man must have a certain freedom of decision over
against God; that God's will is the first cause, man's will the
second cause of salvation. Without this participation of the
human will, Erasmus saw the basis for ethics endangered.

In *The Bondage of the Will* (1525), Luther sharply attacked
Erasmus' position. In matters "among us" there may be freedom of
decision, but not in those matters that are "over us". That the
human will is not free but in bondage over against God does not
make sense to natural man. But in the presence of the cross of
Christ, we must confess that salvation is not at all a human
possibility, but comes from God alone and can be grasped only by
faith in God.

The break with humanism brought the last important
differentiation between the Reformation and the other reform
movements. Although the divisions between Luther on the one hand
and Carlstadt, the knights, the peasants, Müntzer and the humanists
on the other served to clarify the nature and the goals of the
Reformation, they also led to a certain narrowing and hardening.
The great expectations with which many at first greeted the reformer

were dampened and even gave way to resignation on the part of some.
This only meant for Luther and his followers that the real task
of the Reformation was just beginning. The call for a reformation
of the church was heard and accepted by many and yet also rejected
by many. There was little hope left that the reformation of the
whole church could be reached. It was more realistic to look for
partial solutions.

The Diet of Speyer 1526

        This became possible through the Diet of Speyer. Charles
V had defeated France and thought that he could now carry out the
Edict of Worms in Germany. But shortly before the business of
the Diet began, the pope fearing the growing power of the emperor
formed together with Charles' opponents the League of Cognac.
This robbed Charles of the fruits of his victory. As the Diet
began, the representatives of Saxony and Hesse entered with the
Latin watchword of the Reformation: "God's Word remains forever".
They no longer took part in the Catholic Mass. That made it clear
that the Edict of Worms could not be enforced.
        A committee of spiritual and temporal princes worked out
a list of proposals concerning the traditional ceremonies and the
correction of abuses. It stated that the seven sacraments and
the Mass should be kept, but Masses for money were to be eliminated
The texts of the liturgy should be read to the people in German.
The cup should be given to the laity pending a decision by a
council; marriage for the clergy would be better than the widespread practice of concubinage. Representing his brother Charles,
Archduke Ferdinand however rejected these proposals.
        At the same time the Turkish advances in Hungary in the
summer of 1526 caused such a political crisis in the empire that
the Diet, with the approval of Ferdinand, recessed on August 27,
1526 without a unified policy for carrying out the Edict of Worms.
It did say that no changes should be introduced in matters of
faith. And it agreed that a general council or if necessary a
German national council would have the best chance of restoring
religious unity. But it also decided that pending a council, the
estates should live with, rule and take care of their subjects
"in accord with their obligations to God and the emperor."
        Actually this agreement only referred to the enforcement
of the Edict of Worms which was therefore once again postponed.
But in the evangelical territories this decision, against its

riginal meaning, was quickly interpreted as giving the right to
ntroduce the Reformation. On the basis of this agreement of the
iet, work now began in many territories to build up an evangelical
hurch.

Although this interpretation of the "Speyer Agreements"
as not justified as such, the individual territories could hardly
o anything else but make the decisions which neither the pope
or the emperor were in a position to make. The mere fact that a
inal decision had once again been delayed together with the
bvious inability of the church to reform itself left no other
hoice. The Diet of Speyer of 1526 therefore opened the way for
he formation of evangelical territorial churches. That did not
ettle the question for the entire church, in fact it made such
settlement even more difficult.

Translated by Donald Dutton

CHAPTER 2

F.W. KANTZENBACH

THE REFORMATION'S POWER TO ORGANIZE THE CHURCH AND CONFESSIONAL LUTHERANISM FROM 1530 TO 1648

The Expansion of the Lutheran Reformation

The transition of the history of the Reformation from the third to the fourth decade of the 16th century is one of flux. In 1529 at the Diet of Speyer the "Protestants" resisted majority decisions in religious questions and again asserted themselves against the empire. Yet the year 1530 did not form the unambiguous transition to the "realization" of the reforming movement. The ecclesiastical structures of the Reformation which underwent a long period of development, were considered as a kind of temporary arrangement, since there was still hope that ecclesiastical unity might be restored. The Confessio Augustana, the evangelical discussions concerning the council and even Luther's Smalcald Articles (1537) testify to this hope.

Around 1560 the confessional epoch in the strict sense of the term began. Confessional documents, especially Reformed confessions, appeared in quick succession. The Lutherans concluded the formation of their confessions with the Book of Concord of 1580. In distinction to Calvinism, which still engaged in active proselytism, and to Catholicism, which still had to conclude the deliberations of the Council of Trent, Lutheranism by 1560 had already passed through the most important phase of its development.

Lutheranism of necessity satisfied itself with its territorial position in Germany and its expansion in the north and in eastern Europe and directed its total energies on controverted theological questions. In 1555 the Diet at Augsburg sanctioned the confessional division of Germany and with the Peace Treaty initiated the confessional epoch. There now developed a curious confessional retrenchment. A dialog concerning the truth of the Gospel was hardly possible under the existent circumstances. To be sure, there were various forms of confessional confusion and adulteration. The development of the established Protestant church and the reorganization of Catholic ecclesiastical structures through the influence of the Council of Trent progressed parallel to one another and hardly exerted the type of mutual influence that could have issued into a dialog over common needs and tasks. The question concerning the unity of the church was answered on both sides in a perfunctory manner.

In the expansion of Lutheranism between 1530 and the end of the old German Empire (1806) three major groupings may be distinguished; the Lutheran church in Germany and the reform movement in the east and southeast which is in Germany's sphere of influence; the Lutheran churches in Denmark, Sweden, Norway, and Finland which developed as nationally unified Luthern churches in the north; and since the 17th and 18th centuries the Lutherans in North America. The majority of Lutherans are found in these three areas to this day.

The Lutheran Reformation could not take root in Italy, Spain, and France primarily because it could not obtain the support of the princes and the magistrates, who already controlled the church and its riches and therefore the Reformation had little to offer to their interests. In America the Lutheran churches were established as free churches in distinction to the German estab-lished church and the Scandinavian national church. In corre-spondence to the political-sociological circumstances ecclesiastical organization in the 16th century developed almost congruently with the territories or cities in which the Reformation was introduced or rejected. In distinction to modern social mobility, which results in increasing confessional mixing and makes Christianity into a world-wide diaspora, there was in the 16th century a diaspora only in rare instances. There was, therefore, little discussion with people having a different confessional standpoint.

The Peasant War of 1525 did not signify a cessation of the expansion of the Reformation in Germany. To be sure, it produced a perceptible check to the reform movement, but the

Reformation's popular character did not disappear with the
disappointments caused by the termination of the Peasant War.

     The North German Reformation received its impulse from
the preaching of the Lutheran ministers. In his work of organizing
the churches, Bugenhagen inteded to initiate development toward
a congregational church organization and for his task appropriated
already-existing social structures. However, even in the north
German cities the tendency toward an episcopal church structure
finally prevailed. On the whole, the Reformation between 1530
and the Smalcald War could register great successes. The
Reformation expanded into many parts of Europe.

The Self-understanding of the Lutheran Church

     Luther's renunciation of the canon law (1520) was the
consequence of an understanding of the church that was rooted in
the Gospel of Christ. On December 10, 1520, he burned the books
of canon law before the Elster Gate in Wittenberg. The renunciation of the canon law symbolized in this act was more important
than the burning of the bull of excommunication. The question,
whether he had violently sundered the unity of the church, deeply
vexed Luther during his stay at the Wartburg after the Diet of
Worms of 1521. He did not wish to call into existence a "new"
church which was antithetically opposed to the old Catholic
church. Rather, he understood those congregations which were
effecting the Reformation as the one, catholic church. Luther,
therefore, made possible a deeper understanding of the unity of
the church. The unity of the church is not guaranteed by an
organism directed and led by a visible head, nor is it preserved
through the rigid uniformity of ceremonies, the uniformity of all
doctrinal statements, or the centralization of administration.
Rather, the unity of the church is guaranteed alone by the
obedience to the head of the church, Jesus Christ.

     From the beginning Luther thought of the one Christendom,
of the one church. Frequently and impressively he alluded to the
agreement between his teaching and that of the ancient church.
Attempts to reach beyond the boundaries of the western church and
establish contact with the eastern church were not lacking.
Melanchthon's contacts extended beyond Hungary and Transylvania
to the Patriarchate of Constantinople. On account of its ecumenical
significance the Confessio Augustana was even translated into the
Greek language. Indeed, according to the witness of the Confessio

Augustana the reformers stood within the one church. The modern
idea of denomination is to be distinguished from this fundamental
confessional document. On the one hand, Luther tirelessly
resisted any confusion of the church as spiritual reality with
the purely external institution. The true church leads a hidden
life. On the other hand, there exist conflicting claims and
pretensions so that the public proclamation of the Word of God
and its effects must be placed under examination. At this point
Luther is of the opinion that the fight for pure doctrine is
necessary and that this has something to do with the distinction
between the true and false church.

When Luther burned the canon law in 1520 and protested
against confusing it with the divine law, this did not signify a
rejection of the divine law which can found itself upon the Holy
Scriptures, not in a biblicistic sense, but in relation to the
evangelical content of the Scriptures.

In contrast to this human/divine distinction the Confessio
Augustana argues in favor of that which can promote the Gospel.
Augustana 28 summarizes the polemical themes and expresses them
positively. The traditional concept of the divine law actually
is no longer suitable. Therefore, the Confessio Augustana prefers
to speak of the *mandatum Dei*: "for the spiritual power has its
commission to preach the Gospel and administer the sacraments"
(CA 28, 12). Within the Christian communion the divine law
manifests itself in a few, clearly delineated and enumerable
actions such as the administration of the sacraments of baptism
and of the Lord's Supper, the proclamation of the Gospel and the
spiritual office of the ministry, which is appointed to see that
both are fulfilled. The imperial law from 1555 on shows what
disparity later occurred to Luther's thinking concerning confessions.
Instead of the spirit-effected witness to the truth by brothers
and fathers in the faith, there is a confessional document which
is severed from the confessing act and has become a state document
whose validity rests on the power of human decree. Thus, it was
contended before the organs of the Empire whether the *Confessio
Variata* or the *Confessio Invariata* would be recognized by the
imperial power. The choice was relinquished to the empire for
its free, sovereign decision--significant of the process of inner
secularization.

For both Luther and Melanchthon political motives in the
writing of confessions are completely embedded in the religious
perspective. However, in this the two principal participants were
essentially different. Luther is characterized by his prophetic

apocalyptic concept of history and takes account of God's wrath, punishment and grace. He conceives history from the perspective of the battle between God and Satan, and he conceives the history of the church as the opposition between the sons of Cain and the sons of Abel. On the other hand, out of ethical-political responsibility Melanchthon always endeavored for theological consensus. In order to alleviate the demands of his conscience Protestant solidarity for Melanchthon must be rooted in theological consensus. His endeavors for the confession, therefore, were ethically motivated, and to that extent political motives were in no way lacking.

Luther, on the other hand, was little interested in political motives and in all his decisions rather pondered their compatibility with the Word of God. His traditionalism had a different foundation than that of Melanchthon. It was based on Christological and soteriological considerations, while Melanchthon liked rather to use formal, historical critical means to demonstrate the church's unity, which represented an important political factor as well.

The Lutheran Confessions presuppose and affirm the confessions of the early church. They concurred with the early church's confessions concerning the salvific truth of the Gospel, and they emphasized thereby the unity of the church, which they conceived to be obligatory. Towards the end of 1536 when the possibility of a universal council finally appeared certain of realization, Luther intensively occupied himself with the confessions of the ancient church. In the first part of his Smalcald Articles he deals with "the sublime Articles of the divine majesty," concerning which he says that they "are not matters of dispute or contention, for both parties confess them." But since Luther doubted whether his opponents were willing to draw the proper conclusions, he kept only the word "confess" in the final text. Following the high articles concerning the divine majesty Luther expressed himself on the unity of the confession of Christ and belief concerning justification without thereby touching upon the patristic foundations of Christology. *The Three Symbols or Creeds of the Christian Faith* published in 1538 (LW 34, 197), discussed the three confessions of the early church. In this writing Luther wished again to provide proof that he desired to believe and confess that which had always been "kept, read and sung in the whole Church" (LW 34,201). This ecumenical understanding of the faith in continuity with the ancient church entered into the history of Lutheranism. It was only in the Enlightenment that this understanding was weakened and even rejected.

The Advance of Lutheranism in the Political Arena

In Electoral Saxony Frederick the Wise had been more of a protector than a determined promoter of the Reformation. It was different with his successor, John the Steadfast (born 1467), who recommended Luther's "German Mass or Order of Service" (1526) to the clergy of his land. In opposition to the alliance of Catholic princes at Dessau, John with other evangelical princes concluded the defensive alliance of Torgau in 1526. Political success manifested itself in that same year at the first Diet of Speyer. Through its "recess" the Diet provided the first constitutional conditions for the established Lutheran churches. The confessional split within Germany became evident in this resolution of the Diet. Until a council for a national assembly could be called, in regard to the Edict of Worms, each estate was allowed "to live, to rule, and to act in such a manner as each one hopes and trusts that he will be held accountable before God and the imperial majesty."

Although the majority at the second Diet of Speyer in 1529 passed a resolution to retract their support from the decision of the 1526 Diet of Speyer, the development already underway could no longer be checked. Therefore, in 1529 the evangelical estates at Speyer protested against the decision to annul the resolution of the prior Diet, which had been agreed to by unanimous consent, and to assert again the validity of the Edict of Worms. The protest was thus directed against a situation perceived to be one of lawlessness, and a protest was lodged against any forceable execution of the Edict of Worms. However, behind the protest there existed genuine motivation of conscience as well. From reasons of conscience the prince is duty-bound to interfere on behalf of the truth of the Gospel. Therefore, the individual prince assumes not only for himself but also for the people under his direction the responsibility of conscience upon which salvation depends. The nuncio sent by Pope Clement VII to Speyer in 1529 announced the pope's intent to call a council for the summer of 1530. However, the pope could not make up his mind really to summon it. Clement VII, therefore, agreed that the emperor would call an assembly of the German estates to Augsburg in 1530 in order to clear up the religious question at a Diet. Were the Diet unsuccessful in this endeavor, a universal council would be considered.

The Protestants could not present a united front in Augsburg, since their differences concerning the doctrine of the

Lord's Supper had not been resolved in the discussions held at
Marburg in 1529 between Luther and Zwingli. Of the three
confessions--the Confessio Augustana, the Confessio Tetrapolitana
(South Germany) and the Fidei Ratio (Zwingli) -- only the first
was allowed to be read publically before the estates of the empire.
The public reading of the Confessio Augustana was on June 25.
The emperor's decision went in favor of the Roman Catholic party,
which had answered the Confessio Augustana with the "Confutatio,"
or Refutation. Against this Melanchthon replied with the Apology
of the Confessio Augustana, although the Apology was not allowed
to be read publically. Now, as before, the pope had no desire to
call a council. The emperor threatened the Protestants with force.
On September 9, 1530, Elector John of Saxony left Augsburg. He
must have been of the opinion that the emperor would compel the
Protestants to obedience. Yet, Charles V had no money, nor was
he supported by the papal court, by Henry VIII of England, nor
Francis I of France. Moreover, the Lutherans had in the meantime
united in the League of Smalcald.

Toward the end of October, 1530, negotiations in Torgau
led to the formation of the League of Smalcald. The course of
unconditional renunciation of resistance, which had been supported
by Luther, was altered with Luther's consent. His change of
attitude concerning the question of resistance took into account
the fact that the uncompromising imperial decisions at the Diet
of Augsburg in the autumn of 1530 had changed the situation.
Luther called Charles a tyrant who reneges on his promises. He
thereby allowed that there could be instances in which jurists
would regard resistance as an allowable option. The jurists must
investigate and evaluate the legal situation and decide whether
such an instance exists. On December 29, 1530, the signers of
the Augsburg Confession assembled together in Smalcald. Among
those assembled were John of Saxony, Philip of Hesse, Wolfgang of
Anhalt, Albrecht and Gebhard of Mansfeld, direct representative of
George of Brandenburg, and the delegates from ten South German
cities. They bound themselves to a united resistance should the
Gospel be suppressed through power politics. The League was
officially concluded on February 27, 1531. Seven cities from
South Germany and seven cities from North Germany were soon added.
The League immediately had respectable effects, for the election
of Ferdinand as King of the Romans was not recognized by the League
(October, 1531). Furthermore, France and England felt themselves
to be the natural allies of the Smalcald League. In 1532 Charles
V had to concede to the Nürnberg Interim, for among other things

he was in need of the assistance of the Protestants against the
threat of the Turks.

Of significance for the internal and external stabilization
of Lutheranism was the Wittenberg Concord between the Wittenberg
theologians and the South Germans as it was signed by M. Bucer
(1536). The Zwinglians, however, did not participate in this
agreement. Bucer confessed that the bread was truly the body of
Christ and, if the words of consecration were not falsified, was
given to all those who received it, even to the unworthy (although
not to the godless: *impii*). Luther recognized the South Germans
as brothers. The Concord, despite differing interpretations of
it, was no compromise. It opened the way for the South Germans
to join that Lutheranism which was characterized by Wittenberg.

Hope for a Council and Religious Peace

The question concerning the convening of a council entered
a new phase after the Diet of 1530. With the election of a new
pope in 1534 the issue gained pressing urgency. In 1535 the new
pope, Paul III, sent his nuncio, Peter Paul Vergerius, to Germany
in order to gain assent for a council from the Catholic and
Protestant princes. However, any suggestion of a national council
on German soil was in no way to be entertained. Although Luther
could conceive of nothing positive that would issue from a papal
council, he would not refuse to attend a council regardless of
whether it would be held in a Papal-Italian city or some other
city. He wished to defend and validate his opinions publicly.
The nuncio, however, deceived himself if in view of Luther's
willingness he believed that the assent of the elector was also
assured. The elector desired to have guarantees that the council
would be a free and Christian one. Even Melanchthon, who until
this time had shown himself desirous of a council, was suspicious
of the assurances of the nuncio and explained what a free and
Christian council was conceived to be. On June 2, 1536, Pope
Paul III did indeed announce a council, which was to assemble in
Mantua on May 23, 1537. In a disputation held on October 10, 1536,
Luther dealt with the question of a council. He contended that
spiritual authority could not be attributed to a council or to an
assembly of bishops in a purely mechanical way. A distinction
must be made between a church which is representative and a church
which is true and lawful. The claim of a council to represent
the church is, so to speak, an external facade, which God does not

regard. The sole criterion for the legitimacy of the church's
teaching authority is whether there is agreement with the authority
of the apostles, that is, with the authority of Scripture. Luther
continued to maintain this point of view in all his reflections on
the question of a lawful, Christian council.

Luther expressed his attitude toward the pope's plans for
a council in the Smalcald Articles. He had been commissioned by
the Elector to draft these articles for the assembly of the Smalcald
League. In preparation for the council they were there to be
discussed and examined. In his Articles Luther is extrememly
critical of the pope. Christendom, he asserts, is only corrupted
by the pope, and therefore the church can be governed and preserved
in no other way than that "all of us live under one Head, Christ."
Were a council to meet, it would be a matter of confessing before
the pope and Satan.

Luther's Articles were not immediately recognized as an
official document by the League of Smalcald. However, theologians
could subscribe to the Articles on their own responsibility, and
in this way the Articles only gradually prevailed as a confessional
document in Lutheran Protestantism. Due to the publication of
his Articles, Luther added a preface to them in 1538. The intended
council had been postponed by the pope, and Luther gave up all
hope of ever experiencing a free council of the church in his
lifetime. Nevertheless, Luther gave remarkably strong expression
to his enduring and evangelical hope for a council. For despite
his hopelessness of there ever being a council according to his
convictions, Luther was not at all weary of reflecting about
councils. The indisputable highpoint of Luther's theology concerning
councils is his profound and beautiful reflections contained in
his *On the Councils and the Church* written in 1539.

As a complement to Luther's Smalcald Articles Melanchthon
composed his *Treatise on the Power and Primacy of the Pope* (1537).
The discussion of the episcopal jurisdiction and of papal primacy
contained in this treatise was intended to supplement the exposition
of the Confessio Augustana concerning these themes. Melanchthon
was commissioned to write this treatise by the theologians and
secular representatives of the Reformation gathered at Smalcald
in 1537. To this document they attached their signatures so that
the Treatise belongs to the confessional documents of the Lutheran
church. In this treatise the divine right of the papacy is sharply
contested, but Melanchthon had no wish to deny to the papacy a
human right. In the church divine right has to do only with the
ordination or institution of bishops or pastors. As prominent

members of the church, the princes' services were solicited for the work of the Reformation. They have responsibility for the Reformation. In this Melanchthon differs from Luther, for while Melanchthon imposed this responsibility on the princes as secular rulers, Luther had assigned to them only the function of "emergency bishops" (*Notbischof*) in strict distinction to their worldly power.

When in 1538 the attempt to hold a council in Viacenza proved unsuccessful, the emperor himself adopted the strategy of obtaining the agreements with the Protestants and initiated a period characterized by religious conferences summoned by the emperor. Especially interested in these dialogs were those theologians on both sides who had humanistic-Erasmian sympathies. Indeed, on some issues, such as the doctrine of original sin and to some extent also the doctrine on justification, some agreement was achieved at the colloquies held in Hagenau, Worms (1540) and Regensburg (1541). The idea of a double justification, which Luther had always criticized, was to assist in the achievement of such agreement. According to this concept, Christ was conceived as the sole mediator of salvation, yet with the aid of scholastic distinctions complete justification was made dependent upon works of faith. The deliberations held at Regensburg from April 4 until May 31, 1541, adopted the so-called Book of Regensburg, which had originated already in the discussions held at Worms and carried the signatures of the two mediators, Martin Bucer and John Gropper. The papal court sent to Regensburg, Cardinal Contarini, who possessed most nearly the theological disposition and experience necessary for an agreement with the evangelical theologians. Without doubt, Contarini endeavored to meet the Protestants halfway concerning justification, yet for him the sacramental infusion and inhabitation of grace (*gratia inhaerens*) was a self-evident presupposition. Luther had no sympathy with compromises acquired with the help of scholastic distinctions. Moreover, disagreement remained in the doctrines of the church and of the sacraments.

Despite its weakness in leadership and its financial limitations the League of Smalcald for years offered a certain guarantee that the emperor, who was under external political pressures, would not move with force against the Protestants. Nevertheless, in 1543 the emperor became unsettled on account of his doubtful hereditary claim to Geldern, wherein the religious question also played an important role. Duke William of Cleve had joined the Reformation and thereby encouraged the evangelical opinions of the Elector of Cologne, Hermann of Wied. Had Cologne

decided in favor of the Reformation, the Catholic predominance in
the electoral college would have been endangered. All of Catholicism along the lower Rhien could have falled to the Reformation.
The emperor, therefore, decided to use force and seized Geldern.
With this incident he created hope for a military campaign against
the Protestants, although at the same time and up until 1546 he
continued his tactic of convening diets and religious conferences.
It therefore appeared as though the emperor preferred a peaceful
settlement, and the Protestants allowed themselves to be deceived.
As the emperor mobilized against the Protestants, even Maurice of
Saxony could be induced to attack the rear of his comrades of
faith in the mistaken impression that the war had nothing to do
with religion. On April 24, 1547, the military decision went to
the emperor at Mühlberg near Torgau.

The Swabian and Alsacian cities participated in the War
of Smalcald, while some Franconian cities remained neutral. The
cities of South Germany had to bear the burden of the war.

Charles V did not take good advantage of his victory. The
imperial "Interim," which was intended to combine the Catholic
order of service with the guarantee of the lay cup and clerical
marriage, proved itself to be virtually impracticable. A principal
dissenter was Maurice of Saxony, who had been awarded electoral
dignity for his act of betrayal, but who with the support of
France now turned against the "animal servitude" imposed by the
emperor on the princes and the people. In the spring of 1552 he
attacked and gained a surprising victory over the emperor. Soon
thereafter the Peace of Passau was concluded. The princes supported
the Treaty of Passau of 1552. They had served the empire when they
helped Charles V against the Turks, and they had submitted more
than was required to the dynastic interests of the emperor, which
were determined by the necessities of the Hapsburg universal
monarchy. Both Lutheran and Catholic princes were now determined
that there should be peace in the empire. What must be done for
the attainment of religious unity, and whether such unity could
even be achieved at all were now questions of secondary interest.
To be sure, all participants nurtured the idea of a quick religious
settlement. However, the truce and the securing of the concept
of empire only became possible since all hope of solving the
religious question on the imperial level had been abandoned and
the necessity of permitting various solutions on the territorial
and local levels had been recognized. With this territorialization
of the religious problem, which appeared to be the only possible
solution, the groundwork was already laid for the Peace of Augsburg

(1555), which had to solve the problem of the civil recognition
and the regulated co-existence of two forms of "catholic"
Christendom.

Luther always thought of himself as an opponent of the pope,
not as a rebel against the emperor. His adherence to the emperor
and the empire had as its consequence in the last analysis the
fact that in the religious peaces of the 16th and 17th centuries
the Lutheran church became a constitutive element of imperial
constitutional law. In a very general sense "Augsburg 1555"
signified the resumption of Passau 1552 and its development into
imperial law. Although there was heated debate to the very end
of the negotiations, an unconditional "peace" was established
which was intended to establish a "friendly", voluntary, and
final settlement in matters concerning the faith. The emperor,
the king, and all the estates were obligated to administer the
peace and to aid anyone who should be harmed through a transgression
of the peace. The high court of the empire had to observe and
protect the peace.

No sovereign was prevented from allowing his subjects to
live according to the one or the other confession. Theoretically,
therefore, he could either allow both confessions or simply
sanction one of them for his subjects. This option of the
sovereign to determine the religious confession of his subjects
was known in the technical language of the jurists as the *ius
reformandi*, the "right of reformation." Wherever one sovereign
ruled, there one faith was to prevail: *Ubi unus dominus, ibi
sit una religio*. After the Peace of 1555 this was changed by the
jurists to the formula, *Cuius est regio, eius est in religione
dispositio* ("whoever possesses the region possesses the right to
regulate matters pertaining to the religion"). In the 17th century
this was shortened to the motto, *Cuius regio, eius religio*. In
those cases where the sovereign recognized only one confession in
his land, paragraph 23 of the Peace claimed that those subjects
of the other confession were to have the right to sell their
possessions and to escape possible religious compulsion through
emigration. (This was not the case for those living in the emperor's
patrimonial domains, and this fact was to have great importance
for the history of the Netherlands). Bondsmen were likewise to
have the right to emigrate, but their masters retained the right
to consider them their bondsmen despite their emigration to another
land within the empire.

Through provincial treaties between the sovereign and the estates a number of areas had already determined before 1555 whether the Lutheran confession or Roman Catholicism was to be the prevailing religion. The Peace of 1555 neither abrogated such treaties, nor made it impossible for the sovereign to lay down future restricting regulations. Consequently, the *ius reformandi* could be exercised primarily in those places where there were no protecting provincial treaties or territorial privileges. This was the case in a number of ecclesiastical districts and in some smaller counties and estates. Moreover, those areas came into question whose sovereign determined either openly or covertly to breach related ordinances.

The Lutherans had to tolerate the fact that the *reservatum ecclesiasticum* in every form was inserted into Article 18 of the treaty of peace. This was done by imperial order and expressly not as a joint decision of the Imperial Diet. According to the *reservatum* every high ecclesiastic, who left the Roman church for Lutheranism, automatically would lose his spiritual office and his benefices. This regulation, which appeared to be directed at individual persons, meant in reality a far-reaching exclusion of the possibility that an ecclesiastical prince would associate himself with his evangelically-minded subjects and lead his territory over to the Reformation. In the great majority of ecclesiastical districts, especially in South and West Germany, this proved a decisive check to the Reformation. The results could be seen in the confessional topography of Germany until 1803.

The Catholic party could be satisfied with the religious peace to the extent that limitations were imposed on the extension of the Reformation. But these were not as successful as one had hoped in regard to the secular estates. The *reservatum ecclesiasticu* could not significantly inhibit the further extension of the Reformation. Decisive for the preservation of Catholic property in the ecclesiastical districts was the dispute in Cologne over an episcopal election (1580-1583). The evangelical Gerhard Truchsess of Waldburg ran against the Catholic Duke Ernst of Bavaria, who was supported with Bavarian force of arms. In this fashion the northeast pillar of ecclesiastical princes in Germany was secured. At this time the zealous patron of the Counter-Reformation, Julius Echter of Mespelbrunn, ascended the bishop's throne in Würzburg. The Counter-Reformation emanating from the south checked the advance of the Reformation in the ecclesiastical districts of northwest Germany.

The Lutheran Church as Institution

In distinction to Calvin not a single church order of a juristic kind can be traced back to Luther. While there are hundreds of church orders by other authors, only eight come from Luther, namely, three orders of worship, two orders of baptism, two orders of ordination, and one order of marriage. Luther left the work of legislation to his colleagues, especially to J. Bugenhagen, who was the author of church orders for Braunschweig, Hamburg, Lübeck, Pomerania, and Schleswig-Holstein and who influenced the Reformation in Denmark and Scandinavia. It was not the Reformation which first discovered the institution of the established church (*Landeskirchentum*). However, the concept "established church" (*Landeskirche*) received its final refinement through the fact that the organizational unity of the church could not be preserved through the reformation of the proclamation and of doctrine. Therefore, the church of the Reformation broke up into a number of territorial independent churches. Every prince, duke, count, every magistrate of a free-city could, or rather was forced to exercise episcopal rights and duties. If one wished to measure them according to canon law, the visitations represented a real revolutionary act. The princes sought to justify them by asserting that they did not wish themselves to teach but wished to assume the responsibility for that which was taught in the congregations of their territory. Luther never derived these rights from the nature of the state. He had to deal with the de facto existence of the established church, but he wanted no state church. Since 1520 Luther had tried to direct the prominent members of the church to their Christian responsibility without his ever being able to imagine that the authorities would soon understand themselves to be no longer representatives of the church but its masters.

Luther conceived himself to be a preacher and teacher whose task it was to strengthen Christian consciences. He did not think of himself as an organizer of a new ecclesiastical entity, no matter how important his views were. He was neither able, nor did he wish, to erect a uniform, all-encompassing organization of the Lutheran church. Therefore, reforming efforts at organization were directed towards individual territories, from electorates and counties to imperial cities. Through many correspondences in their statements concerning the understanding of worship and doctrine the church orders of the Reformation era very impressively exhibit the peculiarities of the territorial

churches. The external configuration of the church was dependent
upon numerous political and sociological factors.

One of the debits of the evangelical church is that the
Reformation's theological doctrines concerning the church and its
law have been realized only in a very fragmented way within the
judicial order governing the relationship between state and church.
On the one hand, the Reformation assertions were encumbered with
and smothered by the equalitarian, biconfessional nature of the
church law established for the empire by the Peace of Augsburg
(1555) and the Peace of Westphalia (1648). On the other hand, they
were suppressed by the absolute character of that constitutional
law which governed the confessionally closed territories. The
order of 1555 and 1648 brought forth an inpenetrable system of
compromise which included elements both medieval and modern,
theological and constitutional, confessional and political,
ecclesiastical and secular.

When it was a matter of the proclamation and the management
of the church, Luther would have most preferred to use the bishops.
The Confessio Augustana (Article 28) discusses the question
whether and under what circumstances the incumbent bishops, who
were imperial princes, could still be recognized in their spiritual
functions. The Augustana distinguishes between the *potestas gladii*
or *potestas civilis* and the *potestas ecclesiastica*. This latter
potestas is limited to the actual power of the *ministerium
ecclesiasticum*, the preaching of the Gospel and the administration
of the sacraments. In this manner it is demanded from the Catholic
bishops. Thus, they could be recognized as bishops only if they
allowed the pure preaching of the Word and the administration of
the sacraments. Of course, a powerful influence was still exerted
by the centuries-long tradition of an episcopal structure, which
in its sociological context had deeply influenced the Middle Ages.

To some extent, late feudal elements continued in the
Lutheran churches. Nevertheless, behind the view of Article 28
there existed a fundamental insight: in the exercise of the
authority of the Word in preaching and absolution every external
force should be renounced. The *iurisdictio ecclesiastica* as the
iurisdictio episcoporum is by divine law committed to the bishops
as it is to every pastor. Spiritual leadership stands under the
Word of God and is obliged to obey it. Given the Word's superior
position, it is obvious that bishops are not the sole ones who may
ordain ministers. Wherever there are bishops who teach the Gospel,
there these bishops should perform the ordination. However, (and
this is the practice in Germany) wherever no such bishop exists,

the ordination to a spiritual office may be performed in principle
by any evangelical pastor. This is the case even if forms for
a specific office for ordinations would be developed, for these
forms would rest upon human gradations within the one office.
Luther would have liked to have retained the office of bishop
in later years as well. When in 1542 an evangelical bishop could
be appointed in Naumburg, Luther participated in the action.

In complete opposition to Luther's opinion, secular lords
were also appointed as evangelical bishops. For example, in 1544
Duke August of Saxony became the administrator of the bishopric
of Magdeburg, while in 1545 Duke Joachim of Münsterberg succeeded
the Bishop of Brandenburg, who had become an evangelical. Under-
standably, ruling noble families saw a good chance to extend their
territorial domains through the acquisition of bishoprics. The
politics of self-interest conducted by the princes dealt accordingly
with the bishoprics of Magdeburg, Halberstadt, and Minden.
Merseburg and Naumburg had a similar fate. The evangelical office
of bishop in the last analysis foundered on the political self-
interest of the territorial princes.

Luther desired a church founded on the responsibility of
the universal priesthood. Since the secular nobility fully
participated in this universal priesthood, Luther apportioned an
important role to it in the direction of the visitations and in
the administration of the church. In so doing, however, Luther
sharply distinguished between the secular government and the
spiritual government in which at times other authorities play a
role. The visitations were in themselves the duty of the bishops.
However, the bishops evaded this responsibility, and, therefore,
Luther of necessity turned to the princes, who were the most
eminent members of the church. In this capacity, and not as the
supreme officer of the civil government, the prince "from Christian
love" was to guarantee his assistance and summon the visitors.
These were to assume an ecclesiastical office, even if they
participated in the visitations as laymen. The criticism that
in the end Luther delivered the churches to the state by agreeing
to visitations by both spiritual *and* secular officers is somewhat
unhistorical. The local congregations could not independently
order their finances. An authority who centrally guided the
church's financial affairs did not exist. Only much later did
the duty of financial administration accrue to the consistories.
For ill or good, therefore, it was necessary for the reorganization
of the church's finances to harness the resources of the state,
which had acquired a great deal of church property. The visitation

between 1527 and 1529 had to master extensive tasks. Suitable
ministers had to be strengthened in their ministries and given
economic security. The decaying monasteries and church properties
were in need of inventory and administration. The schools needed
to be improved. Luther perceived the essential part of church
administration to be in visitations: *visitatio est gubernatio*,
visitation is governance.

Even if the visitations were commissioned by the princes
and executed in common by theologians and civil deputies, yet the
actual governance of the church was not to be by means of external
power but by the Word of God. On this point Luther never ceased
to insist, and, therefore, he cannot be made responsible for
later developments. His experiences during the visitation in
Electoral Saxony persuaded him to write his catechisms of 1529.

In 1527 within Electoral Saxony the office of superintendent
was created in those cities which served as administrative seats.
Bugenhagen's Church orders from 1528 on introduced superintendents
with episcopal dignity as administrators of both external and
internal church affairs. However, these hopeful beginnings did
not prove fruitful, because by their nature visitations were
practicable only within particular time-periods. In the long
run officers and administrators were necessary to decide pressing
questions of ecclesiastical law, especially those questions
pertaining to the marriage-code.

At the beginning of February, 1539, a consistory was set
up in Wittenberg. Its founders, Justus Jonas and Chancellor Brück,
had wished to make of it a governing council of the sovereign
with all the rights and privileges which appertain to such an
authority, including the power to mete out punishments from
corporal punishment to imprisonment. Due to Luther's protests,
however, the consistory became merely a divorce court and had
nothing to do with spiritual matters. The consistory of Leipzig
was formed in 1543, that of Merseburg and Meissen in 1544. Luther
had good reasons for his opposition to the formation of consistories
to serve as administrators of a church government under a sovereign.
He felt that they provided a menacing competition to the office
of bishop. Such competition already manifested itself during
Luther's lifetime in the altercation between George of Anhalt,
the Bishop of Merseburg, and the Saxon theologians, who were
striving for a consistorial order. Furthermore, Luther felt the
consistories to be the harbingers of the state church. A comparison
of Luther's preface to his *Instruction of the Visitors* with the
Constitution and Article of the spiritual Consistory of Wittenberg

(1542) is instructive. The "Constitution" adopted the Roman
administration of justice, rejects the papal abuses but in
accordance with the early church symbols accepts canon law.

In March, 1544, Duke Maurice summoned a conference of
theologians to Leipzig. This conference produced a comprehensive
opinion paper concerning the question of church order. Of
especial concern was the spiritual character of the consistory.
According to this opinion, the consistory was only to exhort,
advise, and guide. It was not to punish in a secular fashion.
In close agreement with Luther the consistory is here conceived as
an instrument of ecclesiastical self-discipline and not as a
governing organ of the sovereign as it was in the recommendations
of the Wittenberg theologians. Unfortunately, this conception
was unable to prevail. Maurice did not concur with the opinion,
since at that time it appeared to him that for Merseburg spiritual
leadership by a bishop was to be preferred. Further development
unfortunately led to the result that through the struggle of
two contending factions over the structure of the church the role
of the princes became ever more important. Had the Smalcald War
not brought a change, perhaps the episcopal structure of the church
under the nobility would have prevailed.

The *Wittenberg Reformation* of 1545 written by Melanchthon
speaks of ecclesiastical courts and has in mind thereby the
consistories. These were by no means merely administrative organs.
They were penal courts which, to be sure, did not punish with the
sword but "with God's Word and separation or exclusion from the
Chruch." They gave necessary support to the pastor in his exercise
of the power of the keys. Yet, there is now talk of a competence
in cases "which the secular authority does not wish to consider."
Therefore, the consistories became an extension of the penal arm
in those areas which were excluded from the penal power of the
secular authority. Whenever the judges of the consistory pronounced
the punishment of excommunication, the pastors would publicize
this punishment.

Melanchthon wished to enlist the assistance of the state
for the church in the area of the administration of justice.
W. Elert perceives in this a theocratic element in Melanchthon's
thinking. However that may be, matters proceeded quite differently
than Melanchthon desired. There arose church government by the
sovereign, "in which finally the power of the Church became an
appendage of the sovereignty of the princes, and the Church became
a mere department of the state" (W. Elert). In Württemberg J.
Brenz (1499-1570) had attempted to develop the church's organization

independently of the church court and thereby to secure an important role for the congregation. He perhaps at first had even
represented the synodical idea. However, he also succumbed to
the pull of state-church centralization which did not allow
independent responsibility to the congregations. Likewise in
Hesse, where in the Homberg church order of 1527 Count Philip
along with theologian Franz Lambert of Avignon had envisioned a
congregational church, the first attempts were total failures.

Church government conducted by the soverign developed as
the twin of political particularism. As the authority of the
territorial church the consistories gave decisive influence to
the jurists. The Lutheran church became a bureaucratically
ruled consistorial church. In order to be free from the will of
secular officials the new authority, contrary to Luther, sought
an independently administered executive instrument in excommunication, which was conceived as a secular punishment. Corporal
punishment, fines, and imprisonment could also be inflicted.

Thanks to the efforts of Melanchthon the tasks of a
national or general synod were brought repeatedly into the fore-
ground during the 1530s and 1540s. The hope that there would be
a German general synod was thereby kept alive. That, of course,
never happened. Rather, the synods held within the context of
the visitations grew in significance. These synods had to be
summoned by the sovereign, and during the 1550s these synods
took on the character of theological commissions, which, depending
on the position of the prince, guaranteed the numerical superiority
of one or the other party. A general, evangelical synod never
took place, and in view of the theological division the aging
Melanchthon no longer expected any success from one. He placed
his hopes on the universities, which were likewise deeply divided.

The Confessional Era

With the Peace of 1555 at Augsburg the right of reformation
became a right of the sovereign. This was to have important
consequences. It was to play a decisive role in the delineation
of territories and regions. The question of who possessed the
actual sovereign authority was not everywhere determined in 1555.
For example, until the decline of the old empire, there were in
Franconia and Swabia disputes and controversies concerning who
was the sovereign in particular cases. Complete clarity was first
achieved through the modern concept of the state which encompasses

a particular region within itself. The medieval state, which
was founded upon a person, changed into a modern state, which
was founded on land area. In 1555 the empire held fast to the
view that there was only one religion within it. The two
confessions were considered to be two expressions of the one
religion, and neither voluntarily relinquished the claim to be
"catholic." The first step toward a formal tolerance of the
confessions had been made, even though neither party wished to
guarantee to the other equal tolerance within its own sphere
of influence. And yet at the same time the first step toward an
intellectual, internal tolerance had been made, for both parties
had done something which pointed beyond their own wishes and
understanding and which received its final form in the Enlightenment's idea of toleration with its political implications. The
Diet of Augsburg (1555) did not finish the work of stabilizing
the church of the Reformation. Rather, such work began then to
make progress. To be sure, the Reformation did enter into its
confessional phase. After the Peace Treaty Lutheranism developed
as a confessional church with those features which were characteristic for most of the territorial churches until the height of
the Enlightenment.

      The old distribution of parishes with affiliates, benefices,
foundations, etc. remained essentially the same. The spiritual
courts retained the right to judge marital cases, and the obstacles
to marriage for related persons remained the same as those in the
canon law. Nevertheless, the Reformers exhibited a fine sense
for transgressions and excesses. This was clear in the courageous,
selfless struggle against the imperial Interim (1548) when many
pastors preferred to risk their lives than to accept ambiguous
ceremonies and formulations.

      After 1555 the evangelical authorities could often exercise
more power than the old Catholic authorities and the bishops.
They controlled the finances and possessions of the church. Since
they had practically assumed the legal competence of the earlier
bishop, the authorities exercised episcopal jurisdiction. Concerning the retention of cult and confession they had the last word.
The church's wealth was transferred to the sovereign, who sometimes
did and sometimes did not utilize it for ecclesiastical purposes.
According to the theory that efforts on behalf of the evangelical
state or for the general welfare were part of the objectives of
the Reformation it was regarded as permissable to use the wealth
of the church to augment the treasury of the state. Through the
theological controversies after the death of Luther there

unintentionally accrued to the authorities a mediation and
judicial function. This gave rise to conflicts which before the
rise of Pietism elicited within Lutheran Orthodoxy a sharp critique of the supreme episcopacy of the sovereign (caesaropapism)
which continually overstepped its limits.

After the Peace of Augsburg Duke Christopher of Württemberg was the first prince to take steps to settle the inner-
Lutheran opposition between the Flacians and the adiaphorists
and Majorists. At a conference with the Catholics in Worms
(September 9 - November 28, 1557) the dissession showed itself in
a disgraceful manner. The Ernestine theologians departed. The
assembly of princes which met at Frankfurt (1558) and at Naumburg
made no further progress. In this situation the formation of
territorial confessions became more and more prevalent. Leading
in the attempt to work out a definitive confessional document,
which would surmount the *corpora doctrinae* of the territorial
churches, were Braunschweig-Wolfenbüttel and especially Württemberg.
At the end of August, 1568, Jacob Andreae was sent by Württemberg
to Wolfenbüttel in order to solicit support for his plans for
agreement. Since 1570 the path toward agreement became ever
more obvious. In 1575 the Swabian-Saxon Concord was submitted,
and the Formula of Concord completed its development in 1577.

Wherever the Formula of Concord was introduced, one was
on guard for any deviations from this general position. All that
was held to be crypto-Calvinist was severely penalized, even to
the extent of inflicting corporal punishment and in isolated
instances even capital punishment. The idea of absolute truth
and the binding nature of the faith continued to exist within
Lutheranism. The necessity to adopt a protective defensive
posture was no less felt in Lutheranism than in Calvinism and
Catholicism. In this confessional period there was fanaticism
on all sides. Through improper and inapplicable comparisons of
Christians with Jews, Turks, and Mohammedans, one not only abetted
the lovelessness characteristic of these struggles, but also
furthered the secularization of the confessional controversies,
for the foundations common to all Christians were denied.

After the Book of Concord of 1580 in which all confessional
writings of the Lutherans were collected, there arose theological
systems within Lutheran Orthodoxy. With the consent of Melanchthon
a Protestant scholasticism was developed with the aid of Aristotle,
who was at the time indispensable for any school philosophy.
Wittenberg and Leipzig vied with one another, and their teachers
showed differences which were, of only small consequence in relation

to the more progressive Jena. Jena boasted John Gerhard (1582-
1637) who taught there from 1616 to 1637 and produced his
theological Summa, which included the Catholic tradition but
distinguished itself from the irenic and ethical tendencies of
the Helmstadt theology headed by George Calixt (1586-1651).
Natural theology understood as preliminary to the *theologia
revelata* paved the way for the Englightenment.

Both before and during the Thirty Years' War the Lutheran
jurists appealed to the threatened Peace of 1555 and attempted
to develop a state church judicial system from its stipulations.
Before it prevailed as law in the stipulations of the Peace of
Westphalia (1648) an order based on parity was established
from the provisional arrangement of the Peace of Augsburg. The
concept of a constitutional agreement suppressed the unanswered
question of theological truth. The *ius reformandi* was extended
to both confessions and became a purely formal right of the
sovereign. The question concerning theological truth was ignored
and simply postulated by the jurists. In reflections on imperial
law one was not to determine which confession was the true one.
Rather, argumentation was limited to matters concerning the
constitution, even though this was contrary to traditional state
church law and to the medieval view of the emperor as the protector
of the one church. The concept of the church had "to surrender
its absolutism precisely in the endeavor to remain a universal
order" (M. Heckel). The Westphalian Congress of München, where
the Catholics met, and of Osnabrück, where the Protestants assembled,
concluded three peace agreements (1648). The ecclesiastical-
religious norms of the Peace stood under the sign of tolerance and
of parity among the confessions. Until the outbreak of the Thirty
Years' War the relationship between the confessions had been
guided by the Treaty of Passau (1552) and the Peace of Augsburg
(1555). The estates of the empire, which had introduced the
Reformation, were assured that they would on that account have to
endure no force. Likewise, the free choice of religion was assured
to the sovereigns in the future. Against the protest of the
Lutherans, however, the *ecclesiasticum reservatum* was pushed
through. According to this *reservatum* those ecclesiastics who
converted to the Reformation would surrender their *beneficium* and
their revenues. The right to a free choice of religion was not
yet extended to the subject peoples who received only the right to
emigrate.

Nevertheless, the Peace of Westphalia signified a clear
step forward. It endorsed the Treaty of Passau and the Peace of

Augsburg. Instead of 1552 the year 1624 would serve as test date
in determining the property ownership of both sides. Especially
in North Germany a number of ecclesiastical territories had become
evangelical since 1552. The patrimonial domains in Austria,
however, were excluded from the Peace and officially remained
closed to the Reformation.

The Peace brought a relaxation of the rigid axiom, *cuius
regio, eius religio*, which meant equality without toleration.
The use of the year 1624 to determine land ownership implied the
acceptance of some confessional mixing. If a prince changed his
confession, he could no longer force his subjects to follow him,
although he could tolerate others who shared his new faith. Upon
such a legal basis, for example, Reformed Huguenots could immigrate
into Lutheran cities. Wherever those of differing faith could
not worship publicly, private devotions could be allowed. Sometimes attendance of worship services beyond territorial borders
was possible.

The Peace of Westphalia made it reasonably certain that a
reunion by political force was not possible. Furthermore, after
the experience of the war a great consensus had arisen that a
reunion through force ought not again be attempted. What in the
Peace of Augsburg (1555) was thought to be temporary was now
recognized to be definitive, even though the Roman church protested
against the legal parity of the three confessions within the
empire.

Translated by William C. Weinrich

CHAPTER 3

Carl-Gustaf Andrén

The Reformation in the Scandinavian Countries

General Features

The Nordic countries - Denmark, Norway, Iceland, Sweden and Finland - show a great homogeneity from a confessional point of view. This fact is based on the way the Reformation was accomplished in these countries. At the end of the 14th century the Scandinavian countries formed a union under the King of Denmark. However, powerful national independence movements, especially in Sweden but also in Norway, continually called the union into question, and for long periods it was entirely dissolved. Protracted fighting for and against the union also took place during the first two decades of the 16th century. For a short period in 1520-1521 King Christian II of Denmark (1513-1523)* succeeded in conquering the adversaries of the union in Sweden and for the last time Scandinavia formed a real political unity under the leadership of the Danish King. From 1521 onwards there were two political coalitions - one consisting of Denmark, Norway and Iceland, the other of Sweden and Finland. Consequently the Reformation was approached and carried through differently in each of these regions.

At the time of the Reformation the conditions in the church were rather similar in the Scandinavian countries. The

---

*Chronological references indicate, in the case of kings, the years of reign, in the case of other persons, the biographical data.

Roman Catholic Church had long been well established. The richly
developed church life was regulated not only by the canon law
but also by detailed diocesan statutes. The vigorous efforts to
attain greater uniformity within the dioceses had found expression
in among other things the publication of missals, breviaries and
manuals. Artistic decoration of the churches was in progress and
distinguished results were achieved at the beginning of the 16th
century. Church discipline was actually maintained and the
decline of the Church on the continent was scarcely felt in
Denmark, Norway, Iceland, Sweden and Finland.

There were, however, anomalies and they were accordingly
subjected to criticism. Primarily it concerned the political
and economic engagements of the bishop and the sale of indulgences.
Indulgences were sold in Scandinavia by the papal legate
Acrimboldus to find means for the erection of St. Peter's Basilica
in Rome. Poul Helgesen, (1485-1535) a Danish Bible humanist
regarded this activity as the chief cause of the annihilation of
the prestige of the Roman Catholic Church in Scandinavia and as
a gateway to Lutheran faith. The Bible humanism of the great
scholar Erasmus Rotterdamus was wide spread, especially in Denmark.
The Reform Catholic endeavors became a vital basis for reformatory
ideas. Rising nationalism also paved the way for the Reformation.
The king urged certain claims on the pope, especially the right
to appoint bishops.

In the light of these general features we will follow
the progress of the Reformation in Scandinavia.

Denmark

The Reformation was brought to Denmark via Schleswig and
the North-German commercial towns. Its different phases are
closely associated with three kings, namely Christian II, Frederick
I (1524-1533) and Christian III (1536-1559). Two of them had
met Martin Luther in person. Christian II, who in 1521 tried to
get the Elector of Saxony to send Luther and others on a visit to
Copenhagen, resided in Wittenberg in 1523, after he had been forced
to leave Denmark because of a revolt. The future king Christian
III was present at the Diet of Worms in 1521 and was witness when
Luther defended his teaching in the presence of the German Emperor.
He was permanently influenced by this experience. The most
important theological contribution to the Reformation in Denmark
was made by a disciple of Luther's, Hans Tausen (1494-1561), who

was a friar of the Order of St. John. He had been educated in
the spirit of Bible humanism and after his stay at the university
of Louvain he was master of Greek as well as of Hebrew. He got
in touch with Luther through his studies in Wittenberg in 1523.
In the Skiby Chronicle, written by Poul Helgesen, he is described
as "the colour-bearer of all Lutherans in Denmark".

The time of Christian II was a period of preparation for
the Reformation. The king tried to create a Scandinavian Great
Power under the guidance of a strong monarch supported by burghers
and merchants. The most important institution of the country –
the church - would have to conform to the royal power, if this
aim was to be realized. Therefore the king pursued a national
ecclesiastic policy of great importance for the future. At the
same time he wanted to reform the church from within, in accordance
with the spirit of humanism.

As mentioned before, Bible humanism spread quite extensively
in Denmark, mostly because of its eminent representative, Poul
Helgesen, one of the most important personages of the Danish
Reformation, who was also supported by the king. Poul Helgesen,
lecturer in biblical theology at the university of Copenhagen in
1519, strongly criticized the prevailing scholastic theology and
the contemporary activities of the church. Profound humane studies
should reform the church from within. Poul Helgensen accepted
many of Luther's doctrines and therefore was considered a Lutheran.
In the fundamental question of the meaning of faith, however, he
differed from Luther. He meant that faith was the right piety
and way of living. The reformers of Denmark were all deeply
influenced by Bible humanism through Poul Helgesen, who also
found a link between the old and the new.

That Christian II himself was influenced by the Bible
humanists who were favorably inclined toward reform is evident from
his draft of a church code. This influence also seems to have
inspired him to contact Wittenberg from where he wished to bring
not only Karlstadt and Melanchthon but also Luther to Copenhagen.
Karlstadt arrived there in 1521 to become a university teacher,
royal counselor and preacher, but he found that the ideas of the
Reformation had not yet been approved by the Danish King. After
a few weeks he returned to Wittenberg. Not until 1523 did Christian
II become a firmly convinced Lutheran, and then he had already left
Denmark accused among other things of letting heretics preach in
Copenhagen.

When he came to power in 1524 Frederick I promised to
oppose Lutheran heresy. In practice however he followed the

tolerance of the German Diets. This implied that preaching in
accordance with the Bible was allowed until a general synod had
taken sides in the religious controversy. The leading Roman
Catholics as well as the humanists also complained that the change
of government did not lead to the expected improvements for the
church. The social and political changes that Christian II had
started, ceased. Indirectly this favored the Reformation among
burghers and peasants. The German peasants' revolt gave rise to
similar revolts in Denmark, chiefly caused by the reactionary
aristocracy and inspired by an appeal from the exiled king,
Christian II. He also intervened in the future, for instance by
having reformatory publications printed. Of great importance for
the progress of the Reformation was the translation of the New
Testament into Danish, published in 1524. This was the first
reformatory edition in the vernacular outside the boundaries of
Germany. The basis of the Danish translation was the Erasmi
Latin translation of 1516 and Luther's German translation of 1522.

The year 1526 was the real starting point for the Reformation in Denmark. Reformatory sermons were delivered regularly
in many places and there was a formal breach with Rome after the
assemblies of the nobility at Odense. For it was decided that
from now on a newly-elected bishop should apply to the king and
not to the pope for the confirmation of his election. Another
assembly was held at Odense in 1527 at which the king dismissed a
demand from the Royal Council that he should intervene against
heresy. In this way a legal basis was laid for continued free
evangelical preaching. The Danish church stood out as a Reform-
Catholic national church founded on the Gospel and with no
connection with Rome.

At the end of the 1520s a great many parishes were reformed
sometimes very dramatically, as for instance in Hans Tausen's
Viborg, where with royal permission a couple of churches were
pulled down and some abbeys were transformed into parish churches.
In Sønderjylland the Reformation was strongly supported by Duke
Christian, afterwards King Christian III, and in 1528 he introduced
a Lutheran church code, the Haderslev articles,in about 60 of
its parishes. This prescribed among other things that the Mass
should be delivered in Danish. Hans Tausen's literary activity
in Viborg was extremely important for the whole church - not least
his Danish hymnbook, his directions for rites and later on his
book of sermons. Of great importance for liturgy was the so-called
Malmömässan of 1528. It was based on Luther's Deutsche Messe of
1523 and the South-German Nürnbergermesse of 1525.

Following foreign examples, Frederick I summoned an assembly of the nobility in Copenhagen in 1530 for a disputation between the Roman Catholic prelates and the evangelical preachers, as he wanted religion to be reformed and taught everywhere in the same way. The meeting was, however, threatened from abroad and the religious questions were disregarded in favor of the political ones. However, the preachers drew up articles of faith - Confessio Hafniensis (1530) - which were characterized by general Protestantism on one hand and radical Bible humanism on the other. The planned disputation never took place and the meeting did not decide anything about the Reformation, but the articles showed the opinion of the leading reformers in Denmark.

The following years were disturbed by internal political riots. Christian II, who had returned to the Roman Catholic church, was a permanent threat. He landed in Norway with an army but was taken prisoner in 1532. When Frederick I died in 1533 the succession to the throne was still unsolved. That same year the bishops tried to regain their power. A civil war centered in Copenhagen and Malmö broke out, based on religious middle-class democracy and opposition towards the king, the aristocracy and the prevailing Roman Catholic church. Duke Christian was victorious in this struggle for power and ascended the throne as King Christian III in 1536. Several bishops were dismissed as originators of the war and their possessions were confiscated.

Through the decrees of 1536 the Reformation had definitely triumphed in Denmark. In the next year, the ecclesiastical conditions were further settled both constitutionally and liturgically by means of *Kirkeordinansen*, a church code with directions about faith, services and ceremonies, approved by Luther and Bugenhagen, and *Alterbogen* - an evangelical missal. In the same year seven new reformatory bishops, called superintendents, were consecrated by the German Lutheran reformer Johann Bugenhagen. As Bugenhagen himself had not been consecrated bishop this meant a definite breach with the old church. Thus the West-Danish Lutheranism under Christain III, with the sovereign as its supreme head, had conquered the radical and democratic East-Danish Lutheran movement. Christian III's Bible of 1550-51 - for generations the Danis. church bible - and Hans Thomissøns hymnbook of 1564 became the final books of the Reformation. Articles of faith were not adopted until 1665 when *Kongeloven* - a constitutional law - referred to the Holy Scripture and the Confessio Augustana.

Norway

        Politically Norway belonged to Denmark, but in the
religious sphere the dramatic events which took place in the
1520s in Denmark had no comparision in Norway, although Bible
humanism was also known there.   Preachers inspired by Luther
seem to have appeared sporadically at the end of the decade but
there was never a national movement.   The Norwegian church under
archbishop Olav Engelbriktsson (c. 1480-1538) did not become
involved in the Reformation crisis.   Christian II's landing in
Norway dod not bring about a positive result for the future of
the Roman Catholic church and after Christian III's victory in
Denmark the archbishop escaped from Norway.   What happened in
Denmark determined the fate of the Church of Norway as well.
To a certain extent one might say that the introduction of the
Reformation was compulsory.   The fundamental documents were also
made valid in Norway.   *Kirkeordinansen* of 1537 contained a
special section about Norway saying, among other things, that the
sovereign promises to send superintendents to Norway to attend
to the preaching of God's Word.   Part of the property of the
Norwegian church was confiscated and churches and monasteries had
to hand over a large number of their silver and gold treasures.
Officially the Lutheran Reformation was carried through in Norway
at the end of the 1530s, but the education of the people still
remained, and for a long time they seemed rather indifferent.
Norway did not get an evangelical Church Order of its own until
1607 although it had Bible translation and hymnbook in common
with Denmark.

Iceland

        In Iceland, too, the development in Denmark was decisive.
On account of the frequency of commercial connections with Germany
the Reformation became known early in Iceland.   Lutheran sermons
were delivered by two Icelandic pastors.   One of them, Odd
Gottskalksson (1500-1556), translated the New Testament into
Icelandic and it was printed in Roskilde in 1540.   As early as
1538 the Danish *Kirkeordinans* was submitted to the *Allting*, the
diet of Iceland.   The new movement was opposed by the two bishops
of Iceland, but from 1550 all resistance to the new ideas was
relinquished and Iceland joined the Danish Reformation as a
Lutheran national church.

Sweden

During the Middle Ages the Swedish church province had
been able to maintain its autonomy in many respects in relation
to the secular royal power of the country, as well as to the
spiritual power of the Roman Catholic church. As members of
the Royal Council the bishops held a prominent political position
and they took an active part in the government of the country.
When in 1520 King Christian II had successfully defeated the
opponents of the union, two bishops were executed at the Massacre
of Stockholm (1520) together with several other prominent Swedes.
Characteristic of the Reformation in Sweden and Finland
was its dependence on a few men who were for a long time leaders
of the country as well as of the Church. In 1521 Gustav
Eriksson Vasa became leader of the national independence movement
that began after the outrages in Stockholm. In 1523 he was elected
King of Sweden, and his reign lasted until 1560. At the beginning
of the liberation Gustav Vasa made a vow that he would defend the
Roman Catholic church and its privileges, but his aim was to
create a strong royal power in an independent country and his
ambition to achieve his purpose made him keenly alive to the ideas
of the Reformation. He was inspired by the Archdeacon of Strängnäs
Laurentius Andreae (1470-1552), who became Gustav Vasa's chancellor
from 1523 onwards. By studying abroad he had become familiar not
only with the Canon Law and the writings of the Apostolic Fathers
but also with the reform ideas of the late Middle Ages. He had
the talents of an outstanding stateman, which was a great asset
when, in collaboration with Gustav Vasa, he gave final shape to
the program of the Swedish National Church in the 1520s.
The reformer of Sweden, Olavus Petri (1493-1552), active
between 1518 and 1552, had also been a deacon at Strängnäs. After
studying thomism under Peder Galle at the university of Uppsala,
Olavus Petri spent the eventful years 1516-18 at the university
of Wittenberg, where he studied the humanities, law and theology.
Like Hans Tausen of Denmark he acquired a good knowledge of both
Greek and Hebrew. At close quarters he witnessed the most important
events connected with Luther's appearance as a reformer, but he
was also influenced by Bible humanism, which left its mark on his
future activity. Through Olavus Petri's sermons from the beginning
of the 1520s the ideas of the Reformation were introduced and
spread all over Sweden.

Also among the prominent personages of the Swedish
Reformation was Olavus Petri's brother, Laurentius (1499-1573),
who was to be the first evangelical archbishop of the Church of
Sweden, a post which he held from 1531 to 1573. He too had been
studying in Wittenberg as a disciple of Luther. The long
duration of the ministry of these men provided the continuity
that was of such great importance for the development of the
Swedish Reformation.

Characteristic of the situation in the Church of Sweden
was the fact that no less than five of the seven dioceses were
without bishops in 1522. Only the aged Bishop of Wäxjö and Hans
Brask (1464-1538) of Linköping were left. The latter was to be
the foremost spokesman for the Roman Catholic church against
Reformation. Another defender of the Roman Catholic faith was
Peder Galle (c. 1450-1538) learned doctor of divinity at the
university of Uppsala. Only one of the newly elected bishops,
Petrus Magni of Västerås (died 1534), had been appointed and
consecrated by the Pope, in 1524. When applying for confirmation
and consecration of the elected bishops, Gustav Vasa vindicated
the independence of the state against the church by requesting
that the charges in connection with the consecration should be
remitted. The Pope rejected this proposal, and the result was
that the relations between the Swedish state and the papacy were
severed - earlier than in any other state in Europe. At the same
time the influence of the monastic system was counteracted by its
concentration on missionary activity in Lapland. The episcopal
power and authority decreased considerably, partly because the
new bishops had not been consecrated and partly because they
were favorably inclined towards reforms.

The bishop of Linköping, Hans Brask, repeatedly warned
his contemporaries of the Lutheran heresy that was creeping into
the country. Nevertheless the Reformation met with approval. The
main ideas of the new ecclesiastic policy were presented in a
letter to Wadstena Monastery in 1524. In this letter, which was
of the greatest importance to the Swedish Reformation, Laurentius
Andreae maintained that the Bible was the supreme authority, that
consequently what happened in the country did not imply the
introduction of a new faith, that Luther's doctrine must not be
rejected without being examined in the light of the Word of God,
that the church was the Christian people and that the money of
the church therefore belonged to the people.

During the following years a series of events occurred
which showed the trend: Olavus Petri was stationed in Stockholm

and thus his influence increased. In 1524 a German Lutheran, Nicolaus Stecker, was appointed rector of the capital. Next year Olavus Petri married and the liturgy of the mass at his marriage service was apparently evengelical. In 1526 the New Testament was printed in Swedish at the royal printing office in Stockholm. The religious question was brought into focus when the king - in accordance with what happened in Germany - gave notice of a discourse on religion in Uppsala concerning certain practical problems of the church. The disputation never came about, as Peder Galle refused to join in the discussion and only delivered a written answer, which was refuted by Olavus Petri both verbally and in writing.

Pressed by religious and political riots, Gustav Vasa was obliged to summon a diet at Västerås in 1527 with the plea that the king wanted to abdicate and that an agreement must be made regarding the Christian doctrine. The king was prevailed upon not to abdicate; a discourse on religion came about. The diet voted to support the king against the disturbances in the province of Dalecarlia, to concede a reduction of ecclesiastical property, to grant the nobility permission to get back certain estates that had been given to the church and finally expressed a wish that the pure Word of God might be preached all over the country. This meant on one hand that the principle of tolerance was applied and on the other that God's Word was considered the supreme authority in ecclesiastical questions. The resolutions of the Diet of Västerås did not mean a rejection of Roman Catholic faith and liturgy but they laid the foundation for the conversion of Sweden to an evangelical country with an episcopal national church led by the king.

The implementation of the Västerås resolutions ushered in a new era for the Swedish Reformation. In 1528 the elected bishops were consecrated by Petrus Magni, Bishop of Västerås, who himself had been consecrated in Rome. In this way the apostolic succession was guaranteed in the Church of Sweden. Immediately after this Gustav Vasa was crowned. The reduction of ecclesiastical property was carried through, with the result that before long the monasteries were not able to fulfil their functions.

In several publications on urgent theological and ecclesiastical questions Olavus Petri unfolded the evangelical church program in the spirit of Luther, even if Bible humanistic ideas can also be found in his writings. In 1529 there was a synod at Örebro to decide on the uniformity of ceremonies. This was the last time that representatives of the monasteries were

present at a synod. The resolution emphasized the importance of
preaching and teaching as well as of discipline and order. The
liturgy was not altered but was given an evangelical interpretation. Nor was there an immediate breach with the Roman Catholic
tradition, for the synod did not bring about any extensive reforms.
In connection with the Synod of Örebro Olavus Petri published a
service book in Swedish which was a reformatory revision of the
Roman Catholic manual. In 1529 the progress of the Reformation
was disturbed by riots in the south of Sweden where they were
angry that the king had supported the Lutheran heresy. By a
decree of the City Council of Stockholm it was ruled that evangelical services should be held in Swedish and from 1530 this was
the only form allowed in the capital. Olavus Petri now published
Svenska Mässan - a missal based on Luther's Formula missae of
1523 and the Nürnberger Messe - a book of sermons and an enlarged
edition of a Swedish hymnbook, all of them important stages towards an evangelical divine service in Swedish.

        The see of Uppsala had been vacant for a long time but
in 1531 Laurentius Petri was appointed archbishop and consecrated
by the Bishop of Västerås Petrus Magni. Disturbances, both
abroad and within the country, delayed the progress of the
Reformation to a certain extent. The reformers were pushed aside,
the king himself took over as head of the church and the Roman
catholic reform movement increased its activity.

        In the middle of the 1530s, after the political conditions
were established in favor of the Reformation, this movement
entered its third phase. In connection with Gustav Vasa's second
marriage in 1536 the archbishop summoned the other bishops and
some prominent clergymen to a synod at Uppsala, which resolved
that the clergy should preach the holy Gospel, that the Swedish
mass should be introduced in all churches as soon as possible,
that the Swedish manual should be used at christenings as well as
at other ecclesiastical ceremonies and that the law of celibacy
should be repealed. Through these resolutions the reformatory
books had been sanctioned by the church and at the same time the
Lutheran reformers had conquered the Reform-Catholics. The Church
of Sweden stood out as an evangelical Lutheran national church.

        Gustav Vasa's cautious attitude toward changes in the
liturgy also appeared in this case, as there was no official
confirmation of the resolutions. The realization of the enjoined
order for divine service resulted in new disturbances and caused
the king to intervene brusquely, prohibiting too extensive reforms
of the liturgy. The reformers were again disregarded and the king

acquired a new adviser, the Pomeranian theologian Georg Norman (1500-1553), who had been recommended by Luther and Melanchthon. About 1540 an adoption of the Swedish ecclesiastical constitution to the Pomeranian one was in progress. At the beginning of 1540 Gustav Vasa issued a decree that a total reform of doctrine and ceremonies in all Swedish parishes should be carried through. The observance of the decree should be supervised by Norman through general visitations. On these inspection tours art treasures and silver objects belonging to the churches were ruthlessly confiscated. This was one of the causes of the so-called *Dackefejden* (1542-1543), a revolt in Småland chiefly directed against Gustav Vasa's commercial policy. It is true that the Reformation was strongly supported by the publication of the whole Bible in Swedish in 1541, based on the German Bible of 1534, and by the official editions of the Swedish mass and the manual in Swedish. However, revolts all over the country showed that there were still many Roman Catholic adherents and it was therefore necessary to detach Sweden from the influence of Roman Catholicism. This happened at the Diet of 1544 when the members promised never to give up the faith that was now predominant in Sweden. Thus Sweden was officially made an evangelical Lutheran country.

The Reformation in Sweden was consolidated during the remainder of Gustav Vasa's reign. Certain Calvinist elements tried without success to assert themselves during the reign of Erik XIV in the 1560s. In 1571 an important step was taken when the Church Order - worked out by the archbishop Laurentius Petri - was confirmed by the king Johan III, another son of Gustav Vasa. With a motto from 1 Cor. 14:40 "All things should be done decently and in order", the Church Order gives regulations, pastoral advice, and liturgical directions. The Church Order is neither a church law nor articles of faith in spite of the fact that it contains fundamental dogmatic investigations, that was the first officially sanctioned explanation of doctrine in Sweden. The sources of the Church Order are Swedish medieval and reformatory tradition and some German Church Orders. The time of Johan III (1568-1592) was characterized by the so-called "liturgical struggle". The king, who was married to the Roman Catholic princess Katarina Jagellonica from Poland, endeavored to co-ordinate the Church of Sweden with the Roman Catholic church. He felt enthusiasm for the writings of the Fathers of the Church and in 1576 he published a new liturgy called *röda boken* (the red book), that was directly based on the Roman mass but was revised with features from the Swedish reformatory tradition.

After the death of Johan III a synod was held at Uppsala
in 1593, afterwards called the Uppsala Council. It was a large
church assembly in which the Prince Regent Carl, Duke of
Södermanland, the councillors and a few other noblemen participated. The decree of the synod disclaimed the Catholic
aspirations. The Scriptures were accepted as the only rule of
doctrine. The three ancient creeds of the church and the Augsburg
Confession were adopted as the true interpretation of the Holy
Scriptures together with the decree of the synod. By that the
Church of Sweden was definitely joined with Lutheran churches
on the continent and Lutheranism was established as the official
religion of the realm.

Finland

The Reformation in Finland followed the same path as in
Sweden. The leading man was Mikael Agricola (c. 1510-1557), who
in the 1530s had been studying in Wittenberg. He returned with a
letter of introduction from Luther himself and he was appointed
headmaster of the school of higher education at Åbo (Turku),
where the clergy of Finland got their training. His many publications, especially a Finnish translation of the New Testament
in 1548 made from the Greek original, a manual, a missal and a
prayer book, were of great importance for the carrying through
of the Reformation in the spirit of Luther. In 1554 Agricola
became Bishop of Åbo. Paul Juusten, Bishop of Viborg, continued
his task and published a Finnish catechism and a Finnish missal.

The Scandinavian countries show certain differences with
regard to the progress of the Reformation. Only in Denmark was it
a general national movement, and Bible humanism held a stronger
position there than in the other countries. Liturgially Scandinavia
was divided into two groups: Sweden and Finland followed Luther's
Formula missae, whereas Denmark and Norway founded their tradition
on Luther's Deutsche Messe. The apostolic succession was maintained
in Sweden and Finland but not in Denmark and Norway.

Yet the resemblances are obvious. Constitutionally the
Scandinavian churches appear as national churches under the leadership of a sovereign. The episcopal power was economically
reduced not least by confiscation. Politically the Reformation
supported the foundation of strong national states and led to an

economic boom in all of them. Culturally the publication of
reformatory books and still more the translation of the Bible
into vernacular was of fundamental importance for the languages.
But above all the Reformation in the Scandinavian countries
brought about a revival of the church that neither Reform
Catholicism nor Bible humanism had been able to achieve. Confessional Lutheranism has characterized the Scandinavian countries
and given them a considerable ecclesiastical uniformity since the
middle of 16th century.

The Reformation in the Nordic countries displays many
similar traits that separate it from what happened on the Continent.
The relatively painless process of transformation (in the parishes
and on the personal level it must however have lasted for a
generation) was partly caused by the fact that the Reformation
was so closely associated with a strong royal power in these
states with their growing national consciousness, that devastating
civil wars were avoided. At the same time the achievements of
the individual reformers naturally played an important part.

CHAPTER 4

WILHELM DANTINE

THE EXPERIENCE OF HISTORY AND SELF-UNDERSTANDING OF THE LUTHERAN MINORITY CHURCHES OF EASTERN EUROPE

Introduction

Anyone who attempts to describe the historical experiences of the Lutheran minority churches in Eastern Europe against the general background of Lutheranism has to accept from the outset that he can only pick out in a cursory and sketchy way a few important elements of their ecclesiastical consciousness. The formative experiences of the period have been so varied, the areas involved vast and with very different social and cultural backgrounds, and the range of aspects to be considered sometimes apparently contradictory that it is impossible to draw a unified picture. The formative experiences of these churches are reflected like sparks of light in the countless glittering facets of memory, and any attempt to force them into a uniform pattern would be a treacherous deception and a mutilation of the historical reality. Indeed, it is the pluralism and diversity which have to be particularly emphasized as the essential components of the complete picture.

However, this does not mean that there was a lack of fundamentals held in common, and one of these has to be mentioned immediately. All Lutheran minorities are deeply influenced by one painful experience: at a crucial moment they were torn away from the main stream of an all-embracing reform movement in church and society, with all its expectations, and, having been

reduced to the existence of a minority church, they had painfully
to work out an interpretation of their particular confessional
status. Because of their Lutheran confession they lacked the
self-satisfied sectarian pleasure of such a minority existence,
which may be characteristic of some other Christian groups. The
liberating Gospel had always directed them into the world around
them, and made them indifferent to their setting. Even in the
worst times of pressure, under cruel oppression and when driven
from their homes, they were not able to renounce their share of
the responsibility for their society. This attitude is well
illustrated by the emigrants from Salzburg who, after they had
been driven from their country by Prince-bishop Firmian in 1731,
still continued in their services to intercede for this their
"gracious sovereign" until they had found a new country which
would accept them as citizens. Today, this form of subject
loyalty may seem strange and hardly worth copying, because of
the patriarchal and feudalistic structures it manifests. Nevertheless, it is important to understand the way in which these
suffering Lutherans saw themselves bound to society, especially
as we shall see that this suffereing devotion was by no means
the only way of expressing political responsibility. This
acceptance of their responsibility for the world around them
did not glorify their minority existence, nor did it become
their proclaimed aim or some sort of ideology. These churches
did not share the happy fate of others who became regional or
state churches in which the Lutheran faith could play a direct
and decisive part in the social and political developments.
Therefore the minority churches were forced to seek for different,
and very varied, ways of expressing their responsibility for the
world, taking into account the different regional situations
and the possibilities open to them in a given historical situation.

We may draw attention here to a characteristic example:
the Lutherans living in the hereditary Hapsburg lands in the
16th century were denied the firm super-structure of a national
church (*Landeskirche*). But that did not hinder them from devising
a different church order or from building up their church from
below. They managed, for instance, to develop a brilliant and
exemplary system of education (Johannes Kepler in Graz and Linz),
and they also served their country faithfully as loyal subjects
of their sovereign. When their leaders were driven into exile
by persecution, and the congregations had to go underground,
these patterns of life naturally disappeared, but this example
nevertheless illustrates very well the possibilities of a political

and social flexibility which are probably characteristic for such minority experiences.

These preliminary remarks have shown how important historical situations and events have been for the church consciousness of the Lutheran minorities. It is therefore necessary to give a general historical survey of the political developments before trying to work out the main elements in their ecclesiastical self-understanding.

The Fate of the Minority

The Lutheran Reformation had spread quite naturally towards the East and South-East; political and national frontiers represented no obstacles, but just points of transition. And, as the Austrian example shows, latent or conscious resistance from government and church initially scarcely impeded the territorial advance. From Slovenia and Croatia through Hungary and Poland up to its northern-most provinces in Livonia there extended an area of more or less intensive Lutheran infiltration, frequently helped by the presence of a German middle-class which had settled there earlier, or, in the north, by the presence of the German knights. There can be no question of a consciously devised confessional strategy, but for several decades the presence of the Gospel in its Lutheran understanding proved to be most efficient in these newly developed areas. However, one must not forget that the humanism which always accompanied the evangelical preaching was tremendously attractive both for the German middle classes and, especially, for the sons of the Hungarian and Polish nobility who studied in Vienna, Basel and Cracow, and for Melanchthon's sake, also in Wittenberg. This heritage was to be of great importance for future developments, even though we shall find a varied and often contradictory series of effects. In it we find the reasons for the susceptibility to Socinianism and Unitarianism, as well as of the Magyars' change to Calvinism. Here also lie the origins of certain structural elements in Transylvanian Lutheranism and also, only apparently in contrast to it, of the success of the Jesuits, who knew how skilfully to use the humanist ambivalence about confessionalism to further the Counter-Reformation. It has to be remembered, however, that the humanist ferment could only find expression in such varied ways because the universal counter-movements, linked with regional power-structures, know how to use it. Thus there emerged the multi-colored mosaic, a political and confessional landscape which, in spite of many changes of scenes, has largely remained the same to this day. Seen as a whole, these developments represent an essential factor in our theme: the open Lutheran advance was stopped, and the Lutheran confessional churches hardened into their minority status.

It was only in the north of the east European flank that whole Lutheran territories were able to establish themselves, bearing certain similarities to middle European and Scandinavian national churches. This was partly due to the relations between Sweden and Russia, and between Sweden and Poland, both in Finland and in the so-called Baltic States. In the Polish state of 1561, the German Lutherans were granted, in the "Privilegium Sigismundi Augusti", the right to their evangelical faith, and to the use of the German language. This they managed to retain right through their changeable history under Sweden and Russia, in Estonia, Latvia and Lithuania, and up to their "return to the Reich", under Adolf Hitler. A lasting and significant result was their capacity to contribute to the founding and growth of indigenous Estonian and Latvian Lutheran churches.

In Poland, however, the door which once had been wide open to Lutheranism was thoroughly barred. First, it was the competition set up by Calvinistic groups and the growing Socinianism among the nobility and the educated middle class which pushed back Lutheran influences. Later on, the Roman Counter-Reformation created a near-monolithic structure of a particularly national Catholicism which to this day can appear as a mighty bulwark of the Roman church against the east. The Lutheran church was practically pushed into a ghetto, and has long been the minority church par excellence. German-speaking and Polish-speaking groups, often in opposition to each other, both shared this status.

Bohemia and Moravia had been only slightly influenced by the Lutheran church because the Austrian Counter-Reformation had remained victorious, and even the Czech Church of the Brethren, some of whose member congregations had accepted the Lutheran faith, was only able after a long period of oppression to reorganize itself as a tolerated minority, and the fate of the Austrian Lutheran church was similar. An exception is the Slovak Lutheran Church which, up to 1918, shared the fate of the churches under the Hugarian crown, and remains to this day a relatively compact, settled national minority church.

In Hungary, after a strong initial impact on a broad front, and also considerable political success - in 1548, the Diet had recognized the Lutheran confession as "tolerated", but had banned Calvinism and Unitarianism - the Lutheran church was soon involved in a war on two fronts. Calvinism managed soon to become a kind of "Magyar" confession, and crystallized around the intellectual center of Debrecen, after the acceptance of a *Confessio Ecclesiae Debreceniensis* in 1562, and the *Confessio Helvetica Posterior* passed by a synod in Debrecen in 1567. Thus Lutheranism was already pushed into a minority position by the end of the 16th century, when 90 percent of the country was Protestant. The foot-holds in western and northern Hungary were strengthened by the particular national problems arising where German and Slovak groups were settled alongside Hungarian elements, but this particular situation also weakened their general position in the country. The Lutheran congregations were hit very hard by the Catholic Counter-Reformation which the Hapsburgs promoted determinedly at the beginning of the 17th century. But they also benefited from the fruits of the "wars of liberation" fought by the belligerent Hungarian Calvinists who, through the initiative of Transylvanian princes, were able several times to regain their religious freedom.

The Diet of Pozsony/Pressburg* proclaimed religious freedom, and the treaties of Pressburg in 1626 and of Linz in 1645 tried to guarantee it. But soon afterwards, especially during the long reign of Leopold I (1657 to 1705) the Counter-Reformation hit the Lutherans with full strength. It was implemented with particular brutality, i.e. the deportation of pastors to become galley-slaves, and it was only with the greatest difficulty that a law was passed in 1681 which allowed the few "inarticulate congregations" to hold public Lutheran worship services. Thus a small Lutheran minority maintained its precarious existence until Joseph II's edict of toleration in 1781 by which the Austrian Protestants were also at last officially "tolerated", and able to build up their own church structures.

The Reformed churches meanwhile had been able, to a certain extent, to maintain their freedom of religion and their church structures, even if they had had to accept severe curtailments and had lost their numerical superiority in the country to the Catholics. At least the Hungarian Lutherans were spared the fate of the Austrian Lutheran church which, for more than 150 years, had been pushed nearly totally underground, and thus they also avoided total absorption by other "national"

---

*Today - Bratislava in Czechoslovakia.

confessions, i.e. by Hungarian Calvinism and Catholicism. The
small and weak beginnings of a Lutheran church in Croatia were
hit even harder, and were entirely wiped out, whilst only a very
few Lutheran congregations have survived to this day among the
Slovenes.

The autonomous principality of Transylvania which was
under Turkish protection played a peculiar and significant role.
Several different national and religious traditions confronted
each other in its area, and were forced to coexist. As early
as 1437, in order to repulse the Mongol invasion, the Hungarian
nobility, the indigenous people of the Szèkely and the relatively
compact settled groups of Transylvanian Saxons had concluded a
brotherly union. After the great victory of the Turks at Mohacs
in 1526 the autonomous principality of Transylvania was founded.
Through the checkered century and a half of its history under
Calvinist leadership, it managed to be the first European state
to implement the idea of a politically guaranteed freedom of
religion. As we have mentioned earlier, this was of considerable
importance for Hungary, as well as for the Transylvania itself.

In 1557, the Diet of Torda* adopted the principle of
politically guaranteed religious equality which, after a religious
debate in Weissenburg in 1566 explicitly included not only
Catholics, Lutherans and Reformed, but also the Anti-trinitarians
(i.e. the Socinians, called Unitarians since 1600). Since the
later Diet of Torda in 1568 Transylvania was called "the land of
the four accepted religions." For two reasons the additional
recognition of the Unitarians is of special historical significance.
First, because the original Szèkely people began to identify
with this confession, trying to maintain their identity through
it, and second because this special confession has continued into
the present time in the Hungarian and Rumanian States. A large-
scale emigration has considerably strengthened the Unitarian
churches in America.

Protected and helped by these developments, the Transylvanian
Saxons were able to build up their Lutheran church structures, and
maintain them to this day. The close links between German
nationality, language, and culture within this one fairly compact
area were rooted in the *Reformatio Ecclesiae Coronensis* written
by Johannes Honterus in 1541, and transformed into the "church
order for all Germans in Transylvania" in 1547. This national
as well as confessional Lutheran statute - in 1572 the synod of

---

*Today - Turda in Rumania

Medgyes accepted the Augsburg Confession - is in some ways the
classic form of the Lutheran movement on its way to the east.

This brief survey would be incomplete without adding that
although the strength of the Lutherans grew considerably later
on and there were some important individual aspects of this
increase, the general situation did not change. German colonists
were invited by different rulers of the 18th and 19th centuries
and settled in Volhynia and along the Volga, in Besserabia and in
the Dobrutscha, in the Hungarian Danube plain, alongside Lutheran
Slovaks and in the Serbian and Rumanian Banat: these were mostly
Lutherans.

These Lutheran German minorities have much enlivened the
wide spectrum of national varieties and have produced many
regionally characteristic and important changes without, however,
altering significantly the overall picture. Today they often
seem like erratics who have somehow been by-passed in the stream
of time. Some of these churches prefer this image of themselves
while the true faith of the Reformation always seeks and requires
a living expression of church life. We need an analysis of the
original basic motivations of these minority churches in order
to find answers to such questions.

The Struggle to Preserve the Heritage of the Reformation

When looking back in church history, it is very clear
that these minority churches remained loyal to the heritage of
the Reformation, preserving the Lutheran doctrine and the
confessional writings. This fact need not be pursued further.
We are concerned instead to find what is the motivation behind
their confessional loyalty, and to investigate its particular
character. This can be of the greatest importance for the
churches' self-understanding, as it developed through the ages,
and is still relevant today. From the preceding historical
survey a few salient facts emerge.

The general world-openness of the Lutheran faith mentioned
earlier brought with it a strong orientation towards the political
events of the day, which was of necessity further increased by
the churches' external and internal dependence on these events.
Unlike many of the established Lutheran territorial churches,
these minority churches were not relieved of their duty to share

political and social responsibility by the decisions of rulers
belonging to the same confession. Whether they liked it or not,
suffering or fighting, they had to play an existential part in
the political history, even though they frequently showed a marked
lack of the strategic will-power, which was so characteristic of
their Calvinist sister church. This is also true of the Austrian
Lutheran church, although it seemed to have entirely disappeared
from view for a long time. The results of the victorious Counter-
Reformation had left behind a curious trauma for the Austrian
state, so that first the persecution of the Protestants, then
their toleration and later their equality were, and still are,
important political problems. To this day its political role
has always been of essential significance for the Austrian
Lutheran Church, although it may have expressed it in various
ways. One could show in detail how much this small group
contributed to the whole development of the modern Austrian state,
and to the formation of a general political and social consciousness, or even - in order not to shy away from dubious memories -
to the so-called "free-from-Rome" movement, where it seemed to
be in the fore-front of political activity. A similar development can be found in Hungary and especially in Transylvania.

The latter situation is particularly interesting because,
as we have seen, the Saxons, Hungarians and Székely had come
together before the Reformation in a protective alliance which
later bore its fruits in the form of the religious peace. But
these results were only made possible by a skilful political
use of both the Turkish superiority over the Catholic Hapsburgs
and the political verve of the Calvinist Transylvanian princes.
The freedom and independence of the "Saxons" was not a reward for
an apolitical fatalism, but the result of sober, purposeful
political action. It was Honterus himself, the pupil of Erasmus,
who had quite consciously and, in view of his theological
training and inclinations, rather surprisingly turned to the
Augsburg Confession, and decided in favor of Wittenberg, and
therefore in favor of the "German" Reformation. In the long run,
this decision had to mean, and in fact did mean, a conscious
spiritual and political orientation towards the "mother-country
of the Reformation".

Neither had the Austrian Protestants hesitated, in
exchange for their military and financial support, to bargain for
religious and church concessions from the Emperor when he was
beset by the Turks. This Lutheran involvement in politics however,

was somewhat haphazard, as shown by the fact that the battle of
the White Mountain* in 1618 was lost to the Protestants, with
incalculable results for the whole of European history, and gave
the Catholics an epoch-making victory only because the well-armed
relief army of the Lower Austrian Lutheran estates was kept
standing at ease for a long time and left a full 24 hours too late
for the help of the Protestant Elector of the Palatine. The
Lutheran leaders and preachers had not been able to agree before
whether it was right to fight against the Emperor. But was this
"theological" hesitation not also really a "political" decision?

Part of the political dimension of course is the national
element which we have met repeatedly before. No wonder, since
in the regionally different but always present confrontation
between different national groups in these areas the newly
awakening national feelings had to find expression. It was
partly due to the Lutheran command to preach the Gospel to
everybody in their own mother-tongue that the Slovenes, Croats,
but also the Lithuanians, Latvians and Estonians developed their
own independent written languages, and the bases for their
national literature, even if not all of them later developed
their own independent Lutheran churches. In spite of its specific
and unique character, the phenomenon of the German Saxons in
Transylvania is exemplary here, since it had, even later on, to
withstand the growing pressures from the Greek-Orthodox Walachians,
and thus the coming Roumanian nationalism.
Two elements seem to be characteristic for this German
national consciousness: one was the need to form their own
closed society in the midst of the confessionally and nationally
pluralistic world around them, and to withdraw into it. The
other, closely related to the first element, was the attempt to
see the confession mainly as a protective frontier which had to
be stubbornly defended, even when inside the confessional body
its theological content could no longer be clearly discerned.
We need no additional proof that the first element was a basic
expression of the search for national identity which can still be
highly effective when there no longer exists a religious confession
as the cohesive agent. There are examples from other parts of
the world which show that the Lutheran confession could produce
amongst national minorities an unshakeable loyalty to German
culture, as can be seen for instance amongst the Volga Germans.

---

*Today - Bîla Hora in Czechoslovakia.

The other characteristic element manifests one of the factors
which, in some ways, also explains and makes possible the struggle
for religious freedom: the confession seen as a frontier not
only prevents all missionary strategy which could reach beyond it,
as we have seen already, but also produces, together with the
protective national feeling, an introverted confessionalism
which declines to submit the truth it claims for the Gospel even
to an open dialogue with "the others". The reluctance to enter
into dialogue which, in these days of world-wide ecumenism, is
so worrying among wide circles of Eastern European Lutheranism
has its deep roots in this attitude, although we must not ignore
important impulses which have come to it from outside as well.

Other national groups were able to find a similar backing
in the Lutheran confession, for instance the Slovaks and
Hungarians. In the latter case, however, it has to be said that
when the German and Hungarian efforts at national self-preservation
collided with each other, the common Lutheran confession often
proved incapable of withstanding the trend to "Magyarisation",
just as, in the late 19th and 20th centuries, the German
nationalism in Lutheran congreations blocked all dialogue with
Hungarian Lutherans. This can be clearly seen in the congregations
of the Burgenland which came to Austria in 1921. It must not be
forgotten, however, that all these national groups in that period
were under immense pressure from Panslavism which was then
paramount in the Eastern world, and which did not only use the
Orthodox churches as an instrument of nationalism, but also took
advantage of some extremely secular trends.

This unwillingness for dialogue, however, has other reasons
also which are felt more consciously as motivations: the historical
experiences with the Roman Catholic Counter-Reformation. The
memories of the general brutality of its implementation felt not
only by the non-Catholic confessions but also by the national
groups connected with them are deeply rooted. Lutherans in all the
eastern European areas under discussion are still deeply suspicious
of Catholics, and this attitude is strengthened by the fact that
the official Catholic churches of the area also distrust the
ecumenical tendencies of the Roman leadership. Even at the height
of Vatican II they disapproved of its dialogue both within the
church, and with the outside. One could almost say that the
period of the Counter-Reformation in that whole area has not yet
ended, and is still continuing under the surface.

But in order to understand the emotional hold of the anti-Roman feeling to the full, one again must not forget the importance of the political factors. The painfully won religious freedom as a theological fact is of the greatest political importance, as can be seen on a world-wide level by the example of the idea and fate of the declaration of human rights. And this close connection keeps alive the fear of being nationally and confessionally cheated. The memory is still all too much alive that it was only by force of arms that the freedom to practice one's religion was to be wrested from Rome. On the other hand we have to question the Austrian and other eastern European Lutheran churches' ecumenical reserve towards Rome very critically.   We have to examine their own history and the great responsibility they have had for obtaining religious freedom, a theme which we are going to take up again.

The historical context and the great significance of the events in Transylvania and Hungary have been sufficiently stressed earlier. Even though general historical thinking does not yet reflect this fact, it can be stated with some certainty that the politically guaranteed freedom of religion in the middle of the 16th century represented an epoch-making event. The stone which started to roll became one of the basic foundation-stones of society in the modern world. Much later, on the basis of the declaration of human rights of the French and American revolutions, freedom of religion became the first of all basic human rights in nearly all of the democratic countries, and even the Catholic church passed a "declaration on religious liberty" during Vatican II promulgated by the pope. All this is, in the last analysis, the fruit of the early achievement of freedom of confession in Transylvania. A detail of perhaps symbolic significance illustrates what consequences this had, first in the history of south west Europe, but also far beyond. The revolution of 1848 in Vienna is unthinkable without the simultaneous revolution in Hungary.

On March 13th Ludwig Kossuth's famous speech to the Hungarian Parliament was read in the streets of Vienna, in which he demanded a democratic constitituion. Kossuth was of Lutheran origin, and had studied in a Reformed theological college. As a politician, he was much concerned with the reconciliation between Lutherans and Reformed. A year later he announced from the pulpit

of the chapel of the venerable Reformed theological faculty of
Debrecen to the legally called Hungarian assembly the deposition
of the Hapsburgs, and the proclamation of a Hungarian republic.
He became a Hungarian national hero and continued to be re-elected
to Parliament, although he was forced to emigrate, and had to live
and die abroad. Whatever he may have meant to the Hungarians
themselves, he helped legitimate national aspirations to emerge
through his passionate struggle for freedom and independence of
nations, religions and individuals. The Hungarian revolution was
a key to open the door to the freedom of society as a whole:
the Viennese historian Hugo Hantsch, a Benedictine, clearly
confirms in his *History of Austria* that the Hungarian problem
only arose through "the relationship and interplay of liberal
and national, of reforming and secessionist ideas." There is
no doubt that the Reformation idea of freedom had separated from
its origins, but nevertheless it remained rooted in the consciousness of the church and its members, as one can easily see today.
It has become more difficult for present-day theological thinking,
however, to understand the inner links between the often sharply
contrasting positions into which the one-sided representation of
one of these aspects can lead. But perhaps this is precisely the
historical heritage which the minority churches have to contribute
to an established Lutheran majority church.

Conclusions

        The present-day observer of the Lutheran minority churches
may have difficulty avoiding the same feeling of resignation that
the church members have themselves when faced with the question
of the sense and purpose of their existence. He may not be
satisfied with the often used justification for their preservation
as museum pieces. The individual results of our analysis with
its many concrete examples, largely appear as set, calcified,
churchified or secularized structures, isolated from each other,
so that any present horizontal dialogue as well as any dialogue-
based prospects for the future seem to be excluded. On the other
hand, however, the sobering effect of such an analysis could
produce a loosening change, if representatives both of the
minority churches and the large Lutheran churches begin to understand the riches hidden in the minority churches' experience of
history. Up to now, the minority churches have hardly yet begun
to reflect theologically about their own development, just as

ecclesiology in general, including Lutheran ecclesiology has not
yet seriously discussed the problem of minority churches who did
not choose this state of their own free will, but were forced
into it through circumstances. The usual reaction was for the
majority churches to look down with pity and magnanimity upon
the minority churches who, in their turn, would look up to them
longingly and hopefully. That meant that the large churches
became the ideal examples for the minorities. An understanding
of the burdensome but fruitful riches of the minorities could
start a process of learning which would benefit both sides, and
therefore the whole Lutheran church. This would be a way of
starting a dialogue within the Lutheran church, and a necessary
prerequisite for a wider general dialogue, which would also
include the Church of Rome. Unfettered by open or secret
inferiority complexes, the minority churches must insist on their
right to be heard as equal partners within the general world of
Lutheranism.

                                    Translated by Donata Coleman

PART TWO

DEVELOPMENTS IN THE LUTHERAN CHURCH
AND THEOLOGY
FROM THE REFORMATION TO THE PRESENT

An independent Lutheran church became a reality in the second half of the 16th century. Luther died, his hopes of a council to heal the division remaining unfulfilled. In spite of this, he had an unshakeable faith that the church of Jesus Christ would assert itself even among his opponents. Since the religious peace brought only toleration of various "catholic" churches, the Lutheran church was faced with the question of how it could maintain the original drive of the Reformation in a state of division. What profile did this independent church now assume? What had it to continue to represent? How could it preserve and safeguard the idea of the one church? After the hope of reunion with the Roman Catholic church was wrecked and a Reformed church, basically different from the Lutheran church was developing, things took a different turn from what was intended at the beginning of the Reformation. From this point on the Lutheran *church* had its own history, which continues to the present day. What sort of experiences have the changes of the centuries brought for the life and teaching and thus for the self-understanding of this church?

The second part of this book attempts to answer these questions under various headings. It tries to present an example of confessionality and the search for identity. This attempt can only be made by taking a suitable cross section of the various

urrents present in history. The basic question of what type of
dentity is manifested by the historical development of the
utheran church will have to be taken into consideration.
eflection on this problem should help the reader see clearly
he continuing endeavor for the preservation of identity. It is
ot the triumphal affirmation of self, but the enduring struggle
o realise the Reformation of the church - now in our own history
oo - which sets the key for the following essays. Only in this
ay can a renewal which depends on repentance and thus confesses
he one Lord and Savior, be realised anew.

The early search for identity of the Lutheran church,
nderstood in this way, becomes a central problem in the theme of
istorical inheritance. "Scripture and Confession" is a common
utheran emphasis. For this reason the first two essays - although
ndependent - both deal with the above mentioned problem (chapters
 and 6). Luther's theology was designed to relate to the
ituation. This is also demonstrated by the history of the origin
f the Lutheran confessional writings. It must be kept in mind
owever, that this "situation" always has as a prerequisite the
xistential encounter with God, the witness of his Word through
he Holy Scripture in the concrete history of both the individual
 conscience) as well as of the people (before the rulers of this
orld). Thus the principle and significance of Scripture are
just as bound as confessional writings and present confession:
he two pairs of concepts find their full relation to situation
in collective worship of the congregation and the thus closely
related spirituality to which the following two essays are
devoted (chapters 7 and 8).

These emphases in Lutheran identity are more or less
uncontested. But here are found also the essential preconditions
for the specific development of spiritual and ecclesiastical life,
which other churches regard as problems of Lutheran confessionality.
The ordained ministry and church order are often ascribed to the
account of Lutheran theology as a deficit. Therefore the orientation according to which proclamation and administration of the
sacraments already include the ministry as a "divine foundation"
is of essential importance for the understanding of Lutheran
identity (chapter 9). If it is considered that the structure of
the ministry is neglected by the Lutherans, then the parallel
problem of the place of social ethics as that of the life of the
church in this world emerges.

To name only the classic example of theological discussions,
i.e. the doctrine of the two kingdoms, it is at this very point

that a specifically Lutheran basic conviction is criticized, one
which can however demonstrate both its weaknesses and its strengths
Both were discernable in the quarrels with the authorities in
our modern society (chapter 10). Just how far this misunderstood
doctrine is fundamental for the understanding of the mission of
the church and how far it can even offer the key for the church's
missionary task in our "secularized" world will give the reader
an unexpected surprize. However, this contested doctrine can
mean a reason for the universal mission of the church which is
freed from the burden of "mission history" and which is relevant
to the present situation (chapter 11). A new interpretation of
this traditional doctrine of the two kingdoms must be able - in
contrast to the perversions which were attributed to it in the
19th century - to particularly emphasize and articulate the
liberation of the secular and as a result the liberation for the
service of the church in the world.

For this reason we feel it is justified to deal with the
problem of the relationship of the Lutheran church to ecumenism
in the final essay in this section (chapter 12). The confessional
element, which comes to the fore particularly in the identity
of the Lutheran church and which articulates what is Christian in
a specific way, is often played off against ecumenical ideas.
As is shown in the last essay, it is in the interest of the whole
of the ecumenical movement that the basic impulse of the Lutheran
Reformation should be preserved. Through this, the continuity of
the church, enduring throughout history, is joined to the preservation of the Gospel as its sole right to existence.

Thus the Lutheran church bears witness not primarily to
its particular history in the Reformation period, but to the
origin and basic elements of the church as a whole. The tendencies
of the themes previously indicated will be introduced and critically
examined in the following cross-sections both with regard to the
history of the church and to her dogma. The result throughout the
text is the unfolding pattern of spiritual and historical development in the last few centuries. The drive for reform in Luther
and also in the confessional writings embraced tendencies, which
were held together dialectically. In the successive period however,
they disintegrated into a one-sided orientation. Orthodoxy was
not merely a theology which unfolded and channelled problems of
the Reformation period into the canals of school-theology in order
to make them understandable. At the same time the fateful
acceptance of questions took place, dictated by the confessional
controversy and resulting in patterns of thought which were those

of the opponents.

Certainly in Orthodoxy the community and the corporative element of spirituality is preserved by the link to the means of grace but it leads to a superficial legalistic exercise of church practices meeting with the severe criticism of Pietism. Individual experience is now emphasised and described in psychological categories. The doctrine of general priesthood has missed its intention: neither the ministry nor the church structures bound to it are clarified in relation to this doctrine. A church order appropriate to the Reformation message and a social ethic find no association with it.

The mission movements, which have acquired their decisive impetus from this very Pietism, have grown up, exactly as the social diaconical initiatives, in this individualistic soil of Pietism. They are not capable of looking carefully at the collectively growing society, which would enable the proclamation of the church to be witness to God's sovereign work as Creator throughout all historical changes. They failed to appreciate the changing order of society.

The challenges of our time demand a rethinking on the part of the Lutheran church and her theology. She looks back to the Reformation origins, not in order to repeat history and to restore the old ecclesial and social orders but to inspire similar existential decisions, as taken by the fathers of the Reformation in their time, in obedience to the divine call.

The developments in church history manifest with unavoidable severity not only loyalty to a heritage but also the failures. In the "hour of destiny" of present Christianity, the Lutheran church is reminded by her confessional conscience to listen anew to the lesson to be learnt from changes in her history. For the sake of her own identity she is referred to the specific witness of the other confessional families. At present bilateral dialogues are held, at which the Lutheran church offers her full participation. This is perhaps going back in history 450 years, although with new demands and with partners who have been changed by historical developments. It will surely not escape the reader that the essays in this book all strike an ecumenical note. Whether the subject is the task of the interpretation of the Scriptures, of present confession, of present worship, spirituality or the questions of the ministry, of Christian concern for the social problems of our time or the particular mission of the Apostolic proclamation among the people of the world - the same theme is always emphasized: we can only fulfil these tasks in fellowship with ecumenical Christianity. This is an exact return to the historical hour of the Reformation: mutual reference to each other and working together in brotherly fellowship for the work of one church in our present world.

The historically-based essays in the first part of the book have shown us the stages of Christian unity. The divisive forces had been set in motion, although an interim relationship prevailed for a long time between the "two Catholic churches." Today, in the wake of the ecumenical movement and the missionary movement linked to it, there has arisen, through the Second Vatican Council a new opening among the confessions, which contains the possibility of a present interim relationship for the unity of the church. The forces converging today could prepare for the new historical hour, where each will recognize the re-unification of the church and will effect unity in the Holy Spirit.

Such a reconciliation of the diverse charismatic gifts does not oppose the specific confessionality of the Lutheran church. It is not a loss of identity but rather a realization of the original call of the Reformation for the renewal of the whole of Christianity on earth. This is how the ecumenical note, struck in the second part of this book, should be interpreted. The Lutheran church's ecumenical contribution thus becomes evident: in all those churches which confess the name of Jesus Christ, which proclaim his Gospel and administer the Sacraments ordained by him, the one, holy catholic and apostolic church can be found, which we confess with the creed of the early church. Astonishingly enough this specific *confessionality* of the Lutheran church affirms a universal church and provides an opening for ecumenism. To repeat this self-understanding concerning our own churches is the most important task of these essays.

CHAPTER 5

INGE LØNNING

THE HOLY SCRIPTURES

The Scriptural Principle of the Reformation

There are certain historical pictures which are indelibly
imprinted on the memory of Christendom. Among these is the
confrontation scene at the Diet of Worms in 1521, with emperor,
empire, and church on the one side and the solitary monk on the
other side, alone with the Holy Scriptures.

As striking as this picture may be, its historical effect
is nonetheless ambivalent. The modern era sees here its ideal
of the free, moral personality, the individual who, freed from
all ties to external authorities, sees himself bound only to his
own conscience. The Lutheran Orthodoxy of the 16th and 17th
centuries saw in the figure of Luther at the Diet of Worms a
firm and unshakable representative of the absolute authority of
Scripture and, on the basis of this authority, of the truth of
divine revelation. Luther's own self-understanding, meanwhile,
corresponds to neither of these two versions. According to
tradition his momentous response at the Diet of Worms contains
three main concepts: "Word of God," "the Holy Scriptures," and
"conscience". To determine the peculiar theological character
of the Reformation scriptural principle is to define the interrelationships of these three concepts. It is perhaps here that
the origin of one of the permanent inner difficulties of the
Lutheran tradition is to be seen.

We consciously placed the scene from the dramatic break-
through period of the Reformation at the beginning of this

discussion. Anyone wishing to understand the true nature of
Reformation theology must above all take into account the situational quality of theological thought. Every step in Luther's
development can be seen as a theological response to the immediate
emergency situation of the church, and not as produced by well
thought out theoretical, ivory tower philosophizing. Decisive
conclusions, precisely in the realm of the scriptural principle,
are forced on Luther by theological opponents like Cajetan
(Augsburg 1518) and Eck (Leipzig 1519). The insights he achieved
"internally" by intensive biblical study received their actual
theological clarity through the "external" confrontation with
ecclesiastical reality.

The scriptural principle of the Reformation grew out of
the constant effort to achieve a correct interpretation of the
Scripture. This development was introduced with the increasing
concentration by Wittenberg University theology on scriptural
interpretation as *the* theological task pure and simple. With
Luther's theses against scholastic theology (1517), the ideal of
scriptural theology was clearly expressed as the basis for a
thorough reform of theological study: true theology is only
possible as scriptural interpretation. An important historical
precondition for realizing this ideal was the edition of the
Greek New Testament by Erasmus (1516) as well as the general
humanistic interest in the history of the ancient world and in
the biblical languages. What gradually appeared as a methodological
renewal, a new programmatic manner of doing theology, was at the
same time an expression of a new conception of the *nature* of
theology. The understanding of the nature and the method of
theology cannot here be separated from one another.

In the Preface to the first edition of his collected
writings in Wittenberg in 1539 (WA 50, 657-661) Luther describes
"a proper way to study theology." According to this description
a true study of theology consists of: prayer (*oratio*), meditation
(*meditatio*), and temptation (*tentatio*). Viewed formally this
definition is not particularly remarkable. It is remarkable,
however, that Luther connects these three characteristics of
valid theological study exclusively and as a matter of course with
the task of scriptural interpretation. He justifies this connection
with a simple reference to the uniqueness of the Bible's content:
whoever would study theology must above all know that the Holy
Scripture turns the wisdom of all other books into foolishness.
One will therefore never solve the problem of scriptural interpretation with human wisdom and reason. The theological task is

per definitionem polemical, with the polemic directed against the theologian himself. The exclusive binding of theology to Scripture is thus the necessary and permanent presupposition, because only Scripture is capable of surmounting the human wisdom of the theologian.

The allusion to Pauline expressions as well as the theme of the revaluation of all values through God's revelation in Christ according to 1 Corinthians 1-2 is here unmistakable. From the fundamental thought of the opposition of divine and human wisdom arises for Luther an indispensable scriptural principle. Not on the basis of any given observations of a formal nature, but only on the basis of the message of the Holy Scripture as heard and believed can the unique quality of the Bible be recognized. The gospel of God's justice not only lies outside the thinking capacity of man, but must "crucify" man in his existence as sinner. Through the proclamation of the gospel, which continually reaches the person anew from outside himself, the Spirit of God creates faith and thus brings about a new creature. The proclamation, however, remains bound to the Bible, because the necessary *extra nos* of the gospel is only maintained when the gospel remains, so to speak, safe-guarded in Scripture.

Thus no one should approach the Scripture without praying for the Holy Spirit. For the interpreter of the Bible there is according to this only one "method": to meditate. Luther explains what this means in a surprising way in the already mentioned Preface: "that is, not only in your heart but also externally, by actually repeating and comparing oral speech and literal words of the book, reading and rereading them with diligent attention and reflection so that you may see what the Holy Spirit means by them." Whoever practices this theological method gets into the middle of the great battle for the human soul, where God (the Truth) fights for the conscience with the Spirit of Lies (Satan). Temptations are characteristics of theology's proper situation as scriptural interpretation. Where God's Word is at work in this world, the enemy of God is also always at work. Through his attacks the scriptural interpreter becomes paradoxically a theologian of experience who, in his condition of being tempted, really learns "how right, how true, how sweet, how lovely, how mighty, how comforting" the Word of God is. Thus arises the certainty of the tempted faith, which only then makes true theology, that is, true discourse about God, possible.

When Luther expresses the opposition of divine and human

wisdom with the contrasting concepts "Word of God" and "human teaching," it is clear from this background that one should not think of the difference as that between perfection and imperfection. Then the task of Scripture interpretation could be achieved through an increase in human understanding. The mysterious statements of the Bible would then be seen in comparison to everyday human statements as especially profound (and thus hard to grasp) truths of the same kind. If one conceives of the uniqueness of the scriptural statements in this manner, then the logical and only correct method of scriptural interpretation would be the allegorical method. Through this method the expositor is able to leave behind the external, everyday, literal sense of the letter in favor of the deeper, spiritual sense. The human form of the Scripture is thus a first step, the literal sense of the scriptural statements is to be understood as a transitional stage on the way to arriving at the actual divine quality. The concept "human teaching" has however for Luther nothing to do with the human form of the Scripture. Because God really became man in Christ, the human form can in no way be inconsistent with the Word of God. Rather, the human form corresponds exactly to the content of the Scripture, the message that God became man. If "human teaching" is to "Word of God" as water is to fire, then it is only because it has a theological content that is opposed to the good news of God becoming man. "Human teaching" encloses the conscience in the prison of religious works righteousness; the "Word of God" sets the conscience free.

The principle *sola scriptura* is theologically necessary in order to avoid "human teaching" and to safeguard the non-derivative nature of the gospel. For Luther this principle is thus deeply connected with his conviction of the clarity of the Scripture. Rooted in the same context is also the increasing concentration in the third decade of the 15th century on the literal meaning of biblical statements and ever sharper criticism of allegorical exposition. As the doctrine of various meanings of Scripture crumbles, so does that of the exclusive right of the ecclesiastical teaching office to interpret the Scripture authoritatively. The traditional conception of the Holy Spirit as the author of Scripture receives here an unusual interpretation through the assertion that there is no more simple author in heaven or on earth than the Holy Spirit. His words can have only the one, simple, everyday, historical sense, and as witness to Christ they possess exactly in this sense the clarity that frees the conscience because they create certainty.

"Spirit", "witnessing to Christ", and "clarity of the
Scripture" belong for Luther necessarily together. Historically
this is viewed as follows: in the work of Jesus God has completed
everything necessary for the salvation of mankind; the work of
the Holy Spirit consists thus of "promoting Christ", that is,
of distributing the saving gifts of the work of Jesus to faith.
In faith the person is revealed as God's creation and thus for the
first time as really human, when he honors God the Creator and lets
Jesus be Savior. Since Pentecost this happens through the
preaching of the Gospel, which founds the church; God's plan of
salvation, which was sealed in the "Scripture" (that is, in the
Old Testament), was brought to light by the oral proclamation of
Christ through the apostles. In the apostolic Christ-proclamation
(but also through it) the Scripture became clear, and remains so
in the continuation of this Christ-proclamation in the preaching
of the Gospel to the ends of the earth. Thus the New Testament
is to be understood not as "Scripture" but as *revelation of the
Scripture*, and Luther can thus with complete logic refer to the
Epistle to the Romans in his preface to the September Testament
of 1522 as "a bright light, almost sufficient to illuminate the
entire Holy Scriptures" (LW 35, s. 366). Thus it can be said
that the church is no *Federhaus* (pen house) but a *Mundhaus*
(mouth house), and that it is actually not New Testament-like to
write books.

        This insight was once again exegetically produced. From
the opposition between "letter" and "spirit" in 2 Corinthians
3:6 Luther discovered (in sharp contrast to the traditional use
of the same passage as the justification of the theory of the
two-fold meaning of Scripture) the opposition and thus the
necessity of distinguishing between the old and the new covenant,
the Law and the Gospel, the obedience to the Law and the obedience
to the Gospel. The written word as characteristic of the Law
and the spoken word as characteristic of the Gospel are more than
formal and external characterizations, they are based on the two
different but related functions of the Word of God. The written
word corresponds to the mortifying function of the Law, the spoken
word to the Gospel's function of making alive. These two functions
are not simply to be identified with the two parts of the Christian
Bible. The New Testament Gospel indeed unveils the Old Testament
Scripture. The apostolic Christ-proclamation contained in the
New Testament first made possible the distinction between the two
functions and thus presented future theology (i.e., the biblical

exposition of the church) with its permanent task.

From this background the peculiar freedom that characterizes Luther's judgments in matters of the New Testament canon can be understood. The scientific presuppositions of this freedom were present in the general historical findings of the theology of the 16th century, with its humanistic influence. One had also become conscious of the complications of canonical history and tried with historical and literary-critical argumentation to establish and theologically to actualize the ancient church's distinction between uncontested (*homologoumena*) and contested writings (*antilegomena*, i.e. the seven books - James, Hebrews, 2 Peter, 2 and 3 John, Jude, Revelation). The goal of these efforts was to determine with greatest possible accuracy the limits of the New Testament (that is, the limits of apostolic writing). It is above all peculiar to Luther's development of humanistic canonical criticism that this was not his intention. In the first edition of his German translation of the New Testament this becomes clear already in the table of contents: unnumbered, and separated from the other books by an open space, stand four of the traditional *antilegomena*: Hebrews, James, and Jude, as well as the Revelation to John. In the prefaces to these four books little use is made of the traditional arguments. Decisive are neither literary critical observations nor the historical traditions of the church. The decisive factor is the theological criterion of "promoting Christ," (*Was Christum treibt*), which is all that distinguishes "apostolic" from "non-apostolic." If one puts the question whether Luther intended the four separated books to be considered as outside the canon, one finds no well-grounded answer. In later editions the table of contents of the New Testament was standardized, although the conspicuous new ordering of the writings remains to this day in Lutheran editions of the Bible. Nevertheless, Luther never changed the theological judgments formulated in his prefaces to the September Testament of 1522. They soon became so offensive to his followers, however, that they preferred to publish the translation without the prefaces.

To the confessional uniqueness of later Lutheranism belongs the phenomenon paradoxically described in the modern era as an "open scriptural canon." Within the consolidated Catholic theology of the Counter-Reformation the humanistically-colored canonical criticism was dogmatically put to an end by the decree on the canon of the Council of Trent in 1546. The authentic writings were all decided, the Old Testament according to the

reek canon of the ancient church, the New Testament with the
xplicit description of every single one of the 27 writings as
postolic. Most of the confessional writings of Reformed char-
cter that arose during the 16th and 17th centuries contain
arallel definitions of the Holy Scriptures, but with the charac-
eristic distinction that the Old Testament is here established
ccording to the Hebrew canon. In none of the Lutheran confes-
ional writings can one find a doctrinal statement concerning the
xtent of the Holy Scriptures. In the practice of its Bible
istribution the Lutheran tradition has never taken a firm position
n the controversy of the Old Testament canon. Thus the problem
f the exact extent of the Bible has theologically speaking remained
n *adiaphoron* to this day.

This confessional peculiarity refers back to the character
f the Reformation scriptural principle of Luther. The authority
f the Bible is not to be compared (as occurs often in the eccle-
iastical tradition of the church) to the authority of a law
ook which rests on precisely fixed assertions (paragraphs and
tatutes), and which requires a legally established interpreter
n every new situation in order to take effect. The Holy Scripture
s precisely not the law book of a Christian legal society.
ost Christum the Scripture in the Old and New Testament accomplishes
od's Word in both functions, it judges the individual and
stablishes him as conscience. The promoter of this effect is the
oly Spirit, who keeps the Scripture in constant movement towards
erbal proclamation of the Gospel. Thus God's Holy Spirit remains
olely effective through the Bible as the only one who "promotes
hrist." He was active in the formation of the Old Testament writings
nd he revealed the Scriptures once and for all through the Christ-
roclamation of the apostles. The authority of the Scripture can
nly be understood in its theological intention if one takes into
ccount the expression of "the eternal *will* of the Gospel"
perpetua voluntas evangelii, CA Art. XXVIII). This expression
s demonstrated by Melanchthon on the example of the apostolic
ecree (Acts 15:28f.) to be the programmatic statement for an
dequate biblical interpretation. The literal statement of the
ecree ("It seemed good to the Holy Spirit and to us...")
orresponds to the question of the abiding will of the Gospel,
hereby the personification of the Gospel must be understood from
he viewpoint of the indissoluble union between the Spirit and
he Gospel.

The CA does not contain a doctrine of the Holy Scripture.
one of the 28 articles of this fundamental confessional writing

of the Lutheran tradition has the scriptural principle as its
theme. The earliest critics in Augsburg in 1530 called attention
to this fact, as the silence seemed suspicious to them. Later
interpreters tried to solve these problems with the thesis of
Melanchthon's church-politically motivated desire to tread softly.
From the premises of Reformation theology, however, there is no
reason to feel a lack; in fact the scriptural principle is
implicitly present from the first article to the last. There are
perhaps even grounds for viewing the peculiar formulation of the
last article with reference to the apostolic decree as an explicit
statement of this principle. That is precisely the question that
the *sola scriptura* ("through the Word alone") answers: how does
the gospel get through to mankind in such a way that faith is
born which confesses and reveres God as Creator and thus brings
the person as God's creature to his true being? As a formal
principle, that is, abstracted from the recognized eternal will
of the Gospel, the Reformation scriptural principle is not
recognizable, so the "silence" of the CA may be understood.

Theology is that understanding of God and man that describe
God as the justifier and man as sinner. Thus Luther defines the
one inexhaustible theme of theology in his exposition of the 51st
Psalm in 1532 (WA 40 II, 327ff.). This theological assertion is
easy to make, but it must be constantly renewed in the school of
scriptural interpretation and its temptations. To keep the church
in this school of the Holy Spirit is the function of the sola
scriptura. Far from being a rigid principle, this expresses the
inexhaustibility of the theological thematic and the total tension
of theological existence in the context of Reformation thought.

The Controversial Theology of the 16th and 17th Centuries: the
Development of an Explicit Doctrine of the Holy Scriptures

The great controversy of the Reformation period was that
concerning the proper understanding of the Gospel and the church.
It was primarily conducted as a struggle for correct interpretation
of Scripture and consequently for the right doctrine of the Holy
Scripture. The main object of the controversy was the claim for
infallible authority of interpreting Scripture maintained by the
teaching office of the Roman Church. This claim had been rejected
by Luther. In the first phase, around 1520, the position of the
Catholic counter argument was concentrated on the proof of the
necessary and indissoluble bond between scriptural authority and

ecclesiastical authority. This was negatively proved with the example of Luther: whoever starts to doubt the teaching authority of the church logically ends by dissolving the authority of Scripture (as Luther demonstrated in the prefaces to the New Testament). The church established the canon of the Bible on the basis of its teaching authority, and on the basis of this same authority only the teaching office of the church is given the right to interpret the Bible in a definite way.

This position is also maintained by the Council of Trent, 1546, although with a characteristic change of accent. As a defence against Reformation theology, around 1530 and 1540 Catholic controversial theology tended more and more to establish the necessity of the teaching authority of the church by demonstrating the material insufficiency of Scripture. The Scripture contains the divine revelation as it was entrusted to the apostles, but it does not contain the complete truth of that revelation. The one and complete apostolic revelation is mediated only through the two equal sources of knowledge, the Scripture and the oral tradition, such that it can always be present in the authoritative interpretation of the teaching office of the church.

The decretal on revelation of the Council of Trent leaves open the question of how the mutual relation of the two entities "Scripture" and "tradition" is to be viewed in the evolving teaching of the church. In the Counter-Reformation polemic, however, there is an unmistakable tendency to underscore not only the material insufficiency of Scripture but the formal inferiority of a written mode of revelation in general. The oral tradition is superior as a medium because of its living quality and its flexibility when it comes to actualizing the content of revelation.

Antithetically to the Counter-Reformation theology there occurs a gradual explication and formalization on the part of the Lutherans of the doctrine of the mediation of revelation. The scriptural principle is thus given a new theological function in the controversy that not only tends to establish the complete material sufficiency of the Scripture, but also gives rise to an ever broader defence of the written word as divinely willed and corresponding to divine revelation. This development begins in the second half of the 16th century, above all with Martin Chemnitz and Matthias Flacius, and reaches its first culmination in the beginning of the 17th century in the theological system of Johann Gerhard. Chemnitz was the first to refer to the Old Testament Decalogue as an example of the written word as a

fundamental characteristic of divine revelation: God not only
instituted the written word as a medium of revelation, he himself
wrote the Law and thus initiated and sanctified the way of the
written word. The Sinai story shows with unmistakable clarity
that it is God's will to preserve the purity of his revelation
through divinely inspired writings. Gerhard adds to this Old
Testament proof a New Testament parallel: the beginning and main
example of the written word in the New Testament is the apostolic
decree (Acts 15:28), in which the Holy Spirit is explicitly
named as the author.

Around 1600 Lutheran theology became involved in a
controversy with the Catholics in which it became necessary to
refer the words of the Bible directly to God, in order to prove
that the written word was the only medium in which revelation was
possible. Thus the scriptural statements were described with
increasing frequency as *oracula Dei*, and the original Reformation
antithesis between "Word of God" (Christ as our alien righteousness)
and "human teaching" (works righteousness) becomes transformed
unnoticeably into the formal opposition between divine and human,
divine words and human words. This path leads of necessity to:

1) the formal identity between Scripture and Word of
   God,
2) the identification of the quality of divine revelation
   in the Scripture with its verifiable superhuman
   quality,
3) the concentration of all attention on the process of
   the revelation becoming scriptural, and
4) the derivation of scriptural authority from the sole
   efficacy of the Holy Spirit in the act of writing.

The biblical authors are referred to by Gerhard as "organs
of the Spirit", "hands of Christ", and "amanuenses of God".
This minimalization of human activity corresponds to the doctrine
of verbal inspiration that was being further developed in the 17th
century. This doctrine, which reaches its culmination in the
assertion of the divine quality of every letter of the biblical
writings, is bound up with the increasing formalization and
intellectualization of the understanding of revelation. Where
the relation between God and man is primarily understood as a
problem of knowledge, and where further the opposition between
divine and human is understood as a difference between infallibility
and fallibility, there the infallibility of the Scripture is clearly
a fundamental presupposition of all theology of revelation. It
thus becomes a primary task of theology to prove and defend this

nfallibility. The canonical problems of the Reformation period
re dogmatically resolved through the formal distinction between
"canonical books of the first order" and "canonical books of the
second order" (the traditional *antilegomena*), and can thus
ogically be declared by David Hollaz at the beginning of the
8th century as insignificant problems.

One may characterize the doctrine of Scripture in Lutheran
rthodoxy as an antithesis to the Counter-Reformation position.
This theology is structurally similar to the basic dogmatic
rinciples of the opponent. In this pattern of thought, authority
nd understanding of Scripture are separated. The Reformation
thesis of the clarity of Scripture is unavoidably overburdened
when it alone has to make possible, by combination of oral and
scriptural traditions as media of revelation, the same kind of
nfallible representation of the once revealed truths of faith,
which the teaching office of the church claims to realize.

In the dogmatic practice of Lutheran Orthodoxy the increasing
formalization of scriptural authority led to a stricter confessional
doctrine of scriptural interpretation.

The Heritage of the Orthodox Doctrine of Scripture: Pietism, Enlightenment and Neo-Lutheranism

The imposing doctrinal structure of orthodox Lutheran
dogmatics was vulnerable precisely in its foundation, the doctrine
of the Holy Scriptures. The rational understanding of revelation,
the identification of God's Word and Scripture, as well as the
rationalization of the authority of Scripture in the theory of
the infallibility of the verbally inspired Scripture provoked
irrational reaction as well as rational criticism. In relation
to the established scriptural doctrine of the Lutheran tradition,
Pietism and the Enlightenment may be viewed as parallel tendencies
toward disintegration.

As a revival movement and a movement toward ecclesiastical
renewal Pietism revolved more around the use of the Bible than the
doctrine of the Scriptures. The early pietistic reform of
theological study can thus be understood as the restoration of the
original Reformation ideal of *theology as interpretation of
scripture*. Just as the Wittenberg University theology at the
beginning of the 16th century, so the Halle reform at the beginning
of the 18th century takes its stand against philosophically oriented
theology, this time in the form of Lutheran scholasticism. The

line of biblical humanism of the 16th century is furthered
positively in the concentration on the study of biblical
languages and historical biblical research. Theologically there
grows out of this reform a biblicism with a preference for
salvation history concepts in place of the confessional systematics
of orthodoxy. The tendency toward biblical positivism in this
theology, as opposed to Reformation theology, is clearly seen in
the occasionally quite conspicuous interest in Chiliasm.

Pietism does not directly attack the orthodox doctrine of
verbal inspiration. With its biblical theological ideal and its
doctrine of *theologia regenitorum*, directed against the objectiviz-
ing of the orthodox revelation theology, however, it introduces
an indirect corrective in the whole orthodox doctrine of Scripture.
The individualizing tendency prepares the way for the theory of
personal inspiration as well as for the historical and philological
interest which is related to historical-critical biblical research.

Direct and open historical criticism of the orthodox
scriptural doctrine was first actualized within the Lutheran
tradition with Johann Salomo Semler's three volume work on the
scriptural canon in the 1770s. Semler had for a long time been
dissatisfied with the doctrine of Holy Scripture in the "systems
and handbooks" of the dogmatic theologians, because he felt
obliged to assert the incompatibility of this doctrine with the
data of canonical history. For a theological legitimization of
his critical intentions, he referred characteristically to Luther
and the Lutheran theologians of the second generation, as well
as to the theologians of the ancient church. Viewed against the
background of a theology that practiced critical freedom in an
exemplary manner the orthodox doctrine of Scripture should be
regarded as a regrettable historical interlude that should be
brought to its conclusion, the sooner the better.

The emancipation of historical biblical research from
dogmatics by Semler and his contemporaries was made possible
theologically by the distinction in principle between "Christianity'
('religion") and "theology." The reproach that historical biblical
criticism destroys the foundation of faith is rejected by Semler,
not only with reference to this necessary distinction but further
by his deriving the freedom of historical research directly from
Christianity's very nature: "the Christian religion rests on the
freedom to investigate and test, which all false and particular
religions deny and forbid" (*Abhandlung von freier Untersuchung
des Canon*, III, 405). Thus the claim of Christianity to be the
true religion leads to the right and necessity of historical

research on the Bible. Thus it follows on the one hand that the established dogmatic doctrine of Scripture must be continually corrected by ever-improving historical knowledge, and on the other hand that one has to distinguish between divine and human *within* the Scripture. The Orthodox thesis of identity between Scripture and Word of God is replaced by the antithesis that the Bible contains "more than what belongs to religion" (Lessing).

The Enlightenment distinguishes between historical and systematic theology and thus lays the groundwork for the widespread branching of disciplines in theology of the 19th and 20th centuries. Nonetheless historical investigation of Scripture receives an immediate dogmatic relevance just because of this distinction. The presuppositions for this can be seen in the Orthodox doctrine of Scripture; with its externalization of the revelational quality of Scripture it had to promote the historicizing of dogmatic questioning, which actually became the fate of Lutheran theology in the 19th and 20th centuries.

Since the last two decades of the 18th century the suppressed critical observations of Luther became once again part of the vocabulary of Lutheran theology. There was little room in the theological problematic of the Enlightenment for Reformation scriptural understanding, which was pregnantly expressed in the antithesis between "Scripture" and "human teaching". Against the background of Pietism and the Enlightenment, the profile of neo-Lutheranism became clear through the renewal of confessional consciousness in the first half of the 19th century. Against a tendency toward biblicism and criticism, the Reformation scriptural principle was expanded with a second principle that was supposed to reestablish the threatened connection between scriptural authority and scriptural understanding. Expressed in Aristotelian terms, the principle of *sola scriptura* became the "formal principle of the Reformation", and the doctrine of justification by faith alone became the "material principle of the Reformation."

Adjacent to this well-weighed doctrine of the two principles of the Reformation exists also the concept of Scripture as *norma normans* and the Lutheran confessional writings as *norma normata*; only through the derived norm of the confessional writings as correct scriptural interpretation does the Holy Scripture receive its theological clarity. Confessionally speaking it is a satisfying conclusion. It is clear, however, that it is won at the expense of one of the main concerns of the Reformation principle of Scripture: the doctrine of the clarity of the Scripture. With this two-fold division the theological point of the Reformation scriptural principle is inevitably lost.

Historical-Critical Biblical Research and the "Battle for the Bible" as the Fate of Lutheran Theology

The Lutheran church has been described with some justification as the "professors' church." The Reformation emerged from the medieval universities, and the new confessional church consciousness was characterized by the careful preservation of academic theology. There is a natural continuity from Luther as professor in Wittenberg to the state church structure of the universities in Lutheran states today. There is an internal structure that corresponds to the external: Luther's thesis that the literal meaning is the only meaning of Scripture, together with the related thesis of the clarity of the Scriptures, provoked an intensive concern with the task of interpretation. This task, in which Luther envisaged theology as interpretation of Scripture, could not be once and for all "fulfilled" either in the work of proclamation or in theological reflection. A theology that claims with any right to rest on Luther's Reformation can never claim to be finished with the theological task of hermeneutics.

The role of Lutheran theology in the development of modern historical-critical biblical research cannot be explained as a direct derivation from the Reformation. *Both* can, however, be explained with the broader historical background we have sketched here: that Lutheran theology could on the one hand assume a leading role in the development of critical research, and that on the other hand this same research created considerable difficulties within the Lutheran tradition and thus provoked especially strong reactions.

The classical doctrinal tradition of Orthodoxy had bound the authority of Scripture to the doctrine of verbal inspiration. The emancipation of historical biblical research could only be realized through a reactive disintegration of this connection; in opposition to the tendency toward identification of Scripture and revelation the humanity of Scripture had to be asserted here. When one no longer immediately connected divine inspiration with the written letter but rather with the human authors through the theory of personal inspiration, then new freedom was won with reference to the historical variety of biblical literature, without hereby forcing one to surrender the concept of inspiration as he foundation of scriptural authority.

The dogmatic problem that is posed through historical-critical biblical research cannot be resolved by modifying the established structure of orthodox revelation theory. Insofar as the theory of personal inspiration is to be understood as such a modification, it is rather designed to veil the problem than to clarify it; one grants critical research a certain freedom by quantitative reduction of the stuff of revelation, and hopes in return to reserve a trouble-free realm for revelation. With this solution it makes no difference in principle where one draws the line between inspired and non-inspired, between God's Word and human words. The theological decision is already made with the presupposed opposition between "divine" (infallible) and "human" (fallible).

The battle between "liberal" and "positive" theology, a permanent mark of the Lutheran tradition in the second half of the 19th century and the first decades of the 20th, can be seen in its vehemence to be a conflict determined by common presuppositions. On the one hand the conflict leads to a massive historicizing of the dogmatic problems in the expanding science of biblical introduction: such things as dating, authorship, pseudonymity, etc., are immediately treated as decisive dogmatic questions. On the other hand the conflict could lead to a pervasive separation of doctrinal tradition from biblical research, with a complete de-theologizing of biblical research as a consequence. Thus the theme of "the historical Jesus", introduced in the 19th century by the liberals as a corrective to the dogma of Christ, was neutralized for generations until it broke out of its stagnation around 1950, but now with the purpose of making visible the connection of the post-Easter kerygma with the historical Jesus.

In the long run, the historical-critical research of biblical texts allows no limitations to be set on it. With its growing historical knowledge of the biblical environment and with its ever more refined literary-critical and tradition-critical methods, it located the Old Testament in its place in the Near Eastern history of religions and the New Testament Scriptures threatened to dissolve into their disparate parts of late Judaism, Hellenism, and early Catholicism. For understanding isolated concepts and texts, the analytical process of historical research is helpful, but nevertheless in the perspective of a *scriptural principle* and indispensable discourse about *the* Holy Scripture,

the results of this research are increasingly difficult to master
theologically. From this latent conflict arise to this day new
confrontations that can lead to church divisions within the
Lutheran tradition.

The latest example of such a confrontation may be seen
as representative of the 200-year battle for the Bible in the
Luther tradition. In 1973 the *Lutheran Church-Missouri Synod*
adopted a paper, *A Statement of Scriptural and Confessional
Principles*, in which historical-critical research was rejected and
the scriptural doctrine of orthodox theology of the 17th century
was established as normative. On the strength of this statement
the president of their highest theological institution was suspended by the church administration. This led to an open schism
because of the solidarity of the majority of the professors and
students with their president. For these theologians the only
remaining possibility was to establish a "Seminary in Exile."

Such an institutionalization of the controversy is an
exception that is hardly imaginable in most Lutheran churches.
But as a symbol it may well serve to illuminate the problematical
situation of the scientific theology. The pulpit and the rostrum
no longer stand so close together as they did in the Wittenberg
of Luther. One gets the impression, rather, that proclamation
and research are far removed from each other. If that is so,
then academic theology has had to give up its proper task in
favor of a specialized existence on the borders of church life.
The task of interpreting Scripture on which the proclamation of
the gospel depends, is left to church tradition. It may be viewed
as symbolic of a fundamental crisis in modern Lutheranism that a
contemporary church administration uses arguments from 'that phase
of tradition which separates the doctrine of Scripture from the
interpretation of Scripture.

*The Contemporary Challenge: The Scriptural Principle in an
Ecumenical Horizon*

The Reformation principle of Scripture did not arise in
the context of a confessional church, but is profoundly bound to
an understanding of the church as *una sancta*. It is thus totally
logical that Lutheran theology in the 20th century has to assume
responsibility for the cause of the scriptural principle in an
ecumenical context, especially considering the widespread
de-confessionalizing of biblical research. Rigid and hopeless
positions that were laid down in the theological controversies of

the post-Reformation era are able to be transcended, as the Montreal Statement of *Faith and Order* 1963 demonstrated, for the problematic of Scripture and tradition. New formulations of the problem, open to the original intention of the scriptural principle, do not, however, arise spontaneously.

Here lies a challenge that can be seen in the two most important documents for the Lutheran churches in the inter-confessional doctrinal conversations in recent years. In the Catholic-Lutheran study report entitled "The Gospel and the Church" (so-called Malta Report), both partners assert, with reference to the insights of modern biblical study, that the doctrine of justification is no longer a point of controversy between the two confessions -- one must however leave the question open as to what role this doctrine plays within each structure as a whole. The "Leuenberg Agreement" asserts for churches of various Reformation heritages, with similar reference to common exegetical insights, a broad agreement in traditional points of controversy, although it omits the key hermeneutical question of the relationship between Law and Gospel. There is in both cases an unmistakable demand for a truly ecumenical scriptural principle, able to bring about the connection between exegetical insight and dogmatically binding doctrine.

The Reformation scriptural principle, symbolized at the beginning of this essay in the scene of Luther's appearance in 1521 in Worms, raises for us the difficult interpretative question of how the three concepts "Word of God", "Holy Scripture", "conscience" are related to each other. The identity problem of Lutheran theology up to now was that one believed this question could be solved by a formalized doctrine of Scripture. But when the Scripture as theologically authoritative is split off from the spectrum "Word of God" and "conscience" (that is, the person as addressed by God), then the theological point of the scriptural principle is inevitably lost. Since "Word of God" is not a formal category of revelation -- Jesus Christ is the "Word of God" to mankind -- the Scripture has its incomparable and exceptional position not in the area of that which is empirically verifiable or rationally demonstrable, but rather in relation to the person as conscience. Through the Scripture as witness to Christ, the Holy Spirit drives out all "human teaching," that is, all forms of forced self-redemption, and offers the conscience the alien righteousness of Christ. Therefore the task of theology is aligned with the task of the interpretation of Scripture, because the Holy Spirit through the Scripture constantly pushes toward the oral promise of Christ in the public proclamation and in absolution. To be the church means to live from this promise alone, and to be driven by the Holy Spirit to proclaim this promise to all people.

That is precisely what happens *sola scriptura* (through Scripture alone). It is just as inaccessible to empirical verification or rational demonstration as the revelation of God in Jesus Christ. The permanent ecumenical legacy of the Reformation is to maintain the indissoluble triad of "Word of God", "Scripture", and "conscience" and to bring this principle as *the* principle of Christian theology into the consciousness of new generations.

Translated by John Hinderlie

CHAPTER 6

Helmut Zeddies

The Confession of the Church

It is thought to be a characteristic of the Lutheran
church that it has a strong relationship with the confession of
faith. This seems to distinguish it most clearly from other
churches and denominations. "Confession," however, is given a
very special meaning. It is not used to describe the direct,
spontaneous witness of an individual responding to an encounter
with the living Lord. Nor is it the profession of faith given
at Baptism, or the Creed spoken by the congregation gathered for
worship. When the Lutherans speak about the confession of the
church, they mean first of all a statement of doctrine. Of
course, this is implicit in any form of confession. But while
in the confession of the first Christians and through the creeds
of the early church doctrine was embedded in praise, witness
and prayer, it soon began to grow more independent, even in the
old church, and developed into a type of doctrinal confession
with the emphasis no longer on the act of confession, but on the
correctness of the doctrine.

Without these changes of structure, the confessions of
the Reformation would not have been possible. With the exception
of Martin Luther's two Cathechisms which were meant for instruction
within church, home and school, they are doctrinal confessions,
drawn up in face of the acute danger to the faith and the church,
and authentically authorized by signature. They sought to safeguard the unity of the church by a common confession. In
justification of their convictions and suggestions for reform,

they claimed to be in accordance with Scripture and with the tradition accepted by the one church of Jesus Christ. Although the confessions of the Reformation show signs of immense efforts to maintain continuity, both in historical depth and in confessional breadth, it is also quite evident that the Lutheran church has had to cope with a variety of different confessional statements from its origin. There is much agreement, but also much scope for differences between these confessional texts. We will have to examine why it still might be possible to speak of only one, or even *the* confession of the church.

It is important to describe the theological context in which the confessional statements of the Lutheran church represented a very special form of confession. The concept of "confession" included a number of forms of expression, motifs and functions. The doctrinal confessions of the Reformation are only a small and limited segment of the whole, and this must not be forgotten in later discussions. This limitation helps us to understand the intentions of the Lutheran church's confessional statements, and to eliminate expectations and demands which they were never designed to fulfill, because they can only answer the questions which confronted them.

Development and Effect of the Confessions during the Reformation

The Efforts toward Unity and Renewal of the Church.

The conditions under which the confessional statements of the Lutheran Reformation were written are truly remarkable. Although they were meant to be theological statements, nearly all of them were reactions to political events. The Augsburg Confession and the Apology were written for the Diet of Augsburg (1530) where the evangelical princes and the independent cities of the empire tried to achieve legal recognition of their conversion to the Reformation. This had become a political matter when the emperor, at the Diet of Worms (1521), had called the fight against Luther and his movement of reform an affair of the empire. In opposition, the evangelical estates of the realm were concerned to prove to the emperor that their Smalcald League founded in 1531 was a legal association within the body of the empire. This was the intention of the Articles of Schwabach and Marburg (1529), which were also the basis for the unity negotiations among the evangelical estates themselves. The Smalcald Articles (1537) were written by Luther himself for the Smalcald League in preparation or the council planned in Mantua which, in fact, never met. The Formula of Concord (1577) was the result of the efforts to bring together the territories which had been torn by inter-Protestant doctrinal disputes. The 86 German territories who signed the Formula of Concord did not consider this only as a matter of church unity but also as a matter of political obligation. In 1580, all the confessional statements, the Creeds of the early church and Martin Luther's Small and Large Cathechisms were brought together in the Book of Concord. This also includes Melanchthon's tract: "On the Power and Primacy of the Pope". The Schwabach and Marburg articles however were not included.

This, however, does not change the obvious fact that the confessional statements of the Reformation, both in their content and in the intention of the authors, are clearly theological documents, but written for political occasions, serving political aims and primarily valid in the political sphere. This ambivalence is understandable against the background of the idea of the *Corpus Christianum*. The medieval belief in the unity of church and state was largely still unbroken. Like the Roman-Catholic emperor, the evangelical estates of the empire also held themselves responsible for the faith and piety of their subjects. They signed the confessional documents because they took it as part of their task as worldly authority to be responsible for church matters in their territories, and doubtlessly their aspirations to political independence from the imperial central power played a part in their commitment to the Reformation.

It is obvious that the reformers themselves did not try to avoid the ambivalence of their confessional statements. This is significant for their own understanding of these statements. They did not want to produce a new creed on which to build a new church. This is very clear in the Augsburg Confession. It is concerned to prove that the territories which had joined the Reformation still belonged to the one holy Catholic church. In spite of their denunciations of the abuses of doctrine, cultus and piety in this church, they still considered themselves part of it. But they claimed to have a better, i.e. more scriptural knowledge of the Gospel. In this it was important to them to be in agreement with the early church and its creeds. Concerned with this continuity, their efforts were directed to reforming the church, and not to leaving it. For that reason they demanded the recognition of the Reformation in the Augsburg Confession.

*The Formation of the Regional Churches ("Landeskirchen")
in Germany*.

It was only the religious Peace of Augsburg (1555) which
acceded to the demand for a legal recognition of the Reformation.
But it did not grant the evangelical estates the desired unlimited
freedom to preach the Gospel according to the understanding of the
Reformation. They had to be content with the promise that this
would be possible in their own territories, without interference
from the central political power. To the Catholic estates this
agreement was a welcome defence against the loss of further
territories to the Reformation. Thus the peace treaty was a
compromise on the basis of the status quo.

Its effects, however, were considerable. The Peace of
Augsburg spelt the end of the political and ecclesiastical unity
in Germany. The confessional separations favored the development
of largely autonomous regional states which, in their turn, were
drawn into the stream of this political development and went
ahead with the building of individual regional churches. This
arrangement did not imply a mutual acceptance of the freedom of
religious practice, or even state tolerance in questions of faith.
The Reformation may have received official legal recognition in
the Peace of Augsburg, but the treaty also confirmed that the
Augsburg Confession did not achieve its true aim, i.e. to maintain
the unity of the church and to implement the necessary reforms
within this one church.

In view of the political situation it was inevitable that
the church of the Reformation was embodied in regional churches
which, in each case, were confined to the particular principality,
county or free city in which they found themselves. They seemed
to have developed according to the principle that national
frontiers constitute the boundaries of ecclesiastical organizations.
In Germany, the integrating power of the Augsburg Confession,
which originally had been intended to bring together the whole
church of Christ, was only sufficient to form territorial or
regional churches which, to this day, are the characteristic form
of the Lutheran churches in Germany.

It was logical that the confessional statements which had
been testified before the emperor and the empire as the doctrine
of the Reformation, and had partly achieved legal validity, should
also be the decisive influence in the development of the regional
churches. They became the guidelines for the teaching, worship
and organization of the church. Ordination included the obligation

to teach them. The princes and the magistrates of the free cities were required to be responsibile for the organization and leadership of the new church structures as *praecipua membra ecclesiae* (Melanchthon, *De potestate et primatu papae*). Designed as a temporary emergency measure, this arrangement had disastrous results when the princes laid claim to the permanent powers of a *summus episcopus*. Church authority became part of the authority of the state, and church leadership often became an instrument of politics. The church in Germany was increasingly territorialized and politicized.

The Renewal of the Churches in Scandinavia.

In the North of Europe the development was different. It is noteworthy to what extent the spread of the Reformation in the Scandinavian countries was also linked with specific political developments. In every case, the Reformation gained the support of the central power of the state. It was therefore able to take a hold on the whole of these countries. It did not need to found new churches but could renew the existing ones to the extent that they each encompassed at least one whole people. And this spread and unity have largely survived to this day.

In Denmark the Reformation was introduced as early as 1536 by national decree. But the beginnings of a confessional orientation are found as early as 1530 in the Confessio Hafniensis in which the Danish Reformers gave a short summary of the basic doctrine of the Reformation. The Danish Church Order, 1537, elaborated by J. Bugenhagen, introduced the Augsburg Confession, which by civil law was accepted in its unchanged form of 1530 as the confessional statement of the church, and it has become part of the statutory confessional definition laid down in Danish law in 1683. The other authoritative bases of doctrine listed are Holy Scripture, the early creeds of the church, and Luther's Small Catechism. Although, since 1849, the Danish church has no longer considered itself a state-church but a folk-church, it is still the duty of the state to guard against the erosion of the confessional position.

Norway was linked with Denmark through the Union of Kalmar, in the same way as Sweden. It was therefore brought into the Reformation from outside and from above. The Reformation was initially considered as part of the foreign Danish rule, and found little sympathy. It was only when Norway gained its own

church order in 1607 that the Reformation really succeeded. In
1687 the confessional basis of the church was laid down, in terms
very similar to those in Denmark. It was the duty of the king to
watch over the observance of the right doctrine.

Unlike Norway, the Reformation in Sweden was directly
linked with the recovery of national independence. In 1527, the
Diet first decreed that the political power of the Roman Catholic
bishops should cease and that church property should be confiscated.
The church assembly in Örebro in 1529 began the ecclesiastical
reorganization. Since 1544 Sweden has officially been Lutheran.
The confessional basis, however, was only laid down by the church
assembly in Uppsala in 1593. Besides the three creeds of the early
church, the original version of the Augsburg Confession (*invariata*)
was accepted as the standard of doctrine. These decisions were taken
by neither king nor Diet. Unlike Germany or the parts of Scandinavia
under Danish rule, the Reformation in Sweden (which until 1809
included Finland) as well as the confessional developments, were
largely inter-church affairs. It was only after the introduction
of absolutism at the end of the 17th century that the church of
Sweden became a state church, bound for its own legislation to the
political powers.

The Development of the Understanding of the Confession

The Confession as the Doctrinal Basis in Lutheran Orthodoxy.

Soon after the confessional statements of the Reformation
had emerged, church history began to run differently from what
had been envisaged. The Lutheran Orthodoxy of Germany was initially
still very well aware of the intention to prevent the founding of
new churches. Orthodoxy stressed the catholicity of the evangelical
faith. The acceptance of the creeds of the early church was an
important element of proof. But Orthodoxy was particularly
concerned to emphasise the difference between Scripture and
confession, following the Formula of Concord. Holy Scripture for
them was credible in itself. As it was inspired by the Spirit of
God, its authority needed no further proof. The confessions
however, including the ones of the Reformation, had only derivative
authority, and were valid only to the extent that they agreed
with God's Word.

Whilst clearly subordinating the confessions to Scripture,
Orthodoxy however never doubted their general necessity. And

interest in them arose not only as evidence of the faith of the
past. The confessional statements remained indispensable for
refuting doctrinal error. The exegesis of Scripture in the confessions was obviously correct. The confessions were a legitimate
summary of what the present faith of the church should contain,
and were therefore indispensable for the preservation of its
identity. They were given a regulative function for the doctrine
of the church. Orthodoxy could draw upon certain statements in
the Formula of Concord to justify its opinion. This finally led
to the religious oath which had to be sworn on the confessional
statements in places of public teaching like churches, schools,
and universitites.

Lutheran Orthodoxy was active beyond Germany. In Sweden
it achieved the recognition of the Formula of Concord in 1686.
The doctrinal basis of the church of Sweden has since included
the whole Book of Concord, and according to the decision of 1593,
the creeds of the early church and the Augsburg Confession are
authoritative for the doctrine and preaching of Scripture, while
the book of Concord is used to interpret it. In Denmark, too,
the theology of the Formula of Concord prevailed. The official
introduction to the Book of Concord however failed because of the
opposition of the king who did not think it was orthodox enough.
On the whole the question of the confession was not of overriding
importance to Orthodoxy, except when used for safeguarding the
uniqueness of Scripture and the doctrinal system of the church.
This laid the foundation for an understanding of the confession
as the doctrinal basis of the church which came fully to fruition
in the theology of confessional Lutheranism in 19th century
Germany.

Individualizing and Relativizing of the Confession Through Pietism and Enlightenment.

In spite of the difference in their motives and aims,
Pietism and Enlightenment have surprisingly strengthened the
church in very similar ways. Pietism was concerned with the
individual and his personal relationship to God. It aimed at a
testimony arising out of the dedication of the heart. The
historically established confessional statements of the church
were suspected of being intellectual dogma. The direct experience
of salvation was held to be independent of any visible church
membership. It was more important that those who had truly

confessed the Lord should gather and testify. Differences in
confession were therefore not seen as signs of the separation of
the churches, but as forms of expressing the faith appropriate
to the existing diversity.

The Enlightenment was characterized by the same tendency
to relativize and individualize the ecclesiological significance
of the confession. It was no longer prepared to accept theological
ideas of the past as binding on the church, but wanted to re-open
the supposedly direct access to the Bible as the source of
revelation by removing the theological ballast of the Middle Ages
from the early Protestant orthodoxy. It was no longer tenable
that individual faith and convictions should be subject to a
doctrinal obligation taken under oath. Wöllner's *Edict of Religion*
(1788) tried to safeguard the legal validity of the confession
in Prussia by directing all pastors attracted to the Enlightenment
to abstain in their sermons from all utterances which were
contradictory to the doctrine of the church, even if they did
not agree with it. This attempt to shield the confessional
writings from all public criticism showed how insignificant they
had become. Their only relevance was as a legal basis for the
regional church structure until 1794, in the General Law of the
Land, Prussia abolished the legal sanctions of the confessions
altogether and declared the state to be confessionally neutral.

In Scandinavia, Pietism and Enlightenment undermined the
structures of the state-church in a way similar to Germany. The
link between church and people which had been taken for granted
for so long, was now being called into question. Peasants and
the bourgeoisie were alienated from the church. The relationship
between church and state needed reforming. In Sweden and Norway
especially, Pietism led to revival movements in which it was
frequently the lay preachers who worked for the spiritual renewal
of the people and - often against the opposition of the clergy
and the state church - gathered them into small cells. After the
declaration of neutrality, the state in Germany ceased to be
identified with the church in its territory. The regional churches
therefore required a new legal status. For those who had emerged
from the Reformation, this legal basis was the recognition of the
Augsburg Confession. Contrary to the original intent, it was now
given the function of becoming the basis for the existence of
concrete church bodies.

The Church-Constituting Character of the Confession in Lutheranism.

The developments in the field of law and of ideas have not
been without influence on the changing understanding of the
Confession. In opposition to the rationalism of the Enlightenment
there set in a noticeable religious revival in Germany. But
this was soon facing a crisis when, at the beginning of the 19th
century, efforts were made to restore the union between Lutherans
and Reformed, since the differences in confession were no longer
held to be divisive. While the advocates of union knew themselves
to be in agreement with the newly awakened religiosity of their
time, its enemies saw it was the last big attack of the Enlightenment. Consequently a part of the revival movement in the church
was linked with a strongly confessional Lutheran theology. It
went back to the concept of the Confession as the doctrinal basis
of the church, as developed by Orthodoxy, and built on it in a
very one-sided way.

For the opponents of unity, the confessional statements
were not only authoritative for the preaching and teaching ministry,
but also became an element constituting the church, and one of the
indispensable premises for its existence. "A church which has
no confessional statement as the basis of its constituted community
would not be a church, because it is not a community of faith"
(J. Fr. W. Höfling). Therefore the confessional statement was
also indispensable for the efforts towards church unity. Since
"the unity of faith has to show itself in the unity of confession"
(Th. Harnack), the unity with other churches was only possible
if they assented to the Lutheran confessional statements.
Confessional Lutheranism tried to use this very strong concept of
the confessional statements as a dam against the threatening
unionism and its indifference to the confessional bases.

These Lutherans also had a very high opinion of their own
church. For them, the Lutheran church was the embodiment of the
one universal church of Christ "by whose perfect fullness all
other churches live" (W. Löhe). There certainly existed differences
of opinion about the details of the theological understanding of
the church among these confessional Lutherans. But they were
unanimous in affirming the indispensable nature of the confessional
statement, and its church-establishing function which turned it
into a *nota ecclesiae*. This fact, together with the wide-spread
fear of union, explains their strong influence on church and
theology into this time.

Their interpretations however go far beyond the understanding which the authors of the confessional statements of the
Reformation had of themselves and of their task. We have already
pointed out the problems in claiming them to be the doctrinal
basis of a church. And they can never be elevated to the position
of church-constituting documents. CA VII has tried to make it
very clear that the church is constituted solely by the preaching
of the Gospel and the scriptural dispensation of the sacraments.
There is a clear change in interpretation now, away from CA VII,
which was the result of an insufficient regard for the historical
context of the CA. This document had marked the very beginning
of the confessional era and could not, as the confessional
Lutherans did, be related directly to individual, separated,
confessionally conscious churches who did not exist at the time.
The ecumenical horizon which was one of the characteristics of
these early statements had been narrowed down to encompass only a
confessional church.

There are clearly understandable reasons for this
misinterpretation of the Augsburg Confession. They lie not only
in the efforts to build defensive positions against Enlightenment
and unionism, succumbing to the danger of one-sidedness in the
process. The concept of confession in Lutheranism uses "organological" structures of thought borrowed from the philosophy of
German idealism, and which have strongly influenced the Lutheran
church of the 19th century (as well as Schleiermacher, the pioneer
of the Prussian church union). The idea of "organism", as the
principle explaining everything that happens, also was used as a
counter-movement to the Enlightenment and its mechanistic
rationalism. This movement was concerned with the harmony of the
whole which, however, can only be understood through its parts,
just as the individual has always to be seen as part of the whole
community. This thought pattern made it possible to have a
direct, evolutionary concept of history, in which the present
grew out of the past, and the future could be anticipated from
the present. But above all it affirmed the unity of all human
life in constant evolution.

This very idea of evolution inspired the church to apply
the basic "organological" structure to the problems of confessional
statements. This led to the idea of organically developing
confessions, and an understanding of their diversity and of the
differences between them, as well as of their continuity and possib1
further development. But the whole was held together by the one
over-arching principle, *the* Confession of the church, of which the

confessional statements of the Reformation were the specifically
Lutheran expression. Multiplicity and diversity mean nothing in
themselves; they are absorbed by the unified whole. New confessional statements can only claim validity if they develop within
this body. This understanding of confessional statements has
influenced generations of theologians who did not fully realize
that they were thus using philosophical categories which could
not fully do justice to the confessional statements of the
Reformation.

The Unifying Function of the Confessions in the Lutheran Churches of the USA.

It was of course not in all parts of Europe that the church
was changed and reshaped according to the principles of the
Reformation with the support of the regional political powers.
Where the regional rulers continued to adhere to the Catholic
faith, Lutheran churches and congregations formed without their
help, if not against their will. They managed to survive in
spite of the Counter-Reformation, but to this day they remain
without exception religious minorities, e.g. in East, South-East,
Southern and Western Europe. And in spite of their relatively
great numerical strength, the churches which grew out of emigration
from Europe to other continents have also remained minority churches,
when compared with the whole of the population. In that situation
there was also a confessional development which took place without
the help of political institutions. Although the immigrants tried
to transplant the forms of their home churches, and cultivated
their traditional language and culture, their ecclesiastical
identity really crystallized around the Confession. The Lutheran
churches in the USA are a good example of this.

Those who were of German origin had, since 1820, a loose
association through a General Synod. Disagreements over the
question of the authority of the Augsburg Confession as the
standard for the Lutheran faith led to the founding of the General
Council (1867). Its "Fundamental Principles of Faith and Polity"
stressed that the Augsburg Confession was the true measure for the
identity of the Lutheran church without, at the same time,
relinquishing all other confessional statements. It is their task
to protect this Confession from misunderstandings and to interpret
it without adding anything new to its substance. This meant that
the General Council had clearly decided in favor of subordinating

the other texts of the Book of Concord to the Augsburg Confession
in order to be able also to affirm the unity of the Confession
of the Reformation. They therefore denied the possibility of
development, or new approaches or even wrong interpretations
within the *corpus doctrinae*, and a historic understanding of the
confessional writings was excluded.

Unlike the General Council, the General Synod held the
Augsburg Confession to be a sufficient basis for the Lutheran
church. They did not need to claim the other confessional
statements of the Reformation for this, especially since the
Formula of Concord was not generally accepted by all Lutherans,
but rather had led to disagreements among them. But the General
Synod slowly came nearer to the attitude of the General Council
by recognizing the value of the "secondary confessional statements."
Although the differences of opinion had not entirely disappeared,
the majority of the synods belonging to either of these two bodies
joined together in the United Lutheran Church of America in 1918.
Its doctrinal basis contained all the confessional writings.
The common link with these statements was, for the ULCA, a
sufficient basis for joining with other synods into one Lutheran
church in America. It was not felt to be necessary to ensure
true orthodoxy by further doctrinal statements.

This was the basis on which the ULCA, the Augustana Synod,
the Suomi Synod and the Danish American Evangelical Lutheran
Church joined together in 1963, to form the Lutheran Church in
America. This incorporated the Scandinavian confessional tradition
which, although agreeing in principle on the concept of the
confessional statement as the doctrinal basis of the church, still
showed certain differences. The churches of Swedish and Finnish
origin recognize, according to the tradition of their mother
churches, the whole of the Book of Concord. The churches of Danish
and Norwegian origin however - again like their mother churches -
only feel themselves bound by the early church creeds, the Augsburg
Confession and Luther's Small Cathechism.

The different degrees of authority credited to the confessional statements of the Reformation were not without influence
on the Confession of Faith of the LCA. It recognizes the early
church creeds "as true witnesses to the Gospel." The other
confessions of the Reformation, including the Formula of Concord,
are seen as "further valid interpretations of the confession of
the Church." For the Lutherans of Scandinavian origin, however,
the crucial question was never the acceptance but the interpretation
of the confessional statements. Unlike the synods who were

influenced by German confessionalism, they were able to retain the
basic statements of the confessional writings without requiring
a uniform interpretation of all questions of dogma, especially
when these seemed to be of secondary importance.

In this they differed clearly from the Missouri Synod
which had been founded in 1847 by representatives of the German
Confessionalism. It demanded complete doctrinal unity as the
prerequisite for any form of church community. For its own use
it has developed, alongside a consciously congregational type of
church order, a comprehensive and unified system of doctrine and
church life including a rigorously applied church discipline.
Out of their belief in the divine inspiration and the subsequently
established infallibility of Holy Scripture arises their complete
commitment to the Lutheran confessional writings because,
according to the "Doctrinal Declarations", they are the dogmatic
decisions of Holy Scripture itself. The authority of the
confessional statements is valid for all the doctrines of the
church. Holy Scripture and Confession have come so close to each
other that, according to the Missouri Synod, Scripture has to be
interpreted through the Confession, and not vice versa, because
otherwise there would be no guarantee for a proper interpretation.

The American Lutheran Church, established in 1930 by the
union of the Synods of Ohio, Buffalo and Iowa, all mainly of
German origin, has tried to establish contacts with the Missouri
Synod. The ALC, which had also recognized the whole of the Book
of Concord as its confessional basis, worked out a "Common
Confession", together with the Missouri Synod which was to be the
basis for altar and pulpit fellowship. Both churches initially
accepted this confession of faith, but the Missouri Synod later
rejected it as insufficient. The ALC therefore, in 1960, joined
with the Norwegian Evangelical Lutheran Church and the Danish
United Evangelical Lutheran Church, to form The American Lutheran
Church. Its "Confession of Faith" again reflects the different
degrees of authority which different confessional statements
carry. The early church creeds, together with the unaltered
Augsburg Confession, are recognized and confessed "as a brief and
true statement of the doctrine of the Word of God." The other
texts of the Book of Concord are accepted as "a further elaboration
of, and in accord with, these Lutheran Symbols." Further theological
agreement was deemed unnecessary for the founding of the ALC, just
as it had been with the LCA. The fundamental unity which existed
already only needed to be stated and made public. This was done
by giving it expression through the formulation of the present

state of the faith. That in itself is remarkable because of the
concept of Confession behind it.

Confession and Witness - Efforts to Make the Confession Relevant.

The Theological Declaration of Barmen.

How did the confessions of the Reformation actually work
as the doctrinal basis of the Lutheran church? Were they capable
of always responding to the challenge of the moment? Was there
no need, in any particular situation, at least to explain in
understandable language what they meant? In other words: do
the confessional writings not also require an exegesis in order
to be useable? How else can a confession lead to witness?

An example of the common witness required in a situation
of acute difficulty for the church is the theological Declaration
of Barmen (1934). In order to refute the heresies of the so-called
German Christians and to resist the attacks of the National
Socialist leaders, representatives of the Lutheran, Reformed and
United churches in Germany joined together in the Confessing
Church. The threat which all the churches faced equally required
the common declaration. The authors themselves felt that it was
only possible because of their common witness to the Lord of the
one holy church which brought them together in spite of their
differences in confessional loyalty. The faithfulness to their
traditional confessional statements compelled them to speak
together in their common suffering and danger.

In six theses the church-destructive errors were countered
with "evangelical truths", and all opinions which were irreconcil-
able with these were rejected as heresy.

1. Because Jesus Christ is the one Word of God revealed
   in Holy Scripture, the church cannot recognize any
   other truths or events as the source of its preaching.
2. Jesus Christ is God's promise of forgiveness, but also
   God's claim on the whole of our lives. There can
   therefore be no areas in our lives which are not subject
   to Him, and which do not require justification.
3. In its faith and its obedience, its message and its
   order the church must testify to the world that she
   belongs only to the Lord who acts through her now in
   word and sacrament. She therefore cannot make the
   formulation of her message and the shape of her order

subject to her own whims, or to political or ideological demands.

4. The different ministries in the church all exist to carry out the service of the whole church. They do not carry any claim to leadership. There is therefore no place for leaders in the church who assume authority for other reasons.

5. According to God's command, the state has to ensure law and peace in the unredeemed world. But it must not become the sole and total framework for human life. It cannot accomplish the mission of the church, just as the church cannot take on the tasks of the state or become itself an organ of the state.

6. As it is the church's mission to proclaim the message of God's free grace, it cannot use the Word of the Lord for its own chosen wishes, ends and plans.

The authors of the Declaration of Barmen were well aware of what it meant to be able to speak together in this way, in spite of the extensive confessional differences which still existed between them. The Declaraction specifically made reference to the differences in confession, and thus to the theological heritage in the light of which the common declaration had to be justified, and on the basis of which there was the courage to issue it at all. It was not by accident that the call from Barmen was termed a "theological declaration". The term "confession" was avoided on purpose, although in content it really was a confessional statement, and the occasion demanded one. But the authors knew very well what difficulties would arise if they worked with a term which traditionally had been used for a written statement of the faith as documentary basis for the doctrinal position of a church. The Barmen Declaration was less concerned with this aspect of a confession than with witness in the particular situation arising from the falsification of the Gospel.

The Norwegian Declaration: "The Foundation of the Church".

The last comments on Barmen also apply to the Norwegian document entitled "The Foundation of the Church" (1942) which, in its sub-title, is called "a confession and a declaration". The statement of the Lutheran church in Norway was also prompted by an acute threat to the Christian faith and to the work of the church

by church leaders imposed by the National Socialists. In six
parts, it sets out, with reference to the concrete situation,
what is, at all times, the foundation of the church.

1. Holy Scripture is basis and norm for Christian doctrine
   and Christian life, and the Lutheran Confessions the
   "true guide in all matters of faith."

2. Because the Lord himself has founded his church, it
   cannot become a tool of worldy rulers. It is therefore intolerable if these rulers, for political reasons,
   remove servants of the church from the ministries to
   which they were ordained, thus depriving them of the
   right to preach and to administer the sacraments.

3. As the community of the body of Christ, the church
   has to stand by all its members, even those who are
   suffering or persecuted.

4. On the basis of baptism, parents have the right and
   duty to bring up their children in the faith of the
   church. The church cannot allow the children to be
   taught in an ideology which is hostile to Christianity.

5. Referring to the doctrine of the two kingdoms, it is
   stated that both state and church have their mandate
   from God. But they must not interfere with each other's
   sphere of competence. Since, according to the confession, the state "has nothing to do with the soul", it
   is not entitled to prescribe to people what to believe
   and think, and thus dominate their consciences.

6. According to the Norwegian constitution, the state has
   authority over the administration and order of the
   church. That does not mean that it is allowed to
   dominate it by means of political power, but it has to
   protect the faith and support the work of the church.

The difference between a "confession" and a "declaration"
is brought out clearly in the text of the document. While the
first three parts start with the words "we confess", the others
use the term "we declare". These are specifically concerned
with the conflicts between state and church, while the first
three parts deal with the church's doctrine of the Word of God and
of the church. It is probable that the terms "confess" and
"declare" were differentiated in order to make clear which of the
statements were immediately connected with the traditional
confessions. But when, in the face of concrete challenges, it
wants to define what constitutes the foundation of the church,
the Norwegian church also needs "declarations". But the document

has not become part of its doctrinal basis, although its importance
has repeatedly been emphasized. Its links with the confessional
statements of the Reformation have probably not been sufficiently
clarified.

Effects on the Understanding of the Confession of Faith

Beyond their immediate context, the declarations of Barmen
and from Norway have helped to revive the question of confession,
to give it new urgency, and to show afresh the complexity of the
whole matter. Both were acts of genuine witness, the response
to a concrete situation which demanded a new act of confession.
In this situation it became necessary to examine how to express
in a contemporary and relevant way, in face of the challenges,
what was the intention of the traditional confessional statements.
The actual situation had been rediscovered. And another insight
was gained: confession without the act of confessing is sterile.
What was needed was not another reciting of the Confessions of
the Reformation, but their application to the present situation,
so that they would express in new words in a new situation what
was their intention from the beginning.

This naturally raised the question of the relationship
of such declarations to the confessional statements themselves
which they were trying to apply. The texts of the Reformation
must be recognized to be in need of, but also capable of interpretation. But this can only be done by recalling their original
context, the occasion on which they were drafted and their
intentions. It also needs to be settled how the up-dated interpretation of the Confessions is to be understood: is it only to
be an exegesis of traditional texts, or can there be new statements
of equal status? According to a generally accepted principle,
the formation of a confession is never finished, so that in theory
it is quite possible not only to develop, but to add to the
confessional statements of the Reformation. If the confession
is to lead to the act of confessing, is it not possible that this
act may result in a new confession?

Concerning the theological statement of Barmen, the
Lutheran answer has largely been negative. The Declaration was
felt to be insufficient, containing only a minimum of truth, and
too far removed from the fullness of evangelical truths. Barmen's
character of historical contingency was felt to be too obvious.
It was to be taken seriously as a call to confess one's faith, but
not be accepted as a confessional statement. The Barmen

Declaration was judged by standards which purported to come from
the confessional writings themselves, but with which these
writings would find it difficult to comply. The criterion, in
fact, was a concept of confession which saw the confessional
statements as *the* Confession of the church which, as a complete
and integrated system, is the foundation of the church. The
argument tells us less about the pros and cons of the confessional
character of the Barmen Declaration than about the concept of
confession by which the Declaration was judged. The norm used was
nonetheless inadequate for the confessions of the Reformation,
both in view of the conditions under which they arose and of their
real intentions.

Conclusions

        Looking back, it is striking that in different epochs
different aspects of the understanding of confession have been
predominant. It is interesting to see how far this was due to
the historic development and to philosophical thought patterns.
The emphasis on certain points of view has often led to one-
sidedness, and has produced a distorted picture of what the
confessional statements of the Reformation were really about.
        It was certainly their aim to be authoritative statements
about the doctrine and the life of the church. They were
convinced that in the Gospel, as the message of justification,
they had emphasized the only permanent foundation of the church.
The confessional writings were not thereby claimed, however, to
be a constitutive element of the church in themselves. They were
not for the foundation of the church, but for bearing witness to
her foundation. To ascribe to the confessional statements of
the Reformation a church-founding character and, disregarding their
variety and the differences between them, to turn them into the
one unified Confession of the church, as German Lutheran theology
has done, can only be understood as a retrospective theological
legitimization of a development which had not been intended for
the confessional writings (at least until 1555). They were not
to found a new church but to renew the existing one. Their aim
was to maintain the unity of the church. When this failed, the
feeling of ecumenical responsibility soon disappeared as well.
There only remained the pursuit of unity and orthodoxy of the
confessional churches.

It is worth noting that the Lutheran Orthodoxy did not go
as far in its understanding of confession as 19th century
Lutheranism, although it naturally prepared the way. For
Orthodoxy the confessions were important as interpretations of
Holy Scripture. Thus they were somewhat removed, but yet had
considerable authority because, as interpretation of Scripture,
they were virtually infallible. The confessional writings were
regarded by their authors as interpretations of Scripture.
Certainly Orthodoxy accepted this understanding. But the Confessions were only doctrinal statements in so far as they corrected
grave dogmatic errors for the sake of the Gospel. In this they
were always to be submitted to the judgment of Scripture. Here
there is an obvious difference from Orthodoxy which took the
confessional statements out of their immediate functional setting
and turned them into independent doctrinal bases on which to
build doctrinal systems. And it was only a short step from there
to the belief that the unity of the church rests on the unity of
its teaching.

The Confessions as the doctrinal basis - this idea which
had originated in Orthodoxy - was of considerable significance for
the churches in Scandinavia and, later, for the unity movements
among the Lutheran churches in the USA. These churches did not
come together on the basis of identical Confessions. They first
had to determine which of the confessional statements were to
be considered the doctrinal basis. Therefore their differences
are really the proof that the confessional statement was the
starting-point for establishing their identities. But on the
other hand, it was partly due to these differences in confession
that the churches never got beyond an unhistoric doctrinal understanding of the role of confessional statements. This made any
hermeneutic work on them very difficult. In the latest union
negotiations amongst North American Lutherans, however, a new
trend can be discerned. Further steps towards unity are no longer
the results of further doctrinal agreements. Unity was found to
exist already. The common commitment to the creeds of the early
church and to the Confessions of the Reformation was considered
to be a sufficiently firm basis for recognizing organic unity.

After this review of the turbulent history of the Lutheran
Confessions there remains the question of what commitment to the
Confessions means today, if one takes account of their original
intention. With a few exceptions it is difficult to say, looking
at the history of the effects they have had, whether the Confessions
of the Reformation have really led to witness in the past.

Although they are clearly doctrinal confessions, they must at
least partly have resulted from an act of direct witness. The
question of the commitment to the Confessions today is what kind
of freedom will encourage Christians and churches to witness,
using the traditional Confessions. Commitment to the confessional
statement is less seen as an intention, or as a required
declaration, but instead as the acceptance of an established
loyalty. It is being bound to a confession which expresses an
experience of God's coming in Jesus Christ. This is always
happening afresh, and governs both the witness and the service
of the church.

We believe that the Confessions of the Reformation were
really meant to be a help in this "simple" spiritual commitment
which sets people free to confess. This was their aim, for the
sake of the unity and credibility of the church. It is fortunate
that the Lutheran church has rediscovered this aspect now, after
it had been lost for centuries. Since it has joined the
ecumenical movement, the Lutheran church has become newly conscious
of the ecumenical nature of its Confessions.

Translated by Donata Coleman

CHAPTER 7

VILMOS VAJTA

WORSHIP AND SACRAMENTAL LIFE

Luther's Approach

The worship services which have been held in the church of
the Lutheran Reformation through the centuries are closely linked
with the Western liturgical tradition. The Reformation must not
be seen as a "liturgical movement", although it is quite clear
that it had great influence on the liturgy. The early development
of the Lutheran forms of worship have often been misunderstood.
Some still think that the Lutheran church is not much interested
in liturgical forms, while others believe that the Reformation has
had a destructive influence on all liturgical matters. Theological
value-judgments and prejudices are very significant.

It will be our task to try to understand the motivation
for this development from Reformation theology, and to interpret
the changes in Lutheran worship through its basic premises. At
the beginning of "Lutheran" worship services, the acceptance of
a "Christian and pure origin" of worship in the times of the
Reformation struggles went together with the freedom to cleanse
the traditional service from all false additions and make it fit
for reverent use. The introductory sentence of Article XXIV of
the Augsburg Confession about the Mass is not apologetic cunning,
but expresses a basic conviction: "Actually, the Mass is retained
among us and is celebrated with the greatest reverence." This can
be said even though Luther had been violently attacking the ways
in which the church of his time was conducting its services for

a full decade. But the new service which then emerged did not
remain inviolable in the Lutheran church. It is therefore not
surprising that the history of the Lutheran worship service has
gone through a similar dialectical process between divine origins
and liturgical realization.

The Word

"Let everything be done so that the Word may have free
course..." This statement of the year 1523 sums up Luther's concer
for worship in all he was doing (LW 53, 14). When he made any
changes in the order of worship, these were limited to the necessary
consequences of his preaching and teaching. And it only happened
after others had already made more or less successful suggestions
for reforms, and after his friends had begged him to do so.

Seen in this way, the preaching of the Word is a return
to the source of all worship. In each concrete situation, it is
a corrective to what exists, and also grows out of the on-going
confrontation with the existing situation. The Lutheran reformation of the order of worship and the sacramental life cannot be
understood apart from the continuing heritage of the liturgical
life. This is the difference between this reformation and some
others from the same period, and also between it and some later
evaluations which overlook its rootedness in the liturgical
heritage. Luther certainly was no "liturgist", neither in terms
of his own time nor of any later period. But he understood
instinctively that a liturgy which had turned into "works" could
not be replaced by another, "better" one without committing the
same mistakes. It is true that he hardly knew any other traditions
(e.g. the rich Eastern liturgical traditions). But it is probable
that faced with these liturgical treasures which had grown on a
different soil his demands would have been the same, i.e. first
to get the preaching of the Word going, and only as a consequence
of this preaching to create new forms.

He went back to the Gospel as the source of his preaching,
and was always looking for the "Christian and pure origins", but
it was not automatically a "Biblical order" which was put into
practice. The contemplation of the words of institution of "the
Mass" serves to examine the existing practice and to lead to faith
in God's promise. Some of the traditional practices naturally
became suspect. But Luther first asked for patience, so that the
results should grow as ripe fruit out of faith. This shows his

grasp of the history of the congregation, and of its situation.
In the 16th century, faithfulness to the source did not require
an abrupt break with the existing structures, but their
correction. When one considers the liturgical problem in this
light, it is clear that ready-made solutions are not possible.
First there were theological interpretations which could use
the dynamic possibilities of the liturgical forms. Then the
second step brings alternatives to the liturgical forms which have
to be tested in the life of the congregation.

From the very beginning, the main Lutheran concern was to
make real in the congregation the saving act of God in Jesus
Christ, through the preaching of the Word. Therefore a relation
had to be established between God's act of salvation and the
worshiping congregation. This led to a critical examination
of private masses and finally to their abolition. Mass was only
allowed as the mass of the community. The idea of the sacrifice
of the Mass, which had invested the priestly office with a special
dimension, also had to go. But at first Luther tolerated the
Roman canon as a transitory measure, so long as the sacrificial
prayers referred not to the sacrament itself (the body and blood
of Christ) but to the presentation of the gifts. But he soon
abandoned this idea, and finally dropped the prayers of the canon,
as incompatible with the Word of God.

Faith

For Luther, the preaching of the mighty acts of God is in
its essence closely linked with faith. Word and faith for him are
correlated. It has generally been held that his concept of worship
as being an "incitement to faith", and therefore the essential
link between the act of worship and faith, has to be understood
on the basis of his doctrine of justification. But one must not
forget that Luther did not just apply his theological presuppositions
to the worship service. He arrived at the concept of faith through
the study of the biblical understanding of the sacrament. In the
Gospels, it is only God's saving act in Christ which is called
sacrament/mystery. The mystery of Christ which, in different
forms, is present among men, is fundamentally linked with the Word
which reveals this secret, and with Faith which received it into
salvation. Thus for Luther faith is given in the structure of the
sacrament itself. Through faith the mystery of Christ gains
existential significance because man is taken into salvation. It

is the Holy Spirit who works this faith when man dwells with the
different sacramental signs. It is true that the sacrament of
Christ's salvation is offered, independent of whether man believes
or not. If that was all that is contained in the concept of
ex opere operato, then it could find its place within Lutheran
theology. But it is only to faith that the gift can become
salvation. Thus, the sacrament must be *"opus operantis"* (WA 2,
751).

If one were to take this to refer to the ontological
reality of the gift of salvation, one would misunderstand Luther.
He is talking about the salutary effects of the sacrament on
human existence. The acts of worship work no differently from
God's other works, i.e. as salvation to those who believe, but
as judgment on those who reject the faith. It was one of the
main points of the reformer's criticism of contemporary theology
that it ignored the relationship with faith. But faith (*fides*)
must be understood as the sacramental presence of Christ. It
is not a function of man's mind through which he can seize salvation.
Christ acts (*operans*) in man through his Holy Spirit. Thus Luther
gives the worship service of the congregation its true sacramental
dimension. Only if the mystery of Christ, through the hidden
action of the Holy Spirit, can attain its aim in achieving a
believing human existence has the mystery of salvation been used
rightly.

The personal dimension of faith thus described is closely
connected with the question of the use of the gift of salvation
offered in worship. It is known that Luther (and after him his
successors in the Lutheran church) criticised the practice of
the Catholic Mass when it was held to make the fruits of salvation
available to others but the faithful congregation. The sacrament
of the altar, as the promise of the new covenant, can "be
communicated to no one, except only to him who believes with a
faith of his own" (LW 36, 48). This explains Luther's and the
Lutheran confessional writings' negative attitude towards the
masses which are said *pro vivis et mortuis*.

In this context we must, however, mention Luther's
attitude toward infant baptism. In the baptism service the
parents, god-parents and the congregation bring the child before
God, so that he may have part in the death and resurrection of
Christ. In order to justify the practice of infant baptism,
Luther uses the argument of the *fides aliena* which he takes from
Augustine. The congregation of the faithful brings the child
(*offerre*) to God in intercession. Thus, the congregation stands

before God, vicariously in faith, and prays for personal faith for the child. It is important to note that baptism cannot procure salvation for the child without his own faith, but that his faith is made possible "through the prayer of the believing church which presents it" (LW 36, 73). This opens up a new way in which the salvation-gift of worship can be used. The sacramental dimension of faith which is expressed in intercession for mankind could keep the church from becoming a shelter for the believers instead of transmitting salvation to the world, i.e. making sure that the word goes out.

The Sign

In Luther's discussions with the fanatics among whom there existed anabaptist tendencies, the sacramental dimension of faith became relevant in a new way. The arguments about faith revealed an attitude which discards the external acts and made faith into an internal quality of the soul. When he uses Augustine's statement that "not the sacrament, but the faith of the sacrament, justifies" (LW 30, 66: LW 35, 12: Apol. IV, 73) it is quite clear that *fides* is related to the sacrament. The Holy Spirit is not against "external things" but awakens faith by explaining our faith through these very things. Therefore God's promise of salvation always carries with it the sign or seal. The sacrament consists of promises *and* signs (*signum*), and the two are linked by faith. Those who despise these external things, whether it be the water of baptism, or the bread and wine of the communion, reject the way which God has chosen for the work of the Holy Spirit in Jesus Christ. *Sola Fide* is not in opposition to the sacramental sign, but to the idea of merit which considers the external attitude in itself as leading to salvation, without faith, and turns it into a work which is attainable to man (Apol. IV, 73). The correct teaching is the *sola fide* which knows itself linked to the sign.

The sacramental structure of God's acts in the history of salvation emphasizes the special significance of the sign. Whatever the sign signifies really happens according to the promise in every sacramental act. In baptism, for instance, the sign is not the water as such, but the immersion into the water, which signifies both the death and resurrection of Christ, and the acceptance of the death and resurrection in faith (LW 36, 67 and 68). The sacrament of the altar unites into one spiritual

body all the faithful who live by it, just as bread and wine is
brought together and pressed from many scattered parts and then
given to the body as food (LW 35, 51 and 58, c.f. LW 36, 353).

The symbolical value of the sign is thus particularly
emphasized. When the fanatics reject the external things they
show that they cannot reconcile creation with Christ's acts of
salvation. The sign cannot be replaced by an inner movement of
the soul, because Christ himself became flesh. The word is
not "more spiritual" than the external sign which it accompanies
and explains. Therefore physical eating and drinking is a
constitutive part of the sacramental happening. The sign contains
something which cannot be expressed in any other way. Therefore
it has its own, integral value besides the spoken word, just as,
in his love, God did not only pronounce a word of forgiveness,
but gave his Son as a sacrifice on the cross.

Against this background it is easier to understand why
Luther opposed the Roman withholding of the chalice as much as
he opposed those who held water baptism in contempt.   The whole
physical life of the Christians was bound up with this sign: the
community of the body and blood of Christ with the community of
Christians. That is why communion was specifically called "the
sacrament of love." The baptism with water, with its immersion
and lifting out was more than a mere symbol. It was an effective
eschatological sign of the death of the old man and the renewal
of the new man, relevant even to man's daily work. That is where
baptism was practised. Through the external sign the special
celebration of the worship service of the congregation touches
the "worship of everyday life" which thus receives a sacramental
depth.

The Development

When Luther publicized concrete suggestions on the form of
worship, he warned that they should not be seen as "necessary
laws." He was in favor of freedom and adaptability of the forms,
and trusted in the creative dynamism of the faith.

Nevertheless his suggestions became the basic models for
the liturgy in the congregations in the different countries.

His friend pastor Johannes Bugenhagen from Wittenberg was
called to many German and European countries as adviser, although
the theologians who had been captivated by Luther's Reformation
message were able to carry on the work by themselves. Nevertheless

it was inevitable that the emerging church structures imprisoned
the dynamics of the Reformation in rigid forms, and there is a
certain justification in speaking about a "new institutionalization" in the style of the medieval heritage, which was no
longer reflecting the full achievement of Reformation renewal
(L. Fendt).

Pedagogy of Salvation

The theological concerns of Orthodoxy have tried to
preserve Luther's heritage, and have used the concept of *Cultus
Dei* both for the liturgical and worship acts and for the whole
of Christian life. But soon there emerges a terminology which
specially emphasizes one aspect of the Lutheran approach, i.e.
the concept of proclamation which can be understood as doctrine.
Melanchthon already, in his Apology (Art. XV, 42) introduces the
definition that "the chief worship of God is the preaching of
the Gospel." The search for theological clarity in fixed dogmatic
precepts replaces the prophetic concept of the living word of God.
The doctrinal sermon and the teaching ministry will now take its
place.

In the Lutheran church it is Orthodoxy which first studies
the technique of preaching. In the theories which are now evolved,
the medieval theories reappear. Luther's prophetic formlessness
turns into the exact opposite: there are precise methodological
rules for preachers, and the pedagogical element is predominant.
It is true that these efforts can, in some instances, be traced
back to Luther: for him the teaching element was a part of the
whole. This means that there was a shift of emphasis which had
consequences which later were not at all desirable to the orthodox.
It still preserves and even develops a type of Lutheran worship
that maintains the unity between preaching and sacramental actions.
But inside this structure, the teaching sermon turns into an
independent liturgical act (*exordium*, prayers, open confession,
hymn, etc.) which necessarily becomes the center, and the dogmatic
material dominates the biblical message so much that it loses its
dynamism. Technique prevents precisely what it ought to have
protected: the freedom of the word of God.

This orthodoxy which was protected by its doctrine of
preaching watched over the church's sacramental life. Public
confession of the congregation is as much part of the celebration
of Holy Communion as private confession once was part of the

communion of the people in the Mass. In the situation of the
regional churches there evolves a sacramental discipline which
was to have helped the reverent celebration and the examination
of conscience. Under the influence of the standard culture of
a national church however, this church discipline gets tied up
with civil rights, and the constraint of the sacramental life is
back. What was to have been the central concern of pastoral care
became a legalistic structure, and led to the hollowing out of
the spiritual dimension of worship. Where civil rights were
linked with service, attendance and participation in the
sacramental life, the opportunity for hypocrisy among the
community was just as open as in the Middle Ages, and the risk of
an "external work" just as great as in the time when Luther spoke.
The Lutheran worship and the sacramental dimension of faith which
went with it were not easily encapsuled in legalistic structures.

The Inner Life

It was inevitable that there was a reaction from Pietism,
seeking to revive the original spiritual depth of the Reformation.
It went back to Luther, and saw the contemporary practises only
as external forms which had nothing to do with the inner renewal
of man.   In Luther's criticisms of the Roman practice pietists
could find plenty of arguments in favor of the view that the
inner, spiritual life is a pre-condition for the life of worship
and the sacraments. It was not enough to leave Rome and its
"Babylonian captivity". Without spiritual renewal even the
"evangelical structures" were of no use. In its early stages,
Pietism still showed much respect for the structures which had
developed over the 150 years after the Reformation. At first they
only tried to find and make conscious the spiritual significance
of baptism and communion. A deeper study of the word of God was
to rediscover the source. This produced a reaction against
Orthodoxy, and the wish for biblical, exegetical, pastoral and
edifying sermons. In order to achieve this, the right use of the
word of God is specially emphasized. Luther's separation between
Law and Gospel becomes for the various kinds of pietists a concept
applied to different groups of people.
This singling out of the word of God finally leads to a
practice which threatens to destroy the sacramental life according
to Lutheran understanding. As a result, the different groups of
people are classified chronologically in the *ordo salutis*-doctrine

of Orthodoxy, and thus the sacramental unity of God's acts is
shattered. In Luther's doctrine of baptism, for instance,
participation in the death and resurrection of Christ was believed
to be a sacramental and eschatological event, quite distinct from
the empirically effective renewal inherent in it. In Pietism,
however, this renewal often becomes the decisive event and is
identified with the conversion of man. The more radical exponents
of this view can even time it. Seen as a second birth, it is
invested with a significance which in faith is sacramentally due
to baptism.

A similar development happens in the understanding of
communion: only the re-born are worthy to eat and drink. Therefore the importance of the act of preparation for communion and
the penance involved are over-emphasized. The sacramental gift
of the body and blood of Christ are devalued by the spiritual
eating and drinking: the meal has become the love feast of the
small group of believers (the truly converted). It has to be
remembered, though, that in both cases the outer order of service
is not being abandoned. Theologically, this produces a fencing-
off of the small, faithful group from those who are not converted.
Continuing in Luther's arguments, since he wanted a worship
service for those "who seriously want to be Christians", it becomes
clear that his real concern for a sacramental worship service has
been lost.

In a period of exterior, legalistically rigid worship,
Pietism rightly stressed Luther's arguments for the inner,
spiritual life of faith, but neglected its sacramental basis. In
spite of retaining the "external forms" it emptied them from
inside, and thus theologically destroyed the forms of worship.
Although many of these theological statements had already been
prepared by the *ordo-salutis*-doctrine of Orthodoxy, it was only
the call for the practise of the re-birth which made it possible
to disregard the real sacramental act. It almost disappeared by
itself when the rational criticism of the Enlightenment set in.

Tendencies of Disintegration

There is a certain justification in referring to a
"disintegration of the forms of worship" in the period of Orthodoxy,
Pietism and the subsequent time of the Enlightenment and Rationalism
(P. Graff). But it has been recognized early that this thesis can
only be held with certain reservations (Y. Brilioth). The original

forms of Lutheran service persisted in the German regional churches
and even more so in the Scandinavian countries. Liturgically,
very little had yet "disintegrated", and the real break only came
with the Enlightenment, as we saw earlier, and had its (geographical
boundaries. Beside the original Lutheran type of service which
was built on the unity between sermon and holy communion, and
which was undermined by Pietism, there existed another, little
noticed type of service: the medieval preaching service which had
found its way into a few (South German) Lutheran liturgies. This
happened under the influence of the Swiss Reformation (E. Weismann).
Since the time of the Reformation therefore, there had been two
basic forms of service in use. The Swiss or South German form
was found acceptable because the transition to communion every
Sunday from the practice of annual communion in the Middle Ages
was not easy, and because the prominent place given to the sermon
was felt to be characteristic of the Reformation. In a later
development, communion was incorporated into this type of service.
This resulted in a liturgically simpler form of communion service
in some Lutheran churches (among them the minority churches who
had been exposed to the persecutions of the Counter-Reformation).

The Enlightenment and the period of Rationalism drove
the Pietism criticism *ad absurdum* and placed the forms of worship -
without their sacramental content - at the service of adult
education. But this has nothing to do with the pedagogical
understanding of worship of the time of the Reformation. Reason
now becomes the arbiter in questions of religion and of culture,
and the sacramental basis of the service is entirely abandoned.
This widespread cultural development was contrary to every church
tradition; it is even noticeable in Catholic theology.

The liturgical science now developing within Rationalism
inevitably clashed with the orders of worship of the Reformation.
The new theorists held that the old orders of service of the
previous centuries had helped to build up the church. But the
proposals for improvement which they introduced abolished the
congregational and sacramental elements in favor of individualism
and subjectivism. Individual elements of the liturgical tradition
might still be used, but the spiritual impetus of the Lutheran
approach was lost. While in Pietism, liturgical matters were
considered to be indifferent, Rationalism could see in them no
educational value at all. Here we find new beginnings which were
to be important in the subsequent history of the liturgy. An
ordinal (in Lutheran tradition often called service book or agenda)
is seen as an unnecessary tie, and the new private lectionaries

departed from, or at best improved upon the traditional ones.
Since everything had to be educational, there was a lack of
understanding of the representative acts of the liturgy. Holy
communion becomes an appendage of the service and had to be
celebrated after the main service or even completely separately.
All the new suggestions meant a destruction of the basic structure
of the original Lutheran service of worship.

Resistance

This state of affairs must not lead us into misunderstanding of the real situation in the churches. There the
traditional Lutheran worship was putting up a surprisingly lively
resistance.

Different reactions prove this. The orthodox believers
in Sweden rejected the introduction of a new ordinal in 1811, and
requested permission to retain the old one (of 1693). The famous
"Prussion ordinal" of 1821 also mobilized the old Lutherans
although Frederic William III had been influenced by the spirit
of the old Lutheran service, but at the same time linked his
reform to the ordinal with the forced introduction of church
union. The situation became critical because the different
reactions clashed with the stubborn legal provisions of the
authorities. This produced splits in which each partner stood on
his right. But the unity of the Lutheran church suffered badly.
Some groups could only escape persecution by the State through
emigration, a fact which has left its scars to this day. It is
sometimes thought that one can dismiss some historical struggles
with the opinion that there were conservative forces at work.
But one must not belittle the historical role of such developments.
They stopped certain wrong developments and set the right course
for the subsequent growth of the liturgical life.

During the first half of the 19th century, the integrated
communion service was being maintained in the German regional
churches, although the regular celebration every Sunday was no
longer generally practised. In the Swedish church it only became
possible after 1861 to celebrate Holy Communion at a different
time than during the Sunday High Mass. But when the celebration
of Holy Communion in the second half of the 19th century slowly
became independent of the main service, this was largely due to
the growing communion shortage, i.e. the lack of regular Sunday
communicants, and not to the disintegration of traditional forms

of worship. Orthodoxy and Pietism already tried hard to safeguard
the reverent celebration. It was only when, through changes in
society and the legal system that worship and sacramental life
in the church was undermined by rationalist arguments, so that
the celebration in the congregations itself was endangered. It
needed fresh thinking to save the old heritage and to seek a
renewal of the Lutheran service through a return to the basic
convictions of the Reformation.

The Renewal

        Through all the changes in the worship and sacramental
life of the Lutheran churches it must, however, be noted that in
spite of many tendencies to disintegration, the Lutheran approach
has always remained alive. It was always there, sometimes more
clearly visible, sometimes only apparent in a few characteristic
elements or even partly obscured, and withstanding many theological
and cultural currents.
        In the second half of the 18th century strong forces of
liturgical renewal began to emerge. In Germany at the time one
used to talk about a re-awakened Luther confessionalism. But
the Scandinavian countries, too, developed their own indigenous
movement of renewal. The Anglo-Saxon revival movements gained
ground in the Lutheran churches, but were also corrected by the
ideas of the Reformation. The renewal of the church's understanding
of the ministry and of confession had important consequences for
its worship.

        Sacramental Re-awakening

        Two examples shall serve to show the full extent of this
new movement in the Lutheran church of the 19th century. They
emerged quite independently of each other.
        First we should think of Wilhelm Löhe and his influence
on the Lutheran churches. His Service Book for Christian
congregations of Lutheran confession, published in 1844, differed
from the usual private service books which were mere desk works.
Löhe's liturgical ideas came out of his work in the Neuendettelsau
institutions. Subsequent editions of this book, and the new
service books in the Lutheran regional churches, as well as
among emigrant churches overseas which were modelled on it, prove

the organic growth of the liturgical life in these institutions.

Löhe understood the limits of the liturgical work of the Reformation as having been more concerned with cleaning up of abuses than with creating anything new. Therefore he tried to create something new with his congregation. He had a feeling for liturgy as representative action, pressing the arts into the service of God and with pioneering ecumenical openness he re-shaped worship and sacramental life. At the centre of this renewal were communion and a rich prayer life. The service is strengthened in its two dimensions, i.e. God's approach to the congregation, and their approach to him, the encounter between God and his people, and the actual presence of the act of salvation. Thus he takes over Luther's liturgical concerns and brings them up to date. Löhe is also at one with Luther in seeing the serving function of all liturgical orders. As for Luther, the church for him can be the church "even in a beggar's garb" as long as it is faithful to the command of the Gospel.

In the Scandinavian countries, similar movements of liturgical renewal grew out of the reaction against Pietism and Rationalism. In Denmark, one of the greatest Lutheran hymn-writers of the world, pastor N.F.S. Grundtvig, becomes the father of a movement of sacramental and worship renewal. His "discovery" was that Christ is present in his Word *in the church* when it is gathered for baptism or Holy Communion. "Only in the bath (of re-birth) and at the table (of the Lord) do we hear God's word to us". Not Scripture as such, but God's acts in worship and the sacraments are the life-giving word to men; it is essential that they be existentially involved. The baptismal confession (Apostolic Creed) calls into the church where praise answers it. The gathering of the congregation is done through the sacraments: Baptism at the beginning and communion later on turn the worship service, according to Grundtvig, into the central focus of the Christian life. The sermon reminds the person of growing faith of his baptism and at the same time points ahead to communion. A Christian is a "child of the congregation", which means that his life is rooted in the sacramental celebration of the congregation. It was Grundtvig's influence which re-introduced the regular Sunday celebrations of communion in the Danish church, and which helped to re-establish it as part of the service. His influence extended to Norway and also shaped the worship of an important part of American Lutheranism.

This stress on the strong sacramental rootedness of Christian life distinguishes Grundtvig and his disciples from the pietistic,

partly Anglo-Saxon- influenced revival movements of his century.
But it also made him different from the parallel high-church
oriented effort for renewal. For him the church was essentially
the gathered congregation, and not the institution. Thus the
ministry does not have a special position, and considerable
demands are made of the laity in order to ensure openness to all
people and to the life of the world. In these distinctions and
emphases his movement preserves specifically Lutheran characteristics without becoming confessionalist.

Restoration

The 19th century leaves for its successor the beginnings
of the liturgical renewal movements. These feed on the newly
discovered historic sources of the church's liturgical tradition.
It is characteristic of this liturgical movement that it cuts
across confessional lines. It may affect different traditions
differently, but at the same time brings about a certain amount
of exchange between them. By going back to the sources of the
early church, new ways are opened to the understanding of the
different opinions which divide the churches from each other.
The liturgical movement is the beginning of the ecumenical
rapprochement which had its first results in the liturgical
renewal of the first half of the 20th century.
From the beginning of the century, the discovery of the
historic sources of the Lutheran tradition went together with a
demand to put the principles thus elicited into practice. The
liturgical movement was not standardized, but the different groups
with their specific characteristics worked for an official
examination of the valid orders of service in their different
churches. These efforts were to instil a new spiritual content
into the old orders of service, and help to work out the appropriate
forms.
It has to be noted, however, that in its early phase the
liturgical renewal movement stuck close to tradition and was not
prepared to be creative, but only restorative. The texts, hymns
and church music contain a somewhat archaic tendency which tries
to ban subjectivist tendencies and aesthetico-romantic elements
from the liturgy, and to go back to the heritage of the Reformation.
It also discovered to what a large extent the Lutheran liturgical
tradition had fed on medieval and early church sources. Out of this
knowledge the liturgical renewal movement gained the freedom to

adopt the common liturgical treasures of the Western church linked with the basic structure of the Western liturgy, which the Lutheran churches had preserved. The work of renewal in the different Lutheran churches in the 20th century ran curiously parallel although the second world war created considerable difficulties for communication. The new post-war orders of worship however, reflect the same theological and liturgical tendencies. This becomes visible in the work of the different committees of the Lutheran World Federation (between 1952 and 1970).

As a general observation it is true to say that the basic type of Lutheran worship is enriched by the liturgical treasures of the ecumenical movement. A few examples show this clearly:

(a) The form of the introduction. In the course of history the old *Confiteor* (which became an act of the whole congregation at the time of the Reformation) had been enlarged into an act of penitence. This replaced private confession, and turned the whole celebration of holy communion towards penitence. In order to restore to communion its character as a meal of thanksgiving and joy, and to retain for confession its own individual value, many Lutheran churches have separated confession and communion. This provided the possibility of having the confession either as an independent (public) service or as a distinct occasion of pastoral care (private confession). In the celebration of Holy Communion the eucharistic character now emerges more strongly.

(b) The service of the word always kept to the traditional order of the mass (*missa catechumenorum*), but it was often abridged and simplified. The liturgical renewal brings about in all the orders of service a richer liturgical form, drawing on the whole Western tradition (richer variants of the *Kyrie* and the *Gloria* were used, and old collects were preserved and two or even three lessons framed by *Hallelujahs* or praises). Following the patterns of the early church, interesting experiments were made in the United States to develop the *Kyrie* into the prayer of intercession. This shows that there has been a general renewal of the tradition of prayer in Lutheran liturgies as well. The place of the once predominant prayer said by the pastor alone (*prosphonesis*) is now taken by the early Christian forms of common intercession (deacon's prayer, litany) which had also been handed down through the Reformation. The congregation is encouraged to join in the prayers. The liturgical year determines not only the lessons but the whole shape of the liturgy, as it has done since the time of the Reformation. Often church music of the type of the time of the

Reformation is revived, sometimes even Gregorian chant. Under
Anglo-Saxon influence, the singing of psalms in English (chant)
is re-introduced in the United States.

(c) The deepest renewal has taken place in the communion
part of the liturgy. It is important to note, first, that in
nearly all Lutheran service books the main Sunday service is now
considered as a unity of word and communion service.   This is
due to the world-wide eucharistic renewal in the Lutheran churches.
The communion part of the service which, following the protest of
the Reformation against the Roman canon had suffered the most
severe cuts, has once more developed in an ecumenical tradition.

The Lutheran criticism of the sacrifice of the Mass also
removed the *offertory* (both as a prayer and an offering) from the
liturgy. This happened despite Luther's opinion that in the early
church gifts were naturally brought (along with bread and wine)
as a thank-offering by the congregation during the service. The
confusion between this thank-offering and the sacrifice of the
body and blood of Christ (the concept of the sacrifice of the
Mass) had a negative effect on this otherwise legitimate element
of the liturgy. The rediscovery of the idea of Christian stewardship meant that the thank-offering also was reinstated in its
place. This was done by a collection of money, and in some cases
also by the presentation of bread and wine. But this latter custom
is often avoided for fear of a sacramental misunderstanding, and
the thank-offering is separated from the communion part of the
service.

The ordinary (*ordinarium*) with its variants according to the
church's year has usually been kept in the Lutheran tradition
(*praefatio, sanctus, benedictus* and *Agnus Dei*), but the classical
texts were sometimes replaced by a congregational hymn. But the
Lutheran tradition did not hand down a complete eucharistic prayer.
Only the essential elements of the institution were needed, the
words of institution (*verba institutionis*) and communion (*communio*)
in both kinds: these were surrounded by the Lord's prayer and by
a post-communion prayer of thanksgiving. The liturgies of the
renewal movements have extended the big thanksgiving prayer: they
include the prayer of invocation of the Holy Spirit (*epiklesis*),
but it is understood only to refer to the gathered congregation
and not to the elements. The remembrance of the mighty acts of
God (*anamnesis*) also finds its place - the celebration is introduced
by the *praefatio*. A prayer of intercession is added (after the
consecration). Here it is obvious that the Lutheran liturgy has
tried to conform with other orders of service in the ecumenical

movement. This is in no way in opposition to the theological
premises of the Reformation but recovers what had been lost in
the historical polemics, or rather had never been formulated
liturgically.

This short summary shows that we are concerned with a
renewal within the tradition of the church. At a time when this
tradition was largely in danger of being lost it became clear
that a simple renewal of tradition was insufficient.

New Challenges

The developments described above marked the apex of the
so-called liturgical movement. The work which has been done on
the official orders of services would be unthinkable without
this background. The movement reached a similar peak in the
Catholic church through the decisions of the Second Vatican
Council and the subsequently instituted reforms. The new order
of the Mass surprisingly has alternative eucharistic prayers,
modelled on examples from the early church which are a good basis
for ecumenical understanding. Today, it is nearly possible to
talk about a basic ecumenical structure of the eucharistic service
in the Western liturgy which is also to be found in the Lutheran
liturgies.

One might expect this rapprochement between the confessions
to have promoted the search for unity among the churches. Although
it has to some extent, it must not be forgotten that during the
second half of the 20th century the church has become conscious
of problems which have led to entirely new departures in the field
or worship. These have led necessarily to a re-thinking of the
whole question of what worship is and of how it should be celebrated
in our time.

A revival of the traditional church service will certainly
mean a deepening of the faith for those people who have grown up
in the church, and who continue to live in it. But this is no
longer true in a secular world. For people without the liturgical
experiences of an earlier generation the traditional service is
like a *disciplina arcana* which closes access to the faith. The
task of evangelism cannot be done through a renewal of the liturgical
tradition. New ways must be found.

But traditional orders of service become a problem inside
the congregations themselves. For many (especially young) people,
the suffering of the world with its multiplicity of human, political

and economic problems presents a new challenge to Christianity. The traditional services are irrelevant to these questions and only inward-looking. Turning to the world and its problems should, in the opinion of these people, mean breaking out of the traditional framework. The proclamation of God's word should take account of these problems, and carry the Good News into the concrete situation of mankind. The barrier between the worship service of the church and everyday life must no longer be tolerated, but the liturgical celebration must instead be linked with the possibilities of action all over the world. The emergence of groups so orientated confronted the liturgical and ecclesiastical existence of the church with new and very delicate political problems.

Thus the traditional confessional problems shifted. The quarrel about the right form of service was no longer a dispute among the churches but cut right across the denominations. At a time when the liturgical traditions were coming nearer to each other, tradition itself was being challenged by secularism, and by a socially committed Christianity. Added to this there was an inner-church problem too. Different trans-confessional movements created something like an ecclesiastical pluralism. This did not content itself with putting different emphases in preaching, but also searched for the appropriate forms of worship to express their particular brand of piety. This problem in itself was not new, as we have seen from the history of the development of the Lutheran service. But formerly the different emphases in piety were still integrated in the traditional liturgical structures while these new movements are trying to find entirely new forms of liturgical expression, not least because they no longer feel at home in tradition. During the last decades this has led the churches to become fields of liturgical experiment. The challenge has had to be accepted lest the new developments by-pass the churches altogether. Thus the Lutheran churches, together with their sister churches all over the world, find themselves at the beginning of an entirely new stage in the liturgical development, which this time is affecting even the basis of the whole Western development. For this reason the challenge is an ecumenical one, since the discussion about the service for the future asks us all what we can contribute from our own traditions, and what we can take over from others. In this way work on the official orders of service has started again most vigorously in most of the Lutheran churches.

The basic arguments under consideration can be summed up as follows:

(a) Since the end of the second world war, liturgical renewal has been wide-spread in most of the churches. As this mostly went together with a spiritual awakening, the congregation would like to retain this liturgical form. For pastoral reasons the old forms are kept, but at the same time there is a search for transitory structures, and efforts are being made to develop forms which would not, however, entirely supercede the existing liturgies.

(b) There is a great desire to retain the ecumenical and early church structures, but it is felt necessary to make room within these structures for the new liturgical elements. New prayers are composed, new hymns are written, the participation of the laity is being encouraged, and the impression of sterile stability is counteracted by creative acts of faith in the contemporary congregation. Thus the basic structure remains, but takes different forms. Beside occasional variants in the lectionary, there are fully worked out so-called thematic services in use now. The theme can either be a burning problem of the day, or an aspect of the Christian faith.

(c) Some Lutheran churches are also trying to find new structures for the service of the word as well as for communion. These are characterized by great freedom and variety, according to the local situation and the different forms of piety. Beside the preaching service (often with a dialogue sermon or a meditation), prayer services are being re-introduced. These are noted for free prayer and intercession, with the active participation of (if possible) all the participants. The new forms of communion service emphasize the community character (the meal) of the celebration, and extend this beyond the congregation itself, by stressing its links with the whole of mankind. It was natural that new forms of service quickly became models which were repeated. A particularly successful form has been the Bible Mass in Sweden, which has grown out of biblical "communion situations" (miracle of the bread, disciples in Emmaus). Here the liturgy is subject to the biblical text which it interprets. These examples are a healthy balance to the completely free liturgical compositions.

These models of work in the field of worship reflect to a remarkable degree the problems of ecclesiastical structure of the contemporary church. Different strata of the church prefer different liturgical models, and for ecclesiological reasons it is

important that the different tendencies do not diverge but serve
the "edification" of the whole congregation. Through this search
the "consumer congregation" should become a liturgically creative
community. Liturgical traditionalists as well as enthusiasts
for new forms should contribute in their own ways to the church's
praise of God. But this will only happen if, besides the large
church with its traditional services, room is found for other
and more varied groups inside the one *ekklesia*.

1.   Recently, there have sprung up small groups inside the
congregations in which the feeling of community among the members
is much closer than in the anonymity of a large congregation.
Such small groups are well suited to liturgical experiments, because
they are seeking for liturgical forms appropriate to the developing
life of faith in the group. The spectrum of these groups reaches
from occasional meetings of people of common interest (i.e. youth,
women, mixed marriages, Christian charity, etc.) to closely
organized communities of Christian life. In order to deepen their
meditation on the word of God and their common prayer, these small
groups often also practice the eucharistic celebration (often as
table community). These small groups which cut across the
denominations have often produced the impulse to ecumenical services
and therefore repeatedly offer new experiences in the field of
liturgy.

2.   Added to this there is the inescapable task of designing
services with a primarily missionary aim. Small groups can be
most useful in preparing these. In our situation it is the task
of the missionary service to address itself to secular people
who come uninitiated and without any previous knowledge to worship.
Therefore the whole problem of the language of liturgy needs to
be studied afresh. A liturgy which is understandable to all need
not necessarily depart from biblical language. But it must not
become a secret language (as traditional liturgies so often have
been accused of doing in church questionnaires). Apart from words,
the Lutheran church has also discovered the value of other means
of communicating the Gospel, e.g. audio-visual ones. Liturgy as
"play", or as "acting" sometimes communicates the Gospel better
than explanatory speech. "Worship in a rational world" (G.
Schmidtchen) surprisingly needs irrational forms of expression
for the irrational Gospel. They can reach people who have become
alienated from the Gospel by the traditional liturgical structures.

As we have stressed repeatedly before, this re-thinking of the problems of worship has not been confined to one confessional church but has been the fruit of an ecumenical exchange at a time when all the churches are faced with a similar situation. But one can try, nevertheless, to examine this re-thinking in the light of Lutheran theology. We want to try and do this at two points:

(a) The ecclesiological aspect: According to Lutheran doctrine, justification by faith is the article by which the church stands or falls. In other words, where the message of justification does not draw the sinner to whom it is addressed into worship (because worship only exists for the edification of the justified) the existence of the church and its services is in danger. If the worshiping church is split up into small groups with their own forms of service, the fear is that they are on the way to isolation. This could look like a revival of the old pietistic *ecclesiolae* problem. This hesitation is certainly justified, and must be taken seriously. It must be pointed out, however, that the attempt to preserve a uniform culture (and consequently a traditionally handed down uniform worship service) has never been the aim of Lutheran theology. The introduction of the vernacular into worship is proof of this.

In a pluralistically differentiated world it is impossible to deny the church the means by which she communicates with it. Any attempt to do so would turn the church into a small group isolated from the people of the contemporary world. Such isolation would not result from the Gospel but from its incarnation in a previous culture. The feeling of strangeness induced by a traditional liturgy does not mean that there is a lack of readiness to accept the Gospel when it is incarnate in recent forms of culture. Those who hold this opinion and are open to the problem of how to approach the contemporary world often keep a certain distance from the closed congregation which cannot find a convincing way of being the worshiping community in the world. The whole community of the church, therefore, can benefit from these small groups because the manifold task of bringing the message of justification to the whole world has been apportioned according to the particular but interdependent gifts of grace. Christians can therefore pray as "representatives" for the world, and express the "acceptance of sinners" in their worship services. Lutheran theology will have to discover its own intentions, and welcome those services which no longer serve the self-justification of the congregation but the justification of those who are lost, amongst whom the members of the congregation will find themselves.

The unity of the worship of the whole church would only be in danger where the differentiations are no longer seen as the necessary use of the different gifts of grace, for the building up of the one body of Christ. The message of justification must contemplate in all humility the sum of the different gifts, and try to strengthen the unity as the work of the Holy Spirit.

(b) The liturgical aspect: In terms of the liturgical form, the Lutheran approach at first was conservative. It was tolerant of traditional structures, and made few corrections to the existing forms. When the present re-thinking of the purpose of the worship service led to attempts to move on from the traditional structures, this was sometimes considered to be a break with the tradition of the fathers, and therefore to be inadmissable. One has nevertheless to examine the motives behind such a procedure very carefully before making a correct judgment.

The Reformation was liturgically conservative because it was dealing with congregations that had grown up in the orders of service of the church and had got used to them. The liturgy of the Middle Ages was the heritage, and the starting-point of all liturgical reform. In a secular world, however, there can be no tradition to break in the search for a different point of contact, since we are dealing with people who either have lost all the old traditions or find their forms of expression very strange. It is therefore wrong to brand the efforts to find a radically new form of worship for our time *ab ovo* as unLutheran or even fanatic.

It is true that the Reformation had rightly rejected the attempt to reconstruct the New Testament order of worship, based solely on biblical evidence. This was not necessary since unity of ceremonial did not belong to the unity of the church (CA VII).

When the new orders today take the Bible as their point of reference, this is for different reasons. It is an attempt to confront the modern, secular man with the original situation of the church, with the work of Jesus and of his Holy Spirit. It is therefore quite legitimate that the new congregations in faith seek for new and appropriate forms in which to celebrate their worship. Creative liturgical action is not incompatible with the Lutheran approach. Naturally such action should be in agreement with the faith of the church of all times, but this agreement cannot be judged by the liturgical order itself. Only very general guidelines can be given for the establishment of such orders which concretely must safeguard the institution by the Lord of the church.

The Gospel's message of justification in Jesus Christ is
a gift of divine revelation. It is brought to man from the
outside (*iustitia aliena*). Therefore the worship service must
reflect, in its basic structure, God's turning toward mankind.
The Gospel does not grow from human considerations, but is given
in the history of Jesus and his Holy Spirit. The worship service
arises out of divine command, and is not a human invention; it
does not arise out of the actual situation of man, but out of
God's history with his people. The claim that the service should
be relevant to the actual situation does not stand in itself,
but rests in the fact that the actual situation is confronted
with God's work in history. Therefore an article in the news-
paper or an analysis of the situation of humanity (of political
or economic problems) cannot replace the communication of God's
Word transmitted in Scripture. To receive the Gospel "from outside" (i.e. without a logical or experimental method being able to
determine it) is the basis of every worship service in the understanding of Lutheran theology. The human response to God's acts
will therefore produce a liturgy which uses the language of praise
of those who have received gifts.

This is essentially different from some experiments in
worship which start with man and his situation. It has to be
admitted that many of the liturgies worked out for the worship
of the contemporary church know little of these basic rules, and
place man in the center in a way which leaves no room for God to
speak. Some of the contemporary worship experiments have departed
from the simple language of *receiving* man, and have replaced it
with rational expressions of *self-analytical* man (under the name
of prayer and meditation). Liturgy however is not an intelligence
test for the congregation, but a presentation of the gift of
salvation, and the simple thanksgiving for the received gift.
This can happen in various forms, appropriate to the particular
situation of the congregation. The possibility of creative renewal
has been given to a generation in which people receive the Gospel
in its original freshness.

The Church as a Worshiping Assembly

During its history, the Lutheran church has lived by basic
theological decisions which have given worship an important
ecclesiological place. The Augsburg Confession defines the church

as follows: "The Church is the assembly of saints in which the
Gospel is taught purely and the sacraments are administered
rightly" (Art. 7). The Church is defined by its worship. It is
constituted by the worship service which is held in the congregation.
The *congregatio sanctorum* itself arises out of the service in
which it lives and grows. If one wants to find the church one
has to attend the worship. In this sense church is not an abstract,
but a concrete function: the worship service of the faithful.

     The question of what is true worship (and therefore the
true church) is asked very sharply in Lutheran tradition. Since
it is an ecclesiological question, it can never be confined only
to a question of liturgical order. Orders are seen as products
of the proclamation of the word and the administration of the
sacraments. In these terms they are "external things" which do
not have value in themselves, but in their use in faith. Orders,
therefore, are variable and can change their forms in the course
of historical changes (cf. Luther's postscript to the "German
Mass"). What remains constant is the service of the word and the
sacraments in which the church becomes incarnate to the salvation
of mankind. Thus the worship service has been understood as the
sacramental life of sharing in salvation, and in these terms the
Lutheran churches have been very much concerned with it since
the time of the Reformation. The question of salvation was already
closely linked with Luther's approach to the reform of worship
services. The service of reconciliation was not to be betrayed.
The word of the Gospel and the sacramental sign had to remain
inviolately valid and become "incitements to faith."

     In the dialectical changes in the history of the Lutheran
liturgy different parts of the service have been emphasized,
always on the basis of the basic teaching of the Lutheran Reformation. As long as these changes did not touch the divine
institution they were able more or less to maintain the Lutheran
approach. Only where the foundations of the service were attacked
through a denigration of the sacraments or through misunderstandable
preaching is there any question of a "disintegration of worship."
But this cannot be simply gathered from the forms of worship.

     The Lutheran service has not remained unchanged through
history but it has remained alive through many trials, and in our
century it has been renewed and, through the discovery of its
ecclesiological significance, it has come into contact with the
efforts of the whole ecumenical movement. It has retained its
decisive element, i.e. the sharing of salvation in preaching and
administration of the sacraments through faith in the Gospel.

This can be the very important basis for a restructuring of the forms of service in the modern world. History, however, will teach us that even within the Lutheran church this must be seen as a permanent task.

Translated by Donata Coleman

CHAPTER 8

Andreas Aarflot

Patterns of Lutheran Piety

There is a growing interest in the inner dimension of the history of the churches which is reflected in the different modes of spiritual life. The institutional side of the church or the influence of its great personalities have long drawn more attention than the undercurrents of the life of the faithful in the church.

We intend in this study to make an attempt to follow some of the patterns of Lutheran piety. Our first concern will be to reflect on the difficulties of such an enterprise. The methodological problem in the first place has to deal with the difficulty of establishing reliable source material. The inner life of a church, as revealed in the spiritual life of its members, is seldom traceable in the same objective manner as are other factors which are characteristic of the history of the church.

When we search for *expressions* of piety, we may find them partly in written documents, such as letters, autobiographical statements, devotional literature, prayers, and hymns, and partly in forms of activity, religious practices, common traditional life-style, and ethical principles. The main source taken into consideration in this study is the material in which the spiritual feelings, needs and concerns of the different ages are reflected, namely the literature aiming at private or corporate worship or devotion. But in addition to this, we would also like to investigate the more reflected theological analysis and description of the inner life of a Christian and try to outline the trends in this theological material.

If, in the first place we seek a *definition* of the term
"piety", it may be defined in different ways: One application
of the term takes its starting point from a religious-psychological
concept, like in the tradition of Schleiermacher. According to
this concept, piety is seen as the purely subjective side of
religion, as the feeling of "absolute dependence" in relation to
God.

In a wider sense, piety may be described as covering the
different human expressions witnessing to a real submission of
man to the Word of Jesus Christ. It is the response of the Christian
faith to the claim of God - in praise, thanksgiving, supplication,
through words and deeds (I. Röbbelen). To a certain degree the
term "spirituality" may be more useful. It seems to reflect a
wider range of associations and is more neutral as to the subjective
and objective factors in piety. In this study the terms are used
alternately without any strict distinction.

*The Emphasis of the Lutheran Reformation: Corporate and
Objective Spirituality.*

There is a definitely personal note in Luthers elaborations
on the theme of the life of a Christian. Basically, his own
experience through the struggle of his heart "to find a gracious
God" always gave the existential dimension to his description of
the spiritual life of man.

Drawing on his own experience, Luther put the emphasis on
the contrite heart, and the depth of the personal confession of
sins. "The heart in its hardest struggle against despair" (Apol.
XX:8) is seen as the necessary background for the true experience
of the justifying grace of God. The triumphant joy of a Christian,
the victorious faith, can never be fully realized without the
knowledge of sin as something under which man is eternally
condemned, unless he is eternally relieved through the forgiveness
of sins which Christ imparts. Faith is the sole medium of
receiving the grace of God. The relationship between grace and
faith is clearly spelled out in the terminology in which Luther
expounded his theology of justification.

God's grace was seen as *favor* - the merciful attitude
towards men, and the correlation in man's heart was faith as
fiducia - trustfulness, the child-like, fearless acceptance of God's
saving act.

This humble, devout surrender of man to the promising grace

of God is in Luther's theology the only possible expression of
piety. At the same time this attitude includes the spiritual
reality which is usually described as sanctification. The new
birth and the new obedience are part of the justification. Also
included is a new dimension of freedom, a joyful confidence, a
triumphant certainty of being taken into the fellowship of Christ.

In this sense, sanctification in Luther's thought can
never be anything but a new beginning. The life of a Christian is
always, in every respect, dependent upon the grace of God. From
God's point of view grace as related to remission of sins is
favor and grace as related to sanctification is described as
donum - the gift of God as a new power of life. But in both
cases, the only adequate attitude of man is faith. "If you
believe, you shall have all things" is the famous expression of
Luther in the booklet *The Freedom of the Christian* (WA 7, 24:13 =
LW 31, 348f). Outside the dimension of faith, even the good
works of a justified Christian fall prey to the danger of becoming
mortal sins. (WA 2, 410, 35ff.; 8, 68, 25ff. = LW 32, 174ff.).

The progress of a Christian life - the virtual piety is
only accessible by faith. It is always a new start - the advance
is not an increase of life qualities, but it is a more absolute
surrender into the merciful hands of God: "To advance is always
a matter of beginning anew" (WA 56, 486:7 = LW 25, 478).

And still it is progress, not a stampede. But the progress
cannot be measured in psychological terms. There is no such thing
as a real, gradual evolution of human nature from a mere openness
to God's grace to something which can be recognized as a real
achievement of human piety. The progress is not one within the
human abilities of man. And still the life of a Christian is a
steady journey. There is a starting point and a final goal. But
these are factors rooted in an objective reality outside man's
inner experience. The life of a Christian is a process of emerging
from *baptism* to the *resurrection* of the body.

Since this description of the final goal can only be
understood as belonging essentially within the realm of the
eschatological salvation, the life of a Christian correspondingly
always includes this eschatological dimension. The development of
piety and the growth of sanctification can never be anything
different from the repeated return to the "alien" righteousness,
the justification which is transmitted by faith to the sinner by
an act of grace. This is the *faith structure* of Christian piety
as it is understood in the Lutheran Reformation.

This faith structure, however, has its *functional forms*, by which piety becomes incarnate in the life of a Christian person and the communal life of the believers. The practice of piety is expressed in prayer, love and good works. These activities are all seen as worked by the Holy Spirit. The spirit of prayer has its counterpart in faith. The spirit of grace has its counterpart in love. And good works are seen as fruits of the Spirit.

The Spirit of God sanctifies the Christian according to the first and the second table of the law. In his treatise *On the Councils and the Church* (1539), Luther talks about the different means by which the Holy Spirit makes the true church manifest to the world. Here he uses the word *Heiltum* (WA 50, 629:13 and 643:2) in order to express the quality of the different means of grace and manifestations of the life of the faithful in the church. The word indicates something connected with salvation (*Heil*), but also carries the notion of "sanity" or of a remedy by which health can be restored. (The words "Holy posession" in the American Edition [LW 41, 139 and 165]are scarcely adequate to cover the original meaning of the word, though it may strike a note which may be illuminating to one of the aspects included in the term).

In Luther's own theology the application of the term is connected with his understanding of the life of a Christian as a *convalescence*. The cure has been prescribed by the doctor, and the patient is totally delivered into the hands of the physician. His final recovery is something which can only be taken hold of by faith. By trusting the doctor and his predicament the patient already may be sure of his total healing.

In this process of healing or sanctification the Christian is thrown upon the sources of God's grace in the life of the congregation. The *collective aspect* of piety is a very important trait of the matter in the theology of the Reformation. In his Articles of Smalcald Luther lists among the blessings of God through the Gospel what he calls the "mutual conversation and consolation of the brethren" (III, 4). One important dimension of Lutheran piety is that it takes place in a close relationship to the Christian community and the practice of faith and love springing out from the sacramental fellowship. That is why the "means" by which the Holy Spirit sanctifies the believers are identical with the "marks" of the church, i.e. the Gospel, the Sacrament, the Ministry of preaching and the exercise of the "keys", as well as praise, worship, Christian education and the fellowship under the cross (*On the Councils and the Church*, 1539).

Piety, Christian spirituality, the practice of Christendom can never be separated from the sacramental community in which God's grace is at work: the church as the body of Christ. The sense of wholeness, the communal aspect of faith, the collective, corporate element of Christianity is essential to the Lutheran understanding of piety.

From this basic background the practice of a pious life springs like fruits from a tree. Prayer, praise and good deeds are signs of the Spirit being at work in the life of a Christian. The patterns of piety are seen in the dialectic of faith and love. This is the fundamental concept of spirituality in the Lutheran Reformation.

When sanctification is conceived of as the work of the Holy Spirit sanctifying men according to the first and second table of the law, piety cannot be restricted to the spiritual sphere of life alone. The quality of a Christian person becomes manifest in the daily vocational life. In this respect Luther condemns the Roman Catholic idea of the monastic life as the ideal form of spiritual activity. As Christians we are called to serve God and our neighbour in the context of our daily struggle to fulfil God's purpose for a truly human life (WA 10, I, 309, 14ff.).

This line of thought is closely related to the idea of the three-fold order of life in the "estates": the family, the civil administration of society and the public ministry of the word and sacraments in the church. These pre-established structures of life in their interdependence mark the framework within which the true spirituality of man may be unfolded and realized.

New Trends in Post-Reformation Piety: Individual Experience and Psychological Description of Spiritual Life.

The development of Lutheran piety in the post-Reformation era is strongly influenced by the theology of Philip Melanchthon. The main shift of emphasis is seen in the new understanding of penitence. While Luther defined penitence as consisting of two parts: contrition and faith, Melanchthon added a third element: the new obedience. And while Luther saw the sanctification as an intrinsic part of justification, the tendency of post-Reformation theology was to make a logical distinction between these factors, which in turn led to a temporal division, separating sanctification

from justification as two distinctive acts. This finally
developed into an elaborate system of *ordo salutis* - an attempt
to trace the different psychological steps in the development of
a Christian life.

W. Elert has pointed to the fact that the theology of
the Lutheran Reformation holds a concept of man which includes
a dual subjectivity, related to *faith* or *psyche* (In: *Structure of
Lutheranism*). The faith-subjectivity is the transcendental
personality. It is completely empty or void, simply a *punctum
mathematicum*. The righteousness which is obtained through this
faith-subject is strictly an alien or imputed righteousness.

The psychological "subject-soul" on the other hand can
only experience the transcendental reality as accusation. It is
the terrified conscience of man (CA XX:15) which indicates his
natural human psychology. From this latter concept the orthodox
theologians developed their concept of the "order of salvation".

A distinctive feature in the orthodox theology of piety
is the concept of *unio mystica*. The final goal of the spiritual
life was defined as being united with Christ or God in a mysterious
way. The heritage from medieval Roman Catholic mysticism is
obvious in much of the devotional literature of the period.
Foremost in this respect is the noted J. Arndt (1555-1621). But
even in hymns and sermons from the period 1550-1650 the tendencies
and trends towards a more inward-oriented piety can clearly be
seen.

The effect of this development on the understanding and
description of Christian piety can be described in the following
points:

(1) There is a strong emphasis on *personal penitence*. In
his heart or face to face with his fellow Christian the pious
person is expected to deplore his own failures and sins. In the
hymns of the period there are many signs of a tear-dripping self-
judgment which at times has the character of self-flagellation.
The medieval monastic practice of self-punishment has been replaced
by an often affected lamentation of one's own natural situation.
A purge of tears has come instead of the bloodshed of the monk's
whip.

But this feeling is often matched with a strong emphasis
on the new life. Penitence is seen to be of no use unless it
effects a renewal of one's life. While Luther saw the true
penitence as the passive form of self-accusation (Articles of
Smalcald III, Art. III, 2), the theology of Orthodoxy as well as

later Pietism stressed the active attitude which was significant
of the new obedience. By referring the sanctification of man
to this new starting point, the danger of synergism became
imminent.

(2) This tendency is closely connected with a growing
skepticism as to the possibilities natural man has of fulfilling
his purpose in this world. There are on the one hand still
eloquent reminiscences of the bold Lutheran faith in God, the
Creator and Upholder of the world. But this feeling is often
linked with a certain fatalism in view of the prospects of man
within the confines of his worldly life. Death is seen as the
irreversible fate of man. "We start dying the day we are born",
this is the statement presented to the readers of one of the
devotional books of the period. The portrait of Epicur is
materialized in many spiritual pamphlets of the time.

Following this generally sad mood of life is a certain
asceticism, a denial of the life in this world and a longing for
a purely spiritual life in another world. There are elements
of a neo-platonic anthropology involved in this concept, and the
dualism of ancient gnostic writers is called to one's memory while
reading some of the passages of the ascetic literature or some
lines of the hymns of the time.

At the same time the mood of the spirituality of orthodoxy
in many ways matches the sentiment of the contemporary baroque
writers. A certain pessimism, a negative distance to the world,
a spleen and a loneliness of the heart are factors which mark the
attitude of life both in the baroque and in orthodox spirituality.
The general feeling of the time is well expressed in the old
saying of the Preacher: "All is vanity."

Sometimes man is described as a toy in the hands of God.
God is playing with the fate of mankind. He appears to be reluctant
to help. He puts on a make-believe attitude of anger and rebuke
towards men. And still the pious writer tells his readers to
put their trust in God. His purpose is always good. This reminds
us of the famous idea in Luther's theology of the *larva Dei* - the
masks of God. But the earnest application of the concept in
Luther's writing has been watered down to something which is little
more than a stoic fatalism dressed in the vocabulary of orthodox
piety.

(3) Another trend in orthodox spirituality is the *warning
against an outward form* of Christian practice which may be used as
a cover-up for a non-committal religious attitude. H. Müller warns

against the four deceptive "church-idols", represented by pulpit, font, confessional, and altar. The emphasis is put on the seriousness of one's personal faith-relationship with God. A search of one's own heart for true signs of repentance and a living faith becomes essential. Piety is becoming more man-centered. The Swedish bishop J. Svedberg (1653-1735) talked about the need for a *theologia realis* in place of the *theologia verbalis*.

(4) A further feature of the same tendency is the increasing *appeal to human will*. This tendency is especially noticeable in the so-called "English sermon tradition" of the late 1600s. The idea of this tradition was that a sermon should attract the attention of the listeners by employing short slogan-like sayings, unexpected applications of the text, and illustrations. All these elements should aim at the appeal to the will, the admonition to make a serious change in life. "God is willing, if you are willing" - may be a striking expression of this tendency.

The English tradition also strongly influenced Lutheran ministers whose sermons were created according to the same pattern. In a sense the interest of these preachers corresponded to the theological emphasis of J. Arndt, whose four books on the true Christian life aimed at the restoration of the image of God in man. Influenced by medieval mysticism, Arndt also clearly represented a bias towards moralism. Grace was no longer simply the *favor* of God, but was understood more in the manner of Roman Catholic theology as the effective, transforming power of the Spirit.

This tendency is characteristic of a large portion of the devotional literature of the period, and may be typically expressed e.g. in sermons on the Beatitudes from the Sermon on the Mount or in certain hymns, especially by P. Gerhardt (1607-1676) elaborating the theme of the new nature of man. Closely connected with this description of the transformation of the human nature is the wish to become like God or be united with him in a blissful fellowship. According to many hymns, the highest degree of happiness is to be near God, and a Christian life is the remedy against all human disaster.

This exalted atmosphere of orthodox piety may have been a literary form to some extent. Nevertheless it points at a dangerous shift of emphasis in the theological founding of genuine spirituality. The appeal to the will of man and the description of the pleasure of a pious heart delighting in the contemplation of God pulls apart what in the theology of Luther was strictly

kept together in one dimension: for him faith and good works were
like roots, tree and branches. The trust in God included both
his justifying grace *and* his sanctification. Sanctification was
seen as something which was received and contained in the same
act of faith in openness for the forgiveness of sins. In orthodoxy
sanctification in reality tended to become improvement of life,
and the final sanctification was removed to the sphere of the
blessed union with God. Strangely enough there was a danger
both of moralism and quietism in orthodox theology.

And the contact with the objective means of grace was not
clearly defined. As for this last point, however, there were a
few representatives of theologically reflected orthodox piety who
stressed the objective basis of salvation through the work of
Christ *for us*, and at the same time turned the interest of the
believer to the reality of the means of grace. A fine representati
of this trend was the famous theologian J. Gerhard (1582-1637)
with his excellent pamphlet *Meditationes sacrae* (1615).

Patterns of Spiritual Life in Pietism.

In the history of the European churches Pietism (1675-1750)
appears as a movement, a trend, a way of thinking and living, more
than a strictly defined period of historical development. The
heritage which pietism took over was the spiritual Janus-face of
orthodoxy, with its rigid confessionalism on the one hand and its
flourishing devotional literature on the other hand.

The historical situation of Pietism, however, was the
break-through of individualism, the longing for a new world and
the growing trust in the possibilities that were put in the hands
of natural man. In a sense Pietism was the ecclesial counterpart
of the Enlightenment with its philosophy and its optimistic concept
of man and society.

When we wish to investigate the typical ideas of spirituali
in this period, one striking fact is the dependency on the religious
ideas of the previous period. It is illuminating that more
devotional books from Orthodoxy were reprinted in this period than
the pietistic writers themselves produced. Further it is of some
importance to notice that the typically pietistic elements of
theology and practice very often seem to have emerged relatively
independently at separate places or centers of the European church.
The search for originality or the creative origin of an idea or a
practice very often proves to be in vain. There seems to have been

a kind of "Common Market" of ideas and thoughts, and a certain general thought-pattern of the time, which allow for different expressions of the same spirituality at different times and places.

This also includes a certain exchange of ideas between different confessional traditions. It is a well-known fact that English devotional literature of the 1600s passed into the German Lutheran tradition. One typical example is *The Practice of Piety* by Lewis Bayly (1565-1631) which was translated into German and edited in numerous editions on German soil. The book served as a model for many similar books of later pietistic tradition. Even Roman Catholic mysticism influenced certain pietistic writers.

One should be aware of the fact that in Pietism, as well as in Orthodoxy, the question of piety is dealt with indirectly through pamphlets, prayer-books, devotions and autobiographical writings more often than in theological treatises. It is a notable fact that Pietism did not produce a single representative dogmatic thinker. The pietistic theology of conversion, for instance, is more clearly spelled out in the personal statement of A.H. Francke (1663-1727) concerning his spiritual illumination than in any other of Francke's theological books.

How then do we outline the essential elements in the concept of piety during the period of pietism?

(1) First there is a further deviation from the Lutheran tradition in terms of central theological ideas. The main shift of emphasis is from the teaching of justification by faith to the understanding of regeneration as *the restored image of God in man*. This idea was in a way introduced even in the orthodoxy, especially through J. Arndt. But during the pietistic era the thought gained ground. While the main trust of the theology of the Reformation was the objective grace of God in the act of justification, the interest of the pietistic fathers turned to the person who had been justified. While orthodoxy took for its starting-point the objective reality of salvation as God's work with men, pietism focused its attention upon the subjective effects of salvation as experienced by men. The term *faith* was no longer self-evident. It was qualified by other words, like "true" faith, "living" faith, etc.

Thus justification by faith came to be understood as an essential change of the human being, not as previously as an act of acquittance of sins through a jurisdictional verdict by God. This may well be seen as more than a shift of emphasis from the orthodox tradition. In fact, many pietistic writers saw themselves

as deliberately confronting the theological position of their
predecessors, even if they wanted to be Lutheran in their general
theological stand. In opposition to the previous theology they
wanted to put the stress on life more than doctrine, on the Spirit
instead of order, on the powerful realization of a new life
instead of a nominal adherence to church traditions. The pietistic
concept of a true Christian life was in many ways inspired by the
ideal of the apostolic church.

(2) One implication of basic pietistic theological
thinking seems to have been that the pietistic concept of a pious
life became markedly *individualistic*. The communal implications
of salvation did not prevail. In as far as they were reflected,
the society of believers in pietism was seen as a group of
individuals with similar experiences. The church was the sum of
individually restored people gathering to share their insights
and feelings.

The leading Danish poet of the pietistic era, H.A. Brorson
(1694-1764), deals with the church under the heading of "brotherly
love." The church is seen as a building, an edifice where the
single stones are added together. "Thus all the pious hearts unite
and constitute God's temple right." This concept corresponds with
the definition of the church given in the catechism of another
Danish pietist, E. Pontoppidan (1698-1764): "The church is the
community of holy people, a fellowship and unity in the Spirit."
This concept in turn led to a spiritualization of the understanding
of the church and the sacraments. The stress was put on the
invisible church, and the sacramental effect of baptism and Holy
Communion was interpreted in terms of spiritual gifts.

The spirituality of Pietism thus became more and more
rooted in the inner feelings and experiences of every single
Christian person. True faith was nourished, not by the objective
means of grace, but by the inner relationship of the soul with
the Lord. The bride-mysticism found a new shape: the mystical
eros-piety with its heavy sensuality.

(3) Another important element in the spirituality of
Pietism is its attitude towards the world. In the first place
Pietism is marked by a definitely negative concept of man in his
natural setting. The human race is seen as a totally depraved
humanity. The secular society consequently is seen as Satan's
field of operation. Salvation is to pass from death to life. The
quality of the new life in Christ is very much in focus in pietistic
literature. But this quality of life is generally described

in moralistic terms. The interest often dwells on the need for
keeping away from the world. Piety finds its expression in the
abstinence from the so-called adiaphora. The main emphasis is
upon keeping up the borderline between the Christian fellowship
and the world.

But this is not all there is to be said. Like in the
English puritan tradition there is a striking dual attitude also
in Pietism as over against the world. There is a strange optimistic
note, at least in the Pietism of Ph. J. Spener (1635-1705), whose
hope is for better times. (Spener's book: "Hoffnung auf bessere
Zeiten").

The program of Pietism has been described as "improving
human conditions through renewal of men" ("Weltverwandlung durch
Menschenverwandlung", M. Schmidt). There is a recognizable wish
in Pietism to improve the world, to create conditions for a new
humanity, to wrestle with the evil powers of the world in order
to save the secular sphere of life from the dominion of Satan.
This is the main motivation for the practical institutions of
Pietism serving educational, social and economical purposes.

Still it seems justified to state that there is only a
weak notion of appreciation of God's creation in much of pietistic
theology. The first article of the Apostles' Creed is generally
only briefly elaborated upon. The tendency is towards an over-
emphasis of the christological elements in Christian faith.
Consequently even the "Hope for better times" easily gets a
christocratic interpretation. The old Lutheran theology of the
world as God's good creation and the service in daily life of
the Christian in his secular calling as the true form of piety,
is nearly a lost dimension in the spirituality of pietism.

There is a certain apocalyptic note in the program of
pietism for a better world. The improvement of the conditions
of secular life, the relief work, the concern for better social
conditions all aimed at the realization of the kingdom of God.
They were signs indicating that the lordship of Christ was taken
seriously. In this sense the good deeds were testimonies to the
genuineness of the Christian faith in the believers. At the same
time they were expressions of the idea of a Christian society,
which was the final goal of pietistic government. Numerous church
laws and regulations of private and corporate piety bear witness
to the strong desire of the authorities to establish a truly
Christian community on earth. But whatever the motive, the social
ethical impulse of pietistic piety should be recognized as one of
its most valuable contributions.

In this context it is interesting to see that the very
structure of the pietistic fellowship was a sign of broken social
barriers. The *collegia pietatis* were of course first and foremost an attempt to create a new collective form of individual
piety. They served a religious purpose and offered opportunity
for a new sense of belonging together under the guidance of the
Spirit and sharing common experiences. But notwithstanding, the
collegia pietatis also brought together people with different
social backgrounds in an active form of fellowship. It is significant that pietism seems to have affected above all persons from
the nobility and people belonging to the new middle class
bourgeoisie of the growing cities. The social attitude of pietistic
ministers also appeared to be definitely more open and communicative
than that of their orthodox predecessors. At the same time the
pietistic gatherings seem to have attracted lower class people,
unemployed persons, craftsmen, etc. This tendency is even more
typical in the English equivalent to pietism, i.e. the Methodist
revival with its heavy impact upon the working class. The
spiritual kinship between those who were affected by the pietistic
movement seems to have been stronger than social differences.

(4) One may feel a certain contradiction between this
rather outward trend in pietism and the tendency to inward, often
mystical contemplation that is present in the pattern of piety
which is revealed in the literature of the period. It can be
demonstrated statistically that the motif of the soul's mystical
union with Christ dominates in the hymns of the period (I. Röbbelen)
The life of a Christian is seen as a pilgrimage accompanied by
afflictions and tribulations. From this point of view the world
is seen as a strange land through which we journey towards the
heavenly land of joy and peace. Salvation is going to be fulfilled
in the eschatological dimension, in the perfect fellowship with
God. But as we move forward on our pilgrimage, the soul seeks
to anticipate the final union with God through mystical contemplation and meditation. There is every reason to ask how this
attitude of world-neglect can be reconciled with the elements of
world-activism which we have dealt with recently.

The meditative mood of pietism tends to accentuate the
life and work of Jesus Christ more strongly than had commonly been
done in the previous period. The theology of pietism thus has a
definitely Christocentric mark. And the piety of the time may be
correspondingly called Jesus-piety (Jesusfrömmigkeit).

(5) One last aspect of Lutheran piety in a pietistic
setting which deserves mentioning is the universal dimension of
the Christian fellowship. As the main emphasis is on the individual
religious experience, the community of believers is transcending
the confessional borders of a given time. There is an ecumenical
feeling of common features in the personal lives of Christians
from different theological traditions.

That does not necessarily include a disregard of one's own
confessional heritage. Most of the pietistic theologians took
a marked apologetic stand in the theological struggles of their
time. But some of them kept up friendly personal relations with
representatives of other denominations, and a few of them also
openly advocated a willingness to search for common ground in
order to reconcile the theological differences, at least in the
evangelical churhces of the Reformation. But on the other hand
there are many examples of a strict pietistic regulation of
activities carried on by the more radical representatives of
pietism. The conventicle acts which were passed in the Scandinavian
churches are a testimony to this attitude.

A critical evaluation of the main elements of pietistic
spirituality will have to point out a certain theological weakness
in the system.

First of all the piety of Pietism is marked by a fateful
individualism. This may be seen as a distortion of the Lutheran
objectivism which is essential to the concept of salvation as it
is spelled out in the confessional writings of the Lutheran church.
Even as the original Lutheran concept of piety also kept a strongly
personal dimension, the main foundation for the pious life was
sought in the reality of God's acts outside of the human being.
This is the Christ-for-us dimension.

But in Pietism this dimension has given way to a Christ-
in-us-concept which in turn is the foundation of piety in the
heart of a Christian. Piety has become an anthropological matter,
and no more a basically soteriological one. Piety is a question
of psychology more than a question of faith.

A second critical point with far-reaching consequences is
the inability of Pietism to see the true relationship between
creation and salvation. This in turn leads to a confusion of Law
and Gospel. The world is no longer seen as part of God's good
creation, over which he reigns through his Law. The aim of the
pietists is to conquer the world through the Gospel and make the

sovereignty of Christ a realized fact in this world. The Barthian
concept of the kingdom of Christ is in many ways prefigured in
pietistic theology.

A third point in pietistic spirituality which deserves
critical comment is the eudaemonistic or utilitarian trend it
holds. Typical of this tendency is the opening question in the
famous Catechism of E. Pontoppidan (1737): "Dear child, would
you not like to be happy on earth and blessed in heaven?" - Of
course, the child's answer was supposed to be "Oh yes, I would!"
This eudaemonistic way of thinking may account for some of the
activities in social and economical enterprises led by pietistic
church people. But it also accounts for the emphasis on happiness
or bliss as the final goal for Christian piety. The description
of the blessed communion with Christ is a recurring theme in
pietistic literature. The theological structure of this thought
is the medieval *fruitio Dei* of the mysticism where the desire for
happiness is satisfied by the grace. It is far removed from the
service-aspect of genuine Lutheran piety, where the love of God
found its expression not in having pleasure in God, but in service
of God.

Significant Tendencies in Later Lutheran Piety.

It is difficult to evaluate the later development of
Lutheranism from the point of view of piety. There may be
several, often disparate trends coming to the fore in the last
200 years. One complicating factor is the transplantation of
Lutheran churches to American soil, where historical development
often took its own course. With the risk of over-simplifying we
shall concentrate on two tendencies which may be traced in many
Lutheran churches during the last 200 years.

The first is a deliberate turn to the sacramental dimension
of the church as the basis for a truly spiritual life. In the
wake of Pietism and its ideological counterpart the Enlightenment,
a new theological emphasis found its way into the confessional
theology of the 1800s. Here an enthusiastic love of the
institutional church was combined with a strong loyalty to the
church orders and a deep reverence for the sacramental grace
administered through the ministry of the church.

A striking element in this kind of piety was that it did
not aquiesce with the absolute traditions of the church as something

to be admired and venerated. Many representatives of this form
of piety felt a strong concern for mission and for the social
responsibility of the church. The diaconal institutions of
J. Löhe (1808-1872) in Germany or the social activities of
the Swedish "young-church-movement" are indications of this new
trend. The piety of a Christian should be nourished by a frequent
use of the sacraments and an active participation in the worship
of the church. But at the same time true piety was demonstrated
in willingness to serve the needs of the world.

There is little doubt that this kind of church piety, as
for instance expounded in a book by the Swedish writer and later
bishop Bo Giertz has been a remarkable element in Lutheran piety
in different churches until this very day. There is generally a
certain high church element in this piety, and in the theology of
its strongest advocates. But this element corresponds with a
confessional trend in some of the dominating Lutheran theology,
as in the Scandinavian tradition represented by persons such as
R. Prenter of Aarhus, Denmark and L. Aalen of the independent
Lutheran theological faculty of Oslo, Norway.

The characteristics of this form of piety are the attempts
to focus again on the same objectivity which dominated earlier
Lutheran spirituality. The Christian faith, as well as the
functional expressions of a Christian life are rooted in the
objective reality of God's grace transmitted through the word of
God as promise and the sacraments as gifts, through which the Holy
Spirit acts.

Side by side with this tendency we may find different
reminiscences of earlier patterns of piety. Through the great
revivals in traditional Lutheran churches in the last century the
pietistic patterns have been renewed by neo-pietistic movements.
For a long time even some of the Lutheran churches of America
carried on the pietistic traditions of their home churches on the
Continent. Pietism in American Lutheranism has, not yet been
evaluated in scientific research. There seems to be a tendency in
present-day Lutheranism to repudiate the heritage from pietism,
mostly under the impression that American pietism was marked by
negative attitudes. It is probably true that the pietists also
often stuck to traditions which were linked with their domestic
background. The immigrants carried local concepts and attitudes
with them, and maintained these in order to keep up their ethnic
identity. Religious traditions and patterns of piety served as
defense mechanisms for a national self-assertion.

With this background, partly in an attempt to free itself from ethnic traditions and create a truly *American* form of Lutheranism, and partly as a response to new challenges of our time, a new pattern of piety has emerged which has had its strongest representatives in American churches, although it is not without analogies in Europe. This may be characterized as an *activistic* piety, putting the stress on the actions of a Christian as the true demonstration of his inner life. The concept also has a theological basis in the idea of Christian stewardship, and it is linked with certain common standards of social behavior which seem to be prevalent in the minds of Americans.

The critical evaluation of this type of spirituality leads to the question of its connection with the objective reality of the sacraments. In how far is this kind of piety essentially drawing upon the sacramental grace of God? A further problem seems to be how to avoid the danger of moralism in what seems to be an optimistic attempt to change the world.

There are, of course, numerous other types of Lutheran piety which might have been mentioned. It is also obvious that there are many modifications of the forms of piety which have been presented here. There may even be lines leading from one pattern to another. But in the history of the Lutheran churches these patterns of spirituality show how difficult it is to carry on the genuine Lutheran tradition of seeing piety as a miracle wrought to sinful men by the Holy Spirit as he uses word and sacraments like "instruments -- to create faith in men, where and whenever it so pleases God" (CA, Art. V).

                              English text revised
                                by Vanessa Dolbé

CHAPTER 9

Günther Gassmann

The Ordained Ministry and Church Order

The Context

Ministry and church order and the way they are understood
and structured belong to the essential elements in a description
of many churches. In some cases, ministry and church order have
even become the decisive characteristics of these churches. They
have achieved, so to speak, confessional status. This fact is
even expressed in the names many churches have given themselves:
Congregational churches, Presbyterian churches, Protestant
Episcopal churches, Methodist Episcopal churches (in the USA).
In these churches, which also include the Roman Catholic, the
Orthodox and the Anglican churches, ministry and church order, with
their specific characteristics, form a constitutive element of the
ecclesial self-understanding and existence of these churches. In
some cases therefore the world-wide fellowship of such a confessional
family regards the ministry and its structures as an essential or
even as *the* essential bond of her unity. (This is most clearly
seen in the Roman Catholic and Anglican churches).

In comparison to these churches, ministry and church order
in Lutheran churches and in their world-wide fellowship do not play
the same distinguishing and unifying role. The specific Lutheran
identity of the churches that emerged from the Lutheran Reformation
as well as their self-understanding cannot be primarily described
in terms of their understanding of the ministry or in terms of the
structures of ministry and order. It is also obvious that quite

different elements (confessions, common history, etc.) are more
constitutive for the bond that binds the Lutheran churches of the
world together as a fellowship than are ministry and church order.
In the same way, Lutheran churches do not see their essential
differences over against other confessions based on the understanding and structure of the ministry or expressed in it. Other
confessions, however, because the ministry occupies another place
in their thinking, see themselves as distinguished and separated
from Lutherans also in this very question (Roman Catholic and
Orthodox churches) or even almost exclusively in this question
(many Anglicans). These - not always noticed - different presuppositions and their consequences often make present ecumenical
discussions on the question of office between Lutheran churches
and other churches difficult.

          Why is it that in the confessions, in the theology and in
the life of the Lutheran churches on the one hand the ministry
is given an essential and indispensible importance and much care
and interest is devoted to detailed church orders, while on the
other hand the specific forms of ministry and church order are
not considered as essential and constitutive elements of their
own confessionality? The reasons for that can be found in the
theological approach of the Lutheran church. In relation to the
priority of the Gospel, which the Reformation reestablished, the
ministry was given a functional, serving role. With the consequence
that there was no interest in developing an independent basis for
a doctrine of the ministry. The structures of the ministry and
organizational forms were relegated to the *adiaphora*, those things
that could be given many different forms under the criterion of
the Gospel. The results of this basic decision were: a permanent
consensus about the central function of the ministry, a discussion
throughout the whole history of Lutheranism about the institution
of this special ministry and about its relation to the general
priesthood of all baptized, the actual embodiments of the understanding and practice of the ministry, which we today must see in
part as false developments, and a multiplicity of ministerial and
organizational structures which is legitimate as such although some
of their specific forms may call for critique from a theological
as well as form a practical standpoint. This short sketch only
gives us an idea why ministry and church order in their importance
and in their structural formation have not become a constitutive
element and distinguishing characteristic for Lutheran confessionalit

The Point of Departure in the Reformation

The Approach

The critique of the Lutheran Reformation movement on the late medieval church could not but strike at the heart of her understanding, structure and practice of ministry and ministries because the Reformation saw them as forms and expressions of an unbiblical understanding of faith and its consequences. This critique therefore could not deal with the question of the ministry as one individual aspect within ecclesiology, but had to see, unmask and overcome it as the structural principle of a perverted understanding of faith. The heresy of the late medieval church which the Reformers exposed was the reversal of the relationship of "spirit and structure" (cf. the title of the book by J. Pelikan: *Spirit Versus Structure*).

The institutional structure of the church (ministries, sacraments) had ceased to be a serving instrument for the direct encounter of man with the redeeming grace of God in Jesus Christ (Gospel). Instead, the clergy equipped through ordination and status with higher spiritual dignity had taken the position of a mediator between God and man, had taken over the means of grace, had to a large extent replaced the preaching of the living Gospel with the Mass, had arbitrarily set and administered the conditions for achieving salvation, had burdened the consciences of men and women through innumerable laws, had extended their jurisdiction far into the secular realm.

It was thus the aim of the Reformation to put this inverted relationship of structure and Spirit back "on its feet." This, however, did not mean that the Lutheran form of the Reformation replaced the rejected institutional system with a biblically grounded plan of a better system. Ministry, structure and insti-tution were not even considered as independent, comprehensive themes. Since the old relationship between structure and spirit had been reversed, they had to be seen in a whole new perspective. It was no longer possible to understand them in terms of a comprehensive structural, systematic expression of faith. Only after the sovereignty of the Gospel, the free and unconditional gift of God given to man in Jesus Christ mediated through the power of the Holy Spirit through word and sacrament had been clearly reestablished, was it possible and necessary to take up the question of the ministry that serves this grace of God. This

basic concept was worked out in a way that influenced further
development first of all in the writings of Luther and then in
the form which became binding for the Lutheran tradition, i.e.
the Lutheran confessional writings. In neither case, however,
was this concept worked out in a comprehensive, systematic form
on the basis of which all the questions that would later arise
could have been answered.

Luther's Concept of the Ministry

Luther's concept of the ministry has just again in recent
years provoked numerous, sometimes quite different interpretations.
He did not, as we said, develop his views systematically but
formulated them - like his whole theology - always in terms of
concrete situations, questions, needs and in confrontation with
other views. Furthermore, he underwent development in his theological thinking. However the Reformation's basic theme remains
constant through all the different statements he makes about the
question of the ministry. The ministry of the church is determined
in its position, function and dignity wholly by the word of God,
the Gospel to which absolute priority is given. In his wonderful
grace and condescension, God however takes men into his service
so that his living Gospel through preaching and the administration
of the sacraments does not remain by itself, but comes to men and,
through the transforming work of the Holy Spirit leads them to
faith, strengthens them in faith and builds up the whole Christian
community. The word requires the ministry of the word. The
servants of the word, however, do not have an arbitrary function;
their office does not exist for itself and by itself, they are
rather instruments, and through their human speaking and acting
Christ himself speaks and acts. In this sense, but only in this
sense, Luther can speak of a *cooperatio*:   the ministers have
"the office, the name, and the dignity, that they are God's
co-workers" (V. Vajta). But these co-workers of God may not claim
any higher spiritual dignity than other men.

The person in his importance or quality recedes totally
behind the ministerial function through which God ministers to
men through word and sacrament. Where this ministry takes place,
there we have the office of the ministry, even in a heretical
church, even among unworthy and unbelieving office-bearers.

The real and still actual debate about Luther's concept
of the ministry does not center around this basic theme of the

Reformation, which is only a consequence of the doctrine of
justification and which is undisputed in the interpretations.
This debate rather deals with the fact that Luther is claimed as
exponent for two different concepts of the basis of the ministry
and of its relationship to the Christian community; two concepts
that have been present throughout the history of Lutheranism.
Actually they also play a significant role in the debate about
the ministry in many other confessions. In thesis form these two
concepts say: a) the special ministry is based on the general
priesthood of all baptized. For reasons of order, the congregation
transfers functions to the ministry which belong to all the baptized,
to the whole congregation (delegation theory); b) the ministry is
based on divine institution, on the institution of Christ. It is
therefore set apart from the priesthood of all baptized, but not
separated by a higher spiritual dignity of the person (institution
theory).

Both theories can be supported by statements from Luther.
If in the past one line of his thought or the other was stressed
as decisive, recent works on Luther's understanding of the
ministry have attempted to do justice to both. They do this by
either speaking of a tension or of a "bipolarity" in Luther's
thinking about the ministry whereby the emphasis finally lies on
the concept of divine institution (e.g. Lieberg, Gerrish, Tuchel,
Prenter) or by attempting to show a development in Luther's
concept of the ministry (Green). It is in any case obvious that
Luther would emphasize one position or the other often depending
on the position against which he argued. But he can also leave
both views stand side by side without trying to balance them. A
one-sided, isolated preference for only one line of thought cannot
therefore be supported with reference to Luther. Luther was not
really interested in a theoretical answer to the question, whether
the office is based on the general priesthood or on direct divine
institution, whether its authority comes "from below" or "from
above". His statements were shaped by his Reformation goals and
by the actual polemical context in which they were made. We
might say, however, that there is a basic thought behind the
different statements, namely: that ministry and general priesthood
must be seen together as much as possible and that both are based
in God's institution. This leads some interpreters to conclude:
that according to Luther, the ministry is entrusted by God to the
church as a whole. All are consecrated to the spiritual "ordo" and
capable of exercising the ministry. The church, however, calls

only some of its members to this ministry so that it might be
performed publicly (Elert, Fischer).

This "bipolarity" of Luther's concept of the ministry
is also the reason why he at one time can put emphasis on the
call of the office-bearer by the congregation (*vocatio*) and in
other places on commissioning with prayer and laying on of hands
by ordained office-bearers (*ordinatio*). Here too it is the "two
front attack" against the Roman Catholic understanding of
consecration on the one hand and the Enthusiast's view of a
direct call by the Holy Spirit on the other which is to a large
extent responsible for the different emphases. On the whole,
however, we must say that Luther understood and practiced vocation
and ordination either as equivalents or as two homogeneous aspects
of the same thing. And even where he emphasized that the priesthood of all baptized believers is realized in the call by the
congregation, he saw in the act of men the act of God himself
who empowered the congregation to such action.

Because of the basic freedom toward forms of the ministry
which we already mentioned, Luther and the other Reformers were
even willing to acknowledge Catholic bishops. And not only in
the event that they joined the evangelical cause, but already
even if they had only been willing to ordain evangelically oriented
candidates. At the same time, however, Luther and his colleagues
advocated a new concept of the office of bishop. Basing their
argument on the New Testament, they considered the office of
pastor and the office of bishop as *one* office with identical basic
functions. They thus rejected the prevailing Catholic teaching
and Luther could therefore use both designations indiscriminately
for the same office-bearers. That he could differentiate between
offices based on human right and on the concrete demands of the
church's total existence is no contradition. He assigned as an
additional special task to the city pastor the theological and
practical function of ecclesiastical oversight and leadership,
which must extend beyond the realm of a single congregation - thus
the name "superintendent" - and with the development of church
orders certain specific tasks were assigned to him. In preparing
and participating in the consecration and installation of the
bishop of Naumburg, Nikolaus von Amsdorf, 1542, Luther also
acknowledged the possibility and the necessity of an evangelical
bishop's office for a larger region.

The Concept of the Ministry in the Lutheran Confessional Writings

It corresponds to the statements above, that ministry and church order in the Lutheran confessional writings have no independent dogmatic position. There is only one short, basic statement about the meaning of the ministry in the main part of the *Confessio Augustana*, in Article V: "To obtain such faith God instituted the office of the ministry, that is, provided the Gospel and the sacraments. Through these, as through means, he gives the Holy Spirit, who works faith, when and where he pleases, in those who hear the Gospel." From this sentence we can infer some basic facts about the ministry which are supported by other statements:

1. The ministry has functional character. It exists for only one purpose, to serve the means of grace, the word and the sacraments.

2. God alone is Lord of these means, he uses them, he acts through them, he is the subject of word and sacraments. The ministry therefore is no independent ontological or institutional entity, it is no "estate".

3. In this way the ministry serves God in his condescension to men and men in their believing acceptance of it.

4. This ministry is instituted by God. It is therefore not a practical measure placed at the church's disposal. This divine institution was first and fundamentally expressed in the call, commissioning and sending of the apostles.

5. The ministry of the church is a ministry of word *and* sacraments. It is neither a "preaching office" nor a "sacramental office" in the narrow sense.

6. Because of its serving function, ministry is not constitutive for the church (word and sacrament are), but it is absolutely *necessary* for the church because word and sacraments require this divinely instituted ministry in order to be effective.

This ministry which serves the Gospel through the preaching of the word and the administration of the sacraments, *is entrusted to the church* (Tract. 67ff.). The church, however, is nothing other than the royal priesthood of all baptized (*ibid*. 69). "Royal priesthood" means that every baptized and believing member of the church is granted the dignity of the "spiritual estate" and therewith the principle capability to be called to the public

ministry of preaching the word and administering the sacraments.
The church has received the right and the authority to elect,
call and ordain ministers for the public preaching of the word
and administration of the sacraments (*ibid.*, 67ff.). The royal
priesthood of all baptized is therefore the presupposition for the
special ministry - instituted by God and entrusted to the church -
of those called and ordained by the church to this office. The
ministry is thus inextricably bound to the priesthood of all
baptized. To be called to this ministry does not separate from
the general priesthood, but rather the minister appointed and
called by the church serves to build up, advance and fulfill this
priesthood in the name and by the commission of God and with his
means of grace. The minister is neither its initiator nor its
delegate. Both the royal priesthood and the public ministry are
God's gifts and commission to his church.

The essential *task* of the ministry, as has become clear
by now, is the preaching of the word and the administration of
the sacraments. This task is summarized in the Apology 28,13
under the traditional, but now evangelically understood concept
of *potestas ordinis*. It is thus an express rejection of the idea
of a sacrificial office (Apol. 13,9). A second traditional
concept, that of *potestas iurisdictionis*, which was also taken
over and reinterpreted, i.e. in exclusion of all temporal
jurisdiction (cf. CA 28), included the tasks of forgiveness of
sins (CA 25; Tract. 60), of right doctrine and of church discipline
in exclusion of human use of force (CA 28,21; Apol. 28, 13f.).

It does not contradict the serving, functional character
of the ministry, it rather underscores it in a certain way, when
we speak of a *representative* concept of the ministry in the
confessional writings. In preaching the Gospel and administering
the sacraments the appointed minister acts because of the church's
call and not in or for his own person, but in the name of God and
in Christ's place (Apol. 7, 28.47; 13, 12). God preaches through
him (Apol. 13, 12), he himself is the one who baptizes (Cat. Baptism
10) in absolution we are to believe his voice (CA 25, 3; Apol. 12,
40), he blesses the elements of the Lord's Supper through the
words of institution spoken by the pastor (FC: Sol. Decl. 7, 76
and 77-81). The words of Luke 10:16 ("He who hears you hears me")
underscore the serving character of this representation: The word
and action of man is only the instrument of Christ's word and action.
The appointed ministers do not represent themselves, but Christ and
through and with him God. They can do this because God wills to
preach and work through men who are elected by men (Apol. 13, 9

Through their voices they shall let his voice be heard. Where that happens, there God is present in the ministry (Apol. 13, 12).

When the serving representation of the ministry is understood in that way, then a further conviction of the confessions is only logical: One should not listen to false teachers, for they are not in Christ's stead (Apol. 7, 47). Unbelieving and unworthy ministers, however, preach the Gospel and administer the sacraments in Christ's place, which therefore do not lose their efficacy (CA 8, 1-3; Apol. 7, 3.19.28.47; Cat. The Sacrament of the Altar 5, 16). This underlines once again the sovereignty of divine action in relationship to the minister acting in Christ's place. This conviction also includes the assurance and promise to the congregation and to the office-bearer that God also acts through sinners.

The representative nature of the ministry means that we must also say that the ministry and the congregation *confront* each other. The appointed minister confronts the congregation not as one who belongs to a special estate, but as one who bears the commission of God and as the representative of Christ, and in doing this he represents finally the way God's word confronts the church.

The confessions use the concepts of call (*vocatio*), election and *ordination* to describe entrance into the public ministry of preaching the word and administering the sacraments. These concepts are not precisely distinguished. Used together or also singly (as in CA 14) they designate the whole process of election, call, ordination, and installation of the office-bearer. As the ministry is given by God to the whole church, so the whole church has also received the right and duty to elect, call and ordain suitable ministers (e.g. Tract. 67; 69; 70; 72; The Sm. Art. Part III, X, 1-3; Apol. 13, 11 and 12). Only those who have been "rightly called" in this way, may exercise the public ministry in the church (CA 14; Apol. 14). Ordination is carried out by pastors/bishops by divine right (Tract. 65, 72). (The concept of "divine right" is not used in the confessions in the sense of a legal maxim, but as reference to the command and the promise of divine institution.)

The confessions declare that for the sake of love and unity Catholic bishops may still conduct ordination as long as they are willing to be proper bishops. The designation of ordination (and of ministry) as a "sacrament" in Apology 13, 9-13, which was based on a broader concept of sacrament, never gained general recognition in the Lutheran church. But this step of Melanchthon's nevertheless expressed a general conviction about the reality of the ministry that in the church's call and ordination through its appointed ministers, it is God himself who acts, it is he who calls to the ministry through the call of men/the church (Apol. 13, 12). The confessional writings have no interest in the actual procedures of ordination. They were left for the emerging church orders. But the traditional form of laying on of hands with prayer is obviously to be continued (Tract. 70; Apol. 13, 12).

The confessions recognize only *one* public ministry for preaching the word and administering the sacraments. The basis for this view is seen, in reference to Jerome, in the way the New Testament sees presbyters and bishops as equals (Tract. 62). Therefore all are equal in the one ministry, which God has instituted in the church, whether they are called pastors, presbyters or bishops. They all have the same task (Tract. 60-61 and 74; CA 28, 8.21). Thus the confessions often mention bishops in connection with pastors (CA 28; Apol. 28, 12; Tract. 60). It also means that ordination administered by pastors is valid by divine right (Tract. 65 and Apol. 14, 1). For the Reformers in their situation, this argument was decisive. For if the difference between pastor and bishop were based on an institution of Christ so that only the bishop possessed the authority to ordain by divine right, then the developing evangelical church would have lacked a valid ministry.

Seeing pastors and bishops as equals, however, did not imply the rejection of a special office of bishop. The wording of the confessions does not always make it clear if the title "bishop" denotes the pastor of a congregation, the head pastor of a city (in analogy to the episcopal parochial churches *paroikiai* of the first three centuries) or a diocesan bishop, but the willingness - for the sake of love and unity - to accept the existing bishops and also to grant them the right to ordain, in as far as they were true bishops and did not suppress evangelical teaching, point to a readiness to continue even the traditional office of bishop as a superior office of church leadership (Apol. 14; Smal.Art. Part III, X, 1). The more detailed and in part also positive statements about the office of bishop in CA 28, give a basic idea of the tasks that are assigned to the bishop by divine mandate: to preach the Gospel, to administer and distribute the sacraments, to forgive and retain sins (CA 28 calls these three functions also the "power of the keys"), and to preserve pure doctrine and church discipline by God's word. On this account, pastors are bound to be obedient to them (CA 28, 21 and 22). On the other hand, pastors and congregations have God's command not to be obedient to the bishops if they teach or introduce anything contrary to the Gospel (CA 28, 23-28;

Tract. 60-82). By virtue of human right and for the sake of good order, unity and love the bishops (or pastors) have the right to establish certain regulations for the life of the church and its worship to which the people also owe obedience (CA 28, 29.53ff.).

In regard to the essential tasks of the public ministry there is no difference between bishops and pastors; they are two functions of the same office. They only exercise these tasks at different levels because the church of Jesus Christ is found in the local congregation as well as in the fellowship of local congregations. It is thus the special task of the bishop, who is in charge of a fellowship of several local congregations, to provide that in this fellowship the Gospel is rightly preached and the sacraments administered according to their institution. As an expression of the more comprehensive domain of his ministry, which also serves the unity and catholicity of the church, he can also be granted the authority of ordination which belongs to every pastor. In addition to that he has certain tasks of church leadership by human right. The criteria for this acceptance of the office of bishop and of an episcopal structure in contrast to the existing office of bishop are emphasized repeatedly in CA 28: no temporal power (distinction between temporal and spiritual authority), no acting and ordering against the Gospel, no burdening consciences through unnecessary and outdated ceremonies, orders, laws, etc. Whether we can draw a principle demand for an episcopal constitution from all these statments is disputed. It is my opinion that although this question as well as individual questions of church order are left open in the Lutheran confessions, most of the texts show at least an openness for and tendency toward an episcopal structure, rather than the opposite. But if that is the case then episcopal structure means that the episcopal functions - by human right - can be exercised in different ways both by pastors and other office-bearers as well as by bishops.

It is clear that there is a basic agreement between Luther's concept of the ministry and that of the confessions. This is true in spite of the fact that Philip Melanchthon placed greater emphasis upon the divine institution of the office and showed even less interest in the general priesthood of all baptized which is reflected in the confessions. In spite of the general importance of Luther for the theology and doctrine of Lutheranism, it should be emphasized that only the confessional writings have binding character for the doctrine and practice of Lutheranism.

The Development of the Concept of the Ministry in German Lutheranism
        (16th - 19th Century)

        The survey of the development of the concept of the ministry
which can be presented here only in brief outline, must be limited
to Germany. This limitation is possible and defensible in as far
as German Lutheran theology into the 19th century had an essential
and influential impact upon Lutheranism in Europe and upon the
Lutheranism that spread from Europe to other countries. In spite
of many independent developments in the other countries, their
concept of the ministry was very much in line with its development
in German theology.
        The constantly changing intellectual and theological
presuppositions, the development of church constitutions and the
practice of the church led in the history of German Lutheranism
to constant modifications of the concept of the ministry. Thus
Lutheran Orthodoxy of the 16th and 17th centuries, following its
basic tendencies, also systematically developed the doctrine of
the ministry in great detail and strengthened the idea of its
divine institution with biblical proofs. It added a new element
to the duties of the office-bearer, that of moral supervision over
the congregation, it suppressed in line with the forms of church
polity of the time the rights and authority of the general priesthood and furthered an intellectualizing concept of the ministry by
stressing the ministry as a "teaching estate" in the congregation.
Lutheran Pietism brought a reaction to that position. The priesthood of all true believers, independent of the structures of a
state-church system, was reasserted. That meant that the ministry
lost its outstanding position. Its primary pedagogical character
was replaced by the function of spiritual care. In the individualistic and organizational concept of the church in *Rationalism* the
ministry lost any specific theological significance.
        This too led to a conscious reaction in the form of the
Lutheran confessional theology in the 19th century. The questions
of the ministry and polity received broad attention in this theology.
There were, however, different views on this question:
        a) A number of theologians emphasized that the ministry is
divinely instituted through Christ. Through ordination it is
passed on in uninterrupted continuity by those who hold this ministry.
One of its functions is the leadership of the church (*Kirchenregiment*).
This should therefore (against the Prince Bishops!) be put in the
charge of bishops (F.J. Stahl, W. Löhe, A.F.C. Vilmar and their
followers).

b) Over aginst this, other theologians emphasized that
by divine right the ministry is committed to the general priesthood. Out of it arises the special ministry on the basis of
recognized gifts and the express commissioning through the
congregation (in connection with ordination as an act of the
church's blessing). Church ministry and church leadership are to
be clearly distinguished. This eliminates any need for an episcopal constitution (J.W.F. Hofling, J.v. Hofmann, J. Müller and
others).

c) All the different attempts to mediate between these two
positions had to overcome above all the either-or in the question
of the origin of the ministry. They affirmed the divine institution
of the ministry, but now understood it as a gift of the Lord to
his whole church. They made a distinction between church ministry
and church leadership, but the latter was not seen simply as *de
jure humano* or as secondary. It can be understood on one level
with the "office of the means of grace" or as an office granted by
the Lord to his church. The question whether the leadership of
the church could rest in secular hands was nevertheless answered
in different ways (A. Harless, Th. Kliefoth, Th. Harnack and others).

This short survey shows how the different aspects of the
Reformation's unsystematically developed concept of the ministry
led to quite different, sometimes even quite one-sided positions
in the church situation of the 19th century with its specific
needs and concerns.

Ministerial Structure and Church Order in the Lutheran Churches

It has already been shown that no biblically or theologically
based structure of the ministry or of church order can be considered
dominant within the framework of Lutheran Reformation thought.
Within this framework there was to be freedom to find the adequate
form for each situation. This basic decision led to several
results in the emergence and development of Lutheran churches in
different geographical areas and under quite diverse conditions.
It permitted a great deal of flexibility and adaptability in the
face of different situations and conditions. Second, it made
possible a lasting inner union and an outward growing fellowship
of Lutheranism in spite of these different types of ministerial
structure and church order. But it finally also had the result,
that there was often not sufficient strength in Lutheranism to

resist the take-over of its church leadership functions by civil
powers or to avoid imitating secular structures and bureaucracies -
together with their way of thinking.

Germany

In the German territories that accepted the Reformation the
church was unable to reorder the often chaotic conditions without
the help of the princes. These, however, interpreted this "act
of love" which Luther asked of them as an emergency measure, as
their due right. Supported by certain theological theories, they
established "consistories" in their governments, which gradually
took over the leadership of the church. Thus the theory and
practice of the Prince Bishop arose even if the sovereign never
exercised the spiritual functions of a bishop. This transition of
church rule into temporal hands stood in direct contradiction to
the intentions of the confessional writings and of Luther, who
himself reacted sharply to the beginnings of this development.
Until far into the 19th century, however, theologians thought it
possible to justify this development theologically. Only with the
abolition of the state-church system in 1918, which was preceded
by a movement toward a greater independence of the church in the
19th century, could the Lutheran churches in Germany begin a
process of developing independent forms of polity and government
which came to a certain completion after 1945.
The office of bishop, which during the Reformation was
either retained in an evangelical form or reintroduced later in
some areas of Germany - though only for a short period for one or
another regional church - was accepted by all Lutheran churches
as the office of church leadership after 1918. It is associated
in different ways with the synods and the main administrative
offices of the church. On the other hand, the office of "superintendent" (under different names) as an episcopal office in a
small geographical area (above all with visitation rights)
remained alive from the Reformation time until today.

Scandinavia

Quite different from the development in Germany was the
clear desire of the Reformers and also of the kings in Scandinavia
to continue the office of bishop and episcopal church order in
evangelical terms after the Reformation. That the office of
bishop was called a good, useful institution introduced under the
guidance of "God the Holy Spirit" (Church Order of Sweden of
1571), and even though a special "consecration of bishops" was kept
along side the ordination of pastors, it was not considered
contradictory to the Reformation conviction of the equality of
pastors and bishops. It was of decisive importance, however, that
by holding on to a definite concept of leadership and order of
the church a transfer of church rule into the hands of the sovereign
was avoided. Even though the Danish and Swedish kings as "eminent
members of the church" and as sovereigns occupied a special position
in relation to the church, they did not act as "emergency bishops"
or as "summus episcopus" after the German pattern. Even though
the parliaments or Diets in Denmark (and later also in Norway and
Iceland) and Sweden (and since 1809 also in Finland) had and still
possess legal authority in ecclesiastical matters, the church
was not subordinated to the control of the sovereign and his
administration in the same manner as in Germany. In the centuries
since the Reformation the church was able to increase its independence more and more. The close connection between church and state
is increasingly seen today as an anachronism and the possibility
of a separation of church and state especially in Sweden and more
and more also in Norway is being seriously discussed and planned.

Together with the office of bishop (and the office of
archbishop, which is understood in Sweden and Finland as *primus
inter pares*), the dean and chapter of cathedrals were also retained,
while on the intermediate level the provosts supervise several
congregations and in some cases install pastors in their congregations. A special characteristic of the Swedish church is that
even through the Reformation period it has maintained apostolic
succession in the (narrow) sense of an uninterrupted direct
succession of the office of bishop through episcopal consecration.
Some historians hold, however, that this succession was lost in
the second half of the 16th century during a temporary anti-
episcopal wave. The Danish bishops who were newly appointed in
the Reformation were consecrated in 1537 by Johannes Bugenhagen.
Through the death of the three bishops of Finland in one year (1884),

its episcopal succession was also interrupted; but it was reestablished, as some argue, through the participation of Anglican
bishops in the consecration of Finnish bishops in this century.
For a Lutheran understanding of the ministry - apart from high
church circles - the question of the preservation, interruption
and reestablishment of apostolic succession of the office of bishop
has no decisive theological relevance.

Through the ecumenical movement, ecumenical conversations
and negotiations about church union or intercommunion, Lutherans
today are however increasingly confronted with the question of
apostolic succession of the ministry. In several Lutheran churches
in recent decades the office of bishop has been connected with
episcopal succession, e.g. in Slovakia, in churches in Asia and
Africa which came out of the Swedish mission as well as (up until
World War II) in Estonia and Latvia, where the office of bishop
(now the office of archbishop) was introduced after 1918 and the
first bishops were consecrated by Archbishop Söderblom. In any
case these churches along with Sweden and Finland are examples
for the fact that the often quoted Lutheran freedom in regard to
the structure of ministry and church order can also be open for
this expression of apostolic succession.

Southeastern and Eastern Europe and Western Europe

The Lutheran churches of *Southeastern and Eastern Europe*
had to develop their structures of the ministry and of church
order under quite different historical conditions than their
sister churches in Germany and Scandinavia. They were and are
minority churches in predominately Catholic or Orthodox surroundings
and it was only in the first half of this century that they attained
their full independence. Although they were limited in what they
could do for a long period of time, they already soon after the
Reformation were able to form structures of church leadership on
the lower levels of church life through synodical organizations
and episcopal offices.

In Transylvania for instance a certain regional structure
with several superintendents existed already in the middle of the
16th century. Poland, Hungary and Slovakia only a little later
developed structures, typical for these churches (and also for
Austria), with seniorities and districts in which the superintendent
received the right of visitation and soon also the right of

ordination. This structure was connected with a presbyterial-synodical order. The office of bishop or the title of bishop prevailed (with the exception of two smaller minority churches in Yugoslavia) in all the churches. Several relatively early examples for this are Transylvania, where this title for the leading superintendents was used already in the middle of the 19th century, and Hungary and Slovakia, where in 1883 the superintendents received permission to use the title of bishop.

In the Lutheran churches of *France* and *Holland* we find a church and ministerial structure which lacks an office of leadership for the whole church. In France this can be undoubtedly traced back to the special external conditions in which the churches live: the distribution of Lutherans in France into two main areas lying far apart in Paris and Montbeliard and the continuation of the state-church system in Alsace and Lorraine which still only permits one top administrative official for the church. With the office of the "ecclesiastical inspectors" (two inspectors in inner France, seven in Alsace-Lorraine), however, the two Lutheran churches of France have created an episcopal office at the intermediate level which is connected with a synodical structure. In Holland influences of Reformed church order have played an important role, but even here the church constitution provides the task of a *pastor pastorum* to whom the visitation of the congregations and counseling of pastors is entrusted.

North America

The conditions in North America - totally different from those in Europe - influenced the structure and to some extent the understanding of the ministry. They were also the reason that Lutheran churches (synods) developed very slowly. They began with small groups of Lutheran immigrants which were often without a pastor. Slowly organized congregations took shape (in the East already in the 17th century). Several congregations joined in a relationship of counsel and mutual support, in which one of the pastors held a certain coordinating and administrative function (as, for example, since the middle of the 18th century in the *ministerium* in Pennsylvania). After that, congregations joined together on the basis of geographical proximity or national origin into synods (e.g. New York 1786, North Carolina 1803, Ohio 1818). An exception to this pattern is the first Swedish immigrant congregations on the Delaware in the 18th century, which modeled

themselves after the district pattern of a Swedish diocese. The
process of church formation during the great wave of European
immigration in the second half of the 19th century took place,
however, much faster than in the time of the early Lutheran
immigrants.

This growth of the church from "below", from the congregation up, had theological and structural consequences that are still
evident today. These were intensified by the sometimes very
emphatic rejection of the church structures prevailing in the
European homeland and by the often very pietistic character of some
of the immigrant groups. This meant that the individual congregation possessed a large degree of autonomy and that the activity
and authority of the laity became highly important. Out of this
situation arose the tendency to understand the pastoral office as
an office delegated by and dependent on the congregation. There
was no interest in offices of church leadership. Acceptance of
the office of bishop was therefore unthinkable, even in congregation
and churches of Swedish origin. There were, of course, exceptions.
In the middle of the 19th century we find strong episcopal tendencie
in the Buffalo and Iowa Synods which, however, in the face of the
generally prevailing synodical structures gradually disappeared.
The introduction of the office of bishop in the Missouri Synod
failed from the start (1838) through the personal failure of the
first bishop, Martin Stephan.

The consolidation of North American Lutheranism however,
has led to the development of episcopal offices of leadership. The
individual districts/synods within the three largest Lutheran
churches are led by presidents and the entire church stands under
a church president, who functions as its leader and is equipped
with administrative and representative authority. It is significant for the function and understanding of these offices that in
the American Lutheran Church in recent years, the church president
and the district president are permitted to use the title of
bishop if they wish.

Africa, Asia, Australia and Latin America

The formation of ministerial structures and church orders
on these continents presents such a diverse and still fluid picture
that it is only possible here to sketch a few general outlines.

The immigrant churches in *Latin America* and *Australia* took
over the structural models of the churches in their homelands and

adapted them to their new situations. Thus synodical church orders
arose into which the office of president (e.g. Australia, Argentina
and Brazil) was integrated. There are also offices of leadership
at the intermediate level of larger churches which in part also
came out of the offices of leadership of formerly independent
synods after they joined into one church (Brazil). The office of
bishop was introduced in only a few cases. That may be explained
partly because of American influences in these churches, partly
because they included substantial groups of immigrants from Union
churches in Germany.

A whole series of factors have contributed to the present
picture of ministry and church order in the Lutheran churches of
Africa and Asia. The great diversity here is an image of the
diversity among the churches and mission societies in Europe and
America, all the more so as the work of Union mission societies
in Germany was integrated into Lutheran churches.

Second, the missionaries and later the European and
American leaders of these churches, which were gradually becoming
independent, possessed a great personal authority, while synodical
forms of leadership developed slowly and with great difficulty
because of the preponderance of the missionaries, the lack of
local leadership and the differently structured patterns of society.

Third, the personal authority of leadership, prepared by
this missionary background, corresponded to traditional African
and Asian authority structures and so furthered the acceptance of
the office of bishop in many of the newly independent churches.
This development was furthered by the proximity to Anglican churches,
but it was also burdened with many problems and unsolved questions
through the lack of a Lutheran theology of the office of bishop
(and offices of church leadership). Some churches seek to prevent
excessive personal authority in the church by limiting terms of
office.

A fourth aspect is the cooperation of the laity in special
ministries such as catechist or evangelist, which is very important
for the life of these churches, but which at the same time also
raises questions in regard to the relationship between the ministry
of ordained pastor and these other ministries.

Finally, the union of formerly independent mission churches
within a country into one church, for example in Tanzania, led to
the situation that within one church in the different dioceses/
synods there are different ministerial structures, different offices
of leadership (bishops in apostolic succession, bishops without
this succession - and some with limited periods of office - and

presidents) as well as different rules of polity for these offices.
Such a diversity within one church does not contradict Lutheran
understanding of church unity, but it is not without its problems.

In the present transitional situation, the Lutheran
churches of Asia and Africa with their heritage from the mission
past are confronted with the task of developing their own forms of
ministerial structure and church order - which are in continuity
with the Lutheran understanding of the ministry, but which at the
same time fit their situation. The Lutheran tradition gives them
the freedom and thus the chance for such a development. The
theological help which it can offer for the concrete task, however,
is limited.

New Questions and Ecumenical Convergences

In recent years following a general trend, the ministry and
church order have become a focus of interest and discussion in
many Lutheran churches. The reasons for this are to be found in
developments in society, in the church and in the ecumenical
movement.

In the face of radical changes in society and church,
many today feel that there is a crisis which forces us to reevaluate
the traditional forms of understanding and exercizing the ministry
of the church. In order to overcome it, emphasis is put on
developing an active laity and on forming a closer tie between
the ministry of the whole people of God and the special ministry
of the ordained office-bearer. Many churches have established
full-time specialized ministries for social work, instruction,
counseling, youth work, etc. alongside the office of pastor. Lay
men and women can be given the special task of preaching and, in
some cases, even of administering the sacraments. There are now
pastors in special ministries and in team ministries. And many
Lutheran churches of Europe and America have now admitted women
to the ordained ministry even though there is still no basic
theological agreement on this question as the controversies, for
example, in Finland, Sweden and the United States show. Church
administrations are centralized to make them more efficient. These
and many other things are done to relieve the church's ordained
ministry and give it a new, fitting function and role. In view of
the Lutheran concept of the ministry it is obvious that this will
lead to new questions. Is there not a danger that the ordained
minister becomes a functionary of the congregation, a mere theologica

enabler or specialist? Could not the lack of theological reflection
about the offices of church leadership under the present conditions
have the result that bishops, church presidents, superintendents
or other bearers of an episcopal office are pushed into the role
of administrators and ecclesiastical managers? Is there not a
danger that the centralized church bureaucracies will become
increasingly isolated from the congregations?

These necessary changes as well as the problems and dangers
that accompany them call for theological reflection and clarification.
This is happening in many places. That this renewed reflection is
still guided by the Lutheran basis for understanding the ministry
is shown by the following quotation from a study paper of the
Lutheran Council in the USA:

> This ordained ministry is a part of the people of
> God, united with them in the task of mission and standing
> with them beneath the judgment and grace of God. In
> another sense the ordained ministry stands on behalf of
> Christ over against the people of God, entrusted with
> the exposition of the Word of God, the administration of
> the sacraments and the general spiritual oversight of
> the church.

> The authority of this ordained ministry, as that of
> the ministry of all God's people, proceeds from the Lord
> of the church himself. It is God who instituted the
> office of the ministry (CA V) and who has continued to
> call and send his servants to fill it (CA XIV). *The
> Ministry of the Church: A Lutheran Understanding*, 1974.

The meaning and structure of the ministry in Lutheranism
have also become the subject of discussion and of renewed interest
through ecumenical conversations, especially through interconfessional conversations with the Roman Catholic and the Anglican
churches. The Lutheran emphasis on the character of the ministry
as a servant of the Gospel is seen as a positive contribution.
There is an overall agreement on the questions of the divine
institution of the ministry, its essential functions, its relationship to the whole people of God and in the meaning of ordination.
On the other hand, however, the question of the office of bishop
and above all of apostolic succession in the context of a
comprehensive concept of the succession and continuity of the
church confronts Lutheran theology with an issue to which it has
previously given little attention. Concern for closer fellowship
with other churches, conversations on union between Lutheran
churches and "episcopal" churches in Asia and Africa, and the
necessity to give clear guidelines for the understanding and
practice of offices of church leadership do not allow us to dodge
this issue by saying that these are not central questions of faith.

Ecumenical discussions on this and other points might perhaps lead
Lutheranism to a double insight: first, that Lutheranism in the
basic lines of its concept of the ministry is following a way that
has validity even beyond its own realm and that should be kept; but
second, that the freedom it claims in the possibilities of shaping
the structure of the ministry and of church order without clarifying
theological reflection may very easily lead to a narrow (and often
theologically garnished) fixation on traditional or secular models,
structures and ways of thinking. Here the ecumenical conversations
could give an important impulse also for the inner situation and
renewal of Lutheranism.

Translated by Donald Dutton

CHAPTER 10

FRANKLIN SHERMAN

SECULAR CALLING AND SOCIAL ETHICAL THINKING

The Re-Interpretation of the Secular

If we are to discuss the role of the "secular calling" in the Lutheran tradition, it is well to bear in mind that the word "secular" is susceptible to various interpretations. Like the word "humanist," it can be understood either in terms of what it denies or of what it affirms.

"Humanist" can be taken, on its negative side, to imply chiefly the denial of the reality of God and of the transcendent; in this sense, it clearly is incompatible with the Christian faith. However, it can also be taken, on its positive side, as an affirmation of the significance of human life within that flesh-and-blood existence known as "history," and an effort to increase its vitality and meaningfulness. In this sense, humanism not only is compatible with the Christian faith, but may even be a direct implication of it; thus one can speak of a "Christian humanism."

The same is true of the notion of the "secular" or of "secularization." *Prima facie*, it also seems to imply a realm that has escaped from God's domain, so to speak, and has become autonomous. But recent theology has taught us to think of secularization in a more positive light, as a process of humanity's "coming of age" (Dietrich Bonhoeffer), and this in turn as willed by divine providence. It represents an emancipation of the various realms of life not from the sovereignty of God, but from the need

for a special "religious" coloring, or from tutelage to ecclesiastical authority. Marriage, work, culture, politics are freed to
be affirmed directly as part of God's good creation, and as the
theatre in which the life of "faith active in love" is to find
expression.

It is in this sense that the Lutheran Reformation may be
said to have involved a powerful "affirmation of the secular,"
and especially of the holy significance of the secular calling.
Two remarks made by Luther, out of many to the same effect, may
serve as evidence of this. In his treatise *On Monastic Vows* (1521),
Luther offers a number of criticisms of monasticism. Prominent
among them is this: that "Christian obedience and love," as he
puts it, "are drawn from the public arena by these men and forced
into their small corner of the world" (LW 44, 329). The positive
implication is clear: Christian obedience and love are meant to
be exercised not in a withdrawn community, but precisely in the
great arena of civil society, i.e., of the "secular world."

The other remark is made almost in passing, as Luther is
discussing, in the Preface to the Smalcald Articles of 1536, what
attitude to take toward the pope's proposal to call an Ecumenical
Council. He is basically sympathetic to the idea, but he comments:

> Not that we ourselves need such a council, for by
> God's grace our churches have now been so enlightened
> and supplied with the pure Word and the right use of the
> sacraments, with *an understanding of the various callings
> of life,* and with true works, that we do not ask for a
> council for our own sake... (*The Book of Concord*, Tappert
> ed., 290. Italics added).

Thus Luther counts among the chief benefits of the Reformation,
as he views it in twenty years' perspective, the recovery of a
true doctrine of vocation--and, he adds of "true works."

This corresponds with the judgment of modern scholars
who see in the Reformation a turning point not only in the history
of theology and ecclesiology but also in the history of Christian
ethics. Thus Karl Holl speaks of *der Neubau der Sittlichkeit*
("the reconstruction of morality") that resulted from the Lutheran
reform, as the egocentric and eudaemonistic motives that had
corrupted medieval ethics were expelled in favor of theocentric
motives, and the world of ordinary human relationships was recognize
as having constitutive and not merely instrumental significance
for the life of faith. Similarly, Anders Nygren sees in the thought
of Luther a rebirth of the ethics of *agape* (self-giving love) over
against the ethics of *eros* (self-seeking love) or the Augustinian-
medieval concept of *caritas*, which attempted to mediate between

the two. As such, Luther's ethic represents, for Nygren, a return
to the ethics of the Synoptic Gospels and of St. Paul.

The nature of this transformation in ethical perspective
can be seen if we consider the way in which certain key terms were
redefined in Luther's thought. This is true of the two concepts
specially emphasized by Luther in the passage quoted immediately
above ("calling" or vocation and "good works"), as well as of the
closely related concept of "repentance."

Repentance, Good Works and Vocation

It was with the concept of repentance and the concern for
its proper definition that Luther began the Ninety-five Theses,
whose promulgation is usually taken to mark the initiation of the
Reformation as an event in the public sphere. "When our Lord and
Master Jesus Christ said 'Repent,'" Luther writes in Thesis 1, "he
willed the entire life of believers to be one of repentance." And
he continues in the following theses:

> #2. This word cannot be understood as referring
> to the sacrament of penance, that is, confession and
> satisfaction, as administered by the clergy.

> #3. Yet it does not mean solely inner repentance;
> such inner repentance is worthless unless it produces
> various outward mortifications of the flesh.

In thus juxtaposing "penance" and "repentance," Luther, no
doubt, was well aware that the sacrament of penance had originally
been intended not to replace the act of repentance but merely to
provide it, as it were, with a ready means of expression. Yet
he was also well aware of the abuses connected with this system.
The sale of indulgences especially struck him as the hawking of a
"cheap grace" (to use the term of Bonhoeffer) that served as a
substitute rather than a stimulus for true repentance and amendment
of life.

Luther's phrase *simul justus et peccator* ("at the same
time righteous and a sinner") serves nicely as a description of the
Christian's paradoxical status before God, and his utter dependence
on forgiving grace. Less well known, but also very illuminating,
is the threefold formula he offers in his Lectures on Romans:
semper peccator, semper penitens, semper justus ("always a sinner,
always repenting, always righteous"). Here repentance appears as
the dynamic middle term between sin and righteousness. The Christian
life, seen from this perspective, involves a constant process of

moral transformation.

Luther reenforces this conception when he speaks in his
Small Catechism of the meaning of baptism for daily life. "It
signifies," he writes, "that the old Adam in us, together with
all sins and evil lusts, should be drowned by daily sorrow and
repentance and put to death, and that the new man should come
forth daily and rise up, cleansed and righteous, to live forever
in God's presence."

Equally important is the redefinition of the "good works"
involved in the Lutheran reform. This redefinition involved both
a change in motivation and a change of locus for such works. The
motivation was no longer to win merit in the eyes of God or to
atone for past sins committed, but simply to serve the neighbor
out of a "glad and generous heart," while relying for one's own
salvation purely on God's grace. Correspondingly, the locus of
good works was changed from the "religious" to the "secular"
realm, i.e., to the realm of one's daily life and calling in the
context of the social world.

Thus Luther, in his *Treatise on Good Works* of 1520 and
throughout his writings, constantly polemicizes against what he
terms "false" good works. These typically include, for Luther,
such activities as the making of pilgrimages, the observance of
vigils, the endowment of masses, the doing of penances by the
repetition of set prayers--in other words, activities located
purely in the "religious" sphere or based merely on ecclesiastical
ordinances. Prayer, of course, is valuable and essential, but
is to be regarded as a means of grace, not a good work. The true
good works are those which are carried out in the context of the
common life, where God has set before us the neighbor in his need.

But how is the content of such "true" good works to be
determined? In answer to this question, Luther commonly cites
two maxims: "Remember the Commandments" and "Consider your station.
It is the Ten Commandments that provide the framework for his
"Treatise on Good Works" as well as similar discussions elsewhere.
In accordance with patristic and medieval tradition, they are
regarded (at least so far as the "Second Table" is concerned) as
a résumé or republication of the natural law, that is, of those
moral norms that are or ought to be evident to everyone. Luther
does not deal in abstract formulations, however. He interprets
the Commandments as prophetic words, spoken into the present
situation to unveil every sort of human deviousness, and at the
same time to point beyond themselves to the positive ethic of the
Gospel.

This twofold process of interpretation is clearly reflected in Luther's Small Catechism, where each Commandment involving a "Thou shalt not" is first broadened or radicalized in its meaning, and then converted into a positive "Thou shalt." In effect, the Ten Commandments are interpreted in the light of the Sermon on the Mount. Thus for example, the Commandment "Thou shalt not steal" is said to mean:

> We should fear and love God, and so we should not rob our neighbor of his money or property, nor bring them into our possession by dishonest trade or by dealing in shoddy wares, but help him to improve and protect his income and property.

To obey the Commandments in this sense is to fulfill the demands both of love and of the natural law. There is no contradiction between these two, since the essence of each can be expressed in the Golden Rule, "Do unto others as you would have them do unto you."

Luther's second maxim, "Consider your station," moves the question of the content of good works towards a yet further degree of specificity. The first maxim, "Remember the Commandments," may be said to refer to the trans-situational constants in Christian ethics. The second maxim, "Consider your station," refers to the situational variables. One's specific placement in the social order will deeply affect, according to Luther, the range and the nature of one's ethical responsibilities.

Here we encounter the closely associated notions of station (*Stand*), office (*Amt*), and calling or vocation (*Beruf*). Although these terms are often used interchangeably, the former two usually serve a more descriptive function, the latter a more theological and ethical one. Human society, as viewed by Luther, in accordance with medieval tradition, consists in a network of interdependent and interconnecting roles--parent and child, master and servant, ruler and ruled, etc. Each of these roles, in turn, consists in the position (*Stand*) that a person occupies, and the duties or functions (*Amt*) attaching to that position. Thus the "station" occupied by a ruler is that of prince (or premier or president); his "office" is to rule. A medical doctor's "station" is that of physician; his "office" is to heal. The totality of such roles and interrelationships within a given realm constitutes a particular "order" or institution (the political, the familial, etc.). And the totality of such orders constitutes the multidimensional unity of a human society as a whole.

So far, this corresponds to the structure-and-function

analysis practiced by modern sociology. The specifically theologica
and ethical dimension arises with the concept of the calling
(*Beruf*). To have a "calling" means *to acknowledge one's station
as assigned by God, and to carry out its duties* (office) *under
the aegis of the divine command.*

Karl Holl, in a key essay on the history of the word
Beruf, has shown how this theologically weighty term, formerly
applied only to the religious sphere, came to be applied also to
the worldly realm. The predominant medieval usage was to consider
only those entering a monastic movement to have a divine "calling."
Under the influence of the lay mystical movements of the late
Middle Ages, the term was extended also to the various secular
occupations. These too could be considered callings if their
duties were carried out as in the sight of God. But they were
still viewed as spiritually inferior to the religious vocations.
It was Luther who took the further step of declaring all callings
to have equal dignity in God's sight.

Thus in his treatise on *The Babylonian Captivity of the
Church* (1520), Luther states bluntly:

> Therefore I advise no one to enter any religious
> order or the priesthood, indeed, I advise everyone
> against it, unless he... understands that the works
> of monks and priests, however holy and arduous they
> may be, do not differ one whit in the sight of God
> from the works of the rustic laborer in the field or
> the woman going about her household tasks, but that
> all works are measured before God by faith alone.
> (LW 36, 78)

The same theme appears at innumerable other places in Luther's
writings. His doctrine of vocation, as this quotation indicates,
is intimately related to his doctrine of justification. Precisely
because we are justified by grace and not by works, we are freed
from judging our daily work in terms of what the world deems status
or success; it becomes not a means of self-justification, but a
vehicle of loving service to the neighbor. Viewed in this light,
monasticism is, in fact, no calling at all, since it removes men
and women from the arena for such service rather than driving them
into it. Thus the final effect of the Reformation, as Holl's essay
notes, is to deprive of the name of "calling" the one pursuit
that had originally claimed it, while awarding it to those secular
pursuits that had formerly been excluded from this dignity.

As to the specific nature of the duties attaching to the
several callings, this is, for Luther, partly derived from the
traditional (feudal) understanding of the functions of the various
social rules, and partly to be ascertained by a direct inspection

of the nature of the work involved. Thus he can write, in
exposition of the "Golden Rule" in Matthew 7:12:

> If you are a manual laborer, you find that the
> Bible has been put into your workshop, into your hand,
> into your heart. It teaches and preaches how you should
> treat your neighbor. Just look at your tools--at your
> needle or thimble, your beer barrel, your goods, your
> scales or yardstick or measure--and you will read this
> statement inscribed on them. Everywhere you look, it
> stares at you.... Indeed, there is no shortage of
> preaching. You have as many preachers as you have
> transactions, goods, tools, and other equipment in your
> house and home. All this is continually crying out to
> you, "Friend, use me in your relations with your neighbor
> just as you would want your neighbor to use his property
> in his relations with you. (Commentary on the Sermon on
> the Mount, LW 21, 237.)

The secular calling, then, is prized by Luther as both
the *place of discernment* of the will of God and as the *place of
obedience* to that will. The hardships that faithful performance
of the duties of the calling may bring are accepted as a cross
laid on one by God ("Vocation is crucifixion," one modern Lutheran
theologian has written). At the same time, the victorious power
of faith is expressed in and through the calling.

One may note that Luther's concept of the calling is a
static one; he had no notion of social mobility, in the sense of
a freely chosen movement among several occupational possibilities.
One is called *in* a certain station of life, not *into* a certain
station. The theological and ethical roots of the concept, however,
made it freely adaptable to later, more mobile social situations.

Strengths and Weaknesses of the Lutheran Position

The early Lutherans found that the note of "affirmation of
the secular" had to be maintained not only in the face of the
monastic and ascetical tendencies inherited from the Middle Ages,
but also over against what Luther called the "new monasticism"
represented by certain left-wing Reformation movements, movements
that counseled a withdrawal from the common life into set-apart
communities. The thrust of this polemic can be clearly seen in
the Augsburg Confession's Article XVI, "On Civil Government," which
codifies, as it were, the role of the secular calling in Lutheran
thought:

> It is taught among us that all government in
> the world and all established rule and laws were
> instituted by and ordained by God for the sake of good
> order, and that Christians may without sin occupy civil

offices or serve as princes and judges, render
decisions and pass sentence according to imperial
and other existing laws, punish evildoers with the
sword, engage in just wars, serve as soldiers, buy
and sell, take required oaths, possess property,
be married, etc.

Condemned here are the Anabaptists who teach
that none of the things indicated above is Christian.

Also condemned are those who teach that
Christian perfection requires the forsaking of house
and home, wife and child, and the renunciation of
such activities as are mentioned above. Actually,
true perfection consists alone of proper fear of
God and real faith in God, for the Gospel does not
teach an outward and temporal but an inward and
eternal mode of existence and righteousness of the
heart. The Gospel does not overthrow civil authority,
the state, and marriage but requires that all these
be kept as true orders of God and that everyone, each
according to his calling, manifest Christian love
and genuine good works in his station of life.
Accordingly Christians are obliged to be subject to
civil authority and obey its commands and laws in
all that can be done without sin. But when commands
of the civil authority cannot be obeyed without sin,
we must obey God rather than men.

This statement deserves further examination, for we see
in it the combination of a number of factors that have made the
typical Lutheran position on social-ethical questions what it is,
for good or ill. On the one hand, we have the expression, in the
spirit of Luther, of a robust faith in the goodness of the creation
and the work of God the Creator, acting through so-called "secular"
authorities and structures (Luther had called them *larvae Dei*,
"masks of God"). Connected with this is the acknowledgement of
the role of natural reason in the devising of solutions to social
problems (matters may be decided "according to the imperial or other
existing laws"). Not every plan or program, it is implied, need
bear a Christian label; there is always a need for the input of
"secular expertise" into the ethical equation. This has remained
a characteristic emphasis of Lutheranism down to the present time,
as over against those who would find solutions to social problems
directly in the Bible or in ecclesiastical tradition.

Another characteristic of the Lutheran position which is
implied, if not explicit, in the quoted statement, is the willingnes
to accept the element of compromise that is involved in social-
institutional life, to persist in the midst of conflict, to remain
at the place of responsibility even if this involves grave per-
plexity of conscience. This was the sense of Luther's advice to
Melanchthon, "Sin boldly." (His full statement was, "Sin boldly,
but believe and rejoice in Christ even more boldly" [*pecca fortiter,
sed fortius fide et gaude in Christo*] in: WA Br 2, No. 424:84f.).

If these be regarded as strengths of the Lutheran position, the weaknesses which are their reverse side must also be acknowledged. The recognition of the role of secular authorities in the divine governance of history is stated in such a way that it can easily be inferred that the social and political structures just as they are at any given time are blessed by God and are neither needful nor capable of substantial improvement--a position which is always a comfortable one for those already enjoying the fruits of prosperity or power. Further, the acknowledgement of the overlap between that which is Christian and that which is naturally human, a point which serves to forestall Christian exclusivity, may be taken so far as to eliminate any sense of differentia in Christian conduct at all. The Confession's statement that the Gospel teaches only an "inward and eternal" righteousness lends itself easily to such an interpretation. Similarly, the assertion that Christians owe obedience to the civil authorities has often been emphasized without due attention to the exceptive clause, "in all that can be done without sin."

Finally, the salutary realism that pervades Lutheran thinking, based on an awareness of the inescapable ambiguities of history, has sometimes lapsed into a pessimism, and even cynicism, that despairs of any amelioration of the human situation whatsoever. An emphasis solely on sin and guilt replaces the dialectical understanding of the relation between *imago Dei* and original sin, i.e., the acknowledgement that even fallen humanity still bears God's image and is capable of the exercise of rationality and virtue in civil affairs ("civil righteousness"). The result is the "cultural defeatism" that Reinhold Niebuhr, among others, considered to be characteristic of Lutheranism.

It is highly significant, however, that when this sort of pessimism regarding human nature appeared during the Reformation period itself, it was decisively rejected. Matthias Flacius (1520-75), a leader of the so-called Gnesio-Lutheran party, held so extreme a view of original sin that he could assert that the image of God in man has been utterly effaced, and replaced with the image of Satan. Original sin, he maintained, has become man's very nature. Over against this, the Lutheran Confessions (see especially the *Formula of Concord*, Article I) held to the Augustinian distinction between man's basic nature as God's creature, and the corruption--of horrendous dimensions, to be sure--which original sin has introduced into that nature. Thus, despite its strong doctrine of sin, Lutheranism maintained the basic affirmation of the world as God's good creation, and endorsed Luther's assertion

that, despite our impotence with respect to "the things that are
above us" (questions of justification and salvation), we do have
a genuine freedom to deal responsibly with "the things that are
below us," i.e., the whole realm of political and institutional
life.

It is noteworthy that this dispute revolved around the
question of human nature, and not the "Two Kingdoms" doctrine,
even though the latter has often been blamed for the alleged
defeatism of the Lutheran tradition. The Two Kingdoms doctrine
has indeed been highly influential, however, in Lutheran social-
ethical teaching, for good or ill; hence it is necessary to review
its basic elements.

The Doctrine of the "Two Kingdoms"

Studies of the origin of Luther's Two Kingdoms doctrine
have shown that it has antecedents as far back as the Old Testament
period, when the wisdom writers distinguished between the way of
the wise and the way of the foolish, or of the righteous and the
wicked. The contrast was heightened in the apocalyptic literature,
with its concept of the warfare of the "children of light" against
the "children of darkness," a notion that finds a strong echo in
the New Testament. The duality appears in the contrast between
Romans 12, in which Paul admonishes the Christians to govern
themselves by what amounts to the ethic of the Sermon on the
Mount ("Bless those who persecute you; bless and do not curse them"),
and Romans 13, where he endorses the use of punitive measures by
the state. It underlies St. Augustine's concept of the Two Cities--
the *civitas terrena*, created, as he puts it, by "the love of self,
even to the contempt of God," and the *civitas Dei*, created by "the
love of God, even to the contempt of self" (*The City of God*, Book
XIV, Ch. 28).

A factor that already affected to some extent Augustine's
thought, and that became more prominent as the medieval period
progressed, was that under the conditions of "Christendom," the
human membership of these two cities came to be identical--namely,
the populace of Christian Europe. What had originally referred
to two groups of people was thus transmuted into the notion of
two different but complementary functions within one spiritual-
temporal community. One spoke of the "two swords" or the "two
powers," namely, those wielded by the church and the state--by
papacy and empire, respectively. Both of these were held to be

ultimately subject to God; hence these were the two ways in which
God himself exercised dominion in the world.

Luther was heir to this whole complex of developments, and
it is this very complexity, no doubt, that accounts for the fact
that the Two Kingdoms notion does not function in his thought in
a univocal fashion. Sometimes, especially in the early Luther,
it seems to refer to *two realms* in the sense of discrete communities
(the "little flock" of Christians in the midst of an unbelieving
world). More often, it refers to *two forms of rule*, as in the
medieval scheme. Within the one civil and (in some sense) Christian
community, God rules "politically" through the Law, using civil
authorities as his instruments, and "religiously" through the Gospel,
using as his instrument the church. Scholars have distinguished
these as the concepts of *Zwei Reiche* and *Zwei Regimente* ("Two
Kingdoms" and "Two Governments"), respectively.

Yet other pairings can be correlated with these. The
"Kingdom of God's Left Hand," i.e., the political kingdom, is the
realm of "God's strange work," i.e., of wrath. The "Kingdom of
God's Right Hand," i.e., the spiritual kingdom, is the realm of
"God's proper work," i.e., of grace. The former is the realm of
the *Deus absconditus*, the latter that of the *Deus revelatus*. The
former, according to Luther's usual terminology, is the kingdom
of God the Father; the latter, the kingdom of Christ.

One of the chief functions of the Two Kingdoms doctrine
is thus to *distinguish* from one another certain dimensions, entities,
or institutions that ought not to be confused. Such a function was
very necessary in the late medieval situation, when the church
ranked as the largest landowner in Europe, and bishops and archbishops served as temporal sovereigns, while at the same time, the
state, under the aspect of "Christendom," had taken on a religious
aura. Luther employed the Two Kingdoms categories to re-establish
the distinctive nature and tasks of each. He recalled the church
to its servant role as a community of believers ruled only by the
Word, forsaking all worldly pomp or power. At the same time, he
re-emphasized the proper secularity of the state.

The Two Kingdoms doctrine also serves to distinguish the
realm of personal relations in which the Christian love ethic is
directly applicable, and the realm of institutional and political
relations where it must find indirect expression. The Christian
in his own person, according to Luther, is a subject of the kingdom
of Christ; but in his "office" (*Amt*), he is a subject of the worldly
kingdom. Between these two there will inevitably be some tension.

Secondly, and this is an implication of the first, the Two Kingdoms doctrine serves a *limiting* function. Each of the major components of the total reality known as Christendom-- namely, church and state--has an area of its distinctive competence, beyond which its writ does not run. Luther employed this limiting function decisively in his treatise of 1523, *On Temporal Authority: To What Extent It Should Be Obeyed*, which is rightly considered a key document for the study of his Two Kingdoms doctrine. The subtitle indicates the main concern of the treatise. The immediate occasion of its writing was the issuance of a decree by Duke George, of neighboring Ducal Saxony, requiring that all copies of Luther's recently issued German New Testament in the hands of the citizenry be surrendered. Luther's reply, in brief, is that the duke--or even the emperor himself--simply has no authority over such matters. "They have no power over souls," as Luther puts it. In modern terms, we may say that this was Luther's protest against totalitarianism, against the state's attempt to extend its sway over the whole of human life.

The limiting function also cuts the other way, indicating to the church the limits of its power or wisdom concerning civil affairs. In the Lutheran view, as we have already noted, an input of "secular expertise" is always necessary. Solutions to social problems that commend themselves out of the Christian conscience need to be tested against the harsh realities of life, and, often, only an approximation to the ideal will prove possible of realization.

Beyond these "distinguishing" and "limiting" functions, however, the Two Kingdoms doctrine also plays a critical and constructive role which, taken together, we may call its *prophetic* function. In the face of the tendency to conceive of God's sovereignty as extending only over personal life, or only over the ecclesiastical realm, it proclaims that the great world of social-institutional realities, of economic life, of power politics, also is God's kingdom, and hence is also subject to his judgment. Furthermore, it is the task of the church, through its preaching of the Word, to remind the world of this divine sovereignty. For the Word with which the church is entrusted includes both Law and Gospel, and the Law in its first function (the *usus civilis* or *usus politicus*) is specifically intended as a guide to human living-together in organized communities. The law in this sense is pre-eminently the law of justice, whether this be understood as distributive justice, in terms of the classic formula *suum cuique*, "Render to each his due"; as retributive justice, working through the judicial and penal systems; or as compensatory justice, expressed in the prophetic protest against oppression and the proclamation of God's bias in favor of the poor.

Luther's Political Preaching

It is this critical and constructive function of the Two Kingdoms doctrine above all, that finds expression in Luther's own writings on social questions. These writings customarily take two forms. In the first place, Luther's sermons and works of biblical exegesis are full of social and political commentary. Especially is this true of his commentaries on the Psalms, the prophets, and prophetic passages in the New Testament such as the Magnificat. He did not rest, in many instances, until he had applied the text not only tropologically (in terms of its relevance to the personal moral life), but also, we may say, sociologically. If by "political preaching" is meant an interpretation of the Christian message that addresses itself very concretely to the burning human issues of the time, then Luther was a political preacher *par excellence*.

The second form which Luther's social-ethical writings takes is that of tracts and treatises, a good number of which he devoted exclusively to social questions, while others touch on them in passing. His pivotal treatise of 1520, *To the Christian Nobility of the German Nation Concerning the Reform of the Christian Estate*, after dealing with the need for ecclesiastic reform, also runs through a whole gamut of issues in the social realm: the need for reform of education, the luxury and extravagance of the princes, the prevalence of begging and prostitution, the profiteering of the merchants and trading corporations. During the decade that followed, he published one or more special treatises devoted to each of these as well as other such problems. These writings reveal an astonishing range of knowledge of the social, economic, and political situation of the day, together with a willingness to "let the chips fall where they may" in his trenchant criticism of sharp practice, avarice and the abuse of power wherever these may be found.

Luther considered criticism of the authorities to be an inherent duty of the faithful preacher of the Word. As he states in his exposition of Psalm 82:

> To rebuke rulers is not seditious, provided it is
> done in the way here described: namely, by the office
> to which God has committed that duty, and through God's

> Word, spoken publicly, boldly and honestly. To rebuke
> rulers in this way is, on the contrary, a praiseworthy,
> noble, and rare virtue, and a particularly great service
> to God, as the Psalm here teaches. It would be far
> more seditious if a preacher did not rebuke the sins of
> the rulers; for then he makes people angry and sullen,
> strengthens the wickedness of tyrants, becomes a par-
> taker in it, and bears responsibility for it. (LW 13, 50)

In his writings on economic questions, Luther applies
this critical approach to an evaluation of the rising capitalism.
He shows himself distinctly unsympathetic to the new scheme of
things. Referring to the wealthy banking and trading families
such as the Fuggers, he asks rhetorically:

> How is it possible that in the lifetime of one
> man such great possessions, worthy of a king, can be
> piled up, and yet everything be done legally and
> according to God's will? I don't know, but what I
> really cannot understand is how a man with one hundred
> gulden can make a profit of twenty (gulden) in one
> year. (LW 44, 213)

Unlike Calvin, Luther did not accept any modification of the
traditional prohibition of usury. He held also to the medieval
notion of the "just price," a price that is not the highest that
can be obtained but the fairest, according to both economic and
ethical criteria. Economic life also, in Luther's view, was to
be an expression of "faith active in love."

Luther's writings on education, such as his treatise *To
the Councilmen of All Cities in Germany That They Establish and
Maintain Christian Schools* (1524) contain important proposals
for educational innovation and reform. His writings on the problem
of poverty, particularly as expressed in the prevalence of begging,
develop plans which are in many respects the prototype of a modern
social welfare system (see *Ordinance of a Common Chest*, 1523).
In his writings on the question of war, he adopts the lineaments
of the traditional "just war" doctrine, according to which, for
the most part, only defensive wars are justified. The war against
"the Turk" (the Ottoman forces besieging Southeastern Europe) is
justified, for Luther, only on this basis, as such an act of
collective self-defense, not as a holy crusade, despite the fact
that it represented the encounter of the forces of Christendom with
those of Islam. The cause of Christ, Luther insisted, could
neither be defended nor advanced by military means. As to the
individual soldier, Luther advised that a Christian could serve
as such with good conscience if he was convinced that the war was
just, but if not, he should refuse to fight, despite his lord's
command.

On one issue posterity has judged Luther especially
harshly; indeed his contemporaries already did so. This is the
issue of his reaction to the Peasants' Rebellion of 1525. His
three tracts on the subject, published in quick succession
during that year, show that initially he had a strong sympathy
with the peasants' grievances, and did not hesitate to rebuke the
lords for their callous unconcern. But he was appalled at the
peasants' taking up arms to secure their demands; and he also
objected, theologically, to their doing so under the banner of the
Gospel. Reacting with his customary bluntness, he called on the
princes to put down the revolt by any means necessary. The
rebellion was crushed with a great deal of bloodshed. Its failure,
together with the hostility to all such mass-based movements that
the experience engendered, is thought by some historians to have
delayed the development of political and social democracy in
Germany by centuries.

Luther shows himself in this incident unable to transcend
the view that although certain demands of an underclass might be
deemed justified, no fundamental change in social structures or
redistribution of political power could be envisioned. This was
only partially qualified by his later endorsement of the "right to
resist" when, in 1530 and the years following, the evangelical
movement was threatened with extirpation by military action on
the part of the emperor (see *Dr. Martin Luther's Warning to His
Dear German People*, LW 47, 3ff.). Although this tract served to
undergird the Lutherans in their resistance both in the Smalcaldic
War (1546-1555) and in subsequent struggles, the endorsement of
such resistance when the faith itself was threatened did not lead
to the development of a full-fledged theory of democracy, as
occurred in progressive stages within Calvinism, especially
seventeenth century Puritanism. The fact that the government of
the Lutheran churches was taken over by the princes, acting as
Notbischofe ("emergency bishops")--a system that became the more
deeply rooted as time passed--only served to confirm this inherent
conservatism.

Conservative and Renewing Tendencies

In the period of Lutheran Orthodoxy (roughly coinciding
with the seventeenth century) we find these conservative tendencies
yet further reinforced. The horrors of the Thirty Years War, with
the massive loss of life, amounting perhaps to one-third of the

population of Germany, together with the widespread pillage, looting
and destruction of livestock, crops, and property, induced a
profound feeling of gratitude to any government that could preserve
a minimum of order.

A characteristic feature of Lutheran Orthodox theology is
the treatment of social-ethical questions within the framework
of the *Dreiständelehre*, the doctrine of the three "estates" or
"orders." These orders are the "domestic" (or "economic"), the
"political" and the "ecclesiastical," the first two composing what
had been, for Luther, the left-hand kingdom, and the last, the
right-hand kingdom. Each of these orders has been instituted by
God, and each has its specific functions:

> The "domestic" order is devoted to the multipli-
> cation of the human race; the "political," to its
> protection; the "ecclesiastical," to its promotion to
> eternal salvation. The "domestic" estate has been
> established by God against wandering lusts; the
> "political" against tyranny and robbery; the
> "ecclesiastical" against heresies and corruptions of
> doctrine. (Heinrich Schmid, *The Doctrinal Theology of
> the Evangelical Lutheran Church* [Philadelphia, 1889],
> p. 608, summarizing the thought of Gerhard.)

The intention here is very close to the Reformation
notion of *zwei Regimente* ("two governments"): God works in diverse
ways through diverse institutions to accomplish his purposes. In
this sense, the full scope of the divine sovereignty proclaimed
by the Reformation is retained. The note of joy in the goodness
of the created order recedes, however, behind the heavy emphasis
on the ordering or restrictive functions. And the division of
labor between the three estates is so interpreted as to undercut
the prophetic function of the church, which, according to Orthodoxy,
has no calling to interfere in political affairs. This, of course,
fitted in perfectly with the developing political absolutism of the
time. The contrast to Luther's bold use of the pulpit and the pen
to castigate the authorities is obvious.

Pietism, which arose within Lutheranism in the seventeenth
century as a protest against what it considered the spiritual
lassitude of Orthodoxy, may be viewed as, in important respects,
a movement of ethical renewal. The Pietists called for an emphasis
on life, not doctrine; on faith as a personal God-relationship
issuing in acts of compassion, not merely as assent to dogma.
Holiness was fostered, inspired, and confirmed in the meetings of
conventicles (small groups for prayer, Bible study and the sharing
of personal concerns). In contrast to Orthodoxy, which tended to
reinforce class distinctions, Pietism tended to soften them, since

masters and servants, persons of wealth and those of moderate
means, met together in the intimacy of these groups. The virtues
of thrift, honesty and diligence in work (those comprising what
later came to be known as "the Protestant ethic") were fostered,
thus making Pietists very attractive as workers or colonists.

One of the most tangible historical effects of Pietism
is to be found in the works of mercy undertaken under its auspices,
and in the institutions founded for this purpose. Pietists were
active in every kind of charitable venture. At Halle, the great
Pietist leader August Herman Francke (1663-1727) erected homes
for widows and orphans, established schools for the poor, offered
vocational training programs, and operated a publishing house and
a pharmaceutical enterprise. Programs were established elsewhere
for the physically handicapped, for mental defectives, for refugees
and prisoners of war. Pietists also were active in educational
reform, working to introduce a more experiential and practice-
oriented approach. All of these concerns found expression not
only in Germany but wherever Lutherans were to be found, including
the far-flung overseas missions which themselves were inspired
largely by Pietism.

With respect to these dimensions of personal ethical renewal
and the performance of the works of mercy, Pietism may be regarded
as an expression of Luther's own basic principle or paradigm of
"faith active in love." In two very important respects, however,
the ethics of Pietism differed from that of the Reformation. We
have noted above that the Lutheran Reformation involved a profound
"affirmation of the secular," which is to say that it was not
fundamentally ascetical in character. It was able to enjoy natural
human pleasures with a good conscience. With Pietism the motif
of asceticism was reborn. In this respect as well as others,
Pietism had much in common with monasticism; indeed, it has been
dubbed "monasticism outside the monastery." Smoking and drinking
were disapproved of; dancing, card-playing and theatre-going were
prohibited; and frivolity in general was frowned upon. Sexuality
was viewed with suspicion, and even within marriage its expression
was to be characterized by sobriety and restraint.

A second very important difference between Pietism and the
Reformation lies in Pietism's lack of a social ethic in the proper
sense, that is, an ethic for the social orders and institutions
as such, rather than merely for the Christian individual active
within these orders. In fact, even the latter was largely lacking,
since the Reformation emphasis on the secular calling as the major

arena of Christian actions was replaced by the Pietist emphasis
on dedication to the *ecclesiola in ecclesia*, and, beyond that, to
the aforementioned works of mercy. Pietism offered no ethic for
the political life as such. Its view of the world beyond the
borders of the churchly realm was predominantly negative; it
engaged in what a modern Lutheran theologian, Gustav Aulén, has
called the "false blackening of the world." In this sense, Pietism
may be said to have had only a "One Kingdom" doctrine. It knew
only the kingdom of the redeemed, not the kingship of God operating
also through secular structures. If, with respect to the motif
of asceticism, it could be called monasticism outside the monastery
in this second respect Pietism may be viewed as a form of sectarian
appearing on the soil of the church (using these terms in the sense
of the contrast between world-affirmation and world-negation
suggested by Troeltsch).

The Challenge of Modern Society

        Having surveyed Luther's thought on the secular calling
and social ethics, together with the viewpoints of Orthodoxy and
Pietism, we have reviewed the major influences that have determined
the classic Lutheran position on these questions. The story of
the period since the French Revolution is a story of manifold
challenges to this position, some of which have been met creatively,
while others have occasioned only a defensive reaction.
        Undoubtedly one of the most significant of these challenges
was the rapid growth of urbanization and industrialization in
central Europe in the nineteenth century. The rise of the "Inner
Mission" under the leadership of J.H. Wichern (1808-1881) may be
viewed as a response to that challenge. Many of the specific
works undertaken by the Inner Mission were comparable to those
of Pietism, adjusted to correspond to the new conditions connected
with the appearance of an urban proletariat. Hostels and training
centers were established for the unemployed, for delinquent youth,
for the handicapped, etc. What was distinctive about the Inner
Mission was the comprehensive vision that underlay these manifold
activities. Wichern perceived in the alienation of the urban
masses from a church that seemed unconcerned about their plight,
a threat both to the future of Christianity and to the stability
of the social order. It is no accident that Wichern's "Protestant
Manifesto," issued in Wittenberg in 1848 over the grave of Martin
Luther, followed by less than a year the issuance of the "Communist

Manifesto." The Inner Mission was to comprise not only a set of charitable institutions, but a broad social movement that by meeting both the spiritual and the physical needs of the masses would eliminate the appeal of the revolutionary currents of the time.

The annual *Kirchentag*, a mass assembly or conference of Protestant laity, which was initiated at this time, served to highlight the "social question." Later, other movements were developed such as the *Evangelischer sozialer Kongress* (Protestant Social Congress), led by Adolf Stöcker, which addressed more directly the problems of social change. A further step in this direction was the emergence of the Religious Socialist movement under the inspiration of the Blumhardts and others. But from these more radical positions the official Lutheran churches held aloof. More typical of the central trend was the work of Wilhelm Loehe (1808-72) and Friedrich von Bodelschwingh (1831-1910), under whose leadership vast clusters of educational and healing institutions were established at Neuendettelsau and Bethel bei Bielefeld, respectively. On questions of public policy, the lead was given by the great conservative jurist and ideologist, Friedrich Julius Stahl (1802-61).

In the "neo-Lutheran" or Confessional Lutheran theology that flourished during the latter half of the nineteenth century, Luther's doctrine of the Two Kingdoms was interpreted in such a way as to locate the influence of the church on the social order chiefly in its fundamental work of molding the ethos of the people. Any more direct form of political witness or intervention by the clergy or other official representatives of the church was considered inappropriate. Also working to blunt the effect of Christian social witness at this time was the notion of *Eigengesetzlichkeit*, the "autonomy" of the various social realms (the economic, the political, etc.), a notion to which the new social sciences contributed. Each realm, it was thought, follows its own laws, which could, one hoped, be discovered by diligent investigation, but which could not be altered by moral effort. Natural law in this (empirical) sense was of course very different from natural law in the older (moral) sense as held by a Luther. Even those most concerned to awaken a sense of Christian social responsibility in the late nineteenth and early twentieth centuries were inhibited by this notion of the inexorable character of social or historical "laws."

Although most of the above discussion has referred to developments in Germany, which remained the heartland of Lutheranism,

similar trends were to be observed elsewhere, and comparable types
of Inner Mission institutions were developed. A unique feature
on the scene in Denmark was the work of N.F.S. Grundtvig (1783-
1872), which was noteworthy for its combination of impulses
toward cultural and ecclesiastical renewal. Grundtvig's slogan,
"first a man, then a Christian," represented a reassertion of
Luther's very positive attitude toward the natural and "secular"
dimensions of life, in contrast to Kierkegaard's stress on
inwardness and paradoxical faith. The Christian life was to be
premised on the development of a wholesome and robust, not
constricted, humanity. The folk school movement founded by
Grundtvig was a major influence in revivifying Danish culture
and creating a sense of responsible citizenship among the common
people. Likewise in Sweden, Lutheranism proved to be compatible
with the development of what is widely regarded as a model
political and social democracy.

In Germany, however, the alliance of "throne and altar"
endured much longer, and it can be said that German Lutheranism
did not awake to the full range of its social and political
responsibilities until the German nation had experienced the
bitterness of defeat and, subsequently, the catastrophe of
destruction, in the two World Wars. The Lutheran attitude toward
the rise of Nazism was, at best, equivocal. Hitler's efforts to
dominate the church itself by dictating its theology or leadership
were stoutly resisted, but, with some notable exceptions, the
Nazi social and political program, including its anti-Semitism,
was not opposed. From the time of the reaching of the *Nullpunkt*
("point zero") of complete national collapse in 1945, however,
German Lutheranism has seen a remarkable upsurge of Christian
social concern and action. Study committees and synodical assemblies
have issued pronouncements on problems of industry and agriculture,
domestic politics and international relations. And in the
"Evangelical Academies," most of them founded since 1945, hundreds
of thousands of lay persons have been brought together--frequently
grouped by occupation--to discuss the ethical dilemmas arising
in professional as well as public life. Here is a significant
recovery of the Reformation emphasis on the secular calling as
the intended locus for manifesting "Christian love and genuine good
works."

Lutherans, of course, were found on both sides of the
barricades during the Second World War. In Norway, Bishop Eivind
Berggrav (1884-1959), a leader in the resistance movement,
testified that Luther gave him the example and the inspiration for

his defiance of the occupying authorities. This was the Luther
of the cry, "Here I stand, I can do no other;" the Luther whose
treatise *On Secular Authority* was written chiefly to demonstrate
the limits of that authority.

In the United States, the development of a Lutheran social
conscience long was inhibited by the Lutherans' position as a
minority group still largely worshiping in a foreign tongue. For
this reason, as well as on account of theological differences,
the earlier "Social Gospel" movement left Lutheranism largely
untouched. More recent decades, however, have seen intense efforts
on the part of Lutheran scholars and churchmen to develop a
responsible social ethic, the results of which are seen in the
work of national and regional study committees and church assemblies
in addressing the issues of war and peace, poverty, race relations,
ecology, urbanization, and the like, as well as in the action of
local parishes on such issues.

In Eastern Europe, Lutheranism has had to learn how to
co-exist with Marxist socialist regimes, and for the most part has
come to affirm also this form of secularity, while reserving the
right of criticism. Likewise, the Lutherans of the "third world"--
in Chile, Brazil, Argentina, Namibia, Tanzania, India and else-
where--also have faced the challenge of a revolutionary situation,
in some cases retreating to a dualistic form of the Two Kingdoms
doctrine, in other cases espousing a "theology of liberation" that
calls for a considerable revision of that doctrine.

For most Lutherans, the "twoness" still remains, for
salvation cannot be wholly identified with social justice; but
the impact of the realm of redemption upon the realm of creation
and its structures is now seen to be much more pervasive and
dynamic than was formerly understood. As they come to identify
more closely with the aspirations of the urban and rural proletariats
of the world, Lutherans may conclude that the moment has come to
reconsider, as it were, their attitude toward the Peasants'
Rebellion, and to take a much more sympathetic attitude toward
the prospect of radical social change than did Luther at that time.
The development of Lutheran social-ethical thinking still continues.

CHAPTER 11

JOHANNES AAGAARD

MISSIONARY THEOLOGY

Much literature about Luther forgets that his theology is a missionary theology. It is true that one cannot find a separate missionary theology in his writings, but the reason is that his whole mind was fixed upon one thing and one thing only: the coming of the kingdom and its consequences for the world and the church. To him everything hinges on God and God's message to humankind in Jesus Christ. Luther's life story is the story of a man who dedicated everything to the spreading of that message, outside the church as well as inside it.

In Luther's theology the spreading of the pure Gospel is the decisive sign of the church. Again and again he returns to this conviction: The church is known as the church of Christ by its proclamation of the true Gospel, and all other signs of the church are aspects of the Gospel. The *viva vox evangelica*, i.e. the living voice of the Gospel and the spreading of that Gospel is at the center of all Luther's thinking about the church and its relation to the world.

It has, however, been maintained that Luther, because of his eschatological expectation and because of his insistence on "God alone" and "faith alone" - without human assistance - did not have and could not have a missionary theology and consequently no missionary motivation and missionary action. Such a view is totally out of touch with reality. Exactly his eschatological expectancy and his theocentric theology contributed to his evangelistic zeal and missionary passion.

The Coming Kingdom of God.

In his Large Catechism Luther writes (on the second prayer of Our Father) that the prayer about the coming of God's kingdom expects the kingdom to come *to two groups* (p. 427). The kingdom will come to those who are not within this kingdom and on the other hand to those who have received the kingdom and followed it.

The prayer, however, also expects the kingdom to come in *two ways*. It will come in time - here and now - through the Word and the faith. On the other hand it will come eternally through the revelation, i.e. the advent of Christ at the end of time.

The expectant prayer thus asks for the coming of the kingdom to two groups in two ways. First we have to pray that the Gospel will be preached purely and sincerely throughout the whole world. But we also have to pray that the kingdom will reign among us powerfully through the Word and the power of the Holy Spirit. To these two groups the kingdom comes in two ways: in time and as a future reality, as eternal life.

In this fourfold manner the kingdom aims at uprooting the kingdom of the Devil, so that the Devil loses all right and power over people. The fourfold manner of the one kingdom of God expresses *the one mission of God* to save all people from the powers of evil.

This is Lutheran missionary theology in brief. It is as simple as that and still so difficult to grasp in its simple wholeness. In Lutheran missionary thinking however this fourfold model is often corrupted.

The corruption takes place:
1) when the coming of the kingdom is understood as a reality for believers only, as something happening within the church, or
2) when the coming of the kingdom is seen as something relevant for the world only, with no consequences for the life of the church, or
3) when the coming of the kingdom is seen as a reality, here and now only, a kerygmatic event without consequences for the future, or
4) when the opposite tendency prevails and the kingdom is seen as lightning on the apocalyptic horizon without reality in time and history.

One could write the history of Lutheran missionary theology on this pattern, for always - when this wholeness was lost,

sectarian tendencies took over and perverted the expectation of
the coming kingdom and the missionary orientation of the church.
This is an urgent problem in Lutheran missionary thinking and
missionary work all over the world even today.

The Instrumentality of the Church

Luther's theology is theocentric. He recognizes no other
subject for the coming of the kingdom than God, the Father, the
Son and the Holy Spirit. It is correct that a tenor is found in
Luther's theology whereby one could get the impression that God
alone, the Gospel alone, Faith alone is active - without people.
The mission of God is seen as God's own mission to such an extent,
that human beings seem to be entirely unnecessary. Lutherans
often took that consequence from Luther's theology and a specific
Lutheran quietism has been the result.

But this is not fair to Luther. Other statements clearly
express the understanding that God uses people in his mission to
the world. In his brilliant treatise on the *Bondage of the Will*
(*De servo arbitrio*), Luther lets *ratio* (i.e. reason) argue that
as a consequence of the majestic power of God, God could manage
without human beings. Luther clearly affirms this, but adds that
God *will* co-operate with people, that God *will* use people as
co-workers. God could do everything alone, but God does not do
everything along. "Thus it is through us he preaches, shows
mercy to the poor, comforts the afflicted." (LW 33, 243. = WA
18, 754).

Once seen this is obvious, because for Luther the church
as the people of God, the body of Christ and the community of the
Holy Spirit is always God's instrument. The church is saved to
participate in the history of salvation. Luther can express himself
very unguardedly, as when, for instance, he states that people are
to be saved through us, as we are saved through those who were
before us.

In the same context Luther develops what he calls "the
highest and true order of a Christian life". This threefold
order is by nature a missionary order. The first part of this
order is the proclamation of the Gospel which through us comes to
the whole world. The second part is the persecution, whereby the
world reacts against the church in order to test its faith.
Thereby the sins of the church are mortified and the old Adam

exorcised. Consequently the third part of this *Ordo Christianae Vitae* is the emergence of the fruits of the Spirit in loving service to human-kind (WA 14: 6181, 28ff. = LW 9, 184ff.).

This order is another expression of what Luther called *the priesthood of all believers*. This concept may not be explicitly mentioned very often in Luther's own theology, but it is never-theless inherent in all his thinking. His statements about the church always imply that the whole church has the obligation for mission. There are no indications of a theology - as was later developed in Lutheran Orthodoxy - whereby the ministry was taken over by one group, the pastors. In Luther's thinking the ministry and the mission is a dimension in the life of the church as such. The promise and the mandate was given by Christ to all believers, to the whole church, including its pastors. But pastors serve the church in order that the church can serve the world.

Luther uses a variety of terms to signify the nature of the church: congregation, communion, people, body, bride, etc., and he stresses that even a 7-year-old child knows what the church is, namely, the "Holy believers and sheep, who hear the voice of their Shepherd" (Sm. Art. Part III, XII, p. 315).

The important point which Luther stresses by these "names" is the community-nature of the church. Over against the anonymous, institutional, hierarchical church of his time he points to a church consisting of people in community. W. Löhe expressed a genuine Lutheran standpoint when he said: "A human being could not become saved alone...alone I should not like to become saved" (Ges. Werke, Vol. 5, I 1954, p. 88). To be saved means to become a part of Christ's love, and love is impossible, when one is alone.

But in communio - in the church - Christian love is a natural consequence of the Gospel. And this love is by nature a serving love, serving other people with the Gospel in word and deed. For Luther the promise and the mandate belonged closely together. Without the promise, i.e. the Gospel, no mandate, but also no Gospel without the mandate. The whole church - the community of believers was understood in this perspective, i.e. as "a creature of the Word of God" *and* as a preacher of the Word of God.

The church is thus not to be understood as an addendum of individual Christians all having their faith in relation to God alone. The church, as the family of God, implies the mutual love and trust among the members of the family and the reaching out in this love to other people in service. In his "The German Mass" from 1526 (LW 19.72ff. = WA 19,72ff.) Luther describes the

consequences of this communio-concept of the church. Even if he
did not have the necessary people to realize the vision, he looks
forward to the coming into existence of "house-congregations"
which were able "to preach the Gospel with hand and mouth."

The One Mission and the Two Kingdoms

This article stated at its beginning that the one kingdom
of God is manifested to two groups and in two ways. There is
only one aim for the mission of the kingdom of God: to abolish
the kingdom of the devil. The famous and notorious doctrine of
the two kingdoms is to be understood against this background.
Otherwise this doctrine will easily beomce perverted into a
dangerous double-thinking. Where such double-thinking prevails
the two kingdoms are understood as *God's* kingdom operating on
the level of creation in the human and secular world, and *Christ's*
kingdom operating on the level of salvation in the Christian
church. The first level is then characterized as horizontal,
temporal, visible, external, relative etc. and the second level
is called vertical, eternal, invisible, internal, absolute, total
etc.

Such double-thinking has become very popular, although
it sharply contrasts Luther's own theology. Its main inspiration
stems from 19th century liberal as well as anti-liberal ideology.
(*Umdeutungen der Zweireichelehre Luthers im 19 Jahrhundert*, Texte
zur Kirchen- und Theologiegeschichte 21, 1975 and *Die Ambivalenz
der Zweireichelehre in lutherischen Kirchen des 20. Jahrhunderts* Text
22, 1976). One can find support for it in some of Luther's early
writings, but only if those texts are taken out their context
and interpreted without reference to the wholeness of Luther's
thinking.

When Luther speaks about *the two kingdoms* he first of all
speaks about the kingdom of God set against the kingdom of the
devil. This antagonism is at the bottom of his whole theology,
and it is definitely *not* to be identified with the relation between
the church and the world. The kingdom of the devil is at war
against God Luther says, both within the church and outside the
church, and consequently the kingdom of God fights the devil in
both church and world.

The medieval tendency of understanding the history of
salvation as identical with the history of the church and vice
versa was rejected by Luther. His famous concept of *weltlich*

Regiment, i.e. worldly rule, in reality means that God is also
fighting the devil in the world, that God is not only active in
the church, but works for the salvation of humankind in all ages
and all places.

For Luther the concept of creation thus expresses a very
positive understanding of human life. God's creation is life as
it comes to us daily, always inspiring us to work and service.
To live a life in faith does not mean to leave this life of God's
creation; in each person's daily routine (*vocatio*), God has to
be served.

Monastic life and religious vocations are therefore no
more part of the history of the kingdom than life in the world
and in the worldly vocations. In the worldly vocations the love
of God is to be transformed into service for the neighbor. The
way in which Luther picked up the "holy" word *vocation* and used
it for secular and human activities of Christians meant a drastic
change of the concept of the mission of the church. Faith in
Christ was seen as a liberating force, whereby human life became
a meaningful vocation and a joyful gift of God shared with others
in the mission of God.

Vocation thus became a term used for the life of *all*
Christians, no longer reserved for priests and religious people.
To take up one's cross and follow Jesus no longer implied a
denial of the world and its secular realities, for *in* these
realities the vocation of Christ had to be realized. "The cross
in the calling" (Wingren) means the cross of Christ taken up by
all Christians, irrespective of their social and cultural level.
The cutting edge of this *theologia crucis*, this theology of the
cross in Luther's thinking is the acceptance of the true worldliness
of the life of a Christian.

This missionary theology is a heritage given to the whole
church, not just to the Lutherans. From its insights the false
dichotomies can be opposed: the dichotomy between church and
world, between holy and secular, between priests and lay people,
between vocational and profane work.

Luther himself did not engage in a missionary out-reach of
a particularist nature. "A particularist mission would have been
as alien to Luther as a particularist church" (H.W. Gensichen).

Luther did the much more important job of "turning the
church inside out", or rather that was his intention, which can
be seen from his writings. The reality as a whole never fulfilled
his expectation, but the vision was handed down to the coming
generations.

Luther related his preaching of the Gospel and his activity
in the reform of the church to the factual missionary situation,
which was at hand. This first of all is seen in his honest
recognition of the vast missionary task among *the nominal Christians*
of his day. But in connection with this he also considered the
responsibility for the mission to the Jews and the Moslems, the
two concrete groups of non-Christians with whom he had contact.
His early attitude to *the Jews* and his understanding of the
Christian obligation in relation to the Jews is found in his book
"Dass Jesus Christus ein geborener Jude sei" from 1523. His
later writings, however, spoke in the most cruel way against his
own theology and contributed to anti-semitism. Luther's attitude
to the *Moslems* was marked by the defensive attitude of the
Christendom of his time, but Luther quite clearly expresses the
missionary obligation in relation to the Moslem world (C. Simon).

Nationalization and Orthodoxy

Experiencing the corruption in the church and the opposition
from the leaders of the church against the Reformation, Luther at
the same time found it possible to mobilize support and assistance
from the secular princes of his time. This became to him a vivid
demonstration of his teaching about the reality of the devil in
the church and the work of God in the world.

Luther therefore found it quite easy to accept the beginnings
of what later became the typical Lutheran state-church relationship, the unity of state and church, the National Lutheran churches.
This development definitely broke the Catholic unity, and a
nationalization of the Lutheran faith took place.

The marriage between secular powers and the new Lutheran
churches created the climate in which Luther's movement of renewal
was transformed into a rigid doctrinal and scholastic system:
Lutheran Orthodoxy. The churches became pastor churches, and the
pastors became civil servants under the respective kings or
princes. The open and missionary church of the Reformation and
"the priesthood of all believers" simply disappeared, and the laity
became a passive object for the ministry of the pastors and the
power of the government. In this way the church lost jurisdiction
over its own ministry, and, bound to clearly defined nations,
districts or parishes, it matched the situation with a theology
undermining the missionary character of the whole church. Vocation
was redefined as clerical vocation and a lot of specifications
were added characterizing the vocation as internal or external,

extraordinary or ordinary, mediated or not mediated, etc. But at any rate vocation no longer meant the vocation of the people of God in its mission to the world.

Lutheran Orthodoxy found support in some of Luther's own writings. Luther time and again warned against the *Schwärmer* i.e. enthusiasts who neglected their daily duties in order to go from house to house like the apostles in Matthew 10. Luther maintained that such people were *not* apostles and had no apostolic calling to missionary work. Their "calling" was wrong, invalid and harmful.

Lutheran Orthodoxy made the following deduction: to preach the Gospel one has to have a valid and legitimate calling, namely an external calling received in the ordinary way, i.e. mediated by the secular authority. People who argue that God has given them a special vocation and want to obey such a vocation, have to prove their extraordinary vocation by extraordinary deeds. Luther spoke about such heroic people and called them *Gottes Wunderleute*. They were acceptable on the basis of an extraordinary vocation, only because they were extraordinary people.

Lutheran Orthodoxy only mentioned an extraordinary, internal and not mediated vocation in order to reject such a possibility, thereby underlining the ordinary vocations of the pastors, representing king and authority, and of the *status politicus*, by the grace of God governing the country and its obedient people.

An interesting debate in the 1590s between Hadrian Saravia and Johan Gerhard throws light on the understanding of mission within Protestant Orthodoxy. Hadrian Saravia (1531-1613) - "foreign minister" for the Anglican establishment - wrote an important book in 1590 about the mission and ministry of the church (*De Diversis Ministrorum Evangelii Gradibus*...). He argued that the apostolic mandate to mission always belongs to the church and its ministry, and that being the case the ministry has to be episcopal. The episcopal order belongs to the missionary nature of the church. Without the episcopal ministry there is no possible vocation for missionary work. *Successio evangelii* is identical with *successio episcoporum*.

The Lutheran theologian J. Gerhard (1582-1637) attacked Saravia in his *Loci Theologici* (Locus XXIII). Gerhard arrived at the conclusion that neither the apostolate nor the apostolic mandate to mission exist in the church. The apostolate was both extraordinary and temporary and since no ministry today has got the unlimited mandate of the apostles, there is no vocation according to Gerhard, to evangelize the world as a whole.

The basic difference between Saravia and Gerhard turns on the understanding of the church. For Saravia the *church* received the missionary mandate "in the persons of the apostles", and consequently the *church* still has the mandate. Gerhard did not even consider the ecclesiological aspects of the problem. He limits himself to a discussion of the difference between an apostle and a pastor, and since pastors today can only have limited vocations, he cannot see how the missionary obligation should be a living reality in the churches of the 17th century. Gerhard is in this respect very representative of Lutheran Orthodoxy and its "nationalization" of mission theology (W. Grössel).

Further expression of the same theological attitude is found in Samuel Schelwig's (1643-1715) *Leitstern des Gewissens* which became very important in the neo-confessional missionary theology of the 19th century. Schelwig maintains that no missionary could be *rite vocatus*. In 1651 the theological Faculty in Wittenberg in a similar way clearly stated that the missionary mandate only aimed at "the dear apostles and disciples of Lord Christ" because only they had "an immediate vocation" for such mission.

The loss of the church as a corporate and concrete reality standing independently and having its own mission was first of all caused by the absorption of the church into the national establishments, and the ideological result was the understanding of the church as the *invisible church*. The state church and the invisible church fit together perfectly. What was lost in that "marriage" was the mission and service of the church to the world, its world mission and its world service.

Not the church as the people of God, but the individual Christian in his or her direct relationship to God was at the center of Lutheran theology in a way which became a preparation for the mystic trends which later developed into the different forms of Pietism. The most genuine forms of this early orthodox piety is found in the great Lutheran hymns from the 17th century, e.g. those of P. Gerhardt (1607-1676).

By and large the Gospel thus became isolated within the Christian territories as a part of Christendom. But when these territories expanded and the kings thereby acquired new citizens, it belonged to the Christian duty of these kings to make sure that the new areas were Christianized. Thus the Danish king for instance contributed to the extension of the Danish church in the Danish colonies of the Gold Coast in West Africa and Trankebar in India as well as in Greenland.

It is futile to discuss whether such territorial expansion is to be called mission or not. The main point is that the Lutheran churches under the nationalization in Orthodoxy lost their missionary self-understanding and that, of course, was true also of their congregations in the colonies. The church of Luther became so integrated in the national states that the whole concept of the one, missionary church tended to disappear. The church no longer had the character of a community, a people, a body. It became so integrated into the national states that "church" came to mean "the pastors".

Important to remember is the fact of the great confessional wars of the time of Orthodoxy. The "Christian" nations were so eagerly engaged in destroying one another, that as a whole no serious attempts were made to reach the world with the Gospel. Attention was given all the time to problems within the churches.

This statement, however, has to be counterbalanced by the fact that the Catholic church, since the Reformation, had always managed to launch missions to the new worlds. What was lost to the Protestants was to be gained from the gentiles! But this "mission" was most certainly not the best possible inspiration for the Lutherans and other Protestants, embedded as it was in Spanish and Portuguese expansion and part of its atrocities.

Confrontation of Pietism and Confessionalism in the Mission Enterprise

It is often said and with some justice that Pietism brought a renewal of the church for mission. At any rate the various pietist movements meant a revival of the responsibility of some lay people. But not of "the laity." Pietism can not be said to have brought back "the priesthood of all believers." It rather established the priesthood of the specific believers. It did not regain the ordinary Christian vocation as the basis for the life and mission of the laity, but established a specific individual vocation as a privilege of the true, pietist believers.

As a part of the mystic Catholic piety found its way into Pietism, the traditional Catholic concept of vocation as something reserved for the religious elite in the churches was revitalized in the pietist movements. This is not said in order to reduce the importance of Pietism for Lutheran missionary theology and missionary practice. The pietists did what was possible in their time and under their circumstances. A real renewal of the concept of the missionary church was still far ahead.

The Moravians (Herrnhuter), under Count Zinzendorf (1700–1760), functioned in reality as a large religious order, living collectively under strict authority and totally dedicated to their Savior. Their lay missionaries went around the world to find the souls already prepared by the Lord for his salvation.

Also *the pietists from Halle*, under A.H. Francke (1663–1727), lived and worked collectively. Their teaching had more Lutheran substance, and their missionary work e.g. in India took place under the doctrinal and legal supervision of the Lutheran Danish king and his theological establishment.

The pietists from Württemberg, inspired by the genius J.A. Bengel (1687–1752), developed their own strange universe, apocalyptic and partly theosophic. They found their missionary outlet mainly through the Basel-mission which became the first of the long series of 19th century missionary societies.

One is tempted to mention the *Methodists* as the fourth type of "Lutheran" pietistic mission, since the Methodists from the beginning were inspired by Luther and the Lutheran pietists, and since so many Methodists paid back this debt through genuine service to Lutheran churches and institutions. In a number of the new missionary societies from the 19th century one finds Methodist influence and this also holds true of the Bible societies on the European continent.

The neo-pietistic movements in the 19th century came in two mainstreams, one in each half of the century. They meant a revival of Lutheran mission and Lutheran missionary theology. The main focus of these movements was a radical kingdom of God theology, which aimed at regaining the same eschatological expectancy which is found in Luther's own thinking. At the same time these revivals intended to regain corporate Christian community, which could speak and act as the people of God at home and abroad. These movements were, however, so influenced by the individualism and subjectivism of the 19th century liberalism that they in many and important ways became foreign to Lutheran theology. Thereby they became one of the reasons for the neo-confessional come-back, which already from 1836 was an important fact in the life and mission of the Lutheran churches on the European continent. In that year the Dresden mission, which later developed into the Leipzigermission was started (see J. Aagaard I, p. 196f., 328f.; II, p. 526f.).

The specific Lutheran influence on 19th century missionary theology is found in two areas. The first Lutheran protest was

expressed by opposition against the non-confessional character
of the new missionary societies from Basel, Barmen, Bremen,
Berlin etc. which tried to keep their missionary activity at a
distance from confessional definitions of mission. For them
mission as an undertaking of faith and love has its standpoint
neither in Wittenberg, nor in Geneva, nor in Rome, but in
Jerusalem. "When it comes to the expansion of the kingdom of
God among the heathens, the faithful stand with their master on
Mount Olive in the important hour, when the Lord gave the command
to mission and at the same time the instruction of his messengers..."
(J. Aagaard I, p. 253).

The new societies definitely wanted to remain "over-
confessional" or "a-confessional", and therefore they kept away
from the actual confessional institutions. They did not need
their confirmation, because they operated on the mandate of the
Holy Spirit. Their ministry was given directly to them by Jesus.

The confessional protest was first of all directed against
this neglect of Lutheran loyalty. But Lutheran confessionalism
in general rose as a front against the Prussian Union, the unity
movement forced upon the churches by the royal family and the
state church structures. The need to keep a Lutheran identity at
home came to mean a similar need for Lutheran identity abroad.
But also vice versa. When congregations in Asia and Africa became
a reality they were not communities of a-confessional "Gold-
Christians." They tended to look more or less like the normal
congregations at home and to have the same need for doctrinal
clarification and rules for an orderly life. But according to
which order were the new Christians to be baptized, confirmed and
married? Which liturgies were the best for holy Communion? The
confessional answers "came back" in this way.

But the Lutheran protest against the missionary movement
was also directed against *the concept of vocation* which was
dominant in the societies. Trying to be faithful to the Lutheran
tradition, the voices of Johan Gerhard and Samuel Schelwig were
heard again. Almost all the Lutheran leaders in Germany in the
19th century participated in a discussion about mission, confession
and church, which became very influential for the development of
a Lutheran sense of identity. L.A. Petri from Hannover, K. Graul
from the Leipzigermission, W. Löhe from Neuendettelsau, L. Harms
from Herrmannsburg and many others laid the foundations for what
is now considered the specific Lutheran missionary theology,
closely followed by similar missionary leaders from Scandinavia
and the USA.

As a whole they continued the prevailing tendency of seeing missionary work as "a free act of love," not determined by the institutions and the laws of the churches. But at the same time they rejected the parallel tendency to understand missionary work as a private matter (*Privat-Sache*) for those engaged in the work of the societies. The confessional loyalty made such a private understanding impossible. Mission must be the task of the church and as churches are confessionally bound mission loses its mandate if it understands itself as an a-confessional activity.

Through all these Lutheran discussions the major problem of the right vocation of a missionary remained unsolved. Behind the dilemma which is still a real problem in the Scandinavian state-churches, lies the unsolved problem of the nature of the church. The tendency to separate the church as an invisible spiritual reality from the church as a part of state and secular community continued from the times of Lutheran Orthodoxy. In the monumental missionary handbook by G. Warneck, the concept of the visible church is very similar to the teaching of the famous scholar R. Sohm, whose handbook on church law presupposed an extreme dualism between the order of the church and the nature of the church. The visible church in this type of "Lutheran" thinking was estranged from all theological norms. This sort of secularization within the churches no doubt prepared the way for very questionable tendencies in this century in the Lutheran churches first of all in Germany and Scandinavia.

The conclusion which must be drawn from the 19th century material is, that the Lutherans to a large extent came to support conservative tendencies, whereby the Lutheran churches lost a number of possibilities in relation to the new people's movements, liberal as well as socialist. The liberal and socialist movements were by and large understood to be anti-Christian. Consequently these movements tended to see the churches only as part of the established society.

The understanding of *creation*, so important in Lutheran theology, became a conservative notion in the neo-confessional theology. God's institutions of creation were mainly understood as the state and the family, both representing the stable and conservative elements of the world as opposed to the people's movements, in which the democratic and liberating forces were at work. In order to oppose those forces Lutheran church leaders and theologians often joined forces with the powers of the states and created an alliance between altar and throne (J. Aagaard, II. p. 738ff.).*

---

*See note on page 227.

The development of the Lutheran churches in North America
tells us something about the solidity of a doctrinal corpus.
Although the situation changed drastically, the theology continued
almost unchanged. The relations to state and society, so typical
for Germany and Scandinavia, were simply non-existent in the new
world. All the Lutheran churches had to be built up as free
churches with a real basis of lay participation. This new setting
seems, however, to have influenced their Lutheran theology to a
surprisingly small degree.

Still a third type of Lutheran church life is found in
North America, and consequently also a new type of missionary
activity came into being. The new Lutheran churches developed
an integrated missionary outreach, well administered and well
supported by the active congregations. The traditional Continental
split between missionary societies and the institutional churches
is almost unknown in North America.

The Ecumenical Challenge in Mission (during the 20th century)

In order to understand and evaluate Lutheran mission
theology in this century it is necessary to take the ecumenical
dimension of the missionary movement as such seriously. Lutheran
participation in the ecumenical movement was manifested from the
beginning by the Lutheran presence at the Edinburgh conference
in 1910 and at all the following mission conferences. As a
whole Lutherans contributed to the common thinking, together with
the representatives from the other churches, but now and again
Lutherans came up against the general tendency with a specific
warning and protest. This normally took place on the basis of
the doctrine of the two kingdoms.

The general anti-liberal and anti-socialist attitudes of
the European Lutheran churches in the 19th century created a
distance between these churches and the people's movements in the
respective societies. The churches - as mentioned above - tended
to unite with all types of conservative powers, and the last part
of the 19th century brought these Lutheran churches into a real
working alliance with authoritarian and nationalist tendencies,
although some of the revivalist movements continually pulled in
the opposite direction, at any rate in the Nordic countries.

The doctrine of the two kingdoms was rarely formulated in
mission theology but it was understood - in accordance with the
development of this doctrine during the 19th century - to imply a

clear-cut separation between the secular and the spiritual realm,
whereby the political powers were given full authority within
their own area to govern and reign as the direct mandators under
God, while the churches in their area exercised only spiritual
authority. At any rate in the Lutheran state-churches it became
practice that most social and political matters, all problems
dealing with life in community, were considered as irrelevant for
the churches - even by the churches themselves.

This attitude created fatal consequences for the missionary
movements in their relation to the colonial activities of the
states.

The German missions were challenged by German colonialism
after 1884. Dr. Solf from the colonial office stated his attitude
very clearly by saying "Colonization means missionary activity,"
and the general tendency among mission leaders was to accept the
challenge by turning the sentence around, "Missionary activity
means colonization." G. Warneck and his school of scholary
missiologists tried however in *Allgemeine Missions-Zeitschrift* to
establish a clear line of demarcation. The general sentiment in
the churches, competing to prove their true national attitudes in
the new German Reich, lead Lutherans of almost every type (confes-
sionalists as well as unionists and liberals) to consequences which
meant an acceptance and glorification of German expansion in Africa
and elsewhere. Mission and colonialism was supposed to have joint
interests and to support one another (C. Mirbt).

One would have expected the predominant understanding of
the doctrine of the two kingdoms to keep the churches and their
missions at some distance to the state and its colonialism, but
it worked the other way round: the doctrine operated *de facto*
often as the dogmatic reason for non-interference and non-protest
in relation to the colonial exercise of power. When the Germans
in German East Africa or German South-West Africa practically
killed off whole tribes as punishment for non-cooperation, very
little protest was heard from the missionaries and mission leaders.

Although the doctrine of the two kingdoms was understood
to exclude a direct involvement in colonial politics it did not
exclude a close relationship between the churches and the *Volkstum*
of the different people among whom the Lutheran missions were at
work.

19th century Lutheranism developed to a large extent within
the atmosphere of romanticism. The romantic concept of *Volk* was
integrated and used as a Lutheran *specificum*. K. Graul (1814-1864),

the leader of the Leipzigermission, was probably the first to see this idea in missionary praxis. He came up against the radical policy of the Anglicans in relation to the caste system in India and argued that this system - having its roots in the history of the Indian peoples - could not be abolished at once but had to be dissolved in the life of the church under the Gospel.

A number of Lutheran mission leaders such as L. Harms (1808-1865) and W. Löhe (1808-1872) followed in principle the same lines and G. Warneck (1834-1910) integrated this policy in his synthesis of *Einzelbekehrung und Volkschristianisierung* i.e. at the same time aiming at converting the individuals and Christianizing the people.

This tendency was taken to its radical consequences in the 20th century first of all by the two Lutheran pioneer missionaries B. Gutmann (1876-1966) and Chr. Keysser (1877-1961). In theory and practice they developed *volksorganische* and *volkspädagogische* missionary methods whereby they integrated the missionary movement into the lives of the tribal systems under which they worked in Tanganyika and New Guinea. Their results were important and served as an alternative to the pietist missions which in general were indifferent to the cultural and social setting of their converts. Gutmann's and Keysser's missionary methods tended, however, to bind the new churches to the structures in society which had to go, and thus the Christians were left unprepared for the new social and political developments in their countries during the 20th century (J.C. Hoekendijk).

An impressive result of the growing ecumenical movement was the Stockholm conference in 1925. This conference on the "Life and Work" of the churches in relation to the post-world war society was headed by the Swedish archbishop Nathan Söderblom (see B. Sundkler).

This event was partly hailed by Lutherans and partly criticized. In *Allgemeine-Ev. Luth. Kirchenzeitung*, 1925, the conference is analyzed in a number of articles first of all by the Finnish archbishop G. Johansson and the German Landesbischof D. Ihmels. At the conference itself a reservation was expressed again and again by the Lutherans, not least by Ihmels. The Lutheran protest first of all aimed at maintaining that the one and only task of the church is to preach the Gospel; that the kingdom of God is simply otherworldly(*schlechthin überweltlich*); that the natural orders of life (*Lebensordnungen*) are expressions of the divine will of creation and that their autonomy (*Eigengesetzlichkeit*) has to be respected.

A similar reaction came from Lutheran mission leaders in
the Nordic countries in connection with the Jerusalem conference
in 1928, arranged by The International Missionary Council. This
conference had decided to launch a study of the social and
economic questions related to the missions of the churches. The
Nordic Missionary Council met in Stockholm in December 1929 and
sent a letter of protest to the IMC, in which the members expressed
that they could not "help feeling anxious at the growing tendency
of making programmes for solution of rural, social and industrial
problems in the various mission fields". When that is done "beyond
a certain measure there is a real danger of diverting the missionary
zeal from its central objective... We must trust and believe that
this message will, among the various nations on the mission fields,
prove to be the salt that will gradually through the native churches
purify and raise the social conditions".

A second letter was sent from the following meeting of the
Missionary Council of the Northern Churches in September 1930.
Again it was stressed that "the social considerations receive too
much attention in the work of the IMC... and the new Department
of Social and Industrial Research and Council was asked "to refrain
from giving advice or co-operation in the introduction of social
reforms on the mission fields - concerning which reforms there will
necessarily be diverging opinions among Christians of different
nations and denominations". A threat to leave the council was the
final sentence of the letter. At the same time the Norwegian
Missionary Council in a detailed statement turned against the IMC
because it supported the National Christian Council in China,
which for the Norwegians represented "missionary modernism". (The
correspondence is found in the IMC archives in the WCC, Prof.
F. Torm published an article on behalf of the NMC in *International
Review of Missions*, Oct. 1930, "The Place of Social Questions in
Missionary Work", p. 593ff.).

The IMC staff tried hard to keep diplomatic relations with
the Lutheran north, but an unoffical letter from G.A. Gollock to
IMC's leader, J.H. Oldham tells its own story: "I rather love the
strong personality of these tiny countries who from one point of
view have so little to give, from another so much. It is worth
as much to win them as it is worth in education to win access to
the mind of a child" (IMC archives in WCC, Geneva).

Under the perspectives of new ideologies and the fascist
threat against all human values, Lutheran theology took a new
turn. This was partly caused by the so-called Luther renaissance,
partly by the influence from Karl Barth. The "back to Luther"
movement was so diversified that it is difficult to point out any
common denominator, but Luther was at any rate used to build up
a new consciousness of the church and its mission in a time of
crisis.

The influence of K. Barth was to a certain extent a
protest against some dominating attitudes among Lutheran "German
Christians" who supported Hitler and his new ideology using the
Lutheran respect for *Volkstum*, authority, obedience, nation,
family and tradition as a basis for acceptance of the new order
in Germany.

Karl Barth's influence cannot be spelt out here, but
through two great missionary theologians his "theology of crisis"
entered Lutheran missionary theology. W. Freytag (1899-1959) and
K. Hartenstein (1894-1952) brought back to missionary thinking
a radical concept of the kingdom of God, different from all our
human efforts and manifesting itself in congregations of faithful
who are called to obedience and suffering in the world. In
Germany, but also far beyond the German borders, they were pioneers
for a new type of Lutheran mission theology.

The mission to the Jewish people makes a specific chapter
in the history of Lutheran mission theology. Already the pietists
in Halle were engaged in this mission and created in 1728
"Institutum Judaicum", in which genuine research was done in order
to support the mission to the Jews. Also Zinzendorf and his
Herrnhut mission became involved, not least through the work of
Samuel Lieberkühn. The Enlightenment, however, in many respects
meant a radical change for Jewry in Europe, since a large number
of its elite gradually became assimilated into the "Christian"
societies. Jews often came to function as the most intelligent
and progressive critics of these societies, both through liberal,
socialist and communist movements.

As far as the churches united with the opposite forces, it
created a very serious tension between progressive Jews and
reactionary Christians, a tension which in this century contributed
considerably to the antisemitic movements. The Hofprediger Adolf
Stöcker from Berlin began his "christlich-germanische" warfare
already in 1885 as exponent of what he called the "Christian Social
Party", and the Christian front against the Jews continued in various

ways till the collapse of the Nazi regime in 1945. Any meaningful mission to the Jews was of course made impossible where anti-semitism reigned.

But there were other voices. The Lutherans in the 19th century were also represented by F. Delitzsch (1813-1890), the Old Testament scholar, who gave his scholarship and all his talents to the service of a genuine mission to the Jewish people. He was a part of the neo-confessional movement, and to him faithfulness to the Lutheran tradition always implied an openness to the missionary outreach. Probably his greatest service was his brilliant translation of the New Testament into the Hebrew language. "Has Luther given the Germans the Bible, Delitzsch has given the Jews the New Testament" (R. Kittel). But Delitzsch was not the only one. It is necessary also to mention J. Chr. K.v. Hofmann (1810-1877), the scholar who opened up a type of exegesis interpreting the biblical text in the perspective of a history of salvation which includes the salvation of the Jews. Similarly Chr.E. Luthardt (1823-1902), a scholar in dogmatics from Leipzig and engaged in the Leipzigermission, manifested an open and missionary attitude to the Jewish people, at the same time turning against the blind faith of the Lutheran churches in their "Christian culture".

The attitude of the churches in the horrible period called the Third Reich, is a story of the foolishness and blindness of the "German Christians", but also a story about a "remnant" in the churches which stood up against the crimes of the *Obrigkeit* i.e. the political authority. Pastor Martin Niemöller already in 1933 firmly rejected the required exclusion of Jewish people from the churches. But although many church leaders and theologians firmly refused to subject the churches to the politics of the Third Reich, there was a tendency to vagueness when it came to opposing these same claims "in the realm of the state." The interpretation of the doctrine of the two kingdoms again betrayed the mission of the church to suppressed and suffering people.

After the Second World War there have been serious attempts to recognize that the painful history of the German Lutheran churches became possible because of the perversion of the doctrine of the two kingdoms. The Lutheran Institute for Ecumenical Research in Strasbourg brought new perspectives to the inherited question about Lutheran identity, and the Lutheran World Federation'

Department of Studies has completed international research on the
history of the doctrine of the two kingdoms. It has been proved
beyond doubt that what we commonly call the doctrine of the two
kingdoms was in practice an ideological model built up in the
19th century and used for instance by the "German Christians" to
excuse toleration even of atrocities against other human beings
"within the secular realm."

The main development in the Lutheran community during the
last decades is the entry of the Lutheran churches from the two-
thirds world. Some of these churches have fostered church leaders
and theologians who now set totally different priorities for
Lutheran theology. Where churches in Asia, Africa and Latin-
America live in a minority situation in societies characterized
by people's movements and urgent social and political challenges,
their theology must try to get out of its Western framework and
its traditional preoccupation with the question raised by ties
between church and state in Europe.

Not until 1970 did this influence manifest itself
convincingly. At the 5th Assembly of the Lutheran World Federation
in Evian a real *World*-Federation came into being, "world" understood
both as a geographical and as a theological term. Following the
WCC Assembly in Uppsala in 1968 the Evian Assembly let the world,
with all its multitudes of suffering and suppressed people, if not
"write" then at least "add to" the agenda of the churches.

These attempts to regain a vision of the church serving
God's kingdom in mission and service to the complete human being
have not been left unchallenged. P. Beyerhaus from Tübingen is
a key Lutheran figure in a concerted German-Nordic attempt to
deal with today's questions about Lutheran presence and mission
in our turbulent world by means of the 19th century interpretation
of the two kingdoms. Their protests against Uppsala 1968, Evian
1970 and the WCC missionary conference in Bangkok 1973 on "Salvation
today" continue the emphases in the Lutheran protests after
Stockholm 1925 and Jerusalem 1928.

This new protest movement reached it culmination in the
Berlin declaration in 1974. This declaration compares itself with
the Barmen declaration in 1934, by which the Confessing Church
stood up against the Nazis and their theological supporters. The
strange fact is, however, that the type of Lutheran theology which
at that time attacked the Barmen declaration today seems to
support the Berlin declaration, while the type of theology which
was behind the Barmen declaration today is attacked by the Berlin
declaration. All this is illustrated for instance by the attacks

on Jürgen Moltmann, who is a genuine theological disciple of
Karl Barth and at the same time a representative of the theological
attempt at the Bankok conference to reach a more biblical and
challenging understanding of salvation.

The mainstream of Lutheran missiologists of all continents
is not engaged in this conservative movement of protest, but
operates within the wider missionary and ecumenical community
participating in its attempts to clarify the mission of the church
in this period of history. Such Lutheran voices are expressed
for instance in the works of the two Nordic senior missiologists
O.G. Myklebust from Oslo and Bengt Sundkler from Uppsala and the
present "master of missiology" in Heidelberg H. Gensichen.

A unique Lutheran contribution to the wider ecumenical
movement has been made by the LWF Department of Studies through
its studies on *Christian Faith and the Chinese Experience*. This
project together with *Pro Mundi Vita*, Louvain, has not only
succeeded in communicating reliable information on the situation
in The People's Republic of China but also in fostering an informed
theological debate on "The Implications of the New China for the
Christian Mission in the World" (see *Lutheran Theological Reflection
on the China Study*, LWF 1975).

The *conclusion* to this story is obvious: There is no such
thing as a Lutheran theology of mission. There is, however, some
pattern behind all the multiplicity and the often opposing
tendencies, and this pattern dates from Luther's own theology.
It is a very ambiguous blessing to have such a rich heritage,
because it may hamper the endeavours to create a constructive
contemporary theology. In fact this has happened continuously
throughout history. But the heritage can also function as a help
to escape the most glaring extremes of partisan onesiddness.

The story of Lutheran missionary theology is a story of
continued attempts to separate what God has united, but also the
story of the continued impact of Luther's own insights:

- that mission certainly is *horizontal*, for it happens
in this human world of ours, but at the same time it is *vertical*
for God is its subject;

- that mission certainly is a *temporal* and secular
phenomenon for it takes place in time and history, but at the same
time it is also *eternal*, for it happens as a movement towards the
ends of the earth and towards the end of time and history;

- that mission is only ours in so far as we *participate* in the history of God's kingdom at war with the kingdom of the evil one;

- that this history of God's salvation cannot be identified with the history of the church but takes place *when* and *where* God wills;

- that the church in its prayer must ask to be used as an instrument, as a *simple servant* of that salvation, and that if it wants to become more it becomes less.

English text revised by
Vanessa Dolbe

*Note:

From the various Pietist movements – both the non-confessional and the confessional ones – a number of groups decided to leave Germany or Scandinavia and go to the new world, i.e. America, first of all North America. In this way the first series of "young churches" came into being. The problems involved in the combination of colonization and mission in America and Australia were taken up by Lutheran missionary theology in a number of ways and with a number of different solutions. They tended, however, to agree on a positive evaluation of the relationship between Lutheran church life and what the Germans called *Volkstum* i.e. the inherent nature of a specific nation or people. This again was underpinned by Lutheran theological concepts of creation.

CHAPTER 12

HARDING MEYER

LUTHERANISM IN THE ECUMENICAL MOVEMENT

The Basic Ecumenical Impetus of the Reformation

For more than 400 years the Lutheran churches have existed
as separate churches among other separate churches and denominations.
This observation touches on a sensitive point in Lutheranism's
understanding of itself. There is a sort of contradiction between
what the Lutheran churches have beome in the course of history
and what was the basic intention of the Lutheran Reformation.

At no time did Luther and his co-reformers make the claim
to be founding a new church community. Wherever a suspicion or
misunderstanding of this kind arose they protested against it
with great feeling. Nor were they ever of the opinion that the
church of Jesus Christ had ceased to exist under the Roman papacy
and that it was therefore important to establish a new link with
some preceding point in the history of the church. In the *Augsburg
Confession* it is stated "that one holy church is to continue
forever" (Art. VII). This confession of the continuity of the church
is something Lutheranism cannot relinquish. This is why, in the
midst of all the disputes, Luther could continue to maintain that
everything which makes the church the church was present in the
Roman church: "This is true: that the papacy has God's Word and
the office of the apostles, and that we have received Holy Scripture,
Baptism, the Sacrament and the pulpit from them.... Therefore
faith, the Christian church, Christ and the Holy Spirit must also
be found among them.... Therefore we must also say: I believe

and am sure that the Christian church has remained even in the papacy" (LW 24, 304 f.).

That the Reformation struggle did not intend there to be a departure from the church of the time and the formation of a separate church is demonstrated above all by the central concern of the Reformation. It was not a question of exclusive insights or experiences which could best be preserved and nurtured within a limited circle. It was a question of nothing less than the heart of Christendom: of the Gospel of the unmerited and unmeritable grace of God in Christ. This Gospel, which had certainly not been lost in the Roman church although it had been concealed and obscured by late scholastic theology, ecclesiastical teaching and the predominant practice of piety, was to be uncovered, purified and enabled to shine forth again. Thus from the very beginning the Reformation struggle in itself contained a dimension relating to all of Christendom. It would have been the equivalent of a denial of the Gospel to have tried to make it only the concern of a separate church.

Both the lasting confession of the continuity of the church and the concentration of all efforts on the presentation of the pure message of the Gospel give the Reformation a basic ecumenical emphasis. Nor was this abandoned as a consequence of the increasing and more rigid resistance of the Roman Catholic theology and church. The founding of a separate church still appeared to be an unconceivable possibility even when the Reformation challenge met with theological condemnation and ecclesiastical excommunication. At the Diet of Augsburg the Protestant princes and estates represented there made this clear to the emperor and the Christian West. *Sub uno Christo sumus et militamus* ("we are all enlisted under one Christ"), as it says in the preface to their written statement of faith (BC, p. 25), which then sets out point by point how the convictions of the Reformation are not only based on the Bible but also fit into the tradition of the early church.

This "no" to the formation of a separate church is even maintained where the papal church is seen as the "false church" and the supporters of the Reformation confession as the "true church". Although this creates extreme conflict, the individibility and paradoxical belonging together of both churches under tremendous tension is maintained. They are indivisible not only because a "pure" church simply does not exist and even in the true church new false teachers and prophets constantly arise. The two churches

are also indivisible because the true church has a permanent
responsibility to the false church: the task of warning, exhorting
and criticizing. The true church may not escape this responsibility by totally renouncing the false church. This sort of
separation will only be brought about by the Last Judgment. We
cannot perform it. It is impossible, says Luther, "for us or for
the holy church to divorce or separate ourselves bodily from the
sacrilege, the papacy or the Antichrist until the day of judgment"
(LW 38, 211).

        And yet Lutheran churches came into existence which are
aware that they are separated from other churches by their
confession, their structures and their life. In the given historica
circumstances this development was unavoidable, indeed necessary.
It would be wrong to try to undo this development simply by
referring to the Reformation in an unhistorical way. What is
important in this changed church situation is, rather, not to deny
the ecumenical emphasis and impetus of the Reformation in favor of
a self-satisfied separate church existence. The Reformation
confession of the continuity and unity of the church and the
awareness of having a responsibility for Christendom as a whole
make it binding on the Lutheran churches to seek dialogue and
fellowship with other churches. Active ecumenical commitment is
therefore an expression of fidelity to their Reformation origins.

The Specific Characteristics of Lutheran Ecumenical Endeavours

        The ecumenical emphasis of the Reformation and the awareness
of ecumenical commitment have found expression in the confession
of the Lutheran churches, the Augsburg Confession. Article VII
deals with "The Church" but it raises the question of the unity
of the Church in so central a way that the article should really
be entitled "The true unity of the Church". When one considers
that within a few decades the Augsburg Confession of 1530 had
become the basic confession of the Lutheran churches in all
countries and has remained so until today, this also makes clear
how firmly the concept of ecumenism is engraved on the memory and
in the awareness of the Lutheran churches and constitutes an
integral part of their Reformation heritage.

        This Article states, "It is also taught among us that one
holy Christian Church will be and remain forever. This is the
assembly of all believers among whom the Gospel is preached in its
purity and the holy sacraments are administered according to the

Gospel. For it is sufficient for the true unity of the Christian church that the Gospel be preached in conformity with a pure understanding of it and that the sacraments be administered in accordance with the divine Word. It is not necessary for the true unity of the Christian church that ceremonies, instituted by men, should be observed uniformly in all places. It is as Paul says in Eph. 4, 4-5, 'There is one body and one Spirit... one Lord, one faith, one baptism'" (BC, p. 32).

This Article is impressively compact and pregnant. It begins with the confession of continuity and concludes with the - Pauline - confession of the unity of the church. At the center there is the statement about the true unity of the church. It is derived from the preceding sentence on the nature of the church and leads on to a statement about what is not necessary for the true unity of the church.

The main idea is as basic as it is simple: that which is necessary for the unity of the church is the same as that which is necessary for the existence of the church. What is equally necessary for the existence and the unity of the church is the Gospel which is proclaimed and distributed to mankind in the form of the Word which is preached and the administration of the sacraments. In this Gospel Christ is present and unites people with himself and with one another to form his body.

However, here it is of decisive importance that the Gospel is preached in its pure, unfalsified form and that the sacraments are administered in accordance with this Gospel. Where preaching and the administration of the sacraments take place in harmony with the Gospel, there is the church. And where there is agreement on this between Christians and churches, there is the unity of the church and all the prerequisites for church fellowship are fulfilled.

This radical concentration of the ecumenical question in the matter of agreement on the true proclamation of the Gospel in Word and sacrament is the real concern of this Article. This is emphasized in two ways. First, it is underlined that unanimity over preaching the Word and administering the sacraments is "enough" for true unity; and this is then immediately expanded to show that uniformity in ecclesiastical rites and ceremonies instituted by men is "not necessary."

Of course, this "enough" and "not necessary" does not describe all the details of the less important area of that which has developed and been conditioned by history. There is no doubt that this covers forms of worship, church law, church order and

church structures. The confessional formulae and dogmatic
formulations which have developed in the course of history will
also have to be included, however important they may be for the
preservation of church fellowship. The same applies to the concrete
expressions of the ministry, although the ministry as such is
"instituted by God" (CA, art. V) and thus belongs to the constitutive
elements of the church.

It is and remains important and of ecumenical significance
that an emphatic distinction is made here between that which is
absolutely necessary for unity and an area not of arbitrary but
certainly of responsible freedom.

All of this shows that this Article does not merely
represent a general confession of the unity of the church but,
at the same time, provides clear ecumenical guidance and directives.
The Lutheran churches have followed them in their ecumenical
commitment. Their endeavours for the unity of the church take
the form essentially of a struggle for unanimity about the true
understanding of the Gospel and the corresponding proclamation of
the Word and administration of the sacraments. This is where they
see the true and promising way to unity because it is the way
into the heart of Christian existence and church life. If common
ground can be found here, the establishment of church fellowship
can and must follow. Differences in the field of church order,
church structures and forms of worship are fundamentally no obstacle
to this fellowship. They are of secondary importance and can be
resolved or tolerated *within* the fellowship.

This conviction is expressed concretely in the fellowship
which exists between the Lutheran churches of the world. It is
a fellowship the center and fundamental basis of which is to be
found in a common concept of the Gospel but which at the same
time embraces a wide range of obvious differences in church structure
forms or worship and expressions of the church's ministry.

To affirm what is said in the Augsburg Confession about
church unity does not preclude recognizing the limits of those
statements at the same time. These limits result above all from
the fact that the Augsburg Confession was formulated against the
background of a church situation which is no longer our own.
Whereas at that time visible unity and the practice of fellowship
were not yet abolished although they were profoundly threatened,
we have a long history of visible division and fragmentation into
autonomous separate churches which are institutionally defined and
estranged from one another. Today it is no longer a question of
preserving visible unity in a situation of crisis but of

re-establishing it. This means that the ecumenical problem has
acquired aspects which are not directly mentioned by the Augsburg
Confession or were of less importance.

Thus it should be noted, for example, that the emphasis
rightly placed on theological concern for unanimity about the
preaching of the Gospel in Word and sacrament at that time could
presuppose a framework of familiarity and practical fellowship
which for us ceased to exist a long time ago. Therefore work for
unity today cannot be restricted unilaterally to the struggle for
theological agreement. It must simultaneously endeavor to re-establish a framework of mutual familiarity and real fellowship within
which theological activity has its place and can be productive.
And many differences in forms of worship, church order and structures,
and especially different expressions of the church's ministry,
have acquired such weight in the course of the history of division
that they can often no longer be understood as bearable historical
differences and have to be included in the ecumenical endeavor
today.

Nevertheless, even when thus taking account of historical
differences and new aspects which have come into the ecumenical
problem since the Reformation, the central ecumenical concern of
the Augsburg Confession can be maintained uncurtailed.

The Struggle for Unity at the Time of the Reformation

After the hearings and disputations relating predominantly
to Luther himself in the first few years following the publication
of the 95 Theses the first comprehensive attempt was made at the
Diet of Augsburg (1530) to resolve the religious disputes in
Germany between the supporters of the Lutheran Reformation and of
the Roman church by theological negotiations. The Emperor Charles
V called the Diet with precisely this aim in view. The Roman
Catholic side was represented by the papal legate, Cardinal
Campeggi, and princes and theologians with Roman leanings like Eck,
Fabri and Cochläus, and the Lutheran side by the Protestant
princes, representatives of Protestant imperial towns and Protestant
theologians, especially Melanchthon and Justus Jonas. The emphasis
was less on theological disputations or attempts at compensation
which were unsatisfactory and essentially non-productive. It was
of lasting significance that the Protestant estates present, with
the exception of a few towns, agreed during the Diet on a common
confession which was read to the emperor and in the following years

became the basic confession of all Lutheran churches. It was
compiled by Melanchthon who included some documents which already
existed and made sure of Luther's consent who, as an outlaw, was
unable to attend the Diet.

This "Augsburg Confession" was strongly marked by the will
for ecumenical understanding. It attempted to stress what both
sides had in common and to demonstrate that the essential conviction
of the Reformation did not contradict the teaching of the Roman
church. Even at that time there were accusations from both sides
that the Augsburg Confession omitted certain controversial questions
(e.g. the questions of the papacy, of the understanding of the
Scriptures, of purgatory, of the doctrine of transubstantiation).
Nevertheless it expressed the fundamental convictions of the
Lutheran Reformation without making false concessions and in very
satisfactory formulations in some cases, which is the reason why
it has been able to remain the common confession of the Lutheran
churches until today.

The permanent danger of a war of religion caused a series
of religious discussions to be held in the following period, also
promoted by the state authorities. The Colloquy of Regensburg
(1541), which followed on from a discussion in Hagenau (1540), was
of greater significance than the first two discussions in Leipzig
(1534 and 1539). It was called by Charles V, supported by the
Protestant princes of Germany, prepared by a preparatory discussion
in Worms under the leadership of the imperial chancellor, Granvella,
(drafting of the "Ratisbon Book") and conducted by Reformation
theologians like Bucer and Melanchthon and noted theologians of
the Roman church including, among others, Eck and the papal legate,
Contarini. Taken as a whole these discussions were a failure.
This was primarily because it proved impossible to come to an
agreement on central points of controversy, like the concept of
the church and of the church's doctrinal authority and, especially,
on the question of the Lord's Supper. Nevertheless, on the question
of justification, for example, a remarkable degree of consensus was
achieved. However, the agreements reached were not accepted either
in Rome or in Wittenberg. The papal consistory accused the statements of consensus of ambiguity and from Luther, too, there came
a sharp rejection. The dialogue was finally broken off - after a
last colloquy in 1546 - when it had become clear that war was to
provide the decision.

The increased political threat to the Protestants (Diet
of Speyer, 1529) and the desire to form an alliance between the
Protestant territories provided the impetus for religious

discussions between Protestants as well. Their aim was to resolve
the tensions which had arisen between the supporters of the
Lutheran Reformation and Upper German and Swiss Protestantism
which took Zwingli's approach. The most important of these was
the three-day Marburg Colloquy (1529) for which Philip of Hesse
issued the invitations and in which the most significant theologians
from both sides took part. It did not in face achieve its aim of
full agreement. Nevertheless, it made strikingly evident how
broad the area of common conviction was. There was obvious agreement on fourteen of the articles drawn up by Luther himself (e.g.
on the doctrine of the Trinity, original sin, justification,
baptism, confession). It was only on the fifteenth article about
the Lord's Supper - despite mutual understanding on individual
aspects (reception of both elements, rejection of the concept of
the sacrifice of the mass, necessity for a spiritual reception of
the gifts of the Lord's Supper) - that it proved impossible to
surmount the difference which was felt to be essential in the
conception of the real presence of Christ. The fact that this
open question meant that they continued to consider themselves
separated should not obscure the other fact - that here, too, some
mutual misunderstandings were clarified and it appeared that
agreement was not too far away.

In the following years it was Bucer, above all, who worked
to achieve this agreement in numerous discussions and negotiations
and managed to do so to a large extent in the Wittenberg Concord
(1536). From the formal point of view this Concord is a confessional statement about the Lord's Supper by the Upper German
Protestants, which was drawn up, submitted and jointly signed
at a meeting of representatives of Upper German towns and Lutheran
theologians in Wittenberg. This document speaks of a "genuine
and real" presence of the body and blood of Christ "with bread
and wine" and emphasizes that the "unworthy" also receive the body
and blood of Christ. In the opinion of Luther and the Lutheran
theologians this removed the conflict so that they recognized one
another as "dear brothers in the Lord" (Luther). To set the seal
on this, in a sense, they received communion together. Although
it was impossible to win the absent Swiss over to this confession,
the Concord brought about a union of the German Protestantism of
the time.

In addition to the urgent effort to come to an agreement
with the Roman church and to overcome the internal tensions among
Protestants, there was also the desire for fellowship with other
churches.

Even during the first phase of the English Reformation Luther's thinking had been accepted to a surprising extent by groups within the *English church* which were predisposed towards the Reformation. Promoted by the contacts between English and Lutheran theologians but brought about above all by Henry VIII's political efforts to establish links with the Smalcald League, two official encounters took place between representatives of the English church and Lutheran theologians. At the king's behest a small English delegation, led by Bishop Fox, spent several months (1535-36) in Wittenberg and had discussions with Luther, Melanchthon, Bugenhagen and others. The outcome was the 17 "Wittenberg Articles" of 1536 some of which were taken directly from the Augsburg Confession. For their part, they influenced the "10 Articles" of the English church which were adopted in the middle of 1536 and remained binding for the next ten years. The "Bishops' Book" (1537), which was compiled shortly afterwards, - a sort of handbook of faith and ethics which was put together mainly by Bishop Fox and the Archbishop of Canterbury, Thomas Cranmer, who was especially open to Lutheran thinking - was also clearly influenced by Lutheranism, in particular by Luther's catechisms.

In the middle of 1538 a countervisit of Lutheran theologians in England took place. They went at the behest of the elector of Saxony and of the landgrave of Hesse and conducted negotiations with a group of English theologians under the chairmanship of Archbishop Cranmer. On this occasion also the main outcome was a series of Articles, the so-called "13 Articles". They were determined to a large extent by the previous "10 Articles" and the "Wittenberg Articles" and evinced a pronounced similarity to the Augsburg Confession. The strongly Lutheran flavor of the later "39 Articles" of the English church (1563) was essentially a consequence of these English/Lutheran conversations.

An attention to the *Orthodox churches* of the East had already played a considerable part in Luther's polemics against the papacy. In the dispute over the Lord's Supper, also, and especially over the doctrine of transubstantiation there are occasional references from the Lutheran side to the Eastern Orthodox teaching. On this and other points the Lutheran reformers evidenced a conviction about the fundamental concord between the Reformation and the Orthodox tradition. The first attempt to establish a direct relationship to the Orthodox churches was made by Melanchthon with his Greek translation of the Augsburg Confession which was

sent to the Patriarch, Joasaph II, in Constantinople, but there
was no response. Fifteen years later at the initiative of
theologians from Tübingen the Augsburg Confession was again
transmitted to the patriarchal see. During the years 1573-1581
an exchange of letters followed between Tübingen professors,
M. Crusius and J. Andreä, and the Ecumenical Patriarch, Jeremias
II. In two extensive theological documents written by the Orthodox
side, which followed the outline of the Augsburg Confession, very
clear emphasis was placed on the existing differences in addition
to the points of agreement. The Tübingen theologians attempted
to answer the obviously unexpected Orthodox objections and in so
doing particularly underlined the Reformation *sola scriptura*.
The main points in the debate were: Scripture and tradition,
justification by faith and salvation by the joint effects of
divine and human activity, the Word of God and the mystery of
worship. This first encounter between Lutheranism and Orthodoxy
did not yet bring about a real grasp of the particularity of the
other partner. The third letter from Constantinople broke off the
exchange of correspondence: "Do not write to us about dogmas any
more but only for the sake of friendship, if you so wish. Fare
well!"

Ecumenical Initiatives in the 17th to 19th Centuries

The exchange of letters between Tübingen and Constantinople
led up to a time in which efforts for unity yielded completely
to confessional self-aggrandizement and self-sufficiency. It was
the painful experiences of the Thirty Years War which finally
caused the desire for inter-confessional understanding to arise
again. But even now on the Lutheran side this hardly resulted
in any major ecumenical endeavors sponsored by the church. There
were simply a few attempts made mainly by individual theologians.
N. Hunnius (1585-1643) in his paper dedicated to King
Gustav Adolf of Sweden (1632), developed the idea of a *collegium
irenicum* which would resemble an inter-confessional theological
senate and examine and resolve all the theological disputes which
arose. The special virtue of G. Calixt (1586-1656) from Helmstedt,
who belonged to the Melanchthonian and humanist line of thinking,
was his great estimation of the early church tradition. There
and especially in the symbolism of the early church he considered
that the true understanding of the Christian faith had been
preserved in its "fundamental" truths and he did not hesitate to

rank it higher than any dogmatic or confessional statement of a
later period. While he tried at first to use the tradition of
the early church in order to criticize the subsequent doctrinal
development in the Roman Catholic Church, he later recognized in
the consensus of the early church the ideal basis for negotiations
over all points of theological controversy and the foundation for
a reunification of Christendom.   This caused him to be sharply
attacked and accused of syncretism; but he nevertheless found
supporters in other Lutheran faculties of the time as well.

        One of Calixt's students, the Hanover theologian and
church politician G.W. Molanus (1633-1722), made the most significant effort since the Reformation period to come to an understanding with the Roman Catholic Church. With the consent of
his prince and the support of the philosopher Leibniz he tried,
first (from 1683) by negotiations with the Bishop of Vienna,
Spinola, and then (from 1691) in an exchange of correspondence
with the influential French bishop and theologian, Bossuet, to
clarify the prerequisites for a union of the Protestant churches
with Rome. His requirements for a return to the Catholic church
were: the priority of Scripture over the council and the pope,
admission of the laity to the chalice, abolition of private masses,
recognition of the Reformation doctrine of justification as a
variant of the Roman Catholic doctrine, acceptance of marriage for
priests and recognition of ordination. The Protestant concessions
were to be: recognition of the papal primacy as an institution
of ecclesiastical and thus of "human" law, consent to the distribution of bread alone in Catholic eucharistic celebrations,
incorporation of Protestant ministers into the Roman Catholic
hierarchy. It seemed to him essential for any union that the
decrees of the Council of Trent should be set aside. In view of
the resistance of his Catholic partners, especially over this point,
he finally had to recognize the futility of his efforts.

        In a quite different way, attempts by Pietism to overcome
doctrinal conflicts provided Lutheranism with a new ecumenical
attitude and resulted in ecumenical activity. The awareness of
belonging to the fellowship of all reborn Christians aroused a
new sense of the church as a universal spiritual reality. As
formulated doctrine, liturgical orders, sacraments, ecclesiastical
constitutions and structures decreased in importance, there was
less hesitation about entering into contact with convinced Christian
of other confessions and actively establishing real fellowship
with them. Representatives of Pietism like P.J. Spener (1635-1705),

A.H. Francke (1663-1727) or Count von Zinzendorf (1700-1760) conducted extensive correspondence with like-minded people in other countries and churches, did a large amount of travelling across national and confessional borders and spread their own writings and those of others in translation in countries of other languages. Inter-confessional cooperation developed in mission (South India) and diaspora work (North America). Ecumenically conceived educational and training institutions, aimed at spreading the faith all over the world, were founded or at least planned: Francke's orphanage in Halle and his plan for a *Seminarium universale*, Zinzendorf's Moravian seminary and his idea of an ecumenical "academy of sciences". In all of this there was evidence of a new type of ecumenical awareness and ecumenical commitment which found an appropriate expression not in efforts to come to doctrinal agreement but primarily in joint action.

Lutheranism underwent a very ambiguous ecumenical experience with the formation of the Reformed/Lutheran unions at the beginning of the 19th century in Germany. The united churches which came into existence after 1817 in various German states were different both in form and in origin. In certain isolated cases they were the initiative of the parishes and churches themselves; in many other cases the initiative clearly came from the political authorities which sometimes even tried to bring about the union by force. There were unions which considered all the historical confessions to be invalid and only recognised the Holy Scriptures as their doctrinal criterion ("non-confessional union"). Other unions considered their confession to be the content which the Lutheran and Reformed confessions had in common without, however, putting this content into words in a new common confession ("absorptive union"). And in yet other unions the traditional confessions were left in force where they had previously been valid, but it was considered that the doctrinal differences were not serious enough to prevent joint communion and a common church administration ("federative union"). The picture was still more complicated by the fact that, in a number of cases, transitions from one form of union to another took place, or in one and the same church different forms of union overlapped or there was a conflict between different interpretations of the union.

These unions met with growing resistance from a more and more confessional Lutheranism. In certain of the German states Lutheran free churches came into existence. Lutheran groups decided to emigrate, especially to North America, or Lutheran associations

and conferences were formed within the united churches. The
Lutheran resistance was sparked off at first by the claim of the
political authorities to decide for the church. But the real
reason for this resistance was that it was believed that the union
would at least partially invalidate the Reformation confessions
and neglect as unessential those convictions which were considered to
be in accordance with the Scriptures over which there were differences with the Reformed churches (doctrine of baptism and the Lord's
Supper). Thus the unions seemed to contradict the Lutheran
conviction that unanimity about true doctrine and the administration
of the sacraments is essential to the true unity of the church.

This negative experience of the unions established at the
beginning of the 19th century left a residue of aversion to and
distrust of movements for union not only in German Lutheranism.
There was a general inclination to see "unionism" at work within
them whatever happened. As North American Lutherans expressed it
later on (1925), "Where the establishment and maintenance of
church fellowship ignores present doctrinal differences or declares
them as a matter of indifference, there is unionism, pretence of
union, which does not exist" (quoted in: V. Vajta - H. Weissgerber,
p. 184).

The Gathering of Lutherans and Ecumenical Openness

The 19th century and especially the second half was a time
of movements bringing Lutherans together and uniting them which
took place along parallel lines at essentially the same time in
North America and in Europe. They were stimulated by a confessional
renewal of Lutheranism which started already at the beginning of
the century, but to some extent they had their own specific motivations on the two continents. Whereas in North America there
was a concern to go beyond the individualism of the separate
immigrant Lutheran churches and the desire to maintain their
confessional character in the process of cultural adaptation, the
union movement in Europe was to a large extent a product of the
resistance to the regional unions promoted by the state.

It would not be right to deny the ecumenical character of
these movements for Lutheran unity because they were primarily
designed to bring together churches of one and the same confessional
family. That would be too superficial a judgment. In reality,
these links established between Lutherans in North America, in
Europe and finally at world level are important although partial

ecumenical events: churches are released from their local and
regional isolation; there is success in surmounting theological
differences which are a threat or an obstacle to fellowship; the
new fellowship transcends the frontiers and barriers between
nations, cultures and races; an experience of the universal
dimension of the church develops which increasingly oust the
spirit of ecclesiastical individualism. No less a person than
Visser 't Hooft, then the General Secretary of the World Council
of Churches in the process of formation, recognized and acknowledged this in 1947 in his greeting to the first, constitutive
assembly of the Lutheran World Federation when he said, "The World
Council (of churches) is deeply aware of the fact that the ecumenical
task can only be performed if the main confessional federations
and alliances perform their task of bringing the churches of their
confessional family together in close fellowship and so prepare
the way for the even greater and more difficult task of establishing
the wider ecumenical Christian brotherhood" (see Proceedings, p. 186).

Certainly these movements for Lutheran unity were designed
to preserve the confessional heritage and - hand in hand with that -
to define where they differed from other churches and confessions.
But at the same time one can observe how a narrow confessionalist
attitude was compelled to yield as links and fellowship were created
between Lutheran churches with very different emphases from different
nations with different cultural and historical backgrounds and, to
some extent, already existing inter-confessional ties. A very
significant indication of this can be seen in the phenomenon of
a kind of "confessionalist opposition" against these confessionally
Lutheran associations. This phenomenon can be observed both in
the North American and the European movements for unity and continued
later with regard to the world-wide gathering together of Lutherans.
It became especially obvious in 1908 when the German Lutheran Free
Churches and a number of members from the regional churches left
the European General Evangelical Lutheran Conference again and
formed their own association, the "Lutheran League".

Things went along similar lines in North America where even
today the churches of the Missouri Synod prevent a more comprehensive
unity of Lutheranism there. Nor has the Lutheran World Federation
so far been able to bring together all the Lutheran churches of the
world, so that it continues to live with this "confessionalist
opposition". The basic reason why certain churches believe that
they cannot share in the Lutheran movements for unity is of a
clearly theological nature. It appears to them that the fidelity
to the confessions of the churches within the associations is

insufficiently strong and ambiguous.   Therefore these are churches
which are particularly strict about confessional observance and
which see tendencies at work in the movements for Lutheran unity
and the associations which will reduce or even abandon the link
with the historical Lutheran confession. This phenomenon of
confessionalist opposition is an indirect but nevertheless very
eloquent indication that strict confessionalism is concentrated
rather outside than inside the movements for Lutheran unity.
Therefore it is a quite logical and natural development for the
movements for Lutheran unity to allow themselves to be more and
more influenced and virtually brought in by the broader ecumenical
movement.

The evolution of the movement for Lutheran unity, on the
one hand, and of the ecumenical movement, on the other, followed
parallel lines in time after the First World War and there were
both personal and material contacts to and fro.

The foundation and work of the Lutheran World Convention,
the organization which preceded the Lutheran World Federation,
belong to the same period as the development and first major
conferences of the movements for Life and Work and for Faith and
Order. The constitutions of the World Council of Churches and
of the Lutheran World Federation were prepared and formulated at
about the same time - in the years from 1936 to 1947-48 - and were
subject to mutual influences and suggestions. The establishment
of the two organizations also took place almost simultaneously.

Lutheran theologians and church leaders took a very active
part in the ecumenical movement at that time. Interestingly
enough, their participation was evidently more active in the field
of the movement for Life and Work than in the movement for Faith
and Order. This applies not only with regard to the number of
Lutheran participants at the major conferences but also with regard
to the determining influence of the Lutherans present. The
predominant figure was the Swedish Archbishop, N. Söderblom, the
spiritual father of the movement for Life and Work and one of the
very first to have a clear idea of a plan for an "Ecumenical
Council of Churches" which he voiced as early as the Spring of 1919.
Without him, it has been said, there would have been no Stockholm
1925, and without a Stockholm 1925 no World Council of Churches,
at least not in its present form. His son-in-law and later
successor in office, Y. Brilioth, was also involved from the Geneva
Conference (1920) onwards and in 1947 he became the first chairman
of the Commission on Faith and Order of the World Council of
Churches. For Germany mention must be made of such a leading Luther

as W. Elert who gave the opening address on the subject "The
Call to Unity" at the first World Conference on Faith and Order
(1927). North American Lutherans like J.A. Morehead, F.H. Knubel,
the long-time President of the United Lutheran Church in America,
and A.R. Wentz must also be mentioned. Since they were also
among the leaders of the movement for Lutheran unity, they make
the personal interchange with the ecumenical movement especially
clear.

    Thanks to the commitment of the North American Lutherans
the structure of the World Council of Churches is not based one-
sidedly on the principle of geographical church representation as
was originally planned, but includes the principle of confessional
representation. When the cause already seemed to be lost, they
received support from the other Lutheran churches and also from
the Lutheran World Convention whose Executive Committee in 1937
spoke out emphatically in favor of the principle of confessional
church representation. How important this structural question was
and is can be seen from the report of the General Secretary of the
World Council at Amsterdam (1948): "The World Council can only be
a living reality if it really expresses spiritual realities, and
these are to be found, on the one hand, in fidelity to the various
confessions and, on the other, in fidelity to the history, language
or task of the churches in a particular nation or continent" (W.A.
Visser 't Hooft).

    Even though the goals and work of the Lutheran World
Convention place the emphasis clearly on the strengthening of
fellowship, cooperation and mutual assistance between Lutherans,
a broader ecumenical concept is also present. The first World
Convention (1923) even deliberately began with this question.
"Lutheranism and Ecumenism" was the first of its three main themes.
Two addresses on "The Ecumenicity of the Lutheran Church" (Bishop
Ihmels) and on "What can the Lutheran Church do to bring about
that 'they all may be one'?" (President Knubel) took this up.

    The ecumenical question and the idea of ecumenical commit-
ment were not yet expressed directly in the resolutions of the
World Convention or in its constitution of 1929. But in 1936 the
Executive Committee of the World Convention drew up a detailed
statement, which took up the ecumenical theme of the first World
Convention again, and sent it to the member churches for discussion
and acceptance. It was intended as ecumenical "guidance" and
dealt with what had been said at the first World Convention while
developing it and making it more concrete to take account of the
now stronger and more consolidated ecumenical movement. Two aspects

are kept together and overlap: the ecumenical commitment of the
Lutheran churches which, as it says, is a consequence of the
"ecumenical character of Lutheranism" and the "need for Lutheran
solidarity" and fellowship. The recommendations of this document
again demonstrate the characteristic range from a common "evangelical
consciousness" and its corresponding fellowship between the Lutheran
churches to a participation in the ecumenical movement which is
envisaged as fully involving evangelical consciousness and Lutheran
fellowship in the broader ecumenical endeavor.

        When the Lutheran World Federation was founded (1947) this
was also expressed in its constitution: both things belong to
the aims pursued by the World Federation: "to cultivate unity of
faith and confession among the Lutheran churches of the world"
and "to foster Lutheran participation in ecumenical movements".

Deepening and Intensifying the Ecumenical Involvement

        In the period following the establishment of the Lutheran
World Federation and of the World Council of Churches many links
developed between the two organizations most of which were essentially functional rather than structural. In all the major areas
of their activity forms of cooperation and coordination came into
existence. It now happened still more frequently than in the
preceding period that leading figures of Lutheranism belong
simultaneously to the governing bodies of the World Council, like,
for example, the first three presidents of the Lutheran World
Federation, Bishop A. Nygren, Bishop H. Lilje and President F.C.
Fry. For the second Assembly of the World Council at Evanston
(1954) a contribution to the theme on behalf of Lutherans as a
whole was prepared by the Theological Commission of the World
Federation. The Lutheran World Federation was doing what it could
to encourage its member churches at the same time to become members
of the World Council of Churches.

*The Question of Ecumenism at the Assemblies of the Lutheran
World Federation*

        What is still more important is that there was clearly a
deepening and intensification of ecumenical involvement within
the Lutheran churches and the World Federation. This is reflected
clearly by its Assemblies. After the first two Assemblies which

still belong to the period of the construction and internal
consolidation of the World Federation, at the Third Assembly in
Minneapolis (1957) the question of ecumenism became one of the
most important subjects. In the theses drawn up there on "The
Unity of the Church in Christ" a much more imperative tone prevails
than in all the preceding ecumenical statements of World Lutheranism.
They express a warning about "simply being satisfied with the
ecclesiastical status quo" and emphasize: "We may find... no excuse
in referring to an invisible unity of all true believers. We
know that the ministry of reconciliation is jeopardized by the lack
of manifested unity". An appeal is made to the ecumenical openness
and "freedom" contained in the Lutheran confession itself: "Whenever we hear the Gospel preached in its truth and purity and see
the Sacraments administered according to the institution of Christ,
there we may be assured that the one Church of Christ is present.
There nothing separates us from our brethren, and both faith and
love constrain us to overcome our dividedness" (see Proceedings,
p. 86).

The next Assembly in Helsinki (1963) adopted a new form
of words for the ecumenical aim described in the constitution of
the World Federation. Now ecumenical commitment and responsibility
were given much more emphasis than in the original version. Now
it is said that it belongs to the tasks of the World Federation
"to foster Lutheran interest in, concern for, and participation
in ecumenical movements". Along precisely the same lines this
same Assembly decided to establish a joint Lutheran "Foundation
for Ecumenical Research" whose Institute began its activities at
the beginning of 1965 in Strasbourg. The Foundation and the
Institute constitute a tool which, as it says in their constitution,
is to contribute "to the fulfillment by the Lutheran churches of
their ecumenical responsibility in the area of theology". That
a world confessional organization was able to set up its own
ecumenical instrument like this, the effect of whose activity goes
far beyond the realm of its own churches into the broader ecumenical
sphere, is something unique of its kind.

At the last Assembly so far in Evian (1970) the ecumenical
aspect, alongside the concern with socio-ethical questions, became
one of the predominant aspects. In the intervening period the
Lutheran World Federation had started a series of bilateral
ecumenical conversations (above all with the Reformed churches,
the Roman Catholic church and the Anglican Communion) and had thus
entered a quite new phase of direct and concentrated ecumenical

activity. It was a novelty in the history of the World Federation
that of the three major sections of the work of this Assembly
one dealt exclusively with the necessity for and consequences of
the "ecumenical commitment" of Lutheranism. From this point
onwards it is possible to say without reservation that the
Lutheran World Federation no longer exercises its ecumenical
responsibility only indirectly, i.e. primarily via its member
churches, but has become in one jump, as it were, an active
partner in the ecumenical movement and is prepared to devote
considerable effort to this ecumenical commitment in the fullest
sense of the word. The study document submitted to the Assembly
by the Theological Commission, "More than Church Unity" and the
"Guidelines for Ecumenical Encounter" (in *Lutheran World*, 1970,
p. 43ff.) closely related to it are the theological expression of
this new, more active ecumenical involvement of Lutheranism. They
consciously incorporate the stimuli from the Assembly of the World
Council of Churches in Uppsala (1968), for example, and at the
same time attempt to correct something of the traditional and in
many ways onesided type of Lutheran ecumenical involvement.

The New Attitude to Church Union

        In the course of these developments a new attitude developed
to the question of movements for church union which had historically
caused a lot of difficulty for the Lutheran churches. Even before
the Assembly in 1963 the Lutheran World Federation had been called
upon by its South Indian and East African member churches, which
were involved in regional negotiations for union, to declare what
its attitude was to this kind of effort to achieve unity, whether
it could support its member churches in this and how it would react
to a church which was the product of the union of a member church
with non-Lutheran churches. The Assembly at Helsinki took up the
question but postponed a decision and requested the Executive
Committee to work out some appropriate guidelines. These were
drafted in the succeeding period and adopted by the Assembly at
Evian (1970) as a "Statement concerning the attitude of the Lutheran
World Federation to churches in union negotiations."
        For the Lutheran churches with their traditional, almost
traumatic anti-unionist attitude, this statement constitutes a very
important ecumenical breakthrough. Its decisive sentence reads:
"A union of churches must be seen as a proper expression of the

unity of the church when uniting churches have agreed upon a
confessional statement of faith that witnesses to a right understanding of the gospel to serve as a guide for preaching and the
administration of the sacraments". This leads to the assurance
that the World Federation would not "prevent member churches from
participating in union discussions but will rather assist them upon
request". And the establishment of a union "should not lead to
a break in relationships with the LWF if the united church's
confessional statement is in substantial agreement with the
doctrinal basis of the Lutheran World Federation" (*Proceedings*,
p. 142).

Naturally this statement does not imply a blanket consent
to every form of church union. The new attitude itself makes
distinctions and corresponds to the basic lines of the Lutheran
conception of unity. In addition it is clear that church union
is in no sense the only model for church unity which must be
worked for everywhere and at all times. Other forms can also
exist which are also - and perhaps even in a more adequate way -
a "proper expression" of church unity.

The Establishment of Bilateral Inter-Confessional Dialogues

One of the most significant developments within the
ecumenical movement over the past fifteen years has been the
evolution of a far-flung network of bilateral inter-confessional
dialogues. Of course, bilateral conversations between confessional
churches had existed before as well. But it is only in recent
times that they have become so concentrated and extensive that they
can indeed be seen as a new kind of ecumenical encounter. The
World Council of Churches has certainly contributed a lot,
even though indirectly, to bringing about these dialogues; in
certain cases it has even given them direct support. However, these
bilateral dialogues take place essentially outside of the organizational framework of the World Council which tends more to favor
multilateral encounters.

Not only have the Lutheran churches become involved in this
kind of ecumenical endeavor with striking eagerness; they have had
a decisive effect in promoting the development and extension of
this network of conversations. They are just as committed to and
active in this new field of ecumenical activity as they were
hesitant e.g. about union negotiations. It is quite obvious that
this is a type of ecumenical endeavor which is particularly congenial

to the Lutheran churches and their conception of unity. The
"Guidelines for Ecumenical Encounter" (1970) drawn up by the
Theological Commission of the Lutheran World Federation make this
clear: "Bilateral encounter is a necessary and appropriate mode
of ecumenical endeavor. It is suited for treating the problems
of church division in their specific form, their theological
importance and their historical roots, as well as for drawing out
the special points of commonality and agreement which have been
preserved in spite of separation.

"The concentration on that which is specific in the relation
ship of the individual churches to one another, a characteristic
of bilateral discussion, usually strengthens the possibility of
understanding among the partners. This is made more difficult in
multilateral discussions because of the number of partners, each
with their own terminology and their own theological and confessional presuppositions. At the same time, this concentration
creates greater opportunities for reaching concrete results,
ecumenical steps, and decisions" (*Lutheran World*, 1970, p. 53ff.).
It is obvious that here too the conviction which is characteristic
of the Lutheran churches is present in the background, namely
that the way to the true unity of the church must not circumnavigate
the confessions but go through them.

Since the beginning of the sixties in rapid sequence such
a wealth of bilateral interconfessional conversations with various
partners has evolved that it is difficult to keep track of them
today, and now Lutheran churches from Scandinavia to South America
and from North America to the Philippines are involved in dialogues
like these. But it is not only Lutheran churches from different
countries which are engaged in bilateral interconfessional conversations. The Lutheran World Federation as such has also abandoned
its previous role of a mainly indirect promoter of the ecumenical
movement to adopt that of a very active partner in the ecumenical
dialogue. As has already been mentioned, in the years since 1965
it has started official conversations with various churches and
world confessional families, with the Roman Catholic church, the
Anglican Communion and the World Alliance of Reformed Churches.
In addition, there are close contacts aimed at the establishment
of similar dialogues with the Orthodox churches, the World Methodist
Council and the Baptist World Alliance. The conversations so far
have had, in part, very significant and promising results which
constitute new milestones in the relations between the churches:
the statements of consensus from the Catholic/Lutheran conversations
in the USA, the Catholic/Lutheran "Malta Report", the Reformed/

Lutheran "Leuenberg Agreement" and the Anglican/Lutheran "Pullach Report".

It has also, of course, become clear in the process that there is a series of controversial theological problems which still await a satisfactory solution and, above all, that the really decisive matter of turning the results of the conversations into church fellowship is difficult to handle. Therefore it appears urgently necessary not only to persevere in the conduct of doctrinal conversations but also to search for new and complementary methodological approaches. But the conviction remains that bilateral interconfessional dialogue will continue to be of central importance in the future as well.

Prospects and Tasks

If one looks back at the way in which the Lutheran churches have understood and exercised their ecumenical commitment, among other things one significant constant feature stands out time and again: it is the conviction that confessional awareness and ecumenical commitment, confessional fellowship and ecumenical unity are not obstacles to one another and can go hand in hand. The relation between "confession" and "ecumenism" is not seen as the insoluable squaring of the circle which would mean that one had finally to opt for the one or the other and that the way to the unity of the church could only be abandoning the existing confessions. The link between "confession" and "ecumenism" is possible and necessary.

This theory of the compatibility of confessional identity and ecumenical fellowship, which was disputed for a long time and from many angles, has acquired a credibility and convincing force today as a result of new ecumenical theological insights which many did not previously believe it to have. It is also able to build on the background of a changed situation in the sense that the confessional churches - including the Roman Catholic church - are playing a distinctive role, which many would have thought impossible, within the ecumenical movement with their bilateral dialogues. There is no doubt that this development will contribute to the conviction of the compatibility of confessional identity and ecumenical fellowship continuing to constitute one of the major approaches within which the ecumenical involvement of the Lutheran churches takes place.

However, it will have to be clearly recognized in the
process that the confessions as they were and still are to a
large extent are at the most capable of coexistence but not yet
fully capable of fellowship. This is the grain of truth in the
theory, which is certainly false when applied wholesale, of the
antagonistic relationship between confession and ecumenism. The
elements of delineation of one from another and of mutual
condemnation have penetrated so far into the fabric of the
confessions and determined their understanding and shape so much
in the course of the history of division that genuine reconciliation
and fellowship between the confessions is unthinkable without a
simultaneous process of change. Only if the confessions are
prepared to change are they able to enjoy fellowship.

This is a matter of something quite other than the
relinquishing of each side's confessional identity in favor of a
trans-confessional Christian identity. It is in fact a question
of modifications and shifts *within* a given confessional self-
understanding. Identity and change are not mutually exclusive.
Where, as in the major Christian confessions, it is a matter of
historical entities, they in fact belong very closely together,
because in the framework of history identity can only be preserved
and maintained if it accepts change. This is the only way in which
it can demonstrate its vitality and relevance in changing historical
situations.

Interconfessional dialogue aims at this sort of reconciliation
between the confessions made possible by change and renewal. It
does not try to abolish the confessions with their differences but,
on the other hand, neither can it leave them completely untouched
in their traditional form. This process could be described as
something like a "redefinition of confessions through dialogue."
This sort of redefinition will have two features. It will have to
remove the elements of distortion, narrowness and exaggeration
which have made confessional divergences into differences which
divide the churches because they obscured the legitimate and
authentic character of confessional divergences. But in this
process of change and renewal the confessions will take on their
authentic form. They will at last recognize one another as acceptable, legitimate expressions of Christian faith, witness and life.
In this way a reconciliation between confessions will come about
and a fellowship will be created which has recently been described
by the expression "reconciled diversity." It is not a reconciliation
and fellowship which come about by abandoning confessional identity
or by mutual integration or merging of confessional convictions.

It is certainly not a mutually tolerant coexistence which does not deserve the names "reconciliation" or "fellowship". Rather, it is a matter of reconciliation and fellowship resulting from a firm acceptance of the other in his "redefined" otherness which has thereby visibly become legitimate.

This sort of ecumenical prospect, which has as its goal a fellowship in which confessional particularities and diversities are not merged but reconciled with one another, corresponds to the Lutheran conception of church unity. It probably also corresponds to the conception of unity in many other churches and it would be a good thing if the Lutheran churches were to work for this sort of concept of church fellowship in the ecumenical struggle.

Translated by Margaret Pater

PART THREE

LUTHERAN CONFESSION IN A CHANGING WORLD

We concluded the previous section with the observation
that theology and the church can only tackle today's tasks and
help solve them if they work together in an ecumenical spirit.
This assertion is substantiated when we consider that churches
of different confessions exist side by side and are summoned to
joint action as a result of their situation, whatever their
confession.

Right though it may be that we live in *one* world and serve
one humanity, due attention must at the same time also be given
to the manifold situations in different parts of the world. Thus
in this final section the special nature of the problems of
geographically separated areas will be examined more closely.
Naturally, in the following essays we could only examine a few
specific cases, and consider these as somewhat like models of
discovering the identity of the churches of the Lutheran confession.
Then it becomes evident how far witness and service of the churches
are determined by historical, political, economic and ethnic factors
in regional situations. As such they do, however, contribute
specific elements of Lutheran identity in the ecumenical context.

The fact that we begin with the European churches is
first of all historically motivated. It was here that the call of
the Reformation was first proclaimed in the life of the European
nations. In past centuries the church was closely linked with
the life of these nations. A pattern developed in which church
and people, structure of society and life of the church were
intertwined. In Europe the "national church" (*Volkskirche,
folkkyrka*) became the sign of the conversion of whole nations and
lands. As the former Bishop Billing in Sweden liked to express

it, the national church represented "the offer of the forgiveness
of sins to the whole people."

Changes in modern society gave a severe shock to this
phenomenon - in Eastern as well as in Western Europe. Cultural and
political developments revealed the fact of how superficial the
bonds of the people to the church were in many places, so that a
"fellowship of confession" was hardly felt to be characteristic.
For this very reason the "system" of the national church has been
questioned. Has not the Christian church become a piece of folk-
lore in the consciousness of the European nations independent of
their confessional ties? Did she not represent a "decorative"
aspect which should belong to man's life only in times of change
and in crisis situations? The question is justified whether this
claim on the service of the church still corresponds with the
apostolic mandate of the Gospel. If the distinct layers of this
question are surveyed and the West and the East European situations
are dealt with separately, the reasons for this lie not only in
the political but also in the closely linked differences in the
structure of society.

When the essay on Western Europe (chapter 13) evaluates
positive opportunities for the national church (*Volkskirche*)
in a changing world this is in no way intended as an unconditional
defence of the past. On the contrary, the critique in this essay
of the present structures of society recalls the church to her
task. She is exhorted to critically oppose a Western tendency to
state monopoly in the interest of humanity; to summon active help
with the comfort and help of God at "folkloric" contact places; to
present a system of norms and values so that men's lives may become
creative. All this cannot be achieved through demagogic declarations
but in a concrete new community of Christians in solidarity with
the whole of humanity. To get on with this task, the church needs
a theology which takes its norm not from the world situation but
from the Word of God. Thus she may offer a new confessional
consciousness to the nations.

In Eastern parts of Europe the church was forced to rethink
her past in a quite special way. The experience of the German
Kirchenkampf resulted in slightly different positions in the GDR
than those in the minority churches of Europe for whom similar
experiences were mostly unknown. All these churches are embraced
however within the same situation, being determined by political
and ideological factors. In this respect the atheistic element
has put new questions to the churches. However in so far as the
Eastern socialist state ideology excludes an "ideological

co-existence" with Christianity, the churches have an opportunity
of following their specific task as churches in socialist states.
The Christian confession would be falsified if it put itself
forward as an ideological alternative or as a competitor. The
doctrine of the Two Kingdoms, understood correctly, can here be
just the very help which the churches can rely upon in eliminating
the misunderstandings of the past.

The Eastern European churches are seeking jointly with all
men of good will to play their part in solving the great problems
which face mankind today. The example of the GDR (chapter 14)
witnesses this in greater detail. We discover that the way is
neither easy nor straightforward to describe. It leads to
existential decisions between different alternatives which themselves are topics for discussion inside the church. One basic
truth remains equally essential, however, for the churches of
the East and of the West: in affirming new social realities,
churches may not become instruments of the people or of the state.
The problems on both sides are similar but are differently
articulated: the mission of the church cannot be fulfilled solely
in the tasks prescribed by the situation and determined by those
responsible in secular matters, i.e. in the "earthly kingdom".
The churches are responsible to him who is not of this world. To
him they owe their first loyalty. To him they bear their witness.
Thus the "church as a fellowship of witness and service" is the
specific profile in the sense of the Lutheran Confessions.

Luther was already aware that new continents were being
discovered and that the Gospel message had to be got across to
these parts of the world as well. It was not until the emigration
of larger national groups to the new world that the existence of
the Lutheran church became a reality there. In the encounter with
a new world a new Lutheran consciousness was created, but slowly
at first. The encounter with new cultures brought to memory first
only gradually that the Lutheran Reformation had only reached the
Anglo-Saxon peoples indirectly, and had not reached the Latin
peoples (especially the Italians, the Spaniards and Portuguese)
at all. The national and cultural encounter with these new church
traditions has made people more conscious of the problem however.
For a long time the immigrants were able to hold on to their
original culture but modern times have resulted, in this respect,
in radical changes and thus a certain identity crisis.

Two essays portray the North American and South American
scenes with their own unique features with regard to discovering
Lutheran identity (chapters 15-16). What has been fought out

willingly or unwillingly in North America in the last few generations still remained an intensive task on the Latin American
continent. In the north and likewise in the south the problem of
acculturation is only partly a problem of language (in its widest
sense). It is simultaneously the problem of different memory
levels of the immigrants who constantly poured into the new world
as late as the Second World War and who held fast to their own
respective memories as a means of safeguarding their own identity.

This observation, which is true for both Americas, is
made more difficult in the South because here one saw an outwardly
Christianized continent, but which, as H. Meyer says, represented
a "Christianity without Reformation." What was the task of the
Lutheran church in this context? The reason why Lutheranism has
prevailed through the common efforts of Lutherans with "different
memories" in the last few centuries will be of particular interest
to the reader. Missionary experiences from non-Christian countries
were not sufficient in the new situation of discovering identity.
The apostolic and missionary task of Lutheran presence made a
new strategy necessary. It is widely understood as an ecumenical
task in partnership with the dominating Catholic church and with
the other Christian traditions. "The search for identity is not
a self-centered goal, but the sign of a hope for a more extended
discipleship" (Lesko).

The missionary undertaking by the European and North
American churches in Asia and Africa has experienced a special
development in the last few decades (chapter 17). The self-
awakening and with it the closely-linked endeavor for political,
economic and cultural independence have questioned the basic
principles of mission valid till then. This question was put to
the Lutheran churches in a striking way after the last world war.
For the problems of the "Third World" are closely related to the
confession of the Gospel. How should this newly awakened self-
consciousness and the national and cultural wealth of these
continents, which have been shaped by another religious world than
the Christian one, achieve new life which has an indigenous form
of expression? The inherited attitude of "paternalism" towards
these peoples and churches must cease. Room must be made for a
growth in categories of their own self-hood and maturity. But
how can the unchangeable and unique confession of faith be transplanted into the changing elements of an indigenous Third World
identity? The world conferences on both the African and Asian
continents have asked this and other related questions. The way
for common witness with the indigenous churches is sought today

in solidarity with the inheritance of the faith of the fathers.
While these churches are in the process of developing their own
independent lives of faith, they are already capable of bringing
back the Gospel to their European and American mother churches.
Thus begins a new era of missionary exchange between Christians,
who belong to different continents but whose profile has been
shaped by the same confession.

It is natural that the course taken on the different
continents and their respective problems should be concluded by
a description of the Lutheran World Federation's service in the
last three decades. Nowadays the LWF has become the organization
through which the Lutheran churches begin their exchange of
experiences in all areas of theology and church life, a process
which continues successfully to the present day (chapter 18).
Because the Lutheran church lacks a universal, authoritative
organization and because the independence of each individual church
is carefully watched over, the self-understanding of the Lutheran
World Federation is presented as a serious identity problem of
our church on the world-wide level. Attempts have been made to
investigate these problems in various ways. Discussion is still
in progress. It will still have to contribute to the manifestation
of the Lutheran church in united witness and service. The realization of church fellowship in our own sphere will in the end be a
test for the ecumenical consciousness of our church. For at the
source of our own existence, thrust upon us by history, unmistake-
ably lies the ecumenical dimension of our mission.

CHAPTER 13

HANS WEISSGERBER

THE CHANGING "VOLKSKIRCHE"
IN CENTRAL AND NORTHERN EUROPE

On the Situation of the Volkskirche and the State Churches

Anyone analyzing the situation of the *Volkskirche* in Central and Northern Europe must proceed on the assumption that the two ecclesiastical regions are not identical but, despite certain common foundations, differently organized. These common foundations are rooted basically in the historical development of the church system which goes back, regardless of its present structure, to the Middle Ages, primarily to the identity between church members and state citizens. This foundation was not appreciably influenced or impaired even by the Reformation, because it was always whole countries or state structures that either accepted the Reformation or remained with the old religion--freedom of religion belonged only to the prince who, having decided himself for one or the other confession, demanded the same conversion of all his subjects: the identity between state citizens and church members was upheld. This defines the nature of the *Volkskirche* from the 16th to the 19th century.

In the further course of church history a process of dissolution began, fed from various sources and developing differently in the different church structures. This process was connected with the secularization that began with the Reformation and which the Catholic churches could also not avoid. It was further connected with a change in the self-understanding of the state, influenced by the French and North American revolutions.

Finally it must be seen in connection with the population
fluctuations which were at least in part a product of the industrialization of Europe. When it became necessary in the course
of industrialization for large population groups to change their
places of living and working, then the principle of the unity of
state citizens and church members could in the long run no longer
be maintained; then the different denominations were finally given
the right to religious freedom and thus also political equality.
The development in Europe was admittedly limited to the two large
churches, the Roman Catholic and the Protestant; the Anglo-American
free churches and the Lutheran free churches that arose in the
second half of the nineteenth century renounced all connection
with or subordination to the state from the very beginning. They
have never grown numerically beyond a minority status.

In the course of this process of dissolution there
arose, in the second half of the 18th century, the demand for
separation of church and state as it had been consistently carried
through in the United States; this demand was fulfilled in France
in 1904, in Russia in 1918, and after 1948 in the socialist
countries of Eastern Europe, including the German Democratic
Republic, although these situations need not concern us here. Nonetheless the separation of church and state can have different
legal forms and consequences for the church, as a comparison of
France and the Soviet Union shows. The separation does not in
principle rule out the possibility that contracts, agreements or
legal connections may exist between church and state, as is seen
in the Federal Republic of Germany.

The situation is different in the Scandinavian churches,
where the state church still exists, that is, there is a legal
identity between church membership and state citizenship, notwithstanding the fact that Roman Catholic and free church minorities
may exist; and where--this is the decisive element in the character
of the state church--the leadership of the church lies in the hands
of the state.

We have learned, however, that the relationship of
the members to their church must not automatically be influenced
by the legal structure of the state-church relationship: the
frequency of church attendance, and of ecclesiastical rites
(funerals, baptisms, weddings, etc.), participation in church life,
general opinion of the role and tasks of the church in society, the
function of the pastor, and finally the "internal" and subsequently,
the "external" emigration of members from the church does not depend
on whether the church structure follows either the Scandinavian

pattern or the principle of separation of church and state with
the maintenance of contractual and legal connections (as in the
Federal Republic of Germany).

The Weimar Constitution of 1919 maintained in Article
136: "There is no state church." The Basic Law (*Grundgesetz*)
set down in Bonn in 1949 adopted the relevant articles of the
Weimar Constitution word for word and gave them ongoing validity.
The relationship of church and state in the Federal Republic of
Germany, has been defined in the Twenties as a "limping separation";
today one speaks (in the words of Prime Minister Albert Osswald,
Wiesbaden) of a "balanced separation on the basis of freedom of
religion."

The relationship between church and state as described
here has been customarily referred to as the *"Volkskirche."* The
concept is old; it appears already in Schleiermacher, but "after
the demise of governmental church rule in 1918 the whole paper
forest of the church echoes with this word" (W. Huber). The
concept is polemically exaggerated here without doubt, but the
polemic could be directed at the state church structure as well
as the purely pastoral church. *"Volkskirche"* was defined as a
goal, namely the christianization of the whole people, which meant
among other things that the members of the *Volkskirche* were objects
of pastoral care by the church (this leads in the current discussion
to the "functional church concept" of W. Dahm, which will occupy
us later). *Volkskirche* can however be understood also as "church
of the people," "church for the people," and finally as "church
for the whole people" (W. Huber). Especially with the latter two
definitions it is important to observe that the *Volkskirche* is
intimately connected with infant baptism and the Christian custom
of accepting baptism, wedding celebration, funerals, etc. as a
matter of course.

The *Volkskirche* is a church organization with a "native"
membership; this membership is established by baptism. The
regulation of membership rights occurs in independent ecclesiastical
responsibility--different from the Scandinavian state churches,
where church membership is connected initially with state citizenship, although the possibility of a free decision by an individual
exists which would separate the two. The situation of the Federal
Republic of Germany is similar to the Scandinavian situation in so
far as the great majority of the members of the society, or
citizens of the state, are simultaneously members of a certain
church organization (in the Federal Republic 95 percent of the
citizens belong to one of the two "large" confessions). This

formal fact does not indicate the degree and intensity with which
the church members make use of their membership. But even yet--
and here nothing has been changed from the medieval structure--
the membership is seen as an imputed and not an acquired characteristic, and rests on the territorial principle. Every Protestant
or every Catholic Christian is automatically a member of the
national or state church of his residential area so long as he
does not initiate a change.

The situation of the state church or the *Volkskirche*
is not always unquestionably accepted--and never has been. Already
Luther had reservations, as can be read in his preface to the
German Mass of 1526. Also, the emergence of the free churches in
the Anglo-Saxon world and their activity in Northern and Central
Europe, which began in the first third of the 19th century, caused
serious questions at the state church and *Volkskirche* system. It
may in this connection be mentioned that it was precisely Lutheranism,
traditionally viewed as especially true to the state and its
authorities, that set free out of its own tradition the forces that
led to the separation from the state church system and to free
churches, and which found new organizational forms through its
conflicts with the state. This occurred in Prussia with the forced
union between Lutherans and Reformed after 1815 in connection with
the adoption of church functions by the state; it happened in 1875
in Hessen and Hannover (here it concerned the regulating of the
registration of population data, (which in Sweden is still handled
by the church); and it happened also in the Scandinavian lands--
above all in Norway--in connection with the spiritual revival movement of the 19th century.

For some years it has been observable that the
discussion of the problem of the state church and the *Volkskirche*
has reached an especially high degree of intensity. This has gone
so far that a fundamental change in existing ecclesiastical or
constitutional relationships is no longer in principle excluded,
but is in fact brought into the theories and discussions. A
signal for this new orientation of the discussion was the book by
H.H. Brunner, *Kirche ohne Illusionen* (The Church without Illusions),
in which so to speak the worst case scenario was presented:
what does a church in Switzerland look like 25 years after the
complete separation between church and state has been fulfilled?
(I myself cannot endorse the conclusion of Brunner, according to
which nothing remains of the church other than a social service
organization that performs community work; but it is nonetheless
remarkable that someone has projected this situation through to

the final consequences.

In Scandinavia there are deliberations in progress which would modify the state church system; a Swedish delegation visited the Federal Republic of Germany in 1975 solely for this purpose. In the Federal Republic itself the *Volkskirche* is seen more as a mission than as an available "possession at hand" (Rendtorff), although respected experts in the field of church and state relations like A. von Campenhausen claim that the relationship between church and state is nowhere so well regulated as in the Federal Republic. In the course of contemporary debate over a concrete issue such as whether a pastor can also be a member of a Communist party, the problem is clearly seen: how can an understanding of the church as an organization with "native" members that has religious duties to fulfill for the society as a whole be brought into harmony with an understanding of the church as a community of fellow-believers? In a word: the state church or *Volkskirche* has to an as yet unheard-of degree become a problem to itself.

Some details of this process of change will be pursued in the following discussion. The subject itself is so multi-layered that in this presentation only certain aspects can be discussed.

The Volkskirche as an Object of Empirical Investigations

Sociology of religion is a part of general sociology, that discipline that gathers data through scientifically sound methods and only afterwards draws conclusions. Sociology of religion began in the '50s in certain limited fields to investigate the facts and the practice of church membership, although broad conclusions were at first not to be reached. The scene changed at the beginning of the '70s when broader investigations were initiated by the Protestant as well as the Catholic churches; the results of these studies are now available: *Wie Stabil ist die Kirche?* (How Stable is the Church?), edited by Helmut Hild, and *Gottesdienst in einer rationalen Welt* (Worship in a rational World), by Gerhard Schmidtchen, as well as the inquiries edited by Karl Förster, *Befragte Katholiken--zur Zukunft von Glaube und Kirche* and *Priester zwischen Anpassung und Unterscheidung* (Asking the Catholics--on the Future of Faith and Church, and: Priests Between Conformity and Distinction).

It is not possible here to go into the details of these studies; they permit the conclusion, however, that the question posed in the volume edited by Hild, can be answered positively. Regarding the number of members, the latent desire to leave the church, and the fixation on the pastor as the reference person for all church activity, the *Volkskirche* can be seen despite all its problems to be extraordinarily and surprisingly stable. Those questioned showed only a slight desire to leave the church; they see the pastor in every way as the decisive reference person for church activity, which contradicts, interestingly, the efforts in theology and church that would relieve the pastor of his traditional duties in favor of a stronger participation of lay members in church life. The identity of church members and state citizens shows cracks and limitations, but seems basically not to be threatened.

The editor, H. Hild, has adequately warned us in the foreword to the study against overemphasizing the positive results. For despite the positive testimony of the church members it is clear that a change in the *Volkskirche* status is inevitable in the long run. This study was made in the densely populated Rhein/Main region, but it can be projected over the whole Federal Republic of Germany because of its representative quality. In view of existing comparable structures it is very probable that a corresponding study in the Scandinavian countries would come to similar conclusions. In the following discussion I proceed on this assumption.

The *Volkskirche* consists of people who participate in church life in varying degrees. The people who are ready or willing to leave the church are also identifiable: at the most they comprise 17 percent of the total membership. Anyone who thinks this amount would begin a healthy weeding-out process in the church should consider the following: that 17 percent who openly or in the long run are thinking of leaving the church belong to that social level which Schelsky referred to already 20 years ago as "the society-determining middle class" that in the future will determine the life of our industrial society. But not only this. When the class of middle and leading white collar workers is shown to be the most likely to leave the church and if they in fact do so, then the class of those who are likely to leave the church that are still only 17 percent of the total will at least then grow considerably when a) they actually take this step, and b) the children of this generation of those possibly leaving the church in turn have children who have no ties to the church. It

is thus easy to conclude that at the latest within one generation
the exodus from the church will dramatically increase. In other
words, the *Volkskirche* is shrinking.

The situation is similar in the Scandinavian countries.
Indeed, leaving the church is made less easy since (in Sweden)
anyone leaving the church must still pay 60 percent of his church
tax, because the church performs functions which would otherwise
fall to the society or the state. But on the other hand, no matter
how one evaluates the results of such studies individually, it is
not possible to deny that the *Volkskirche* in the future will not
be able to represent the vast majority of society, because these
people will no longer be made members of the church by baptism in
the former proportions. One will rather have to act on the
assumption that there is a certain percentage of the population
that will consciously decide to distance itself from the church
and a certain percentage that will consciously be ready to enter
the church. The numbers and percentages do not here play the
decisive role; the determinant and decisive factor in the change
of the *Volkskirche* is simply the fact that the church in Central
and Northern Europe in ever-growing measure will consist of
conscious members and not only of baptized members.

The Legal Aspects of State-Church Relationships

The legal arrangement between state and church in
Scandinavia rests essentially on traditional law that provides for
a state church. That means that the highest leadership posts of
the church are in the hands of the state, that is, the king, the
parliament, or the responsible ministerial department. Even where
there is a Bishops' conference, a Synod, or archbishops, the church
lacks an independent representation toward the outside world and
an independent legislative power on the inside. Thus the Swedish
government still decides on the appointing of bishops, and the
Danish minister for church affairs decides on the removal of a
pastor who no longer accomodates himself to the traditional customs
of the *Volkskirche*. But the state church structure has already
been broken through, especially in Finland, where the varied
history of the country has led to church-state relationships that
correspond more to those of the Federal Republic of Germany than
a state church, and the church of Finland has a greater independent
voice in external matters. But even in the countries with the
classical state church system, like Denmark, Norway, and Sweden,

a process has begun that seems to be changing the state-church
relationship.

    Church News from Denmark (December 1975) gives infor-
mation on the situation in Denmark, and I include the full text
here:

"The Evangelical-Lutheran Church is the Folk-Church of Denmark
and is as such supported by the state," it is said in the Constitution of the Danish Kingdom. Most people in Denmark - about 95
percent - are members of this church.

The thoughts of the men who gave the constitution were that the
Folk-Church should have its own constitution which was expressed
in the so-called promise-article: "The relations of the Folk-
Church shall be fixed by a special law." This promise-article,
however has been fulfilled in a very special way - or never
fulfilled. The goal naturally was to create a church constitution
with congregational self-government, but this has never been
realized. Instead we have the practice that when problems arise
in the church, they are solved by current legislation. It is
very important to know this historical background to understand
how the Folk-Church of Denmark is working.

It is most simple to look at the official Folk-Church as a frame
system, a very elastic one, inside which the life of the church
takes place.

Most of the resources of the Folk-Church are raised from the special
church-tax which is paid by the members of the Folk-Church. It is
collected by the municipalities.

It is the parish council who makes the budget of the local parish.
The parish councils are expressions of the local democratic
government in the Folk-Church. In practice the tasks of the
council are limited in several ways. The most important tasks
are:

Administration of the freeholding churches. Account and budget.
Right and duty to build churches according to the growth of the
cities. Decisions concerning confirmation, permission of collections
in the church, agreement to changes in liturgy and time of service
etc. Election of pastor. Election of bishop - together with the
other parish councils in the diocese.

The free organizations of the church:

The free organizations play a very important role in the Folk-
Church. They can be gathered in the groups: Children and youth
organizations, deaconical and social institutions, educational
institutions. Most of the free organizations only exist because
of private resources. As a main role, the free organizations work
on a free basis inside the frame of the Folk-Church, spread across
the country and at the same time fitting into the local life of
the congregation. They are children of the great awakening in
Denmark in the last century, especially the Home Mission.

One of the free organizations is "Kirkefondet" - the Church
Foundation. Today a considerable part of the work of Kirkefondet
consists of putting new life into congregations. Under the title

"Aktion Ansvar" - "Action to Responsibility" - programs have been planned in the course of the past few years in nine congregations, and in six congregations - among them one which is Catholic! - preparations are being made for the introduction of the program. Kirkefondet's General Secretary, Gunnar Hermansen, says of the goal of the program: "-We want to call each member to activity and co-responsibility in the church and the congregation to which one belongs. Action to Responsibility is sober and realistic because it only points toward a certain group of people, namely the people we already have some contact with, and who are not strangers to the church. The program wants to start a dialogue with these people and motivate them to activity and co-responsibility, in order that they can make decisions concerning what has to be done in their own congregations. So far the results of the action have been very positive."

The problems signalizing a profound change can be seen in these places:

a) The state universities have theological faculties that are responsible for theological research according to scientific standards and also for the training of pastors of the church. The character of these theological faculties as carrying out true science as criticized from both sides, university and church. This is justified as far as theology does not draw the foundation of its research from theology itself.

b) The Scandinavian legislation concerning the church makes it possible at any time for the state to interfere in the official pastoral duties of an individual pastor, even to remove him from his office if he no longer complies with the church laws established by the state. Example: a Danish pastor who refuses to baptize children without parental instruction, and in fact requires the parents to take part in a five-hour baptism instruction, must face the consequence that he will be released from church service, since the ruling state church system presupposes unconditional infant baptism. The latest report on this subject makes it clear that the particular pastor has shown an exaggerated stubbornness for the sake of his cause, but on the other hand the state organs, even those democratically elected, show no readiness to withdraw their rights over against the church. This case shows two things:

1. Orthodox Lutheranism is in certain instances (as in Germany in the 19th century) prepared to act in opposition to the state (this despite the general opinion of dutiful, loyal Lutheranism); and

2. The state must re-investigate its relationship to the church in order to insure that it is not simply concerned with maintaining its power over the church.

Besides his traditional ecclesiastical and spiritual

duties, a Swedish pastor also has the function of municipal registrar, which has little to do with his spiritual office but much to do with the connection of the state with his church.

On the other hand certain ecclesiastical acts--for example the naming and installing of bishops--require state approval of confirmation in order to be fully valid. In the Federal Republic of Germany the legal situation is different for the different confessions: according to the Prussian Concordat of 1929 and the *Reichskonkordat* of 1933 a Catholic bishop must swear loyalty to the constitution after being named and installed, whereas the naming or election of a Protestant bishop or church president must simply be announced to the responsible state government; it is sufficient afterwards that an inaugural visit be made in order to document the friendly relationship between church and state (as expressed in an exemplary way in the so-called Loccum Contracts of 1955).

Independently of a state church or *Volkskirche* system as regulating the relationship between state and church, the public influence of the churches on state actions, for example in the area of legislation and administration, has receded. The voice of the church is not so binding even in the Scandinavian state churches as it once was. This can be seen very clearly in the case of the Norwegian bishop Per Lönning, who resigned his office precisely at the moment when the Norwegian Parliament would not follow the church's conception of abortion law reform. The point here is certainly not the abortion laws as such, but rather the question of the extent to which the state, in its legislative function, is bound by the opinion of the church. If the state is not prepared to be bound by this opinion--as in this concrete case--then the question of a new regulation of the state-church relationship is posed with special urgency; at this point the resignation of Per Lönning is in fact justifiable.

It should be noted that the efforts to change the state church system in the Scandinavian countries primarily come from the church or, as is shown by the visit of a mixed Swedish commission in the Federal Republic of Germany, from the state and the church together, because the situation is in general seen as unsatisfactory and a solution is sought from both sides that does justice to the transformation in the society. It is different in the Federal Republic of Germany: here the official churches of both the Roman Catholic and Protestant confessions are satisfied with the *Volkskirche* situation and with the contractual regulation of the relationship between church and state, and thus

do not initiate changes. This applies as well, incidentally, to
the two main political parties of this country, the CDU and the SPD.
This does not necessarily stop the parties from occasionally
exercising criticism of the churches in concrete cases, of course.
Thus, for example, the general secretary of the CDU stated on the
occasion of the issuing of the new Roman Catholic statement on
sexual morality: "The church is making itself ludicrous" (Deutsche
Presse Agentur, German Press Agency from 19.1.76).

Excursus: The Demand for "Separation of Church and State" in
           the Federal Republic of Germany

           The Free Democratic Party (FDP) has made itself the
advocate of all those who feel that the intention of the German
Constitution of 1919 is still unfulfilled. The principle of
separation of church and state is rooted there, but existing
contractual ties between state and church are said to hinder the
realization of this constitutional mandate. What are the concrete
concerns of those holding this view?
           With the misleading slogan "a free church in a free
state" the FDP demands not the separation of church and state,
which is in any case long since completed, but rather the elimination of remaining church privileges and the retreat of the church
to the realm of private piety. The so-called FDP church paper of
1974 envisages the following:
a) the classification of religious communities as normal groups
of society in an organizational form yet to be developed;
b) the removal of all religious "relics" from public life, such
as crosses in classrooms and courtrooms, religious oaths, the right
to participate jointly in public welfare, such as kindergartens
and hospitals (N.B.: In the Federal Republic of Germany 70 percent
of all *kindergartens* are run by the churches!);
c) the renunciation by the state of its right to intervene in
church affairs, such as in the oath of loyalty to the Constitution
spoken by Catholic bishops, the political clause in the appointment
of leading officials in the Evangelical church, the appropriate
representation of the churches in the governing bodies of public
organizations such as radio/television stations;
d) the elimination of religious instruction in the schools in
favor of an informationally-oriented religious study program; and
not least
e) the organization of the military chaplaincy in the Army
(Bundeswehr), in the prisons, and in other public organizations on

a private basis.

This is just a sample from the voluminous catalog of 14 original demands of the FDP, which has been, interestingly enough, reduced to 13 because the party itself could not agree as to whether the theological faculties should be eliminated as educational training centers for pastors of both confessions or if they should be transformed into more or less neutral departments of religious studies.

The theses of the FDP can be reduced to threee fundamental statements:

1. The organization of the church should no longer be in the form of a public corporation, but rather a form yet to be developed;

2. All rights and privileges which the church still enjoys as a consequence of historical developments or present social contributions should be eliminated;

3. Religious confession and religious expression should be restricted to the private sphere.

What is being offered under the label "separation of church and state," namely the elimination of the privileged *Volkskirche* and the relegation of religious expression to the private sphere, is at the moment not a topic of political or ecclesiastical debate. These demands however might have a long term effect politically when the *Volkskirche* has shrunk to such an extent (as is predicted by current empirical investigations) that its social role and its service functions for the population must have a different, better, motivation as at present is pursued by its existence as such. At this time there is no reason for the social function of the *Volkskirche* or the contributions of the state to the church to be reduced. There are so many social necessities that point to the validity of maintaining the present state of affairs. Just to give one example, the state educates pastors who afterwards enter the service of the religious communities. It also educates economists and businessmen who enter the service of industry that is organized on the basis of private economy and the maximation of profit without having to contribute anything more than the regular taxes for the education of their own successors. The state also trains lawyers and doctors, who upon successful completion of their studies exercise their duties independently and on a private basis. It thus follows that the education of pastors who represent social reference persons of considerable importance, cannot be viewed separately from the education of those exercising other key social functions.

Change in the Legal Relationships Between State and Church

In the area of social services the situation is similar: the state simply cannot accomplish all the services which society perceives as needed. And reversed: church activities can be considered legitimate because here something is done that no one else does (Robert Geisendörfer).

It is in fact so, but it must not remain so. The alternative would be the omnipresent welfare state, which it is the duty of the church to resist on the basis of the biblical understanding of man. Here the church may oppose any encroachments, not for its own sake, but for society.

The existing legal state and church relationships secured through contracts, are historical products; there is at the moment neither a practical nor a political necessity of changing them. This does not of course rule out possible changes on the side of the state or the church. The social services of the church in the Federal Republic of Germany (and similarly in the Scandinavian countries) presently save the state large sums of money. The takeover of such services would cost the state, and thus the taxpayer, not only more money, but would in the long run reduce the potential numbers of workers who as servants of the church are not devoted to acquisition and profit but with Christian motivation place themselves in the service of a cause, i.e., in the service of needy people. The state, if it were to assume all the social services that the church now offers, would of necessity have to give up this potential, which would cause not only financial but above all enormous human problems.

In weighing all the facts, one can assume that there is at the moment no purpose in changing the existing *Volkskirche* regulations, that is, the state-church relationship and the orderly exercise of the social services through the church. The state can, as legal experts have established, unilaterally cancel the state-church contracts or even give up the state-church-system itself. The state can further--assuming it has enough money--take over the social services of the church, and it can finally legislate an organizational form for the church that corresponds more to civil law than the corporate, public structure or state church form in which the church, and thus the church-state relationship in Central and Northern Europe, is presently organized. The question is only if the state itself would at the moment be best served by such actions.

There is at present a tendency toward a social welfare state in Central and Northern Europe; the state is inclined or even eagerly moving towards the assumption of total responsibility for providing the vital primary and secondary service needs of the individual citizen. That could--as the example of Sweden shows-- work well, as long as the state makes no irreversible claim to power, as happened in the socialist states of Eastern Europe; that is as long as the state does not insist on keeping all those functions and areas of work for itself that it once took over. This assumes also that the means for providing a state-regulated, total welfare system can and will be produced from the whole society.

The existence of *Volkskirchen*--no matter how their church-state relationship is legally defined--counteracts the tendency toward monopoly of the state. The socialist states grasped this long ago, and have accordingly banned the churches to the area of private religious exercises. The Western democracies have not at present taken this step, and with good reason. If the state practices wise self-limitation this will be respected, and the church will retain what belongs to the church. If the state inclines towards taking over all areas of primary and secondary social services, it will *à la longue* experience the church as a disrupting foreign element and attempt to curb its public effective-ness. Certain signs of this are recognizable in Scandinavia and Central Europe. The reduction of ecclesiastical privileges that has already begun and is being continued is a characteristic of the change in the *Volkskirchen*.

Social Services of the Churches

The church has up to now done pioneering work in the area of social services. In the Reformation period the assets of churches and cloisters, above all in the cities, were turned into relief funds (*Armenkasten*) and could thus be used to aid the socially disadvantaged. The Enlightenment produced a type of pastor who not only was concerned with the salvation of souls, but also with the economic well-being of his congregation; for example by introducing new agricultural or industrial methods (potato cultivation, and hat and glove manufacturing in Central and Northern Europe are originally due to Christian initiatives, even though this is no longer recognizable), taking care of the sick, caring for children in kindergartens, caring for wayward and unemployed young people, the psychologically ill and--a great problem today-- care for drug-dependent people. All these are social tasks that the churches above all have assumed; the churches were of course

at the same time ready to give up the exercise of these functions
when other state or social agencies declared themselves willing to
take them over. On the other hand, attending to public and social
needs is legitimate for the church so long as no other agency does
this. Here is a characteristic public function of the church,
which can best be accomplished in the form of the *Volkskirche*.

A *Volkskirche* deprived of its human, financial, and
social resources will not be able to perform its services to the
degree to which it was accustomed. Yet these services are expected
from a *Volkskirche* or a state church by the public. That means
that over against its own members a church, whether organized as
a *Volkskirche* or a state church, legitimizes its claim to be the
church for all the people less in orthodoxy than in orthopraxis,
it will come into question less for what it teaches than for what
it does.

To be sure, when the members of a church expect social
services they expect at the same time something more, because these
services must naturally be substantiated and justified. But what
is this "more"? We have learned that a Protestant hospital is
distinguished from a municipal hospital by something other than
the pious phrases on the walls; and a Protestant kindergarten is
distinguished from a municipal kindergarten by more than the sign
on the door. The difference lies in the message that God has
accepted all people for the sake of Jesus Christ and that this
message leads to social consequences.

One must, however, not limit the social services of
the church to the narrow field of Christian deaconic tasks. The
studies in sociology of religion have shown (and here some theore-
ticians, e.g. Dahm, have developed a "functional church theory")
that the expectations of the people from the church, apart from
immediate social services, fall in two important areas of life:
first, accompanying and assiting a person through the critical
stations of life--birth, maturity, marriage, and death. It is
precisely the services of the church that are offered at these
crucial moments and, apart from minor variations, they still enjoy
the unbroken affection of the people.*   Here lies an important

---

*According to information from the church chancellery
of the Evangelical Church in Germany, the vast majority of church
members in the Federal Republic still clings to the principle and
practice of infant baptism.
90% of all the children of whom at least one parent
belonged to one of the two large confessions were baptized in 1973.
The assertion that in Hamburg only 46% of all children were baptized
for example, is false.

task of the church, which must probably be understood more as
service to the person than as a missionary possibility.

The second expectation that one has of the church
today is the mediation of a norm and value system. Admittedly,
it characterizes the change in the function of the church in
Central and Northern Europe, that it is no longer the sole source of
norms and values on the market, but is in an intensive competition..
Typical for this situation are the reverberations produced by the
latest declaration of the Congregation of Faith of the Roman
Catholic Church on sexual morality. Only a few voices were in
agreement, all the others made clear that they no longer would
follow the Vatican line. The general secretary of the CDU,
Dr. Biedenkopf, said that the church is making itself ludicrous,
he was criticized by his party superiors for tactical reasons, but
he had given expression to a mood widely held by the people.

Facit: The role of the church as purveyor of a
value system is not disputed, but the values it purveys must not
be those of yesterday. The person of today expects from the
church guidance for today!

It is one of the decisive characteristics of the North
and Central European societies that the competitive conditions
on this market are not disadvantageous to the churches, which is
completely in contrast to the Eastern European countries. The
values, norms and orientation system that the church has to offer
must not necessarily become part of the total social consciousness
and they must not necessarily be integrated into state regulations.
But they are there, they are requested and required, and they are
sometimes even followed.

This is of course to be distinguised from the public
influence of the churches on state legislation and social order.
This influence is obviously receding, as we know, but nonetheless
the people still often ask "what the church says about this"--
even then, when one is not necessarily ready to follow what the
church has to say about it.

Two examples of this point:
1. In a lengthy documentation in 1968 "What Do the Germans Believe?"
Werner Harenberg empirically established that theological and
confessional statements are much less rooted in the consciousness
of the people or even accepted by them than is expected by the
church authorities or assumed for the normal structuring of congregational life. Even further: the emancipation from the statements
of faith of the Christian Confessions does not necessarily conflict
with a deep inner connection to the church.

2. The Catholic part of the population in Central and Northern
Europe has failed by far to increase to the extent one would have
expected from an observance of the strict Catholic regulations on
birth control, above all the encyclical of Paul VI that places
even ovulation control under ecclesiastical verdict. In other words
even Catholics who feel themselves bound to the church take the pill
despite papal instructions to the contrary.

This once again characterizes an important change in
the *Volkskirche:* it cannot by its very nature be a community
based on common understanding of faith. It is rather now by
necessity organized on the basis of pluralism: This of course,
evokes the task of defining the borders of such a pluralism.

This change can be exemplified in the development of
the Deutscher Evangelischer *Kirchentag*.* It arose in the spiritual
and material situation of the post-war years, and was originally
a manifestation of the Protestant church, designed to strengthen
the faith of the participants and give a missionary impulse for
those on the fringe. For this form of Protestant manifestation it
was important to emphasize unity, first of all the ecclesiastical
but also, before 1954, the political. In the '60s there occurred
a transformation - influenced among others by the student movement
and the spread of the so-called "critical theory" - to a sort of
Protestant Forum, that none of the different and partly polarized
groups succeeded in controlling. The manifestation of Protestantism
that the *Kirchentag* reflects is rooted consciously in a pluralism
that offered room for the different directions, positions and groups
within the Protestant Church. It was not the *Kirchentag* that had
changed, but rather the *Volkskirche* whose manifestation it is.

At this point new tasks arise for theology. Regardless of whether the work of theology is organized in state
universities or church-owned seminaries, the critical task of
theology will undoubtedly intensify. Theology must do more today
than merely interpret the tradition and establish the normative
and binding Christian tradition. The sociology of religion, so
important for illuminating the situation of the church in society
as it may be cannot make the claim to be a normative science. The
constant researching of the sources and the historical achievements
of the Christian faith can, in confrontation with the results of
empirical social research, provide the possibility of preaching the
gospel to modern man within the changing conditions of the *Volkskir*
and of calling him into the (likewise changing) structures of

_____

*A modern Protestant lay movement, organizing mass
meetings every second year.

ecclesiastical and Christian community. If the rejection of the
church as a community of faith corresponds to the expectations of
a changing *Volkskirche* and the church is viewed more from the
perspective of its services to modern man, then theology must among
other things provide for a church not degenerating into a social
service agency for the religious care of the people. In other
words, the proclamation of the gospel for modern man and the
expectation of modern man toward the proclamation must be brought
into a balanced relationship. At the same time the *Volkskirche*
must develop and offer new forms and possibilities of Christian
community, of which the traditional worship is just one (although
the central one) among many. In other words, a changing *Volkskirche*
requires also changing and new forms of Christian communication
and community.

In the framework of our topic and the function of theology
in the *Volkskirche* can only be hinted at. But this is the task
of the theology in a changing *Volkskirche* This church itself will
have to draw its consequences from the results of a theological
effort so understood. Even the development of a form of communication is unthinkable without such theological work.

Conclusion

What was presented in the foregoing discussion as
marks of change in the *Volkskirche* may be briefly summarized in
the following statements:

1. As far as membership lists are concerned state citizenship
and church membership are no longer identical; church membership
is not a given fact as has been taken for granted up to now, but
rather an acquired status.

2. This can have implications for the re-ordering of the state-
church relationships. It may further lead to the reduction of
church privileges; the process of reduction is ongoing. Therefore

3. The churches will investigate whether they can and should
continue to perform their social services to the same extent as
they do at present. This does not however mean that the work and
the opportunities of the church will be restricted, but

4. The expectations forwarded to the church are focused on
accompanying man in the critical moments of his life and conveying
to him a norm and value system. These expectations can be met
within the framework of the biblical mission of the church for
proclamation and pastoral care. This leads to two further consequences:

5. The *Volkskirche* is not an association of like-believers, that
is, a community of people committed to the same declaration of faith
and doctrine. Both institution and term of *Volkskirche* leaves room
for a necessary pluralism. And

6. Theology is challenged to bring into the balance the church's
mission and man's expectations, and at the same time to define the
limits of this pluralism and of developing new forms of christian-
ecclesiastical community.

7. A *Volkskirche* that can no longer count on a membership identical
with the nation's population but that nonetheless meets human
expectations in keeping with its given mandate, must assume a
critical function over against a constantly expanding state monopoly. It can in the sense of its continuing public role, however,
demand from the state that it give room for the church's right to
exercise the role of a critical watchdog.

8. It must be thankfully noted that this is the case in the
democratic constitutional states of Central and Northern Europe.

Translated by John Hinderlie

CHAPTER 14

GÜNTER KRUSCHE

THE RE-DEFINITION OF THE RELATIONSHIP TO STATE AND SOCIETY (IN SOCIALIST COUNTRIES)

The Lutheran Churches in the German Democratic Republic

The way in which the churches in the GDR redefined their relationship with state and society was of particular interest for the ecumenical movement. As the model case of an evangelical *Volkskirche* in a socialist society, their actions took on exemplary significance. While the Lutheran churches in Eastern Europe throughout their history had always been minority churches, socialism met in Germany with an evangelical church with a long tradition of being the state church or *Volkskirche*. The history of the churches in the GDR is, therefore, a very impressive and informative example of the relevance of the social situation for the preaching and work of the church.

The *Situation after the Second World War*

With the unconditional surrender of Hitler's Germany on 8 May 1945, the Third Reich ceased to exist. This was the irrevocable end of a historical era. The partition of the remaining parts of the Reich (without its Eastern territories) decreed by the victorious powers started a development which finally (in 1949) led to the

formation of two German States whose reunification became increasingly unlikely because of the antagonism between the capitalist
and socialist societies. The cold war finally resulted in the
integration of the two part-states into the respective power blocks.
The border between the two states, once only a demarcation line
between zones of occupation, now became part of the iron curtain.

The GDR which arose in the territory of the Soviet
occupation zone developed from a "transitional structure" into a
political reality which eventually received diplomatic recognition.
The principles of the Potsdam agreement, i.e. de-nazification,
demilitarization and expropriation of war criminals, were rigorously
applied in the Soviet occupation zone, and in the process of
reconstruction the foundations for a new social order were laid
after the socialist pattern. In those days the example of the
Soviet Union was of prime importance. The first phase of social
reform was seen in terms of reconstruction, reunification and
alliance politics. The SED (Socialist Unity Party of Germany)
which had sprung from the merger of the Communist and the Socialist
parties (KPD and SPD) insisted from the beginning on close cooperation with the anti-fascist and democratic forces, especially in
the so-called "block parties."

The complete breakdown meant that the evangelical churches
also were back at "square one." Not only had the destroyed
churches to be re-built, and the scattered congregations gathered
but the churches, especially the Protestant ones, were faced with
the task of restructuring their whole life after passing through
the severe crisis of the *Kirchenkampf*. Not all Christians had
rejected the pernicious spirit of National Scoialism, even if not
all had followed the "German Christian" movement which had stood
for a synthesis between Christian belief and German national
spirit. It was particularly their propagation of the "leader
principle" which provoked the protest of the "Confessing Church."
Against it, they drew up the much-quoted Barmen Declaration of
1934, containing the following significant phrases: "We reject
the false doctrine which states that there are areas of our life
which do not belong to Jesus Christ but to other masters...."
(Thesis II). Although the historic developments seemed to have
proved the Confessing Church to have been right, its representatives
still knew that, together with all the other evangelical Christians,
they were called to repentance: "We accuse ourselves for not
having confessed more courageously, not having prayed more faithfully,
not having believed more joyfully and not having loved more
burningly." (Stuttgart Declaration, 1945).

During the first years after the war the churches were as much concerned with coming to terms with the past as with the rebuilding of functional structures for the regional churches and with the union of the whole church. Because of the Ansbach Recommendation of 1934 which even Lutheran voices (e.g. G. Voigt) had called a "misleading document", the Lutheran churches were suspected (as followers of the doctrine of the two kingdoms) of being more susceptible to the pernicious spirit of the time than the followers of Barmen (and Karl Barth) with its emphasis on the lordship of Christ. This explains to a large extent why the disagreements over the past still influence the quarrels about the political responsibility of the church today.

The undisputed lesson from the *Kirchenkampf* however was an understanding that the church has to witness "through its faith as well as its obedience, its message as well as its order" (III Barmen thesis). On the basis of this understanding the evangelical churches started energetically to draw up an "order for church life." They clung to the basic orders of the church even when this began to be politically inopportune. In the period of growing alienation between the two German states the church was the only remaining functioning all-German organization, since both the EKD and the VELKD drew their members from the whole of Germany. Thus the church was drawn into the vortex of political tensions, was branded a "military church" and even suspected of being the fifth column of the West. (A chief cause was the agreement arrived at with the Federal Government in Bonn on chaplaincy work in the army for which members of the Synod from GDR had shared the responsibility).

The measures taken to establish political frontiers to safeguard the state border of the GDR on August 13th 1961 virtually spelled the end of the church unity, although the EKD continued to see itself as a "unity", and found it difficult to agree to regionalization. It was the Barmen thesis No. III which made it so difficult for the churches in the GDR to draw conclusions for church order from political facts or demands, "as if the church could make the form of its message and its order subject to its own pleasure, or to the ideological and political convictions of the day." The heritage of the church struggle together with the still unresolved "German question" have given the development of the churches in the GDR its specific character, different from the churches of the other peoples' democracies.

The Challenge from the Marxist Ideology

At first the tensions of state politics and church politics determined the relationship between state and church, but the ideological problems quickly became more prominent. As the socialist society was further developed and the SED leadership grew stronger, the Marxist-atheist propaganda also increased in sharpness. The doctrine of Marxism-Leninism became the basis of science, economy and education, and this raised the urgent question how far atheism belonged to the center, the substance of Marxism-Leninism, or whether it was an "additive." According to a statement of July 1958, the church was willing to "respect" the building of socialism, and to recognize the existing state as true authority, but it was impossible for the church to accept atheism as an ideology.

The confrontation over this question came to a climax over the youth dedication issue, which, as an act of dedication according to the order of church life had to be seen as being in direct opposition to confirmation, and therefore had consequences in church law. But in the whole sphere of education and in the question of Christian youth work and childrens' work there again arose severe disagreements which led to the suspicion that a second "church struggle" was imminent in the GDR. As in 1953, the administrative measures taken against the churches were soon abandoned for reasons of political common sense, but the impression remained that the GDR was trying to build an atheist ideological state, and this fear obstructed the process of learning and integration within the churches. During that time, political reservations about socialism were actually given Christian and theological reasons, and it was the "atheist component" which apparently justified this identification.

The official representatives of the state and the advocates of the ideology always insisted on the "incompatability of scientific world view and religious prejudice" and increasingly stressed: "There is no ideological coexistence!"

The Christians were slow to understand that the atheism of the socialists had its origins in the attitude of the church towards the "fourth estate" and arose out of the "context of the development of Western thought." It slowly became clear that "atheism was a question to the church" (the title of a pamphlet published by the VELKD in 1962), and that a simple confrontation with an apologetic intent could not be justified. At that time the realization began

to grow, albeit among only a small number of people, that the
Christian faith need not necessarily go together with the bourgeois
order of society, the Western life-style and the democratic
constitutional state. It was necessary to discard traditional
models: gone forever was the century-old tie between throne and
altar; it was replaced by the consistently implemented separation
of state and church. Gone also was the vision of a Christian
society; the building of socialism became the leading idea instead.
And gone was the unity between church and people; this hit the
Volkskirche of the Lutheran tradition in a sensitive spot.

The Changing Volkskirche

The political upheaval of 1945 had altered the appearance
of the established churches, but on the whole left their structures
unchanged. In spite of the de-nazification inside the church itself,
in spite of the exclusion of the "German Christians," the regional
churches with the exception of those affected by the territorial
changes in the East remained as they were, and their internal
structures also stayed the same (as for instance in the Evangelical-
Lutheran church of Saxony) unless they had been modified and brought
up to date according to the understandings of the church struggle
("law of the confessing church").

The breakdown was therefore followed by a consolidation of
the regional church establishment, similar to that in the Western
member churches of the EKD which was founded in 1948. The churches
in the Soviet zone of occupation (and later in the GDR) used their
constitutionally guaranteed independence to put their affairs in
order. The "order for church life" was a result of such a reorganization. It soon became clear, however, that it prescribed an
ideal situation and overtaxed the majority of its members' *Volkskirche*
consciousness by testing the reality of the *Volkskirche* with the
demands of a confessing church. Many church members did not live
up to these standards and therefore escaped the nets of the newly
organized church discipline by leaving the church. For ideological
reasons this was made very easy during the '50s and citizens in
certain occupational groups were urged or even required to do so.
Nor on the question of youth dedication, did the church win the
power contest. Only in exceptional cases did the parents of the
children being canvassed have the courage to withstand the urgency
of the recruiting. Even the refusals were not always based on a
real concern for the church as its cause, but on some political

motivation. Most children followed their parents and went in for
both, rejecting the church's demand for an either - or. Meanwhile
the process of shrinkage continued but the hope that the church
in the GDR would "shrink itself back to health" (Rudolf Augstein)
did not come true. Even with decreasing numbers the idea of being
a *Volkskirche* was kept alive: the church might be shrinking, but
not into becoming a confessing church, only into a *Volkskirche* with
a reduced scope of experience. But the degree of conscious
commitment also increased, even in official functions pertaining
to the *Volkskirche*, and small groups of convinced Christians
permeated the traditional congregations, often as "para-congregations"
outside the official program.

It was of great consequence that during the first years of
reorganization the tensions with the state and the question of
church unity in a divided Germany absorbed nearly all the church's
energy. Thus the churches were not free to come to terms with the
social situation, let alone perceive their new opportunities. But
this had to change.

Common Factors when Faced with Society

The measures of August 13, 1961, made visible the irrevocable nature of the partition of Germany, and showed that the
hoped-for re-unification belonged to the realms of Utopia. They
forced the churches to face the facts. They also compelled them
to act together, irrespective of confessional traditions.

The Lutheran churches have consciously shared their common
responsibility in the conference of church leaders in the GDR. Any
differences of opinion when it came to practical action or church
politics were usually caused more by non-theological factors than
by the confessional character of a regional church. One only
needs to remember the differences over youth dedication or of the
evaluation of statements by church leaders. It is therefore
difficult to find a specific contribution which the Lutheran
churches have made to working out the relationship to state and
society.

In the GDR there were and are eight regional churches
(Landeskirchen), five of them United (Berlin-Brandenburg, Province
of Saxony, Anhalt, Greifswald, Görlitz) and three Lutheran (Saxony,
Thuringia, Mecklenburg). They share the experience of facing the
state and the ruling ideology. But in the long run this is not
enough. During the first post-war years the assistance they had

provided had mainly had an apologetic character: they wanted to
supply arguments in the struggle of opinions, correct historical
misinterpretations and defend Christians against the accusation
of political dissention. But now more differentiated voices made
themselves heard. In 1957 Johannes Hamel raised one such voice
in a booklet entitled *The Christian in the GDR*. Karl Barth's
"Letter to a pastor in the GDR" (1958) supported him. It began
to become evident that the job of the Christian was not necessarily
to opt for the West, but that the situation had to be judged
afresh through the Gospel, and that through it there should come
freedom to serve. The interest in Bonhoeffer which began to
develop in the literature of the GDR also gave some help:
"Religionlessness does not separate us from Christ"; "Atheists are
our brothers"; "under grace we are in solidarity with the unbelievers."
These and similar phrases were used in those days, mixed with
criticism of the church.

A first statment from the churches came in the *Aids of the
EKU* of February 1959. It dealt with the testing situation in
which the congregations found themselves, and looked at it in terms
of the Gospel. A retreat into the inner life is rejected as
strongly as the politization of the Gospel. By referring to the
lordship of Christ it links up with the Barmen Declaration and
limits political obedience. From the basis of the Gospel, the
situation is accepted as a challenge. A result of such consideration
was the appeal issued by the Synod of the Evangelical Church of
the Union in 1960 to "stay in the GDR", consciously directed against
the stream of refugees from the country. And the Lutheran regional
churches thought along similar lines (i.e. the Bischofswerda
working group in Saxony).

All these efforts were based on Romans 13. "Authority",
"God's gracious dispensation" in the sense of the 5th Barmen thesis
also existed in the GDR. Quite irrespective of its ideological
component the socialist society was placed under the challenge of
the word of God. The Christians began to find positive elements
in socialism, especially after the discussions between W. Ulbrich
and Professor E. Fuchs (9 February 1961) and the Wartburg discussion
with Bishop M. Mitzenheim (August 18, 1964) which seemed to contain
an open offer to the Christians: they were called to cooperate in
the spirit of "common humanist responsibility," leaving aside all
ideological opposition. The significant role of the churches in
the service for peace was formally recognized. This pragmatic
change in official church policies made it possible for socially
committed Christians, of whom there were a few, to contribute their

experiences to the thinking of the church.

"Seek ye the best for the city" (Jer. 29) was discovered
as another key word for the congregations, but the Christians
committed to the CDU (Christian Democratic Union party in the GDR)
and the National Front also claimed it for themselves.

Lordship of Christ or Doctrine of the Two Kingdoms

The pamphlet of the EKU of 1959 had deliberately taken up
the doctrine of the lordship of Christ. But what about the Lutheran
tradition? We should mention in this context the two pamphlets
issued by the VELKD, *The Christian in the GDR* (1961) and *Atheism
as a Question to the Church* (1962). In answering our question, the
first of these is particularly relevant. The most important points
of this pamphlet can be summarized as follows: Referring deliberately to the doctrine of the two kingdoms, linked with the
distinction between law and gospel, it lays particular emphasis
on the "right of the church" and the special task of the congregation
which cannot be simply reduced to social responsibility. The
existence of the church as such has a critical function because it
limits every aspect of salvation and every totalitarian claim. In
the reference to the doctrine of the two kingdoms there seems to
be something specifically Lutheran which has been revived recently
in discussions of the "Alliance of Evangelical Churches in the
GDR". It must be admitted that this insistence can be difficult
and can lead to apparent opposition. More recent studies of the
doctrine of the two kingdoms (E. Wolf, U. Duchrow, W. Huber) make
it clear that it converges with the doctrine of the lordship of
Christ at some essential points, and even G. Voigt, one of the
co-authors of the pamphlet, states: "the doctrine of the two
kingdoms is not contradictory to the doctrine of the lordship of
Christ, but rather the right way of speaking about it" (1974).

The doctrine of the two kingdoms can also be used to
separate the spheres of responsibility, so that the church is
confined to its own ecclesiastical sphere, i.e. to the cultic
area of "its own humanization" (G. Bassarak). Members of the CDU
prefer this version. But from all we know this is a complete
misunderstanding of the meaning of Luther's doctrine which is
concerned with the difference between the spheres of responsibility,
but not with their separation from each other. In this sense the
Lutheran churches are also following the spirit of Barmen.

In this way it became possible for all the eight member
churches in the GDR to accept joint responsibility for the "Ten
articles on the Freedom and Service of the Church" (1963). This
was the first joint statement of the United and the Lutheran
churches in the GDR. And in it a deliberate attempt is made to
reconcile the mission of the church with the given situation. The
affirmation of service to mankind becomes more important than the
rejection of the ideological component of this society. Certainly
the obedience of the Christian has its limits, especially where
the particular mission of the congregation is concerned, and also
for order and law. "The church falls into unbelief ... when she
leaves the shaping of her order to the changes of the respective
dominant social conditions of the moment" (Article IX). The
ten articles were designed to guard against the wrong kind of
synthesis; therefore they very strongly stress the critical distance.

And it didn't take long for them to provoke the opposition
of the "Weissensee Working Group" who, in their "Seven Clauses
on the Freedom of the Church to Serve" emphasised more strongly
the church's mission to serve society, preferred the concept of
"church for others" and warned against the opposite danger, i.e.
the withdrawal from life as it is being lived. And, as we have
seen, the fear that an attitude of political disagreement could be
legitimized by taking recourse to the Gospel was not altogether
unfounded. While the "Ten Articles" emphasized the lordship of
Christ, the "Seven Clauses" stressed the self-sacrifice of Jesus.
It was not the concern for the life of the church, but for man in
a socialist society which dictated these priorities.

The debate between the two approaches has never been
finished. The tension between witness and service was already
apparent, and has been with the churches in the GDR ever since.
Within this field of tension, efforts were made which led, in
1969, to the foundation of the BEK (Federation of Evangelical
churches in the GDR).

Between Ideological Demarcation and Open Dialogue

It will have become clear that the evangelical churches
and their members had at first been obsessed with the "atheist
component." The propagation of atheism in party and school, the
proclamation of socialism as the kingdom of men (W. Ulbricht), the
promulgation of the Ten Commandments of Socialist Morality pushed
them into an ideological confrontation, and the Christians who for

that reason were branded enemies of peace and fifth column of the West rightly felt themselves to be misunderstood.

This situation started to change a little when, in the 1960s the thesis of the socialist community of men promised a certain flexibility. The cooperation of the Christians was now warmly welcomed. Through the discussions in the churches themselves of the church's service to man grew the willingness out of their faith to contribute to the building of socialism. Certain elements in block politics now came to the fore, supported by the positive experiences made by Christians, all suggesting pragmatic solutions without touching on the ideological premises. The dialogue between Christians and Marxists seemed to be on the wane.

A certain contrast to this was found in the ideological reservation of the established churches. This immediately elicited a wave of protest from within the churches themselves which borrowed the language of the partners in the Salzburg Discussions: Machovec, Garaudy, Kolakowski - greatly over-estimating the room for maneuver which really existed, as we know today!

In the circles of the CDU and CFK (Christian Peace Conference) the friends of dialogue also stirred, and the ranks of Christian groups of the National Front were swelled by interested Christian ministers and lay people, often against the will of their church leaders. The idea of the "socialist community of men" appealed to "our common human responsibility" without asking ideological questions of conscience. In those days there was much talk of the compatibility between Christian and socialist humanism, but the sudden end of the open dialogue after the events in Prague in 1968 seemed, with hindsight, to prove those right who had never abandoned their ideological reservations. Thus it was inevitable that the ideological incompatibility between Christianity and Marxism became more obvious again, especially since the 8th Party Congress of the SED (Socialist United Party of the GDR) in 1971 had coined the formula of the "ideological demarcation" and promised to fight any theory of convergence. This was, in the first instance, meant as a blow against revisionism and a "superfluous attitude to reconciliation", but mainly hit the Christians who were prepared for dialogue. "There is no ideological co-existence."

Since that time there has been no more dialogue, with the exception, however, of some informal contacts. The ideologies stand irreconcilably alongside each other. This has been repeated very clearly by the leadership of the party, and the church leaders are only too glad for this clarity. There is a negative consensus between party and church.

Between Politically Negative Attitudes and Critical Solidarity

It cannot be denied that in the'50s the majority of the Christians had uniformly adopted a negative attitude. It must be remembered, however, that the churches were still suffering from the trauma of the unresolved church struggle, and that socialism had been imported under the most unfavorable conditions, i.e. as a consequence of a lost war. There was also the national problem of the partition of Germany.

But the churches could not remain in their attitude of resistance if they wanted to take seriously their service of men. A more differentiated way of judging the situation therefore slowly gained ground. New and better experiences became known. Further thinking was influenced by a sense of reality among the mature laity and by a political sense of proportion among the church leaders. There was a growing awareness of what was possible. Young Christians especially urged their churches to be open to the given situation. Acceptance of the socialist society made a re-thinking of their own mission in this society imperative. The church had no political mandate, but shared the responsibility for the whole of society.

The Lutheran churches found it hard to agree to a global acceptance of socialist society. They recognized their "solidarity in sin" (cf. *The Christian in the GDR*), but they were afraid to mix opposites if they recognized unqualified solidarity. They especially avoided any form of legalizing or legitimizing of existing situations. They stuck to a "respect for socialism."

In this situation there arrived the formula of "critical solidarity" (Bishop Krummacher), which also gave rise to quarrels. Some thought it went too far, while for others it did not go far enough. But it left the churches sufficient room to say "yes" to the socialist society as long as it serves man, and to retain the critical "no" for individual cases. We must not forget that this gave a new quality to the statements of the church, even if the representatives of the state saw in this formula another expression of the "watchman's function of the church" to which it had no right. But from where did the church leaders get their "yes" and their "no" - from the situation or from the Gospel? That was really the question which needed an answer.

Between Social Reality and Mission of the Church

The church in the GDR has always resisted the demands for unreserved acceptance. The lessons of the church struggle had gone too deep. This explains some of the differences from the churches in other Eastern European countries. But the churches did take the given situation seriously, and took account of the irrevocable facts: in the end they accepted socialism, resigned themselves to the partition of Germany and, in 1969 - however painfully - abandoned the organizational unity of the EKD. Even if the church in the GDR has never agreed to the principle that the frontiers of the state are the frontiers of the church, it has learned to accept the frontiers of the state as the frontiers of organization.

The regional synod of the EKD had declared on April 5, 1967, that "The evangelical church in Germany exists...We as evangelical Christians in the GDR have therefore no reason to destroy the community of the EKD. We have good reasons for holding on to it...". But the constitution of the GDR of April 8, 1968 created a new legal situation, and the churches in the GDR were faced with the question whether they should hold on to their church orders in defiance of the constitutional law of their state or not. They therefore started preparations for the founding of the BEK.

The churches of the GDR have often been accused that they capitulated to the force of circumstances and simply conformed. Those who were involved in the founding of the BEK know this is not true. On the contrary, it was a conscious response to a given situation for the sake of the mission. The situation is not the norm, but the place for Christian witness and responsible service. Because the church wanted to be obedient to its Lord even under changed social circumstances it chose the way of the possible. There was no alternative in sight. The order of the church is not an end in itself. Its purpose is to serve. This is important to remember for further developments.

Between Inner Emigration and Social Co-Responsibility

As an institution, the church in the GDR is barred from taking a direct share of social responsibility. And the willing-ness of individual Christians to take on social tasks is constantly

frustrated by the fact that specifically Christian contributions
are unwelcome. It is only as a motivation that the Christian faith
is seen to have some relevance. The constant rejection of specific
contributions brings the danger of an "inner emigration" which is
particularly momentous at a time when the church has just rediscovered its responsibility for society. And it would be contrary
to the ecclesiastical consciousness of the evangelical church to
become a "cultic church" of the Orthodox pattern.

The demand for a program of a theology specific to the
GDR (Herbert Trebs) did not meet with the desired response. It
mainly foundered on the impossibility of bringing together the
ideas of reconciliation and partisanship.

Here we must mention the rediscovery of the laity. What
is denied to the church as an institution constitutes their whole
situation: they are present in society. The offer of responsible
cooperation is addressed to them. Their - on the whole recognized -
social cooperation happens concretely in specific sectors of
society. This can be wholly practical work, and therefore escapes
falling under any totalitarian claim. The atheist ideology can
provide no alibi for social abstinence by the Christians. But it
is the task of the church to equip its members for this service in
society. By doing this the churches in their turn receive valuable
experiences, among them the understanding that the ideological
level is not the only one on which witness and service can happen.
As a state the GDR exists for everybody, and the humanizing of
society is very much in its interest.

The consensus among the evangelical churches in the GDR
can be summed up as follows:

1) the church sticks to its mission
2) the state remains subject to God, irrespective of how
   it sees itself
3) society needs the Christians in their witness and
   service

The Founding of the Federation of Evangelical Churches in the GDR

After the constitution of the GDR came into force in 1968,
the existence of the EKD became not only politically but legally
dubious. Furthermore, any unity among the regional churches in
the GDR was threatened by separate agreements with each of them.
Thus the foundation of the BEK remained the only solution if the

regional churches wanted to continue operating in their common task.
The order of the BEK of June 10, 1969 looks back to the decisions
made by the first confessing synod in Barmen. It also remains
faithful to the basic conviction of Barmen by repeatedly stressing
the serving nature of all church orders. The wording of Article
4 (2), which talks about the independence and self-sufficiency of
the federation must be read against the background of the third
Barmen thesis.

        The inner freedom of the church in the GDR was expressed
above all in the controversial Article 4 (4) which regulates the
relationships with the former sister churches in the Federal
Republic of Germany: "The Federation affirms the special community
of all evangelical Christians in Germany." Common tasks which
could no longer be accomplished because of the lack of organized
unity, were to be undertaken "as partners in freedom." Bishop
Schönherr refuted the accusation that the unity given in the EKD
had been abandoned: "... this is not conformism nor even cheap
opportunism, but a responsible decision about the kinds of institution
and structure which will enable the churches in our opinion best to
carry out Christ's mission." But this means that unless the church
takes seriously the social reality and its own empirical situation
it cannot produce an ecclesiology which takes account of the church
as a community of service and witness. This is the ecclesiological
consequence of the foundation of the BEK.

Community of Witness and Service

        From the outset the churches in the GDR have structured
themselves as a community of witness and service. But opinions are
still divided about what this implies. The existence of the church
in socialism can never be without tensions because the witness and
service of the church as an independent contribution meets fierce
opposition. The unequivocally formulated leadership claim of the
SED, the "party of the working class" logically limits the church's
effectiveness in society. In the field of education there were
many cases of discrimination against Christians, and these produced
widespread disillusionment, expressed at the BEK synod in Dresden
in 1972. H. Falcke described the understanding of the separation
between state and church current on that occasion as the "retirement
of the church." In his paper on "Christ frees - therefore church
is for others", he said however, "Because Christ frees us, the
church can exist for others," and "We may believe that the socialist

society is also subject to Christ." About the cooperation of the Christians he said: "This is clearly not an ideology of holding aloof, or of a third way. It is the way of mature cooperation out of faith, upheld by a better promise than the one socialism can give, recognizing a command more binding than any men can give, and which is therefore concretely committed."

Many openings and possibilities for witness and service by the churches have appeared since, there have been also consciously accomplished acts of Christian responsibility, but there were many impossibilities and obstacles. The church as an institution has spoken on social questions: it has strongly supported the World Council of Churches' program to combat racism, and has also raised considerable funds through the program Bread for the World, channelling them to the countries of the third world with the help of the state. It has also worked for the setting-up of the conference on European security and cooperation, and for the implementation of the Helsinki decisions. Through official representatives it has participated in the world congress for women's year in Berlin in 1975.

Some criticism has arisen inside the churches themselves against these involvements, and against the participation of bishops and representatives of the churches in the events to celebrate the 30th anniversary of liberation. These seemed clearly to be going beyond the task of the church. Bishop Schönherr very carefully sounded out the extent of the elbow-room when he said in his address at the above-mentioned event: "When we are concerned with a more just, more peaceful and more friendly world, and when we know that to work for it is God's will, then we do not need to take the limits of ideology more seriously than our common task."

The churches in the GDR also got involved with the problems of human rights. The study produced by the theological commission of the national committee of the Lutheran World Federation in the GDR on "The Normative and Relative Character of Human Rights" is a contribution from the Lutheran churches. This study strongly insists on the historic character of human rights - a result of digested historic experiences. The social aspects of human rights are also emphasized - this means they took seriously an impulse given by the Marxist discussion of human rights. Human rights are not only seen as rights of the individual but also as rights of others. Many congregations in the GDR see themselves as being significant examples of the realization of human rights as congregations freed for true humanity.

On the Way into the Minority Situation

        This describes a further stage in the educational experience
of the church in the GDR. The shrinking of the congregations has
produced in some regional churches symptoms of de-churching which
in their turn have induced resignation among the clery and fatigue
in the congregations. The experience that Christians are becoming
rarer is more common than a decade ago. This carries the danger
of a narrowing of the horizon of experience, and also of theological
limitations. As the church lives in a condition of social assymetry
to society, its picture of the world risks becoming distorted. Its
members are no longer representative of the whole population,
whether socially or in their consciousness. The church in the GDR
is now faced with the task of developing a new self-awareness.
Bishop W. Krusche has coined the slogan "diaspora" for this situation. It shows that the church in the GDR has seriously entered
the post-Constantinian era. Not only the state church, but the
Volkskirche is fading into the past.
        The situation is a challenge particularly to Lutheran
ecclesiology. It is necessary to resist both a sectarian isolation
from society and uncritical conformism. It would help the churches
in the GDR to recognize the possibilities in this diaspora-situation,
between conformism and isolation, if they could take their bearings
from a correct understanding of the doctrine of the two kingdoms,
i.e. one that stresses its wholeness. If the church sees itself
as the diaspora in the missionary sense, and follows the movement
of God's love for men, then it will live with a great promise, even
in dispersion and as the little flock. As salt of the earth and
light of the world it learns to accept and make sense of any given
situation. In many shrinking congregations there are small groups
on the way to discovering new horizons for the church, free from
the worries about the survival of the church, and ready for witness
and service.

The Lutheran Churches in Eastern Europe

        It is hardly possible for an outsider to give a detailed
and differentiated account of the conditions of church and society
in the socialist countries of Eastern Europe. Our descriptions
will have to be very cautious. The empirical reality in these
countries is extremely complex. If we are nevertheless attempting

briefly to analyze the developments in some of the East European
countries, we do this because the relationship between tradition
and situation, between Lutheran heritage and social challenge has
led sometimes to similar and sometimes different answers.

Hungary: Theology of Service

The Lutheran church in Hungary looked back on a long history
of suffering as a minority church when it entered a period of
re-orientation in 1945. In response to the challenge of a socialist
society this church has developed a theology of service, in which
the church understands itself as the serving church following
Jesus Christ, the *kyrios - diakonos*. They therefore reject both
the idea of Christocracy and a basically critical attitude toward
state and society because that would imply "knowing everything
better than others." Rather it is the task of the church "through
serving love to contribute to the establishment of a juster order
of society" (Bishop Kaldy, Amsterdam 1975).

This concept is based on the doctrine of the two kingdoms
"which enables the faithful to participate in the construction
of society without claiming a leading or dominating position" (Prof.
Pröhle 1975). The lack of the "critical element" in the relationship with state and society can be partly explained by the fact
that this church had not gone through the church struggle, and had
no Barmen to fall back on. However its path since 1945 has not
been without difficulties, as proved by the fate of Bishop Ordass,
and the measures taken against him in the '50s. But the church
remains the church, and politics remain politics. This distinction
allows the church to find its identity as the servant church.

CSSR: Affirmation of the Heritage - Affirmation of Society

For the churches of the reformation in Czechoslovakia, the
political and social upheavals during the years of 1945-1948 meant
liberation in a very specific sense: from the preponderance of
the dominant Catholic church. This is true for the Slovak Evangelical
Church of the Augsburg Confession and, even more so, for the smaller
and less known Silesian Evangelical Church of the Augsburg Confession
which, after a turbulent history during the Polish partitions in
the Teschen area ended up with the majority of its congregations
on Czechoslovak territory. For the first time in its history it

was given a constitution (1948) recognized by the state. These
churches did not emerge from the Constantinian era, but from a
history of suffering and a minority situation. In the lee of the
disputes between the socialist state and the Roman Catholic church
it experienced a time of comparative calm and reconstruction for
the church.

But naturally these churches had to come to terms with
the Marxist ideology and the rapidly spreading secularization.
Their response was a theology of service. This position enabled
them to accept socialist society "although ideologically it can
never identify with it" (Bishop Michalko 1974). It is on the
basis of this position of service that the Lutherans in the CSSR
organize their relationship with socialist society: "The Christians
do not exist to condemn the shortcomings of the growing society,
but to see and clearly support the aim and possibilities of
socialism" (Prof. Gabris 1975).

Poland: Church in a Double Diaspora

Two factors have influenced the history of the Reformation
in Poland from the very beginning: the predominance of the Catholic
church and the link between Lutheranism and its ethnic German
origin. The Polish Lutheran Church was always a minority in the
diaspora. For this reason it never had either power or influence,
especially since its identity was often in danger through strong
personal and financial ties with Germany. The partitions of Poland,
too, prevented the establishment of a Polish national church of the
Lutheran faith. Through the Second World War and its aftermath,
especially the deportation of ethnic Germans, the church shrank to
about 120,000 members. At present (1975) the membership is given
as 74,995. The position of the Evangelical Church of the Augsburg
Confession in Poland is mainly characterized by its opposition to
the Roman Catholic church, while its relationship with the state
is relaxed. Ideological disputes are rare, and fundamental tensions
about education hardly occur. The state has an unmistakable interest
in furthering church minorities. The opposition to the Catholic
church makes the ideological opposition to Polish socialism less
apparent. The Bishop of the Lutheran church J. Narzynski, writes:
"The sense of sharing the responsibility for the common fatherland
is the basis of the social co-operation between Christians and
Marxists in Poland" (Luth W 1976 Nr.2).

Rumania: Between Volkskirche and Confessing Church

The history of the Lutheran Churches in the Socialist
Republic of Rumania is another example of how Lutheranism works
out according to its specific situation. These churches found
their particular character as recognized ethnic minorities through
establishing their identity as German Lutheran churches, and
retaining it through the many momentous changes of the last
centuries. Confessional and national frontiers coincided. The
church in Rumania is the Orthodox church. This fact limited all
missionary efforts from the very outset. On the other hand it
also leads to an intermingling of the confessional and national
problem: to marry into a Rumanian family meant contracting a
confessionally mixed marriage. The integration of German or
Hungarian speaking nationals into the Rumanian society leads to
a disintegration of the Lutheran congregations just as much as
the growing wave of emigration of Germans to the Federal Republic
of Germany. "This happens in the course of the reunification of
families ... but leads to ever more separation of families, so
that there seems to be no end to this movement" (Bishop Klein 1974).
The tension between the Lutheran heritage and national tendencies
is a constant challenge to the witness of these firmly established
churches. In addition, the process of secularization and urbanization is hitting this church, specifically the *Volkskirche* of the
Germans, particularly hard.

The church in the Transylvanian area wants to face this
challenge "by shifting the emphasis of the concern of the church
away from the institution and impersonal order, to the personal,
pastoral, human and neighborly" (Pastor G. Ambrosi as cited by
Bishop Klein). The relationship with the Rumanian state which
obviously is governed more by pragmatic considerations than by
ideological presuppositions, has become increasingly relaxed during
recent years. The future will show whether the Lutheran church
in the Transylvanian area will manage to preserve its tradiational
heritage in the midst of a foreign, socialist and urbanized
environment. In the face of the possibility of emigration to the
Federal Republic of Germany, and of the government's policy of
integrating other nationalities, the existence of the Lutheran
church cannot be based in the fact of being of ethnic origins.
"The Gospel remains. If the church remains faithful to it, then

eventually its way will not be without promise" (G. Ambrosi).   This
can be said of all the churches in socialist countries.

Translated by Donata Coleman

CHAPTER 15

ROBERT H. FISCHER

RECENT LUTHERANISM IN NORTH AMERICA

Changed Appearance

In the 20th century, and particularly since the Second
World War, American and Canadian Christianity has remained restless and changing within a restless and constantly changing
society. Lutheranism also has been changing. Let us look
first at the surface evidence: church growth and organizational
patterns.

Since early in the century Lutheranism has been the third
largest Protestant family (behind the Baptists and Methodists).
Between 1945 and 1968 Lutherans maintained a growth rate outpaced
among the mainline Protestant families only by the Southern
Baptists: (in 1900 about 2.5 million baptized members) in 1945:
5.87 million, in 1968: 9.24 million, including about 300,000 in
Canada. This growth is especially significant because it was
long assumed by many Americans that Lutheranism grew by immigration
but not by evangelization. Immigration, however, had been virtually
cut off between the world wars. The mid-century influx of refugees
added materially but by no means decisively to the Lutheran population. Some of these refugees have settled down in independent
bodies whose statistics are not often identified in general surveys
of church membership.

Growth in American Protestant membership tapered off in
the 1960s. While the Southern Baptists and many smaller ultra-
conservative groups continued to grow, the mainline Protestant

churches actually went into a decline in membership. Along with
them, Lutheranism in the USA and Canada slowly shrank from 9.24
million in 1968 to 8.93 million in 1975. Signs are appearing,
however, that this trend is about to be reversed.

The face of Lutheranism also has changed organizationally.
In 1945 eight bodies (comprising two-thirds of the Lutherans of
North America) were cooperating in the National Lutheran Council
(founded in 1918), while five bodies (comprising the remaining
third, led by the Lutheran Church - Missouri Synod and the Wisconsin
Synod, second and sixth in size respectively) cooperated in the
doctrinally orthodox Synodical Conference (1872).

Mergers in the early 1960s reduced the NLC bodies to two.
In 1960 *The American Lutheran Church*, with Fredrik A. Schiotz as
president, was formed from three midwestern bodies previously
associated in the American Lutheran Conference, a confederation
(1930) claiming a "bridge" role between the Synodical Conference
and the theologically diverse United Lutheran Church in America.
Merging were the Evangelical Lutheran Church (formerly Norwegian
Lutheran Church), the American Lutheran Church (German in background
with centers in Ohio and Iowa), and the United Evangelical Lutheran
Church (formerly United Danish, a conservative pietistic group).
They were joined three years later by the Lutheran Free Church, a
small decentralized Norwegian body.

In 1962 the four remaining NLC bodies established the
Lutheran Church in America, with Franklin Clark Fry as president:
the large ULCA, whose main strength was still in the east of the
USA, the Augustana Lutheran Church (Swedish in background, the
next most Americanized Lutheran body), and the smaller Suomi Synod
(Finnish) and American Evangelical Lutheran Church (Grundtvigian
Danish).

As these merger efforts were nearing fruition, negotiations
were opened to replace the NLC with a cooperative agency which
the Missouri Synod could join. The *Lutheran Council in the USA* was
formed in 1966. Member churches were to be free to decide in
which joint activities they would cooperate, but were obligated to
participate in discussions to bring about full doctrinal unity among
Lutherans. Missouri and its little Slovak satellite, the Synod
of Evangelical Lutheran Churches, joined the LCUSA, and a Missourian
C. Thomas Spitz, became the first general secretary. The Wisconsin
Synod, the Evangelical Lutheran ("Little Norwegian") Synod and some
splinter groups objected to such fraternization, and by 1961 the
Synodical Conference was virtually defunct.

In the LC-MS itself, the election of Jacob A.O. Preus in 1969 signaled a challenge to the synod's trend toward modifying its rationale of church relations. The result of the increasingly bitter and painful polarization was a schism in 1976, when a sizable minority of "moderates," resisting the synod's return to rigid doctrinal isolationism, formed itself into the *Association of Evangelical Lutheran Churches*. This development and its results for inter-Lutheran relations will engage our attention later, as will the topic of Lutheran ecumenical relations.

Canadian Lutheranism, meanwhile, moved toward autonomy and closer fellowship during the 1960s. The *Canadian Lutheran Council* (1952) was reorganized in 1966 in similar fashion to the LCUSA. In the same year the ALC Canada District became the autonomous *Evangelical Lutheran Church of Canada*. Affiliates of Missouri and the LCA in Canada assumed semi-autonomous status. In 1971 the ELCC proposed merger negotiations among its council partners. Hopes for a quickly united Canadian Lutheranism proved premature, however, as the old dissension persisted over the nature of fellowship and the way to attain it.

There yet remains to be mentioned the small but slowly growing Lutheranism of the countries and islands in the southern part of the continent. LCA has a Caribbean Synod of 9400 members concentrated in Puerto Rico and the Virgin Islands. Affiliated with LC-MS is the Mexican Lutheran Church (autonomous since 1958) with 1600 members. LC-MS also has a Caribbean Area mission with 3500 scattered in several Central American countries. The ALC assists the Mexican Lutheran Church, and jointly with LC-MS supports the Augsburg Seminary in Mexico City. Two faith missions chiefly of Scandinavian-American membership, the Latin American Lutheran Mission and the World Mission Prayer League, also have missions in Mexico and Central America.

The Setting: A Time of Chastening

Recent developments of Lutheranism in this part of the globe must be seen against the background of recent North American life. This we may characterize as a period of chastening especially in the USA, to a lesser extent in Canada.

The USA emerged from the Second World War confident of its continued growth, its internal soundness and its ability to shoulder the responsibilities of international leadership -- ready to export American paterns of human development and to take the lead in containing communist expansion.

At every point this confidence has suffered heavy blows in the past quarter-century. Only with difficulty are North Americans coming to realize that their material resources, their human resources, their technical and political and moral powers are not unlimited. The civil rights struggle which took shape in the 1950s and 60s forcibly revealed to America and the world that large segments of our society, particularly the blacks but also others, were being systematically excluded from fair opportunities to pursue the "American dream" of "liberty and justice for all." American foreign policy launched some very creditable efforts such as post-war reconstruction in Europe and elsewhere, and the up-building of the United Nations as an instrument for world cooperation and order.

Frequently, however, the USA misread the aspirations of developing nations, and in its enterprise to contain communism in Southeast Asia involved itself in an increasingly unpopular war from which it extricated itself with embarrassment. The forced resignation of a US president in 1974 became a symbol of deep-rooted corruption in society. In our time, indeed, the long-evolving critique of authoritarianism in western culture has advanced to a point of permissiveness, individual and social, which may well cause people to wonder whether society can still establish persuasive standards of morality and integrity.

It would be a foolish misreading of this picture, however, to conclude that the national integrity and the moral nerve of the USA, much less Canada, are at the point of collapse. Indeed, deep reservoirs of social intelligence and moral energy have been tapped precisely in the facing of these crises, even though the crises are far from past. At all events, one must be aware that North American society is living through a time of intense testing if one is to understand how Christian church life, and specifically that of American Lutheranism, have been shaped in recent decades.

On the church scene, it is just in this era -- the middle of the century -- that American Lutheranism (particularly in the midwest) became fully Americanized and established its credentials to share in the leadership among the churches. Lutherans won respectful attention first by their large-scale, skillfully handled, patiently continuing work for post-war humanitarian aid throughout the world. From 1940 to 1975, led by Paul C. Empie, they raised over $120 million in the USA and Canada through Lutheran World Action, and managed the distribution of a much larger valuation of material supplies through American and Canadian Lutheran World Relief. In the 1940s American Lutherans were providing leadership

not only for the formation of the Lutheran World Federation (1947)
but also for the launching of the World Council of Churches (1948)
and the National Council of Churches of Christ in the USA (1950).
In all three movements the name of Franklin Clark Fry stands out.
Lutherans simultaneously were beginning to produce an impressive
array of influential theologians spanning the whole range of
academic scholarship and practical expertise. They were tackling
more penetratingly and realistically than ever before the deep
problems of Christian social responsibility, and showing notable
creativity in the fields of the arts and the mass communications
media. To such activities we shall have to devote a closer look.

It is ironic, meanwhile, that by the 1960s, just when
American Lutherans were clearly establishing these leadership
credentials, American Protestantism itself began to experience a
serious loss of momentum and an acute crisis of identity and
mission. Lutherans themselves have shared in the malaise.

Lutheran Church Life

Congregational and Intra-Church Activity

1.　　　The traditional neighborhood parish, so well sketched by
E. Th. Bachmann in the 1957 edition of *Lutheran Churches of the
World*, remains the model of the real church, no doubt, in the eyes
of most American Lutherans. This fact indicates something of
both the strength and the weakness of grass-roots American
Lutheranism. Our people in many kinds of parishes still know that
the church gathers around the ministry of word and sacrament. The
deep stability that results from this sense of churchliness
nourishes Lutherans, and exercises a quiet attraction upon others.

The model of the stable parish, however, becomes increasingly
problematical. As the mobility of population accelerates and more
and more neighborhoods change, in country and town as well as city,
ever fewer of these traditionally stable churches are to be found,
and those that remain can hardly be made the norm for the church's
mission in changing and deteriorating communities.

The traditional church, moreover, has long tended to be
socially restricted and restrictive -- in our time predominantly
a middle-class institution, often more self-serving than outreaching.
Even its "church-centered" activities often insulate its people
from a mission to the world around it.

The traditional symbols of the church -- its vocabulary, its action patterns, its authorities -- become ever less intelligible to modern society, if they are merely repeated in traditional forms.

This kind of analysis comes from careful studies instituted by various church bodies. The LCA's Task Force for Long Range Planning (1965-68), for example, produced studies on current trends in LCA congregations, social change, and theology, and finally it issued a report on *Significant Issues for the 1970s*. The task force recognized that "participation in existing congregations has become increasingly marginal for large numbers of people," including many creative and committed Christians. Even so, it declared its conviction that "the congregation is and will continue to be the primary locus for the expression of life together within the Christian community." It identified "being a community of believers" and "participating in the human community" -- in short, the questions of *identity* and *mission* -- as major areas where the creative attention of the church must be focused. Specifically needed in congregational life, it suggested, are (1) lay involvement in significant ministries of the congregation, (2) variety in congregational program, (3) a personal experience of the community of believers -- i.e. a sense of "belonging."

The example cited illustrates the widespread concern in American churches, including Lutheran, for "church renewal." The popularity of this term, especially in the late 1960s, indicated that the church was being energetically summoned to bold openness in reassessing its nature and its program. At its extreme, "renewal" was virtually equated with experimentation in new forms of activity. Does the quieter mood of the 1970s mean a rejection of that call for openness in patterns of church life? or, more hopefully, a greater realism which balances openness to the new with recovery of the positive values of the tradition, with its continuities and sense of identity? Both motivations, no doubt, are at work.

Three examples of recent developments directly affecting the internal life of the congregation may be mentioned. First, a joint commission from LCA, LC-MS and ALC prepared a report on the "Theology and Practice of Confirmation" (1967), which redefined confirmation as "a pastoral and educational ministry", "encompassing all of the educative experiences from Baptism to mid-adolescence," designed to help the baptized child "identify more deeply with the Christian communitiy and participate more fully in its mission." The report recommended admitting children to holy communion at about the age of 10 or 11, and concluding the confirmation process at age 15 or 16. After considerable discussion in the congregations, LCA and ALC adopted the report in 1970; LC-MS simply urged congregations to "study their practice" of confirmation and communion. Actual implementation of the new proposals in The ALC and LCA remains mixed.

Second, at the invitation of the LC-MS all three large bodies and the SELC and the ELCC formed an Inter-Lutheran Commission on Worship in 1966, to prepare "common worship materials." The eight bodies of the National Lutheran Council had published the *Service Book and Hymnal* in 1958, after 14 years of cooperative effort. Widely used, the volume "served the cause of unity at the congregational level," says one historian, "in a manner which no amount of theological treatises could ever have accomplished." Now the formation of the ILCW raised the hope of advancing Lutheran unity still further.

At work in our time has been a curious combination of a veritable liturgical renaissance and a groundswell of anti-traditionalism in American culture. In an effort to address the legitimate concerns of both tendencies the commission has deliberately reached out both to ancient and to modern ecumenical liturgical expression in order to deepen and enrich that of the Lutheran tradition; it has modernized liturgical language, eliminated archaisms, introduced (optionally) the new ecumenically established English texts, e.g. of the Lord's Prayer and the creeds; drafted a wide variety of liturgical orders and musical settings; prepared a diversified lectionary and calendar; and broadened the treasure of hymnody far beyond the old traditions of Germany and Scandinavia and the long-familiar English tradition, by reaching even to idioms of the third world, of folk music, and of jazz. Working thus with boldness of ideas, but also with caution by testing in the congregations every new worship order and every suggested list of hymns, the ILCW has recently submitted a final draft of liturgical forms and hymns to the churches for their approval, and hopes to publish its hymnal by 1978.

A third example is the efforts of church bodies to draw up statements to provide inspiration and guidance for revitalizing congregational life. Two of these deserve special mention. First is the LC-MS "Mission Affirmations" of 1965, which declared that "the church is Christ's mission to the whole world -- to the whole society -- to the whole man. The whole church is Christ's mission." Churches should cooperate except "when it would deny God's Word." Secondly, when the LCA in 1972 launched a two-year project to put into popular expression the church's "theological affirmations,"

it produced not another formal statement (like its brief "Manifesto"
of 1966) but a study booklet designed for congregational exploration:
"In, Not Of" (i.e. the world). "We are baptized!" is its key
affirmation; our theology is our guide to "living our baptism in
the world."

2.   In the realm of polity and church administration also,
important developments have taken place in recent years.

Deeply underlying the changes are perennial questions
regarding the church's identity. All Lutheran bodies have devoted
enormous energy to studies of the church and its ministry. One
outcome has been the ordination of women in the LCA and The ALC
since 1970, an action offensive to the LC-MS. Another result has
been an energetic effort to develop a more flexible concept of
the ordained ministry. In addition to their normal parish ministry,
churches are attempting to establish guidelines for "experimental
ministries" in order to reach and serve persons untouched by the
traditional ecclesiastical channels. One form is the "tent-making
ministry," where the minister earns his livelihood wholly or
partially in another occupation. An example, pioneered in The ALC:
a minister may serve as manager of a large apartment house, and at
the same time provide pastoral service to its residents.

A third intense concern of the churches is the development
of "the ministry of the laity," to encourage creative leadership
and witness and service on the part of the body of believers, and
to establish a corrective to clericalism. The laity are the church,
the people of God, not an appendage to it. Many pastors, therefore,
like to regard their role as that of an "enabler" of laypeople's
ministries. In view of all these developments, of course, the
relation between laity and ordained ministers will need further
reappraisal.

In the area of church polity there are divergences among
the major bodies. The ALC declares that "the Lord of the church
has committed to the individual congregation the ministry of Word
and Sacrament and therewith basic authority." Congregations
delegate authority and power to the national body. The LC-MS has
traditionally insisted that it is simply an advisory "agency of
the congregations with no authority other than that specifically
granted by the congregations." The LCA has an "elliptical" theory
of the church: "The Church exists both as an inclusive fellowship and as local congregations... This church [LCA]...derives
its character and powers both from the sanction and representation

of its congregations and from its inherent nature as an expression
of the broader fellowship of the faithful...". Membership of The
ALC consists of congregations; of LCA: congregations and ministers;
of LC-MS: congregations, ministers and teachers.

The ALC recently approved optional use of the title of
bishop for its presidents. The LCA rejected a similar proposal.
Both actions were taken without great enthusiasm.

Vast structural and administrative changes have been made
in the last decade. In 1972-74 the LCA achieved a major revision
of "function and structure," with a view to "purposeful inter-
dependency" and greater corporate efficiency without undue centralization. Eight boards and seven commissions were restructured into
four divisions (carrying out program responsibilities) and three
offices (providing support services for the divisions), along
with two boards (publication and pensions). Notably new features
are the Office for Research and Planning and the Office for
Administration and Finance. -- In the same period The ALC revised
its structure along rather similar lines.

By contrast, a great upheaval in polity is currently taking
place in the Missouri Synod. Determined to eliminate the dissent
blamed for creating "doctrinal chaos and undertainty," the majority
in the synod voted the Preus administration vast powers which have
altered the former picture of a strictly advisory synod. Actually,
the "moderate" dissenters recognized the legitimacy of the so-called
"conservative" doctrinal position in the synod as well as their
own; the Preus side denied that the dissenters' position is toler-
able in the church.

Landmarks of the crisis leading to the 1976 schism are
four: (1) In 1972 the president composed a fundamentalistic
"Statement of Scriptural and Confessional Principles," which the
synodical convention in the following year, by a 55-45 percent
vote, declared binding. A large "confessing movement" of moderates
promptly formed in protest, under the name "Evangelical Lutherans
in Mission." (2) The Concordia (St. Louis) Seminary Board of
Control, having already dismissed or retired several faculty members
in a campaign to eradicate alleged doctrinal deviation in the school,
suspended President John Tietjen in January 1974. Over 400 of the
600 students withdrew, accompanied by 45 of the 50 faculty and
staff. The dissidents set up "Seminex," Concordia Seminary-in-
exile, nearby. (3) President Preus, armed with a mandate from the
1975 synod convention to discipline district presidents who failed
to carry out the resolutions of the synod, that is, who supported
ELIM and approved the ordination and placement of Seminex graduates,

vacated the offices of four of the eight "insurgent" district
presidents in April 1976. (4) Concluding that their mission in
the world as evangelical Lutherans was no longer possible within
the Missouri Synod, a number of ELIM congregations in December formed
the independent *Association of Evangelical Lutheran Churches*,
adopting a congregational polity. The new body continues to grow.

For the first time in American history, crusading funda-
mentalism has captured and rigorously purged a major Protestant
denomination. The way presumably will now be open for LC-MS to
revive fellowship with the Wisconsin Synod. On the moderate side,
even before the schism ELIM had declared itself for pulpit and
altar fellowship with both The ALC and the LCA.

Activity among the Churches and in Society

1.   Inter-Lutheran Relations.

Over the years the National Lutheran Council painstakingly
won the confidence of mutually suspicious Lutherans. It became
the focus of American Lutheranism's most practical and most
creative efforts, not only through its notable work abroad but
also through dozens of activities at home. These included planning
for the urban and the town-and-country church, social welfare,
Hispanic work on two continents, immigration service, campus
ministry, military and hospital and prison chaplaincies and clinical
pastoral education, public relations, radio, television and movies,
and co-operation with the Lutheran World Federation. On important
public issues the NLC not only produced some able studies and
statements, but also in a few instances exercised discernible social
influence, e.g. upon the US government's immigration policies. In
the field of ecumenics it led Lutherans into an age of bilateral
dialogs, as we shall see below. -- This list of cooperative
achievements, of course, should not detract from the Missouri
Synod's impressive creativity in similar endeavors, e.g. radio
evangelism ("The Lutheran Hour") and the arts.

It is difficult to exaggerate the importance of the NLC in
producing the seismic shift of North American Lutheranism from
ethnic clannishness to a concern for the whole of society, from a
sense of social inferiority to a willingness to share the risks
of leadership in the mainstream of American and Canadian life, from
jealous guarding of individual church autonomy to an increasingly
generous spirit of inter-Lutheran and ecumenical cooperation.

By the late 1950s Missourians were cooperating to some
degree in nearly every major area of the NLC's work. The softening
of Missouri's position of aloofness during the era of Oliver Harms'
presidency (1962-69) made possible the formation of the Lutheran
Council in the USA in 1966. Though high hopes were expressed for
this new stage of Lutheran co-operation, the Preus backlash in
the LC-MS, accompanied by a period of economic stringency, has
brought serious curtailment of the programs of both the USA and
Canadian Councils in the 1970s. Missouri reinterpreted its "Mission
Affirmations" to recover its traditional doctrinal isolationism.
The presidents of the three large churches agreed in 1975 to
discontinue their "Consultation of Lutheran Unity."

A major response to these developments has been a powerful
(though not precipitous) groundswell of union sentiment between
The ALC and LCA. Even the structural revisions of the two bodies
were accomplished with an eye to further rapprochement. In most
enterprises the two bodies now cooperate in planning and in practice.
The ALC and LCA seminaries in St. Paul, Minnesota were "functionally"
united in 1976, and cooperation is becoming ever closer elsewhere.
A joint committee on communion practices proposed in 1976 that
Lutheran communions "should be open to all communing Christians
present." This controversial proposal, it will be noticed, abandons
the principle of "Lutheran altars for Lutheran communicants only" --
which for The ALC (as well as Missouri) had implied that doctrinal
unity had to be worked out in formal statements before mutual
recognition could be accorded in eucharistic fellowship.

2.   Inter-Church Relations.

Strong loyalty to the Lutheran tradition in North America
to a large degree explains the historic rivalry of church bodies
over the true identity of the name Lutheran. As with other Christian
traditions, the mood of "triumphalism" has characterized the
Lutheran missionary drive at home and abroad -- the competitive zeal
to convert not only the unchurched but also fellow Christians to
our faith and to chart the growth of Christ's kingdom in terms of
our institutional success. The threatening drift toward both anti-
Christian secularism and indifference among Christians has stimulated
this zeal.

In our time, under the impact of the great human cataclysms
of the 20th century and the ecumenical experience of Christendom,
Lutherans have in some measure outgrown their self-preoccupation

and defensiveness. To some Lutherans the "ecumenical question"
has meant chiefly the question of Lutheran unity. Now, however, a
concern for the wholeness of Christ's body and a deeper realization
of the character of Christ's mission to the world have taken
hold.

Two features of Lutheran ecumenism are noteworthy.

(a) Lutheran participation in ecumenical organizations
has been mixed. Deeply suspicious of the ecumenical movement, the
Synodical Conference and most members of the American Lutheran
Conference bloc in the NLC insisted on the principle of doctrinal
unity before practical cooperation; the ULCA and Augustana took
a different position. Five NLC bodies now in the LCA and ALC,
however, shared in establishing the World Council of Churches, and
American Lutherans such as Franklin C. Fry, O. Frederick Nolde,
Fredrik A. Schiotz and Robert J. Marshall and many others have
taken leading roles in it. The same churches and persons have also
been leaders in the LWF. Meanwhile, when the LCUSA was formed,
Missouri's abstention from Federation membership necessitated the
creation of an LWF - USA National Committee (and another for Canada)
to administer LCA and ALC/ELCC cooperation with the Federation.

On the other hand, only the LCA is a member of the National
Council of Churches of Christ in the USA (1950) and the Canadian
Council of Churches. Dr. Fry helped persuade the former Council,
which merged the Federal Council of Churches and several other
agencies for specific areas of cooperation, to adopt constitutional
safeguards which Lutherans called "the evangelical principle"
(acknowledgment of Christ as "divine Lord and Savior") and "the
representative principle" (provision that a council of churches
must directly represent and be accountable to churches, not simply
to churchmen and independent organizations). F.C. Fry and A.R.
Wentz had been influential in establishing these principles also
in the WCC and the LWF. But though the former ALC had been
affiliated with the National Council, the new ALC (1960) declined
to join it. Suspicion of "liberal" theological and ecclesiastical
influences and of social activism reinforced traditional objections.
Especially in our recent times of confusion and of ecumenical
experimentation, these suspicions have become more intense in
conservative areas.

A principle of limited cooperation came into play, meanwhile,
in both The ALC and LC-MS. Without joining the National Council,
these churches have taken part in many of its enterprises and even
furnished some leadership in them. Missouri has acted similarly

with the World Council and LWF.

A major breakthrough in ecumenical thinking took place in 1974. The LCA, which continues the tradition that had pioneered in devising the rationale for a discriminating ecumenism expressed in the "evangelical" and "representative" principles, restated and extended them in "more affirmative terms" in a new document, "Principles Governing External Relationships of the LCA." In essence the new statement emphasizes where we *should* cooperate with others, rather than where we *may not*, and it extends its purview to matters of common inter-religious and humanitarian concern. Directly opposed to this attitude is the present Missouri policy.

A test case for Lutheran ecumenical policies came after the formation in 1960 of the much-publicized Consultation on Church Union, an elaborate scheme to merge ten American denominations (including several large ones). Proponents a little belatedly urged Lutherans to take part in the consultations. Lutherans did send observers, through the LCUSA, but they judged the COCU blueprint ecclesiologically unsatisfactory. While COCU should not be regarded wholly as a failure, it has not in fact reached its primary goal of a great church merger.

(b) The 1960s, meanwhile, inaugurated the age of bilateral dialog. For North American Lutherans this began with the Reformed-Presbyterian invitation in 1961 and with the Catholic dialog in 1965. Lutherans including LC-MS have been among the leaders in this movement, on both national and international levels and at the grass roots as well. In the latter part of the 1960s dialogs were begun also with Anglicans, Orthodox, and Jews. Dialogs continue on a broad front in the '70s. Three observations stand out. (1) With the Reformed and the Roman Catholics the theologians found no insuperable obstacles to communion fellowship. (2) Closest rapport has developed with the Catholics, among whom the Lutheran sense of historic catholicity finds sympathetic resonance. Ecclesiastical-procedural reasons for separateness may persist, but doctrinal differences are no longer the chief obstacle. (3) High-level theological agreement may be difficult to translate into practical church-wide action and attitude. The Reformed/Lutheran theologians' hint in 1966 that communion fellowship should be considered is only now approaching the stage of formal ecclesiastical decision. The face remains, however, that we live in a far more open and friendly ecclesiastical atmosphere than we did twenty years ago, and progress is likely to continue.

3.   The Church's Mission

If triumphalism is being effectively criticized in the
Lutheran churches, it is due in large part to recent ecumenical
experience. The emergence of an able and articulate world-wide
Christian partnership, the hard facts of international relations
unfavorable to the old free-wheeling western missionary enterprise,
the long-lasting economic recession in North America, newly
critical social problems at home, an institutional religious
recession generating doubts over our own identity -- all have
brought Lutherans and others to greater sobriety in their thinking
about the church's mission.

Lutherans, meanwhile, remain deeply and creatively committed
to mission, as the response to Missouri's "Mission Affirmations"
shows. By and large we have resisted the suggestion, recently
widespread, that Christians should attempt simply to be a freely
serving "presence" in the world, rather than try to convert people.
Since World War II, it is true, American and Canadian Lutheran
World Relief has skillfully distributed material aid (exceeding
the mark of one billion pounds in 1963) wherever critical human
need appears, regardless of nationality or faith -- in contrast to
the policy fifty years ago of trying to confine our assistance to
"true Lutherans."

But Lutherans keep this humanitarian concern in tension
with the compulsion to share the whole Christ with the world.
Particularly The ALC is noted for its fervent interest in evangelism
Well over one-half of the income of the Lutheran church bodies still
is devoted to World Mission and American Missions. In addition,
The ALC in 1975 launched a United Mission Appeal for $25 million,
to be equally divided between these twin causes. It received $37
million. The LCA intends to imitate the campaign.

Present policy for *overseas mission*, for a variety of
reasons, has drastically altered the traditional pattern of sending
out primarily evangelistic missionaries. American and Canadian
personnel from the LCA serving overseas in 1974, for instance,
numbered 194 (38% ordained), compared with the high mark of 548
in 1967. With national leadership now determining policy in overseas churches, North American boards basically respond to requests
for fraternal aid, particularly for short-term specialists in
education, medicine, agriculture, economics, etc. Changes in church
structure and terminology furnish a clue to the change in outlook:
the Lutheran Foreign Missions Conference of North American dissolved
itself in 1966; its functions were assumed by the LCUSA Division

of Mission Services.

To encourage overseas churches in their assumption of autonomy, the LCA Division of World Mission and Ecumenism is even phasing out "permanent" affiliations with "daughter" or "sister" churches, in order to work on a free partnership basis, responding to needs of highest priority wherever in the world they are found. Closely related is the effort to replace the "sending church" mentality with an effective pattern of also *receiving* the richness of witness which our fellow Christians all over the world have to offer us. The "Mission on Six Continents" visitation, begun in 1973, is a pioneering venture which will be further developed in the future.

An exception to this outlook is found at present in the LC-MS, which in its current crisis has exercised heavy pressure to keep overseas affiliates doctrinally in line.

In regard to the churches' *mission at home*, similar changes have taken place. Planting new congregations -- formerly called "home (or American) missions" and "church extension" -- has remained a high priority, but it suffered a sharp decline in our period. At the height of post-war expansion American and Canadian Lutherans were forming a new congregation every 54 hours. In the first half of the 1970s the large LCA, for instance, averaged only 24 new fields a year, reaching its low ebb in 1971.

Structural revisions in the 1970s may be illustrated through the LCA: Boards of American Missions, Social Ministry, and College Education and Church Vocations were consolidated into one Division for Mission in North America.

Of all its areas of responsibility the most challenging frontiers are found in church and society and specialized ministries. Faced with staggering problems in contemporary society, the essentially conservative Lutheran churches on the whole have made remarkable progress in opening themselves to new ways of thinking and action. No longer does the ingrained Lutheran tendency toward social individualism and quietism dominate the churches' leadership. Along with many others, Lutherans used to maintain that the social responsibility of the church (apart from its works of mercy) was to inculcate principles of righteousness and then leave civic action to Christian individuals in their several callings. The American tradition of the separation of church and state was often invoked to argue that churches as such have no business in the political and social arena. Post-war Lutheranism, however, is reaching clearer insights and forging more realistic programs to exercise a more faithful social responsibility.

One such basic insight is found in the LCA statement of
1966 which describes the proper relation of church and state as
"structural separation, functional interaction," rather than a
completely impenetrable wall. While this principle is no master
key to the problems of church and society, it has helped unlock
the churches' social creativity and their social conscience.

On a broad front Lutheran churches have moved with vigor
to deal responsibly with modern social problems -- although a
large gap admittedly exists between a massive "business-as-usual"
attitude in the churches and the progressive efforts of responsible
leadership. Lutherans have recognized institutional racism as our
most urgent domestic problem, along with the many-faceted urban
crisis. Characteristic of Lutherans and most other churches now
is the policy of facing such social problems corporately (the
church itself *does* have responsibilities to act), ecumenically
(social problems must be faced with concerted efforts, not simply
by individual traditions), and a great deal more realistically
than in the past (churches are trying to tackle fundamental problems
of justice and the structures of society, not merely symptoms of
injustice).

Lutheran social ministry has three dimensions: social
studies and statements, social ministry agencies and institutions,
and other specialized ministries.

In recent years the studies and statements of the major
Lutheran churches and the NLC/LCUSA, which have the force not of
church law but of "position papers" for information and discussion,
have evidenced great penetration and sophistication especially when
compared with the often simplistic and idealistic productions of
the past. The statements cover a vast range of current issues:
the recent bibliography, "The Churches Speak, 1960-1974," fills
56 pages.

Lutheran churches are speaking to social issues in another
way through the Lutheran Resources Commission - Washington. This
new agency (1969), now an adjunct of LCUSA, was established to
provide liaison for Lutherans with "government departments and
agencies, voluntary agencies and foundations in the interest of
social progress." The United Church of Christ and the United
Methodists cooperate with it.

Traditional church institutions such as hospitals and
homes for the aged continue; new forms of child care have largely
replaced church orphanages. Other forms of service now have
mushroomed; LCA, for example, lists 11 different categories of
health and welfare agencies and institutions. All such institutions

are tightly regulated by government.

Pioneer efforts are proliferating to bring human concern and the gospel of salvation to people not traditionally served by Lutherans. Only a sample can be mentioned. Cooperative ministries are expanding in the inner city; coalitions of congregations and agencies are often inter-Lutheran or inter-denominational. The churches have involved themselves in "community organization" efforts and other para-parochial enterprises. There is an increasingly lively engagement with the concerns of Blacks, Hispanic Americans and American Indians for justice and self-determination. These minority groups are experimenting with methods of organizing to advance their interests; Lutherans are beginning to find ways to be helpful to them, and have discovered some Lutheran leadership arising in all three groups. LC-MS has been the leader in Lutheran ministry among the Blacks, and ALC among the American Indians. In the recent resettlement of Vietnamese and Cambodian immigrants, 900 Lutheran congregations have sponsored and welcomed 1000 families.

In summary, LCA President Robert J. Marshall in a recent address has sketched the character of Lutheranism in a way which the vast majority of North American Lutherans would endorse:

1. We are a biblical church; we are also a confessional (but not a fundamentalistic) church: our devotion to the scriptures leads us to confess our faith.

2. We are a charismatic church: that is, we seek to be guided by the Holy Spirit; but we are also an evangelical church, in that we try to use *all* the gifts of the Spirit in a mutually enriching and corrective way.

3. We are a diaconic church; we perform our service in an ecumenical way.

CHAPTER 16

Béla Leskó

The Discovery of Identity
in a New Culture and Society:
In South America

Martin Luther was a nine year old child in Mansfeld when Christopher Columbus "discovered" the Americas. Unlike a child of our age, he was not kept up to date on the latest events by the mass media. None the less, at the early date of May 29, 1522 in his Ascension Day sermon on the extension of the Gospel and the missionary mandate to the whole world, he noted that: "in our time new islands and lands have been found" (WA 10, III, 139, 19f. WA 10, I, 1. 21, 16), and that the preaching of the message will be expanded throughout the world in spite of the difficulties and hinderances in its way (WA 10, III, 140, 7f.).

At this time Luther could not have known that this expansion of Gospel preaching to the new islands also meant the expansion of Europe to Central and South America, the expansion of a colonial power over territory and idigenous populations and the expansion of the European people, nations, culture and of the church allied with the colonizing powers. He could not have known that a great part of the people who became an object of evangelization also became a target for total extinction in many regions. Nor could he have dreamed that only twenty four years after his death an edict against his teaching and writings would be read in Lima, Peru, or that his followers one day would discover in these "new lands and islands" the need to struggle and search for an identity.

There is one important point to note. Luther is preaching about the expansion of the Gospel and not about the expansion of his followers or of "Lutheranism" or the "Lutheran Church." However, history puts us in the context of the facts and evolutions which could not have been foreseen but which exist as part of a process within Christianity's struggle to find the right preaching of the Gospel. We are part of that humanity which in different ways and in different places intended to be an agent in the making of history and also in the preaching of Jesus Christ.

Therefore, the search for identity by the persons and communities in South and Central America, who today call themselves Lutherans, has to be seen in the light of this expansion process of Western Christianity, initiated in Europe, and in the more recent context expanded through inter-American relationships. When Europe projected herself toward South America at the time of the first colonizations, she carried on her endeavor alone. Later, however when within the Americas a new force was born in the North, the new trend of expansion toward the South presented it- self as a second door, opening for the preaching of the Gospel. The message coming from the North, however, was already the fruit of a new identity, of a new "memory" (1 Cor. 15:1) with the original European element as part of it but re-thought in a new context. This explains how, within the same confessional family of Christians, two different kinds of "memories" can arrive at the same place and participate as additional elements in the process of the definition of a third identity and the formation of a third memory.

The search for identity is one of the most notable charac- teristics of the Lutheran churches on our continent today. Such a search is not only a creative process however, but also a situation of struggle and repentance. How did these churches arrive at this point in their history? We shall briefly point out some aspects of this historical process.

From an American Christendom toward a Latin American Church and the Arrival of Lutheranism.

When European Christendom as an expanding force on the new continent took its first steps toward the establishment of the Roman Catholic Church, first in its Spanish and some time later in its Portuguese form, the news of the Reformation reached Latin America only in a negative way, through the edicts of the inquisition. The short Protestant efforts at missionary work on this continent

during the first three centuries of its history did not remain
important historical contributions. There were a few exceptions
where the establishment of a Protestant church was also backed by
European countries as in Jamaica, the Danish Antilles and Surinam,
but in no case did Protestantism make an impact on those parts
of the new world where the Iberian influence maintained the ruling
hand. The sporadic presence of missionaries in other parts, like
the Calvinists in the Bay of Guanabara (Rio de Janeior, 1555-1567),
the Dutch Reformed in Northern Brazil (1636-1649), the intentions
of the Lutheran baron Justinian von Weltz (1665), the efforts of
the Brethren of Herrnhut to establish themselves in Dutch Guayana
(1738-1748) and the proved presence of Lutheran and other Protestant
Europeans in Brazil and other places, did not lead to the introduction of any Protestant church into this new Latin-dominated
world.

Meanwhile the new Latin-American Christendom, composed of
the Roman Catholic Church and the Spanish and Portuguese states
and cultures in close cooperation, produced a historical effort
in both a negative and a positive sense from the point of view of
the extension of the Christian faith, its confrontation with
other cultures and its reaction to the changing nature and trends
of the political power. Protestants have generally very little
understanding of what the significance was for example, of the
change of power from the House of Austria-Hapsburg to the Bourbons
(1700), the change from the Viceregal system to the system of
Intendancy or the expulsion of the Jesuits (1767). During the
17th century the Roman Catholic Church, especially in her work of
evangelization, suffered serious confrontations with the pretensions
of the Patronate, with the immigrants and with the privileges
claimed by the Hispanic civilization in the new world.

At the same time the missionary effort was struggling to
adapt the Christian message for the man nourished by the pre-
Christian cultures and religions. When the decadence and declin-
ation of the Hispanic power started in Europe, the consequences
were also felt by the church on this continent, and the arrival of
independence at the beginning of the 19th Century made her situation
critical. "The disorganization of the Corps of Bishops was total,
and resulted in the absence of ordinations of priests and monks,
the plunder or destruction of the archieves, the isolation of the
parishes...". "The same way as the 'Medieval Christendom' lost
its unity by the centuries, Latin America was losing its unity
during only one decade" (Dussel).

When independence arrived, an ideological, political and economic vacuum was created. It was filled with the ideas of the French Revolution, with the concepts of liberalism and with the economic and political dominance of foreign powers, first Great Britain, then the United States and for a period both. The continent, with the complacent collaboration of many of its leaders, became an open field for new projects, basically as the potential producer of raw products and food for the more and more industralized Northern Hemisphere.

For the realization of these projects new immigration was needed and organized. The groups of new immigrants who came to Latin America became innocent participants in the economic imperialism, mostly of Great Britain, which extended over the whole continent. This unknowing complicity has naturally influenced the whole history of the Lutheran immigrant church, including its ecclesiastical and political attitudes in the past and even today. At the time of the great immigrations and also after the colonial time, South America was dependent, in one way or another, on one or more European powers. This condition was accepted since both sides apparently benefited. Consequently, when the immigrants sought a relationship of dependence with their home churches, they were acting in the spirit of the Latin American countries and governments where they lived. The problem was that the local powers did not maintain relations with the nations of their origin, but with others. This is why, for example in Argentina, the first Lutheran services were organized under the protection of the English or Scottish churches. This is also the reason why other evangelical churches, if they had a missionary vision, established themselves by the way of the mediation of the Anglo-Saxon colonies and the Freemasonry monvement.

The continent was at that time also open for new Protestant missionary attempts. Such efforts were not undertaken without difficulties and without sometimes very severe restrictions, but the task was not completely impossible as in former centuries. At the same time immigration brought the first Lutheran groups to this continent, who organized themeselves in congregations. It started in Brazil (1824) and led to the period of synodical organizations in Brazil, in the River Plate countries and in Chile (1886-1912). North American Lutheranism made contacts with the continent in the 1890s, bringing the German language by way of the Missouri Synod in Brazil and Argentina at the beginning of the 20th Century. They took up the problem of the mission to the South

after 1916 and intensified their efforts following the First
World War. The idea of systematically using immigrants as part
of a church-building project was considered by world Lutheranism
only after the Second World War. This historical development
closed an important period of our history and started a new one,
which was characterized by the arrival of new immigrants (who in
this case were often refugees), by the foundation of the Lutheran
World Federation and its projects with regard to Latin America,
the achievement of autonomy of both missionary and immigrant
churches and the preparation of a new generation of pastors, for
the most part born on this continent. Today Lutheranism is present
in Central and South America.

But this presence is still influenced, more and more
consciously, by the changing history of the continent and its
nations, by the arrival of new ideologies, by the developments in
the Roman Catholic Church from transplanted "Christendom" to a
transformed Latin American Church and by the general religious
life (other Protestant churches, the Ecumenical Movement, the
charismatic movements and the birth and rebirth of many different
kinds of popular religiosity). In this historical perspective
and in the maturity process of self-reflection the question arises:
Who are we?

A Transplanted Christianity

Latin American Christianity as a whole is a transplanted
Christianity. When we accept this as a reality for Catholicism,
we find that it is even more true of Lutheranism in Latin America.

There is a difference when the Christian faith is transmitted to the people by the work of missionaries, or when it
arrives through immigrants. It is true that both types of transmission of the Gospel existed on other continents also, but
Central and South America is the only area where the missionary
enterprise began with conquest *and* colonization, and eventually
resulted in a continental occupation by European immigrants,
primarily Iberians. Following the independence of Latin America,
immigration continued to be encouraged and the new immigrants
(including Catholics) arriving from all parts of Europe brought
their own ecclesiastical structures and traditions. In conclusion,
when the first missionaries arrived to preach to the indigenous
population, colonists arrived at the same time and transplanted
their church from Europe.

This is the case of the Roman Catholic Church. It can be noted in the whole of Catholic history in Latin America how – under the same central authority in Rome - in reality *two* types of "churches" arrived on this continent, the missionary church and the immigrant church. Both these tendencies can still be seen, and possibly contributed during the last decade (espeically after the first South American conference of Roman Catholic bishops at Medellin 1968) to the very different interpretations of the socio-political reality made by various groups within the same church. Because of this situation, our question is not what Christianity brought here, but rather, what the Christians brought with them. The colonization itself was also the starting point of a process which ended with the present heterogeneous picture of Latin America as a continent, with a continental Christianity, which often has a contradictory nature. The different periods of massive European immigration and the varied results of racial and cultural mingling between the immigrant colonies and the indigenous population produced different kinds of religiosity and different types of churches.

The same thing happened with the transplanting of the various types of non-Catholic churches to this continent, with the difference that in the case of the Lutheran church the dissimilitude between the churches transplanted by the way of immigration and those transplanted by the way of mission is much more obvious. The other great difference between these two main streams of Christianity (a third, the Orthodox line, is also present but exclusively in the form of immigration of ethnic groups) is, that the Roman Catholic Church arrived with its own culture and participated in the formation of the Latin American culture from the beginning, giving a basic historical contribution which formed part of the personalities of the new nations. The transplanted Protestant Christianity, on the other hand, arrived from quite different cultural settings and brought with it cultural characteristics which at the moment of arrival were predestined to die out or be contributions by a minority. When the acculturation of the churches is required, this includes the inevitable obligation to confront the message of the Reformation with a culture whose characteristics Hispanic Catholicism carried to this continent.

The well-known Argentine Roman Catholic scholar, E. Dussel, shows how this continent had its own Latin American Christendom before the time of independence. This new Christendom had three fundamental roots: Hispanic Christianity and its church, the Hispanic culture and the culture and heritage of the American Indian. These basic elements represent two worlds, the world of Hispanic

Europe and the indigenous world of America. All this flows through
Latin American Christendom and is seen in the church's influence
on the immigrant Hispanic population, especially in the cities,
the introduction of Christian preaching to the Amerindian world
through mission efforts and the armed conquest of the frontiers.

Naturally this description does not intend to explain a
process already completed, nor deny the regional mutations. The
content and meaning of the evolving Latin American culture is
still being discussed and the same is true with regard to the
definition of the various nations' identities. "When a nation
comes to express itself, arrives at a genuine self-consciousness,
i.e. the consciousness of its cultural structures and its ultimate
values, through the cultivation and development of its tradition,
it possesses its own identity." (Dussel) The search for this
identity is behind many cultural, social and political movements
in our continent.

None of the basic factors indicated by Dussel can be ignored.
They are deeply rooted in the spirit of the continent and the cross-
fertilization is still in process, as can be seen in the cases
where splits and new church formations occur, when parts of the
original Amerindian population again become conscious of their
cultural heritage. It is obvious that to these basic elements new
contributions were added by way of the organized immigration.
The origin and the intensity of this immigration could change the
picture of a region and add new elements to the culture, mentality
and religiosity of Latin America.

None of the newcomers, individually or as churches however,
can forget the presence of the basic elements and the influences
of the Latin American Christendom.

The new elements added to the cultural picture and to the
struggle for identity often come from non-Iberian countries and
streams of thought - streams in which Lutheranism forms a part.
As a result of these trends it is difficult for a non-Iberian
European immigrant to find his identity, but the problem of identity
was no less difficult for the Latin American who became a Lutheran.

A Transplanted Church, the Gospel and the Quest for Identity.

As early as 1932 Werner Elert wrote in his classic *Morphologie
des Luthertums* (2nd Ed. Vol. 2, p. 126f.) that for the Reformation
"Die Anpassung des Kirchentums als solchem an das Volkstum sollte
dem Evangelium dienen - nicht umgekehrt." The Bible was translated,

the German language was introduced into the people's worship life
and a new type of hymnology was created, but all these originally
had two basic motivations: "der Betonung der evangelischen
Verkundigung als der Zentralfunktion und des Gemeindegedankens
als der lokalen Konkretisierung der Kirche."

From the writings of immigrant groups we can see a position
which states the opposite.   It maintains that it is only the
church which is able to conserve the heritage of the different
ethnic groups; and so the different forms of the transmission of
the Gospel have to serve the *Volkstum* rather than the *Volkstum*
serve the universal expansion of the Gospel.

Lutheran immigrants in Latin America are going through an
identity struggle.   In the environment where they are living,
German, Danish or Swedish become synonymous with the Lutheran
Church.   However this does not necessarily mean that those who
use these expressions and talk of a German church or of a Danish
church really know these churches represent the same Lutheran
tradition.   Where both an ethnic immigrant church and a missionary
church are present in the same place, the word "Lutheran" can also
be used as a synonym for "North American".   The two identities
are given by the national origin of the people or of the missionary,
but not by the testimony of the Lutheran message.

The origin of a person is part of his identity, and if a
member of an ethnic group is forced by a church which is working
towards cultural assimilation to renounce his origin, he loses
one factor which makes up his identity.   The same is true when
someone is forced to renounce a religious tradition or when this
tradition is lost in a new environment.

The fact that in the main Lutheran churches in Europe
Volkstum and church went together, made it difficult for the European
Lutheran churches to consider Latin America as a missionary
continent, and not just another place where their own *Volkstum*-
church brothers and sisters were a living continuation of the
home church.

Here we would like to make a distinction between the concept
of the geographically transplanted church or congregation which
is a continuation of the home church and the continuity of a
tradition within new contexts, with new challenges for witness and
service.   The first means *dependence* and is an obstacle in the
process of maturity towards self-reliance and a new identity.   But
the second means *interdependence*, where a new identity formed
within a new context does not reject the "memory" of the tradition
but can transform it into a positive heritage and recognize it as

one of the basic elements which compose this new identity. In
this case the relation of conscious interdependence can transform
the receiving churches into giving communities. Interdependence
means receiving but also giving.

The old identity which the immigrant churches brought with
them does not respond adequately in the context of changes and
new realities. The crux of the problem however is not the "value"
of the old identity, but its applicability for the future. This
is the moment when the Gospel itself, and the Lutheran confession's
strong orientation toward the Word of God and its proclamation,
does not allow us the luxury of an easy resignation, but rather
forces us to model some elements of our old identity.

A continuing problem in many communities with immigrant
backgrounds is that an unnecessary tension is created. The pastor
and some younger members try to force the older generation to
renounce their identity while the older members of the congregation
make it impossible for a new identity to be expressed.

*The quest for a new identity is not served by a simple
change, but a change does take place because of one's growth in
discipleship*.   What can be the motivation for conscious growth
towards a new identity? During the last decades we have experienced
different kinds of motivations while searching for a new identity.

One is derived from our ecclesiastical and confessional
beliefs. In faithfulness to our fathers we have to ensure that
the Lutheran Church continues to exist in our country.

Side by side with our confessional ideas arises the idea
of "representation". The Lutheran church is a universal *catholic*
church and it is still the living sign of the 16th century
Reformation. Therefore we should see to it that our church is
represented by at least one congregation in every republic of the
Central and South American continent.

The missionary motivation is similar to, but more extensive
than the idea of simple representation. Many people were never
baptized, while others are only nominally Christian. Our mission
is to offer a better church. In this case, however, tension
between mission and proselytism arises which for many years was
not solved theologically.

Another motivation is an ethnic consideration. The church
has to survive to conserve our language and culture. The socio-
political motivation is especially strong today. Many theologians
and lay people maintain that becoming a political factor in the
continent's search for a new type of society is of utmost importance.
This identity, however, is often defined by non-Lutherans or by

Lutherans from other continents and does not arise as an organic
concern of the churches here. Both the Latin American churches
and their "First World" counterparts realize that political
concerns do not touch the living nerves of the churches here. At
times there has been a lack of confidence in the people who must
live this political mission here. For example the decision to
transfer the LWF Porto Alegre Assembly to Evian, 1970, was made
in Europe and in the USA. In a much more important case one has
to ask how many of the elements leading to the split in the Chilean
church arose among the Chileans and how many were imported from
the "First World"?

While each of these different motivations belong to the
totality of a church identity, none of them provides the solution.
On the contrary, within each of the issues there are powerful
counter-arguments. At times there have even been conflicts between
these motivating forces for they were not sufficiently flexible
to allow the expression of another reason for change. They will
be valid only if they become tools of the Gospel, of the Good
News of Jesus Christ. All these aspects can be causes for new
growth if they are servants of the Gospel which aids the process
of maturity and growth of men, churches and nations.

None of these motivations alone will give life to the
church, nor can they foster its mission and the fulfillment of
its task. The Gospel has to be the fundamental motivation. When
Latin American theology and preaching today underline the importance
of the Gospel for the whole man and for every aspect of human
needs and life, the quest for identity is included. Only faith
can transform me, with my heritage and my abilities, into an
obedient servant. Obedience to the Gospel of Christ will open
the doors and show the way.

Transformation is not a negation of the continuity. It
is evident that all church bodies are the fruits of the proclamation
of the Gospel by *others*, but they can only be transformed into
mature churches if, under the influence of the Word and nourished
by the Sacraments, they take over their responsibility for the
universal proclamation of the Gospel. Where this is not present,
there is no identity.

The Missionary Approach and the Identity Crisis.

Lutheranism has never arrived as a strong missionary force
to Latin America and for various reasons, many still unexplained,

the few Lutheran missionary enterprises among the indigenous people never achieved a significant numerical growth compared to the pentecostal movements of today and other missionary enterprises of the past. How can we explain this phenomenon?

The starting point of our mission is and always was the same as for any other church - to preach the Good News of the redeeming and liberating Jesus Christ to mankind, to baptize and make disciples of every nation. However, we have to bear in mind that the Lutheran missionary projects, which generally were started by foreign mission boards with experience on non-baptized continents, arrived here to an almost completely baptized population.

The question arose as to whether this work could be considered traditional mission work or simple proselytism. Were the missions converting Christians from another church to ours or non-Christians to Christ? Many missionaries struggled with this question alone, without clear guidance from higher levels. Today it is theologically clear that it is our shared responsibility, with Catholics and other Protestants, to provide a context in which *all* baptized Christians can grow in faith. This is not proselytism. But Lutheranism in Latin America did not always have this aim clearly in mind. What today is generally accepted was questioned during the past decades.

The immigrant church accepted the presence of other churches and passed the whole responsibility for evangelization on to the Roman Catholic Church or to other evangelical churches which, they felt, were more suitable for the task when the language of the new country was to be used. The missionary churches, or better missionary enterprises, saw other denominational groups as competitors rather than co-workers. While they questioned the authenticity of the other churches, they de facto refused to recognize the baptism of others, especially that of the Roman Catholic Church. However, they did not commonly rebaptize converts to Lutheranism.

The result of this time of theological insecurity was a message which can be characterized by two factors: a) a negative interpretation of the teachings and ethics of the "others", and b) a personal conversion *from* the world *to* the salvation offered by a "better" and "cleaner" church. This message, which was intended to be a positive contribution, became in the long run a heavy burden which influenced the future development of our church in a negative way.

We are used to talking about a missionary mandate, which is closely connected with pretensions about the extension of a church, a denomination or of the power and influence of an agency. What happened was that the great mandate of Jesus Christ was transformed into a legalistic demand without the freeing message of the Gospel, used with the aim of replacing one church, in particular the Roman Catholic, and was not a contribution to the christianization of an increasingly semi-Christian, pagan or indifferent population.

This narrow interpretation of the mission mandate even resulted in fighting within the family of Lutheran churches, especially after the Second World War, when new Lutheran immigrant communities were attacked by the fledgling mission churches. For example in Argentina the members of the missionary church were educated in the spirit of a threefold opposition - against the Catholics, against the immigrant Lutherans and aginst some other Protestants. It is clear that this basically negative approach could not bring the dreamed-of fruits. We can observe today that the results of this education, and of the loyalty to this "memory", are congregations struggling for survival but without any force for extending themselves, and pastors who fulfill the given traditional tasks but who often cannot attract new members.

However, even within these congregations there are people working for a new interpretation of mission. They argue that the fulfillment of the task will only be possible, if the missionary mandate of our Lord is interpreted as Gospel - as the bearer of Good News. Where the missionary mandate is a legal demand, couched in negative language and actions and not an offering of gifts and services, love and grace, this mandate does not give any hope. Without the promise of this hope there can be no future and no universal dimensions of the Christian faith. The community will become a closed group of individuals with a faithful pastor but without a future.

This self-centered attitude has various roots not always easy to detect. The self-reflection and self-criticism of Latin American Lutherans, which is one of the positive turning-points of the last decade, indicate some possible reasons.

It is important to know that the two periods, when Lutheran missionary enterprises for Latin America were started in the United States and Canada, coincided with other secular historical events. In particular we are thinking of the two World Wars and the impossibility of continuing traditional missionary work in some parts of Asia. When mission-fields have to be closed, the search for new fields is not always the fruit of a well-based theological decision. Most Lutheran missionary projects in Latin

America have been characterized by a feeling of insecurity and
by continuous changes in their aims and methods. Manpower and
funds were many times sacrificed with little chance of success.

The missionary with problems regarding his own identity
arrived to work in a project which lacked a clear identity, during
important moments of social and institutional transition, and
failed to take these "moments" into consideration. Lutheran
missionary work in Latin America was, generally speaking, a late
attempt. Other Protestant missions had shared at least the past
100 years of history of the new nations. The participation of
Lutherans from the United States oscillated between non-participa-
tion at the 1916 Pan-Protestant Congress of Christian Work in
Latin America and the participation of a small group resulting in
the organization of the short-lived Pan-Lutheran Missionary Society
for Latin America. This shows the insecurity of the North American
mission boards as they looked south.

When Lutherans went to Latin America they went in opposition
to the position taken at the Edinburgh Conference (1910). One
of the fundamental questions regarding their ministry was whether
they go as *foreign* missionaries or to do their "home-missionwork
abroad" within the Pan-American scene.

The idea of Pan-Americanism and the later influence of the
two World Wars often aroused anti-European feelings in the missionary's mind. He considered as negative baggage what his forefathers
brought with them from the old continent. When he arrived and
discovered the presence of European immigrant Lutherans who were
related to the "enemies", his previous rejection of the folk-
church or state church heritage came to the surface and made this
rejection part of his message. The preaching also became
individualistic. The pietist tradition of the missionary, critical
of the life style of the surrounding population, called the individual out of his context and invited him to be a member of a new
community with an "evangelical culture" and with a new life-style
which in fact was that of the missionary.

Who was the converted person? He was generally a member
of a large family, which lived within the very broad family context
of Italian style (much broader than in the United States or in
northern Europe), or a new immigrant from the European Latin
countries who looked for a replacement of the lost big family; or
a Lutheran from Europe who for some reason or other did not
maintain his relationship to his ethnic group.

It is well known, that the broad Latin family group is a
very closed community of interests. The local congregations

transformed themselves into "families" along this line, with some
leading laymen as "heads of the family" and the "owners" of the
congregation. When urbanization and industrialization began
breaking down this traditional extended family, the family group
tried to defend itself - and individual local congregations did
the same. The congregation becomes self-centered or pastor-
centered, often around a national pastor who is not less individualistic than the missionary was. The goal is not to reach out
but to remain. The hard drive towards self-support imposed on
many mission congregations and churches in Latin America has
accentuated this self-centeredness. As congregations develop a
survival mentality, they are unable to grow. This attitude of
self-defense can hardly serve as a missionary motivation.

We have to have the courage to admit that Lutheranism
today in Latin America is not a missionary force of importance,
and it is not comparable to the efforts of many other evangelical
churches or the Roman Catholic Church.

However, there is an important Lutheran presence in Latin
America, which owes more than 90 percent of its existence to the
Lutheran immigration. The immigration itself is the consequence
of historical events and situations. There have always been some
very clear reasons why a stream of immigrants is pushed out of
the home country or why immigration is planned and promoted by
the receiving country. It was not an accident when the immigrants
came to South America. Nor was it an accident that the different
economic, political and national immigrations brought their love
and faithfulness to their church with them. The present existence
of Lutheranism on this continent is the result of the hymnbooks,
prayerbooks and Bibles, which were included in the immigrants'
baggage. The pastor often came later.

The new situation for Lutherans of this continent is the
beginning of consistent collaboration between mission boards and
immigrant churches. This tendency started in Chile and Brazil
during the 1960s and has added a new element to the search for
the identity of these churches. The missionary attempts offer
stimulation and new questions for the immigrants - and they in
return give the historical continuity of the Lutheran tradition.
The two different kinds of "memory" can lay the groundwork for the
next "new memory" of the coming generations, when both, side by
side, struggle with the same basic question: What was the intention
of the Lord, when he allowed churches of the Reformation heritage
to exist on this continent?   And since we do exist: What is our
contribution in message and service which we should and can offer

our new countries and fellow human beings?

Some years ago we summarized the basic thoughts for our new missionary approach in the following sentences:

The message of Jesus Christ for our continent awaits our contribution - our witness;

that we are a church that knows how to spread the testimony of its members within this given context;

that we are ready to bring baptism to those who have not yet been baptized, and act as Christ's heralds for those who still do not know him or have separated themselves from him;

that we can prepare a spiritual home for those who have been baptized and educated into the same faith but who today live outside of any spiritual community;

that we will communicate the Gospel message of the remission of sins and salvation to the whole society, while serving that society by means of our members, who are renewed in Christ;

that we are prepared to practice good stewardship in the distribution of the tasks of the church between those who share our faith;

that we will demonstrate our unity with the universal church of Christ, which is known by its pure preaching of the Gospel and its proper administration of the sacraments;

that we are willing to work with all humility, making ourselves servants of the goal of Christian unity, which was given to us by our Lord, Jesus Christ.

Identity, Memory and Unity

Our position in regard to the search for identity, the discovery of the active roles of the various memories and the differentiation between the concepts of continuation and continuity, are fruits of the Lutheran reflection started with the Hannover Assembly of the LWF in 1952. This period brought in or inspired many new projects and has also seen their realization or discontinuance, e.g. in the field of theological education or of publications. Today it is clear to us, that the reasons for the discontinuities were too optimistic functionalism and the ignorance of the variety of memories in the years of initiations. Where new creations remained with success a healthy continuity worked within the change.

The diversity of identities has until now resisted the creation of regional or continental unity. The five continental Lutheran congresses* could reach joint resolutions, declarations and recommendations but not abiding actions. The variety of memories and loyalties, and the ecclesio-political situations, projected often from the outside into the continent, obstructed the necessary decisive steps.

However, this period of the last 25 years, its projects, experiences, realizations and failures, and their teaching, laid down the foundations for the future. Our eyes are open and the Gospel is preached and we are reflecting on the definition of our call, urged also by the political, social and ideological struggle.

There are many elements, e.g. the vigorous experiment done by the representatives of the theology of liberation, which proves the presence of the search for a new identity in the whole of Latin American Christianity.

In spite of our disunity, new horizons open up and a Latin American Lutheran conciliarity is in the making as a part of the ecumenical one. The search for identity is not a self-centered goal but the sign of a hope for a more extended discipleship.

---

*They were held at Curitiba, Brazil, 1951, Petropolis, Brazil 1954, Buenos Aires, Argentina 1959, Lima, Peru, 1965, José C. Paz, Argentina 1971.

CHAPTER 17

JAMES SCHERER

GROWTH TOWARD SELF-HOOD AND MATURITY: IN AFRICA, ASIA, AND AUSTRALASIA

Common Characteristics

Lutheran churches in Africa, Asia and Australasia (apart from English-speaking Lutheran communities in Australia and New Zealand, and four small German-speaking churches in Southern Africa) have a common character that sets them apart from the majority and minority Lutheran churches of Europe and the diaspora churches of North and South America. Lutheranism in these regions was introduced under the sign of colonialism as part of the Lutheran missionary movement from the West. The struggle to eradicate the residual effects of colonialism, both on the economy and the human spirit, and to remove the last vestiges of mission-ary dominance in the life of the church, is a marked feature of these churches.

A second common characteristic is the high degree of poverty, illiteracy and under-development to be found in most of these lands. Countries like Ethiopia, India, Madagascar, and Tanzania fall on the list of the world's least developed countries with per capita incomes averaging about one hundred dollars. Countries like Malaysia, Taiwan and Korea belong to the group of "middle income" countries averaging three hundred dollars per capita per year. Japan, the industrial giant of Asia, is the obvious excep-tion to the general picture of poverty and under-development.

A third common characteristic of these churches is the high population growth rate which places such a heavy burden on resources of food, housing, education, health services and jobs. Asia, with an annual population increase averaging between two and one half and three and one half per cent, is expected to have four billion people by the year 2000, when it will be the home of 60 per cent of the population of the world. Africa, with an annual population increase of three per cent, is expected to double its present population of just under 400 million by the year 1990. Correlated with these high rates of population growth are also high rates of infant mortality and shortened life expectancy.

A fourth common factor is that these churches are all in the process of transition and development toward a new identity-- from mission churches to indigenous churches, and from foreign spiritual outposts to authentic local expressions of Christian community. This process of transition will be illustrated below.

During the 19th century some leading Western missiologists held the view that a young mission church could make the successful transition from dependency status to independence by following the so-called "Three-Self Movement." The "three-self" marks of a church, as taught by Henry Venn and Rufus Anderson, were: self-government, self-support and self-propagation. An indigenous church, by these standards, is one capable of governing itself under national leadership; capable of supporting itself out of local resources; and capable of continuing the missionary task in its own environment.

This understanding of the process of indigenization as applied to Lutheran churches in Africa, Asia and Papua-New Guinea is by no means wrong, but it places an undue emphasis on changes in constitutional structure to the neglect of other important issues. When the Gospel enters a new socio-cultural environment, it remains what it was before but at the same time produces something new and different. "Transplantation is mutation" (B. Sundkler).

Independence or self-hood is not something artificially granted or imposed by a foreign mission agency. Properly speaking, it grows out of the church's obedience to Christ and his mission in a particular time and place, and within the existing social, political, economic and cultural context. The emerging identity of the church is a spiritual process that involves the struggle to understand, express and put into practice what God reveals to a Christian community through his Word and in harmony with Lutheran tradition , though not in literal dependence on it. It develops

through an interaction between God's promise and command and the
challenges and demands of the local situation.

Self-hood expresses itself in distinctive forms of worship,
theology, confession of faith and ministry; in the utilization
of indigenous cultural elements that are counted worthy and beloved
by the people; in a critical appraisal of inherited traditions and
a freedom to set them aside without disloyalty; and in an increasing
determination to find resources through the local community for
carrying out a suitable Christian ministry and giving a witness to
the whole Gospel. In some cases, as the experience of Lutheran
churches in Southern Africa shows, the price required may include
suffering, martyrdom, and the willingness to take up the cross
in defense of the whole Gospel.

The fallacy of the older "three-self" approach was its
naive assumption that indigeneity could be fostered even while
colonial beliefs and values went unchallenged. Churches would
become independent, not in spite of, but because of European moral
and educational superiority, western managerial techniques and
missionary paternalism. The African and the Asian would succeed
by imitating the missionary and taking over his system. This
approach had very limited success. It succeeded in creating little
replicas of Western church life, complete with European doctrinal
formulations, American efficiency, foreign architecture, centralized
and top-heavy administration, paid professional ministry, and
costly institutions. These churches were independent in form but
not in spirit. The Gospel was preached and the Christian community
was planted, but it was a case of the boy David going to battle
against the Goliath in Saul's armour. "I cannot go with these,
for I am not used to them" (1 Sam. 17:39).

As long as the colonial system remained intact, churches
in Africa and Asia could not develop a true self-hood or be clear
of their actual identity. The real struggle for self-hood began
only after the colonial framework had collapsed or been destroyed--
through successful wars of liberation or through the decline and
voluntary withdrawal of a European power. The 90 year history
(1885-1975) of European colonialism in black Africa illustrates
this. The partitioning of black Africa by European powers at the
Conference of Berlin (1885) created arbitrary national boundaries,
disrupted tribal and ethnic unities, and bound African people to
political and economic identification with European colonial powers.
It frequently led to the imposition of European languages, manners
and customs on subject peoples. Under the protection and with the
encouragement of Belgium, Britain, France, Germany and Portugal

the church was introduced into virtually every part of Africa. As
late as 1920 only three countries--Ethiopia, Liberia, and South
Africa--stood out as exceptions to the prevailing rule of colonial
domination. One of these countries, the Republic of South Africa,
practiced its own internal colonialism.

In the 1950s movements for national liberation and growing
concern for human dignity and self-determination were on the rise.
The 1960s were marked by de-colonization and a transition to self-
government, sometimes peacefully but in other cases violently. In
1975 the oldest foreign colonial empire in Africa, that of Portugal,
was totally liquidated. By that year, 45 African countries had
achieved political emancipation and been admitted to the United
Nations. Only three areas in Southern Africa remained under
precarious white minority rule: South Africa, Namibia (Southwest
Africa) and Zimbabwe (Rhodesia). All three of these countries
have Lutheran constituencies. Southern Africa has become a global
symbol for the struggle against racism and minority rule and the
continued quest for self-determination for all peoples. The
struggle against colonialism, foreign or internal, and the pursuit
of self-reliance are among the major catalysts accelerating the
growth of Lutheran identity in Africa.

The situation of Lutheran churches in Asia is determined
not simply by the reaction against colonialism but also by the
persistence of ancient culture patterns and religious beliefs and
the chronic problems of poverty, under-development and over-
population. Asia is much larger and more populous, as well as
culturally and religiously more diverse than Africa. It has a
history of Western colonial penetration going back to the Vasco
da Gama era at the end of the fifteenth century. It has known
Asian forms of imperialism practiced by the Chinese, the Moghuls,
the Turks, and more recently by the Japanese. It is the birthplace of all of the world's great religions, as well as the home
of great cultures from antiquity and important technical achievements.

Even though Christianity came to Asia under the protection
of imperialism, the great cultures of Asia have not embraced the
Christian faith to the same degree as the nations of Africa. With
notable exceptions, Christianity in Asia bears the appearance of
an alien minority faith. Outside Sumatra and Papua-New Guinea,
Lutheranism is a minority within the Christian minority. In the
scattered Lutheran communities of the industrialized countries
on the rim of East Asia, Lutheran church members tend to be middle-
class, urban and well educated. Elsewhere, Lutheran churches have

not been gathered from the dominant social groups or higher
religions of Asia. They have come from among the backward and
marginal groups, the outcastes, hill peoples and tribals seeking
identity and fulfillment through incorporation into the larger
Christian community. At the same time, "new religions" continue
to thrive and gain adherents in Japan and some other countries.

In contrast to Africans, it might be said that Asian
Lutherans tend to be politically quiescent except where they
attain a position of social recognition, as among the Bataks in
Indonesia and the people of New Guinea. In Asia, the period of
political awakening and emancipation together with the emergence
into world community participation through the United Nations
began earlier than in Africa. In 1975, Papua-New Guinea, the
major remaining colony, achieved its independence. Today only
British Hong Kong and Portuguese Macao remain under colonial rule,
and these at the sufferance of the People's Republic of China.

The Asian independence struggle after World War II was a
powerful unifying factor. Asian countries took the lead in
developing the politics of "non-alignment" in the 1950s. Today
much of the momentum for Asian solidarity has been dissipated for
a variety of reasons: the failure of ambitious agricultural and
industrial development plans in India and elsewhere, the decline
of parliamentary democracy in India, the rise of military dictator-
ships and the imposition of martial law in countries like the
Philippines and Korea, and the fear of communism in Indonesia,
Southeast Asia and Korea, accentuated by the struggle in Viet Nam.
Overshadowing all else is the rise of the People's Republic of
China as an Asian "super-power" with nuclear capability.

Without question, the identity of Lutheran churches in
Asia is being deeply affected by the growing political stagnation
that has set in in many parts of Asia. Except for Papua-New
Guinea, the potential for creative Christian participation in
nation building and shaping the pattern of the future is generally
not present in Asia, where Lutheran identity and mission has
expressed itself in other, non-political ways.

The growth of African and Asian Lutheran churches toward
self-hood and maturity is certainly an indigenous process in which
each local community remains accountable, under the Holy Spirit,
to its Lord for the faith delivered once to the saints. But in
this process, as there have been political catalysts, there have
also been enabling factors. One of the most important enabling
elements has been the growth of solidarity and joint witness among
Lutheran churches on a national and regional basis; increasing

fellowship between Lutherans and other Christian bodies sharing
the same cultural and political context; and links of partnership,
mutual consultation and inter-church aid between Lutheran churches
in Africa and Asia and the other member churches of the world-
wide Lutheran World Federation. Both at the regional and global
level the most important enabling instrument has been the LWF
through its departments and commissions for Church Cooperation,
Studies and World Service and its liaison agency for Community
Development Service. For the 45 LWF member churches in Africa,
Asia and Australasia, growth toward self-hood has been stimulated
by ecumenical participation.

Structures and Advances in Partnership

Africa

Even before the Organization for African Unity (OAU) was
formed at Addis Ababa in 1963, or the All-Africa Conference of
Churches (AACC) was gathering African churches at Kampala in 1963,
the LWF had taken the initiative of bringing its member churches
in Africa together for mutual inspiration, fellowship and planning.
In 1955 the LWF convened the first All-Africa Lutheran Conference
in Marangu, Tanzania. It sought to bring Lutheran churches and
mission groups out of isolation into contact and to enlarge their
vision of a wider church fellowship throughout the entire continent
of Africa. Another aim of the Marangu Conference was to "speed
up the transition in Africa from mission work to fully oriented
African churches" and to give African church leaders experience in
international partnership. This conference marked the beginning
of Lutheran unity in Africa. Marangu sounded the call for a new
advance of the Gospel in Africa. It was noteworthy for focusing
attention on "a possible new Lutheran Confession for Africa" which
would not only safeguard the historic faith but also provide a
guide for dealing with African traditional religions, practices
such as polygamy, and the challenge of Islam. A stirring of
enthusiasm for the evangelization of all Africa was felt. This
great missionary task could be accomplished only through fervent
prayer, better pastoral care, the Africanization of leadership,
equipping of laity, and upgraded theological education.

A second All Africa Lutheran Conference was held at
Antsirabé, Madagascar, in 1960 in the full tide of the African
independence movement. A dozen new countries had become independent,
and African church leaders spoke with growing frankness and less

diffidence to Westerners. Two hundred delegates from nine countries
were present, two thirds of them African nationals, and speaking
40 tribal languages. The atmosphere was far more politicized than
at Marangu. These African churches, it was clear, would not be
willing to view the role of the church passively in terms of withdrawal from the struggle for peace, justice and human rights. A
resolution strongly condemning racial discrimination was passed.
Christians were called to practice obedience through "responsible
citizenship" as active participants in government service and as
members of African political parties. "We confess the lordship of
our Saviour over all the world." The church was urged to pursue
its opportunities of Christian service in relation to industrialization, urbanization and the development of agriculture, as well
as in the traditional roles of education and medicine.

A second group of issues related to the "faith of our
fathers" was also discussed. The conference asked that matters of
church practice not clearly spelled out in the Lutheran Confessions
should become subjects for study. Among these were the urgent
question of church-state relations, the use of African elements in
liturgy and worship, and guidelines for Lutheran churches considering
union with non-Lutheran bodies. It was said that Lutherans should
come to internal agreement on matters of faith and order before
entering into wider ecumenical negotiations. A case in point was
the Lutheran attitude toward episcopacy, which was particularly
attractive to African churches and was then being introduced in
several variant forms into Lutheran churches in Africa.

A third All-Africa Lutheran Conference was held in Addis
Ababa, Ethiopia in 1965 on the theme "A Living Church in a Changing
Society." This conference took place shortly after the collapse
of the East African Church Union Consultation negotiations in
Dodoma, Tanzania, early in 1965. The church union proposal would
have brought together Lutherans, Moravians, Presbyterians and
Anglicans in East Africa in a trans-confessional union through the
mutual adoption of the "historic episcopate", which the Lutherans
were unwilling to accept. A special study on the nature of unity
and the causes of disunity was included in the Addis Ababa conference. The conference recommended that Lutherans should clarify the
true basis of church unity and having done so, seek to enter into
dialog with other churches in order to share the Lutheran conviction.
That conviction was that a common faith, rather than a common
structure, was the prerequisite to true unity. Lutherans would
become active participants in the work of AACC and the World Council
of Churches. However, the abortive experience of the East African

Union negotiations would lead Lutherans to seek closer fellowship relationships and unity primarily with sister Lutheran churches in Africa.

The LWF has also arranged regional consultations in East Africa (1973), in South Africa (1975), and for the French-speaking African churches in Madagascar (1975). It has provided consultative services on urban industrial mission and marriage counseling. Visitation programs and leadership exchanges between African countries have been arranged. It has cooperated in the "New Life For All" campaign, a joint evangelization effort involving the Lutheran Church in the Cameroon and sixteen other Protestant Churches.

The Radio Voice of the Gospel (RVOG), LWF-operated short and medium wave broadcasting service based in Addis Ababa which started operating in 1963, has also facilitated closer relations among partner churches through the production and follow-up of religious broadcasting. Cooperating with eight feeder studios throughout Africa and others in the Near East and India, RVOG conducts audience research, trains local church personnel and generally stimulates the interest of the churches in the utilization and follow-up of the mass media.

Asia

Turning now to Asia, let us note the distinctive accents and emphases of Lutheran cooperative work there. Although lacking the cultural unity and geographical proximity of Lutheran churches of Africa, the twenty-four LWF member churches in Asia have shown enthusiasm for Lutheran cooperation and for the enabling role of the LWF. In 1956 the first Asia Lutheran Conference was held at Gurukul, Madras, South India, to commemorate the 250th anniversary of the beginning of Lutheran mission work in India, and also to consecrate Rajah B. Manikam as the first native Lutheran bishop in Asia. Over 90 persons from nineteen churches in Asia attended, the largest delegations being from India and Indonesia. This was a historic meeting which signaled the coming of age of Lutheranism in Asia.

In his keynote address on the subject "Building the Church in New Asia", Bishop Manikam labeled the Asian churches he had seen as "pale imitations" of Western churches, too Western in their theology, and needing to stand on their own legs. He called for bold experiments and new ways of communicating the Gospel in Asia. Bishop Manikam, in a proposal which foreshadowed the development of

"Six-Continent Mission", suggested the initiation of a two-way
traffic in personnel between Eastern and Western churches. A
group of Asian churchmen speaking to Western delegates at the
close of the conference, said: "We thank you for the Gospel of
Christ which you have brought. . .it will be a day of special
rejoicing when God calls *us* to serve *you* with the same Gospel which
you have first given to us." The mood of the conference was positive
to bold forward steps in the work of the kingdom, but the initiatives
taken were not quickly followed up.

        The Dean of Japanese Lutheran Theologians, Dr. Chitose
Kishi, delivered an address on "The Relevance of our Confessions
in Modern Asia." Kishi stressed the value of creeds and confessions
in preserving the Christian heritage for Asian churches. Taking
the Bible as the source, and with the confessions as guides, Asian
churches in new situations might be called on to develop new
confessional statements. This same theme had been discussed at
the first All-African Lutheran Conference at Marangu in the previous
year. Also on the agenda at the Madras meeting were ecumenical
relationships, the Christian approach to the non-Christian environment (nationalism, communism, and Hinduism), evangelism in the
parish, church autonomy, stewardship, and cooperation between pastors
and lay people. This conference broke new ground in bringing Asian
churches out of isolation into contact around common issues.

        A second Asian Lutheran Conference meeting at Ranchi,
North India, in 1964 attracted 50 delegates and 30 observers from
twenty-three Asian churches. It was taken as evidence of "a growing
desire to think and act together." The churches themselves
selected the four major topics under discussion: I. Evangelism in
a Changing Society; II. Lutherans in the Ecumenical Movement;
III. The Economics of the Church; IV. Mass Communications in the
Work of the Church. The discussion on evangelism demonstrated the
complexity of evangelism in a changing society which must take
account of divergent religions, problems of nation building and
socio-economic development, responsible family-planning, needs of
higher education, and possibilities for mass communication. The
section on ecumenism was notable for its strong emphasis on manifesting the unity of the people of God in outward fellowship.
Lutheran churches were called to seek for agreement in doctrine and
practice with churches from which they were separated. It was
recommended that each Asian church should establish a commission for
ecumenical action and enter actively into programs of regional,
national and international ecumenical organizations. The recognition
of ecumenical obligation as a mark of the emerging identity of a

church was certainly a major emphasis at Ranchi.

Another key issue lifted up at Ranchi, and strongly emphasized in subsequent discussions, was the role of economics in church identity. "It is important for the life and total commitment of a particular church that it be self-supporting." Achieving and maintaining self-support was dependent upon a variety of factors including stewardship, education in the congregation, and re-thinking the ministry of the church so as to depend less on salaried professionals and to make better use of "tent making ministers" and gifted laity. Stress was laid on the importance of criticizing organizational structures so as to make them indigenous, adequate, and capable of self-support. The role of missionary institutions, policy toward profit-making ventures, and the use of funds from overseas also came under discussion. More recently the Asian churches have undertaken a whole series of self-studies on stewardship and church economy looking toward the identification, development and use of local potentials for ministry in each country.

A fourth emphasis at Ranchi which is indicative of the special interests of Asian churches was "mass communication in the work of the church" through literature, radio and television. The church was called to utilize fully every available means for communicating the Gospel, including the written word, and to promote literacy where it does not exist. Each church was urged to develop a local board for literature and mass communications, training specialized workers and giving full attention to effective means of literature distribution.

Radio and television broadcasting were also commended as valuable instruments of evangelism. Religious television programming has been successfully conducted in Taiwan for many years, and also exists in Japan on an occasional basis. Lutherans make extensive use of radio broadcasting in India and throughout the Far East. In Tokyo and Hong Kong the Lutheran World Federation Broadcasting Service maintains regional offices of communication. The LWF has taken the initiative in holding study workshops for mass media workers and consultations on mass media and ministry in the Far East. Thus in both Asia and Africa evangelism through the mass media and follow-up by the churches are a mark of Lutheran identity.

Another area of crucial importance for fostering church identity among Asian churches is theological study, research and training related to the mission of the church and the understanding of the Gospel in the Asian setting. The diversity of cultural situations and the minority status of most Asian Lutheran churches

has thus far impeded their theological development. Only in India,
Indonesia and Japan has there been significant theological research
and publication related to the world of cultures, religions and
socio-economic problems, and the needs of church unity or ministry.

In 1951 the Federation of Evangelical Lutheran Churches
of India produced its own doctrinal statement, taking into account
the Indian religious milieu. For more than ten years this Federation also conducted theological conversations looking toward union
with the Church of South India, and leading to the issuance of
"agreed statements" and a joint catechism. In 1952 the Batak Church
(HKBP) of Sumatra, in connection with its membership application to
the Lutheran World Federation, developed its own confession of
faith, a critical adaptation of the Augsburg Confession to the
problems of paganism, Islam, sectarianism and nationalism in
Indonesia. The Japan Evangelical Lutheran Church (JELC) has
carried on special research in Luther studies and methods of
evangelism. In general, however, the theological contributions
of Asian churches have been meager in relation to the needs, a
fact which tends to reinforce the alien character of Asian Lutheranism.

The LWF in collaboration with its Asian member churches
has now addressed this problem by establishing an Asian Program
for Advanced Studies (APAS) which became operational in 1975. APAS
is a decentralized regional program of faculty and student exchange
and congregational stimulation for the promotion of theological
education, training and research at various levels, both practical
and academic. Under APAS, local churches are encouraged to identify
concrete issues in theology and ministry and to devote resources
of scholarship and personnel for the deepening of church identity
and mission. Such programs assist isolated churches with the
solution of expressed needs while at the same time strengthening
ecumenical links among churches scattered across a broad arc
stretching from Korea to Papau-New Guinea   and thence to the Near
East.

Portraits of Six Churches

We shall conclude this examination of the growth of
African and Asian Lutheran churches to self-hood and maturity by
offering selected sketches of churches in six areas working out
their identity in the contemporary situation amid threats, crisis,
or special opportunity. These are: Ethiopia, Tanzania, Southern

Africa (including Namibia), India, China, and Papua-New Guinea.

    1. Ethiopia -- Lutheran work was begun in 1866, and in 1958 the Evangelical Church Mekane Yesus (ECMY) was formed with four geographical synods, 194 congregations, but only 31 ordained Ethiopian pastors. Between 1958, when ECMY had 25,000 members, and 1976 when it listed 283,000 members, the church recorded a remarkable tenfold growth. This rapid growth, part of a Christian mass movement sweeping across many areas of Africa, placed heavy burdens on the ministry and resources of the ECMY which led the church to invite partner churches in the LWF to assist in the in-gathering and pastoral care of new converts. The church was at the same time heavily involved in community development and literacy programs in rural areas. In 1972 the ECMY Executive Committee addressed its now famous Pastoral Letter on "The Inter-relationship of Proclamation and Human Development" to the LWF Executive Committee for consideration by member churches. This prompted a world-wide discussion of the meaning of development and its relationship to evangelism, and the proper criteria for the use of resources from abroad. In itself, this pastoral letter was a valuable expression of the emerging identity of an African church.

    Late in 1974 the feudal monarch of Ethiopia, the "Lion of Judah, Elect of God", was overthrown. Feudal governors and aristo-cratic landowners were imprisoned or executed. A military revolutionary government declared its solidarity with the landless peasants, abolishing high rents and nationalizing rural lands, at the same time prohibiting hired labor. The ancient Coptic church was stripped of much of its power. Banks and key industries were nationalized under the "Declaration of Economic Policy of Socialist Ethiopia" (1975). Young people were dispatched to rural areas in a kind of "cultural revolution" to engage in literacy and rural development. Civil war raged in Eritrea over the issue of secession. For a time, the lay president of ECMY, Ato Emmanuel Abraham, was himself imprisoned as an officer of the former government, but then released. The church's Executive Committee under the leadership of the General Secretary, Gudina Tumsa, took emergency steps to guide the church through its crisis situation.

    The political crisis in the country prompted ECMY to under-take a major review of its structure in the light of social and political changes "with a view to devising new strategies for contributing to nation-building and setting an example in moving boldly toward self-reliance." Some of the major policy steps taken, which illustrate the radical change in the church's identity from

the older feudal situation to the new climate of socialism are the
following:

(1) To adopt a functional rather than a proprietary
institutional approach to Christian service to the needy. ECMY
should be prepared to divest itself of church controlled service
institutions and community development projects at the proper time.

(2) To decline the proposal for a moratorium on foreign
funds and missionary personnel in view of the great tasks of evangelism and the theological reality of interdependence, but at the
same time to increase local ministry and stewardship resources to
achieve the goal of local self-reliance by 1980.

(3) To accept a reduced salary scale and to simplify
patterns of housing and living for church leaders in order to
achieve local self-reliance.

(4) To reaffirm ECMY's standing commitment to the spread
of the Gospel through use of mass media, congregational nurture,
Bible study and house meetings, and to make church members aware
of the "cost of discipleship" in the new revolutionary situation.

2. *Tanzania* -- If Ethiopia illustrates a crisis in church
identity brought on by a violent political upheaval, Tanzania
demonstrates a social and cultural transformation in the church
which is no less profound for having taken place in a non-violent
way. Tanzania offers the Lutheran church an unsurpassed opportunity
for Christian witness and service during the transition to a full
economy of African socialism. Lutheran mission work in Tanzania
was originally begun by German missionaries in 1887. In World
War I, German East Africa became a British colonial territory.
During both world wars German missionaries were interned, an event
which produced a temporary "orphaned mission" status for the
Lutheran church and led to the rapid internationalization of the
mission force. In 1958 the Federation of Lutheran Churches in
Tanganyika (FLCT) was formed out of seven regional synods. In
1963 these synods formed the Evangelical Lutheran Church of Tanzania
(ELCT), which today consists of eleven synods and dioceses, each
completely autonomous, and having a total membership of over 750,000.
The ELCT has its own theological seminary, operates an extensive
network of medical and educational institutions, and maintains
departments for evangelism (including radio broadcasting), theologica
training, religious education and curriculum development. It has
sent missionary pastors and evangelists to work in neighboring
Kenya.

In 1961 Tanzania received independence from the United
Kingdom. It is a one-party state by law, with the Tanganyika
National African Union (TANU) under President Julius Nyerere
being the ruling power on the mainland. Tanzania is essentially an
agricultural country with 93 percent of its population consisting
of poor farmers living a marginal existence. In 1967 TANU issued
the "Arusha Declaration" on socialism and self-reliance, which
set the basic direction of Tanzania's economic and social development. Dependence on foreign aid and foreign development models
is eschewed. Hard work, land, intelligent leadership and self-
reliance are described as the foundations of true development.
Therefore, TANU members and government leaders are expected to
lead exemplary lives of discipline and sacrifice. Farmers are
encouraged to move from isolated homesteads to "Ujamaa villages"
in order to live and work together and to practice self-reliance.
Ujamaa symbolizes family-hood and sharing of resources to build
a more decent human community. Government encourages "villageiza-
tion" by giving priority in agricultural services and credit to
communal villages. Universal primary education is the goal, and
mass campaigns for adult functional literacy are underway.

The challenge to the ELCT is to make the transition from
a heavily subsidized, Western-style church to one that fits an
agricultural economy and the peasant culture of a very poor country.
Western missions have bequeathed to the ELCT the burden of costly
institutions, a centralized administrative structure, and an
elitist ministry which is dependent on outside subsidy. Although
the ELCT has officially endorsed the Arusha Declaration, which
abolishes class privilege, many local congregations face the
temptation of continuing as elitist bastions of personal privilege
in the midst of poverty. The government positively welcomes the
participation of the ELCT in shaping the country's future. Many
Christian leaders help to staff government ministries. In an
experiment in the Central Synod, the church has sent teams of
pastors, medical and social workers and agriculturalists to Ujamaa
villages to help establish a Christian presence in the midst of
transition. The ELCT gradually moves toward a new identity under
African socialism, but not everywhere at the same pace, and without
the stimulus of a political emergency as in Ethiopia.

3. *Southern Africa* -- The issue which overwhelmingly shapes
the contemporary identity of Lutheran churches in Southern Africa
is not revolution or socialist transformation but racial differences
within the household of God which nullify pulpit and altar fellowship, and the struggle to eliminate racism as a determining element
in church identity. Allied with race are other socio-economic,
cultural and political factors. In Southern Africa there are
thirteen Lutheran churches (two of them actually Moravian) with
approximately 950,000 members in all, roughly 585,000 in the
Republic of South Africa and 371,000 in Namibia (Southwest Africa).
Eight of these churches are black, one is colored, and four are
exclusively white and German-speaking.

Lutheran missionary work began around 1850 and led in 1957
to the organization of two black indigenous churches in Namibia,
and somewhat later to the formation of large black regional churches
on synodical lines in the Republic of South Africa. In 1966 the
Federation of Evangelical Lutheran Churches in Southern Africa
(FELCSA) was formed as a platform for common action and dialog, but
without power to legislate for the churches. In 1965 the four
German-speaking white churches formed their own union. In 1972
two large black churches in Namibia united, and in 1975 four large
regional churches in the Republic also united. At this writing,
polarization on racial lines among Lutheran churches is nearly
complete.

While the struggle against racism in the churches is a
common factor in both countries, the legal and juridical situation
for blacks in Namibia is very different from that in the Republic.
In the Republic a white minority of 16.7 percent holds complete
political power over a population of 70 percent black, 9.4 percent
colored and 3.0 percent Asian. Eighty-seven percent of the land
is reserved for Europeans, and thirteen percent for blacks and
other races who form the industrial base of a pyramid held in place
by *apartheid*. The goals of apartheid are to preserve white minority
rule, to allow each racial group to develop separately and to halt
the de-tribalization of blacks. Thus discrimination against blacks
is legal and mandatory under the laws of the Republic of South
Africa, and blacks have no political recourse to change these
policies. Therefore the struggle against racism in the Lutheran
churches assumes a crucial importance.

In Namibia, by contrast, with a white minority population
of sixteen percent among a majority of blacks, the legal situation
is more favorable to the black people. South Africa's legal claim
on Namibia was limited to administering the League of Nations

mandate of the former German colony after World War I. The United
Nations General Assembly in 1966 terminated the South African
mandate and placed Namibia directly under United Nations administration. In 1971 the International Court of Justice gave its
landmark ruling: "The continued presence of South Africa in
Namibia is illegal; South Africa is under obligation to withdraw
its administration from Namibia immediately and put an end to
occupation of its territory." In 1972 the joint heads of the
United black Lutheran churches of Namibia petitioned Prime Minister
Vorster for the opportunity of dialog concerning the legitimate
rights of black Namibians which were being suppressed. Intensified
liberation activity by *Swapo* provoked anti-terrorist measures and
led to the arrest, trial and imprisonment of countless Namibians
accused of terrorism, many of them leading church members.

Meanwhile, world opinion, both religious and secular,
condemned South Africa's illegal occupation of Namibia, its racist
system of Apartheid with the "divide and rule" strategy, the
contract labor system, pass laws, and artificial constitutional
conferences. The spiritual and material support of world Lutheranism together with the legal backing of the United Nations has
prompted Lutheran leaders in Namibia to mobilize their people around
the defense of the Gospel and to seek a new identity for the church.

Today, Lutheranism in Southern Africa, after years of
political neutrality and silence, has at last made the discovery
that the Gospel has something to do with the daily life of people
under oppression. In the past ten years a progressive radicalization
has taken place in the theological perspectives of black Lutherans
as seen in FELCSA-sponsored pastoral institutes and church leaders'
seminars. Some black churchmen now appear to embrace the view
that the black churches have no alternative but to go the way of
a "confessing church" prepared for martyrdom and crucifixion. In
1967 a discussion on the theological implications of "the Two
Kingdoms" doctrine led to the conclusion that the policy of separate
development limited the human rights of non-white citizens. "We,
therefore, reject the policy of separate development." In 1968 a
discussion on "State and Church" relations pointed to the need to
keep social and political structures under the continuous direction
of the Gospel. Churches had the freedom and duty to express themselves on such issues. In 1971 a church leaders' seminar on "Church
Fellowship and Human Fellowship" insisted that Christian fellowship
could not simply be understood spiritually but must take shape in
daily life. "Every action of the church has to give expression to
the meaning of the Gospel in its impact on Christian freedom." The

1970 LWF Evian Assembly had said that Lutheran church members of
all races "should be willing at all times to receive communion
together" and stated that churches deviating from this principle
were guilty of departing from the "essentials of Christian faith
and life." The church leaders' seminar of 1971 commented: "There
must be no separation or division in the church which reflects
the division of our society because the church belongs to God and
not to man." Black Lutherans increasingly espoused the black
theology of liberation.

In 1975 at the Swakopmund Consultation these discussions
culminated in "an appeal to Lutheran churches in Southern Africa"
to denounce "alien principles" which were undermining doctrinal
integrity, the witness and practice of the Lutheran churches and
threatening the faith. These alien principles were identified as
(1) primary loyalty to an ethnic group, (2) belief in church unity
as something spiritual only, (3) belief that the Gospel has nothing
to say to the social structures and the political and economic
system, and (4) refusal of pulpit and altar fellowship, thereby
destroying the unity of the church. The task of the church, as a
super-natural community created by God, is to bridge the divisions
between human groups, to perform the task of pastor and watchman,
to preach the Gospel of reconciliation through non-violence, and
above all to witness to fellowship in Jesus Christ as the unconditional basis for mutual acceptance and brotherhood. Such statements are typical expressions of the contemporary mission and
identity of black Lutherans in Southern Africa. Who would dare
to predict the end result of such convictions, deeply held and
faithfully put into practice?

4. India -- India is a complex and culturally rich and
diverse country with a profound spiritual contribution still to
be made to Christian witness in the world. For this a genuinely
Indian inculturation of the Gospel is needed. The birthplace of
Protestant and Lutheran missionary activity 270 years ago India
today boasts nine Lutheran churches joined in the United Evangelical
Lutheran Churches of India and numbering 902,000 baptized members.
Lutheranism in India has had a longer and richer experience than
in any other Asian country. India is the acknowledged leader in
ecumenical movements, and Indian Lutherans have led others in their
constructive and responsible approaches to wider church unions
embracing Christians of different confessional backgrounds through
careful doctrinal discussions. From 1948 to 1959 South Indian
Lutheran churches engaged in theological conversations with the

church of South India, leading to the issuance of "Agreed Statements" on major issues of faith, and opening the door to church
union negotiations and the drafting of a new church constitution
during the 1960s. After more than 25 years of negotiations there
now seem to be good prospects for inaugurating a new united church
of Christ in South India on a limited basis by 1980, with present
institutions and jurisdictions unaltered for the first four years,
to be followed by full union about 1984. Meanwhile, the nine
member churches of UELCI are seeking to strengthen their Lutheran
identity and solidarity in order to make a stronger ecumenical
witness in India.

Indian Lutheran churches have made pioneer discoveries
and conducted experiments in evangelism, "tent-making" ministries,
witness and service to the poor and handicapped, and tackling
problems such as poverty, malnutrition, illiteracy and backwardness.
They have also initiated efforts at translating the Gospel into
authentic forms of Indian spirituality and indigenous forms of
worship and praise. They have demonstrated the meaning of the
Gospel to Muslims and even won some Hindus to the Christian faith.
Yet despite creative efforts by many individuals, corporate
Christianity in India remains alien in character and has failed to
penetrate deeply into Indian culture. Lutheran churches, while
acknowledging a great evangelistic task, have seemingly become
more introverted and perhaps more concerned with their own survival
than with their mission. Growth rates have slowed markedly, internal
church schisms are not uncommon and there is today much hesitancy
about making conversions for fear of offending Hindus. The true
identity of Indian Lutheranism, and the spiritual gifts of its
people will come into focus as Indian Lutherans are grasped by a
passionate concern for mission. Equipping local congregations for
outreach and witness to their neighbors remains a prime task.

5. *China* -- LWF statistics continue to show the membership
of the Lutheran Church of China in the People's Republic of China
as 53,000 persons, even though nothing is known of an organized
Lutheran church on the mainland, nor has there been contact since
foreign missionaries were expelled as agents of imperialism over
25 years ago. Lutheranism lives on in Hong Kong, Taiwan, Singapore,
Malaysia and elsewhere in the Chinese diaspora, but the church on
the mainland is more conspicuous by its absence than by its presence.
Yet China as the most populous country in the world, and the most
successful model for socio-economic development by a poor agricultural country, exerts tremendous fascination for world Lutheranism.

China's remarkable opening to the West in 1972 touched off a series
of national conferences and international consultations, partly
sponsored by the LWF, aimed at evaluating "theological implications
of the New China" and relating "Christian faith and Chinese
experience." These lessons are not so much based upon Lutheran
identity as on the non-identity of Lutheranism in China and the
universal implications for Christian faith of the virtual disap-
pearance of organized institutional Christianity from the People's
Republic of China.

The phenomenon of the New China confronts Christianity
with a series of tantalizing questions. How has the New China,
after centuries of famine and civil unrest, succeeded in feeding,
clothing, housing, governing and putting to work 800 million people,
as well as motivating them to spirited participation in the building
of a self-reliant nation? What is the peculiar character of the
ideology, known as "Mao Tse-Tung Thought", which evokes this
positive response and which makes citizens of the New China desire
to "serve the people" rather than pursue personal self-interest?
Can human selfishness be eradicated and people be motivated to
social goodness simply by furnishing them with socialist hero-models?
If the Chinese people have in fact experienced a rebirth of hope
for human beings and human community, yet without reference to
salvation in Jesus Christ, what does this say about the claim of
the Gospel? Can a people find fulfillment in hard work and mutual
service and problem solving without God? Is God at work in
revolutionary China? Finally, what went wrong with the work of
Christian missionaries who preached free and unmerited salvation
in Jesus Christ, invited people to repent and believe, and themselves presented practical examples of human betterment and concern
for the unfortunate? Was the Lutheran Church in China a sign of
salvation to the Chinese people? Why was the Christian mission
not accepted? What can we learn about the nature and purpose of
the Church from this?

It is generally agreed that the study of the New China
confronts us with more questions than with answers. Too little
time has elapsed for a clear perspective to develop. The politics
of China remains in flux. The social, economic and cultural
gains of the revolution, while unquestionably enormous, cannot yet
be properly evaluated in terms of their permanent worth. Moreover,
the viewpoint of Chinese Christians who remained in China throughout
the revolution is not, apart from official spokesmen, well enough
known.

The issues of the relationship of Christian faith and mission to Chinese history and culture are complex and ramified. Nevertheless, a few conclusions can be tentatively drawn. (1) The Chinese revolution confronts Christian faith with a powerful challenge to re-think itself in terms of modern, secular, humanistic goals and aspirations. (2) The gap between the traditional Christian profession of love and our actual historical practice should challenge Christians to self-criticism. (3) In too many parts of the world, the Christian church is identified with preserving the status quo, protecting the rights of the privileged, and supporting oppression rather than promoting justice and liberation for the oppressed. (4) The forms and structures of Christian ministry and community, and the approach to power and possessions, may have to be radically de-institutionalized in order to survive in a society like the People's Republic of China. The true calling of the church is to be a "serving church", not saving itself but existing in and for human society. (5) Christians can learn much about education for real life, the liberated role of women, the participation of youth and the provision of health care for all from the New China. We can see that the New China raises questions about human identity everywhere, not simply in China itself.

6. *Papua-New Guinea* -- The Evangelical Lutheran Church of Papua-New Guinea (ELC/PNG) is a young church in one of the world's youngest nations. In 1975 the country made the peaceful transition from Australian trust territory to independent nationhood after barely 90 years of contract with the outside world. Papua-New Guinea is inhabited by people of Melanesian stock speaking over 700 languages, 250 alone in the area served by the ELC/PNG. The terrain is rugged and mountainous, making access to some interior highland areas extremely difficult.

German Lutheran missionaries brought the Gospel to Papua-New Guinea beginning in 1886. After a slow start the church began to grow in the coastal areas. A characteristic of this growth was that conversions almost always took place by group decision. In 1930 the Gospel was taken by native evangelists and missionaries from the coastal areas to the interior highlands, where it now flourishes. During both world wars the work experienced disruption because of the internment of German missionaries. This has led to extensive internationalization in the supporting mission groups. Since World War I American and Australian missionaries have also been extensively involved.

The Japanese occupation during World War II posed a severe
test to the young church, which suddenly found itself an orphan.
All missionaries withdrew, some of them meeting their death at the
hands of occupation forces. The young Christian community quickly
matured as a group accepting responsibility for its own church
life and Gospel witness. After the war the church grew rapidly,
attaining a membership of 400,000. Baptisms averaged 20,000 each
year. The church was known for its active lay witness. In 1956
the ELC/PNG was organized as an independent church under a missionary
bishop. Since 1973 a Papua-New Guinean, Bishop Zurewe Zurenuo,
has led the church. The church leadership structure is almost
totally "localized", with national pastors heading all six districts
as well as most of the three seminaries and six vernacular schools.
As the country approached independent nationhood, the church was
well prepared.

The coming of independence poses a new identity crisis for
both nation and church. Papua-New Guinea's extensive network of
educational, medical and other public services have been heavily
subsidized, up to 40 percent, by Australia. The country must now
rapidly increase its internal revenue by broadening its tax base
and encouraging local industry. It can no longer live by massive
infusions of foreign aid. Self-Reliance has become the key to
survival.

Similarly, ELC/PNG is able to support itself only to the
extent of 3 percent from voluntary contributions by members. Up to
97 percent of the church's income has come from foreign church
subsidies or from the church's own economic enterprises. Unique
among Lutheran churches, ELC/PNG owns ships and airplanes and
operates regularly scheduled services; has income-producing
plantations; maintains repair services and engages in construction;
manufactures furniture and building parts; prints and publishes
both religious and commercial books, and owns and operates hotels,
tourist buses, commercial buildings and a housing development.
These economic enterprises provide income for the church and
developmental job training for church members.

Today the ELC/PNG is passing through a crisis of transition.
It seeks to simplify its complex and costly mission-oriented
national church structure. It must increase stewardship education
and voluntary giving in order to be free from foreign subsidy and
independent of income from economic enterprises. Migration of
young people to cities and towns in search of employment creates
social problems but also opens up new opportunities for witness
and service. The level of training for pastors and evangelists

in highland villages needs to be up-graded. Faithful to its missionary calling, the church will in time find a new identity as it adjusts to its new life situation.

LUTHERAN CHURCHES OF AFRICA, ASIA AND AUSTRALASIA

(National Totals for Baptized Members in Thousands)

	1958	1963	1969	1976
ETHIOPIA & ERITREA	25	54	97	297
TANZANIA	320	404	462	758
LIBERIA	5	6	15	27
MADAGASCAR	219	243	328	463
NAMIBIA (SW AFRICA)	202	242	276	371
SOUTH AFRICA	427	454	514	585
INDIA	662	717	797	903
INDONESIA	717	800	1257	1683
PHILIPPINES	3	5	8	12
JAPAN	13	18	21	25
PAPUA-NEW GUINEA	202	228	394	460

CHAPTER 18

E. THEODORE BACHMANN

THE FUNCTION OF THE LUTHERAN WORLD FEDERATION

The Lutheran World Federation means many things to many people: a worldwide confessional family, a channel for helping others, a means to strengthen struggling churches, an enterprise requiring support, and so on. But to most people - Lutherans included - the LWF is an unknown. Indeed, it was probably better known in the late 1940s (founded in 1947) and early '50s than in the following decades when its presence was assumed, and its programs tended to be seen as routine. The same was true of its predecessor, the Lutheran World Convention (1923-47). Each time, in the wake of a world war, Lutherans responded to widespread need. Like certain other individuals they showed themselves better at coping with adversity than in dealing with the seemingly simpler but equally serious long-term issues of proclaiming the gospel or tackling root causes of injustice, poverty and the like. Yet to those already conversant with the LWF - and to those who would like to know something about it - a short recital of its nature and function will fill a felt need.

A seeming contradiction underlies the relationship of Lutherans to each other throughout the world and to other Christians. On the one hand, the LWF is by definition "a free association of Lutheran churches" (Constitution III, 1). On the other, Lutherans have been called the most highly organized of the world's confessional families. The contradiction is more apparent than real. An accurate description speaks of contrast; a contrast inherent in the

relationship of freedom and responsibility. The fact that three
out of four of the world's estimated 70 million Lutherans are in
member churches of the Federation says something of the volition
and the use of freedom responsibly.

The nature or ecclesiological character of the LWF has been
debated, notably in the early 1960s. Some argued that the Federation is more than a "free association" and in effect is - or
could become - a world Lutheran church. The issue was discussed
in the Federation's quarterly, *Lutheran World/Lutherische Rundschau*
(1960, 1961), and aired at the 1963 Assembly in Helsinki (*Proceedings*,
pp. 276-95). A major concern was that Lutheran churches accord
each other full pulpit and altar fellowship, in preaching and in
the celebration of holy communion. Considerable progress towards
this end has since been made, although some exceptions still remain,
for example in North America's inter-Lutheran relations (the
Lutheran Church-Missouri Synod).

This, then, provides a lead toward understanding how - in
this closing chapter - the function of the LWF is understood.
Earlier authors in this book have treated Lutheranism in the
ecumenical movement, saying something about the rise of the LWF
and its antecedent LWC. Likewise, something of the process whereby
Lutheran churches have emerged outside the original European matrix
has occupied various contributers. It is appropriate, therefore,
that this symposium of accounts conclude with a consideration of the
function of the LWF.

Guiding the Federation have been those functions which
have laid emphasis on witness to the gospel, unity of faith,
cooperation in study, ecumenical participation, and response to
spiritual and physical needs (Constitution, III, 2). To anyone
asking why a global confessional body like the LWF should continue
to exist - and this is a pertinent question - there is a fourfold
reply: the member churches desire it; small churches and minority
groups are more readily heard in it than in a bigger and more
diversified context; a common spiritual heritage and extensive
practical experience enable swift action; bilateral dialog with
other confessions - Roman Catholic, Anglican, Orthodox, Reformed,
and others - advance the concern for unity within a catholic
context.

This account falls into three parts. The first deals with
the legal instrument, the Constitution, which governs the way the
Federation carries out its function. The second summarizes the
Assemblies held between 1947 and 1970, mentioning also the presidents
and general secretaries who have led the Federation. The third

describes the Federation at work.

The Governing Instrument

At its first assembly, held in Lund (Sweden), June 30 -
July 6, 1947, a decisive act of the LWF was to adopt a constitution.
This marked a turning point in the history of world Lutheranism
according to the veteran American churchman and historian, Abdel
Ross Wentz. "The constitution expressed clear and long-range
purposes, set conditions for membership, established methods of
procedure in interchurch aid, and as a doctrinal basis took the
brief Eisenach statement of 1923. It provided the Lutheran forces
of the world with a more systematic and more durable integration
than they had ever known before and opened the way for a new era
in Lutheran history."

Some Functional Aspects of the Federation

Before turning to the constitution itself, three other
matters deserve notice. First, why Geneva as a site for the headquarters of a worldwide Lutheran enterprise? Geneva's international
significance provided the answer. The World Council of Churches
(1938-48 "in process of formation") was based there. To American
Lutherans Geneva was already in 1945 a logical center where
Lutheran relief and reconstruction efforts - emanating also from
such distant and diverse places as Sweden, Australia, Canada and
elsewhere - could be unified and also coordinated with those of
the WCC. Key persons in the success of this arrangement were the
WCC's general secretary, Willem A. Visser't Hooft and his counterpart in the emerging LWF, Sylvester C. Michelfelder. Ecumenically
Geneva also fostered closer relations with other confessional
families. For example, the World Alliance of Reformed Churches
(founded in 1875) reorganized in 1948 and located its headquarters
in Geneva; unlike the Lutherans, however, the WARC followed the
policy of most other communions and channeled its energies for
relief and reconstruction through the WCC. The Geneva location
early aided Lutheran approaches to the Roman Catholic Church; a
process furthered by the LWF-affiliated Institute for Ecumenical
Research, Strasbourg, opened in 1965. Most recently, the opening
(1975) of the Orthodox Center of the Ecumenical Patriarchate in

Geneva/Chambesy promises to foster further contacts with Lutherans and other communions.

Secondly, like many other international bodies based in Geneva, the LWF is a legal entity incorporated in Switzerland. According to the Swiss Civil Code (Article 60ff.), the LWF is authorized to own, or take over as trustee such property as member churches or their agencies (such as missionary societies) may desire to entrust to it. In case of international conflict, such property would be placed under the protection of the neutral Swiss consular authorities.

Thirdly, the LWF is operative internationally as a Non-Governmental Organization (NGO) recognized by the United Nations. This dates back to the years when the LWF became extensively involved in the care and resettlement of displaced persons and refugees; a task which eventually aided not only Europeans but also Chinese in Hong Kong, Middle Eastern Arabs, sub-Sahara Africans, and others. The challenge, as LWF president, Franklin Clark Fry (Lutheran Church in America) told the 1963 Assembly in Helsinki, is that through this work the Federation was reminding all Lutherans "to do good to all men, not only to those of the household of faith."

The Design and Content of the Constitution

Many who have examined the LWF constitution find it a remarkable document. Its 12 substantive articles, with a 13th providing for amendments, combine clarity, simplicity, and flexibility. This makes it a ready instrument to describe the nature and to guide the function of a global "free association of Lutheran churches." As a German historian has observed, this consitution could hardly have grown out of the ample legal theory surrounding European church law; for this law has traditionally been bound to the confines of a given territory or country. Instead, S. Grundmann sees the LWF constitution as growing out of the practical experience of American churches, exercising their freedom and responsibility in a nation whose own constitution was the first to provide for separation of church and state. The LWF constitution follows the general pattern of an American style Lutheran synodical constitution. Modified, it is capable of practially unlimited extension. A basis for this document was laid by the experience of the LWC, whose executive committee (New York, 1936) called for the drafting of a document that would help draw Lutherans everywhere into closer partnership. However, rising difficulties between nazi totalitarianism

and the German churches as well as World War II intervened. The
actual drafting was completed only in 1946 for an initial
Scandinavian, American and German scrutiny in Uppsala.

Consider now the design and content of the constitution.
Its *name* (I) denotes a federation of churches holding the same
confession of faith; an on-going association, stronger than its
legal predecessor, the LWC.

Its *doctrinal basis* (II) remains the one adopted at Eisenach
(1923); so phrased as to be acceptable to most confession-conscious
Lutherans, it debars Lutherans holding membership in union churches
(like Lutherans and Reformed united in the Evangelical Church of
the [Old Prussian] Union), yet fails to convince strongly confessional bodies like the Lutheran Church of Australia, or the
Lutheran Church-Missouri Synod.

The text bears repeating here: "The Lutheran World Federation acknowledges the Holy Scriptures of the Old and New Testaments
as the only source and the infallible norm of all church doctrine
and practice, and sees in the three Ecumenical Creeds and in the
Confession of the Lutheran Church, especially in the Unaltered
Augsburg Confession and Luther's Small Catechism, a pure exposition
of the Word of God."

In *nature, function and scope* (III) the purposes of the
LWF are delimited. Its nature as a "free association" enables it
to act as agent for matters the churches assign to it; yet it
shall neither exercise "churchly functions on its own authority"
(like sponsoring the Lord's Supper on its own initiative), nor
legislate for its member churches or limit any member church's
autonomy.

Its scope, however, allows the LWF to take action on behalf
of one or more member churches "in such matters as they may commit
to it."

Its functions (alluded to earlier) continue most of those
exercised by the LWC in a more limited way. Formerly called
"purposes", these functions get at the heart of the Federation's
intention and are six-fold. They are to:

(a) Further a united witness before the world to the
gospel of Jesus Christ as the power of God for salvation.

(b) Cultivate unity of faith and confession among the
Lutheran churches of the world.

(c) Develop fellowship and cooperation in study among
Lutherans.

(d) Foster Lutheran interest in, concern for, and participation in ecumenical movements.

(e) Support Lutheran churches and groups as they endeavor to meet the spiritual needs of other Lutherans and to extend the gospel (i.e. formerly called education and mission).

(f) Provide a channel for Lutheran churches and groups to help meet physical needs (i.e. formerly called spiritual and material aid).

These first three articles form the self-identifying part of the constitution. *Membership* (IV) in the Federation is open to churches which accept the doctrinal basis (II) and also accept the constitution at the time of application for membership. Reception into membership is decided by the Assembly or, in the interim, "if not more than one-third of the member churches raise an objection within one year, by the Executive Committee."

Its *organization* (V) enables the LWF to exercise its functions through four interdependent instrumentalities: (1) The *Assembly* (VI) - "the principal authority in the Federation" - consists of delegates from all the member churches and determines the fundamental lines of the Federation's work. Normally it meets every six years.

The *Executive Committee* (VIII) comprises 22 members plus the LWF president; conducts the business of the Federation in the interim between Assemblies; meets at least annually; elects the General Secretary and assigns him his duties (IX); represents the Federation in all external relations.

National Committees (X) include the member(s) of the Executive Committee in the given country, represent the interests of the LWF in a given country and report annually concerning these matters to the Executive Committee.

Commissions (XI) are established under the authority of the Federation and are appointed either by the Assembly or the Executive Committee. Their purpose is to discharge designated functions of the LWF. Commissions report annually to the Executive Committee, which exercises general supervision over them.

The Commissions and their respective operational Departments, as well as the General Secretariat (the enlarged work of the General Secretary's office) together comprise the means whereby the Federation carries out its announced function. The matter of *finance* (XII), and of how the work of the LWF is supported, is integral to the story which follows below.

Finally, *Amendments* (XIII) to the constitution may be made by a two-thirds vote of those present at any regularly called Assembly, provided due notice is given the preceding day. This provision keeps the constitution flexible. While the number of

amendments has been noteworthy from the first Assembly (1947)
onward, none of these amendments have resulted in major changes
in content. The constitution in 1977 still bears strong resemblance
to that of 1947, yet structure and function of program units -
guided by Terms of Reference determined by the Executive Committee -
have changed with the changing times and needs of the churches.

The Assembly and the LWF Story

        Like the church universal and the ecumenical movement, the
LWF is people. Never is this more evident than at an Assembly.
The Sixth Assembly in 1977, for instance, will have over 260
delegates. Counting consultants, observers, staff, visitors and
others, some 700 people are scheduled to meet on the University
campus overlooking Dar es Salaam. The Executive committee determines the number of delegates, allocating them with due regard
for "numerical size of the churches, geographical distribution by
continents and countries, adequate representation by Younger
Churches and Minority Churches." Each completely independent
Member Church is entitled to at least one representative in the
Assembly. Readjustments, upon request of the churches, are provided
for. (VI). The following table shows how there has been a steady
revision in representation in favor of proportional increases from
the newer churches in Asia, Africa and Latin America. This change
has been at the expense of the larger churches in Europe and
North America. But this has contributed to the sense of belonging
to a "Lutheran World Family" - as, for example, Bishop Zurewe
Zurenuo, of the Papua-New Guinea Evangelical Lutheran Church explains
"LWF" to his people.

	Total Delegates: Number and Percent from Asia, Africa, Latin America (AALA)					
Assembly	1947	1952	1957	1963	1970	1977
Total No. Delegates	170	201	240	262	216	267
From AALA Churches	13	19	31	49	71	102
% AALA Participants	8%	10%	13%	19%	33%	38%

Africa was a late starter. But a comparison with Asia
shows an accelerated increase for Africa.

Assembly	1947	1952	1957	1963	1970	1977
Asia	10	13	14	23	30	37
Africa	2	0	5	15	30	51

This change is especially significant in view of the Evangelical
Lutheran Church in Tanzania being host to the 1977 Assembly.

However, not only the AALA churches are a concern. The
largest groups of Lutheran congregations outside the LWF are those
in Germany's Union churches. These may be represented on a
consultative basis, with voice but no vote (II, VI, above). This
second class relationship has long been a problem, and for many
the ecumenical movement makes it difficult to understand lines
drawn long ago.

The First Five Assemblies

Consider the Assemblies. They are vantage points from
which to follow the LWF story. They have certain common features,
such as agenda items which the constitution requires of an Assembly
(VI), plus rules of procedure, plenary sessions, specialized
sections, small groups, public events and, above all, worship and
Bible study. Channeled through the Executive Committee come the
reports of the General Secretary, of the Commissions Departments,
and others, giving an account of their stewardship since the
previous Assembly. Issues are debated, actions taken, elections
held, and guidelines for the future set down. An often bewildering
volume of papers usually provides the delegates with more than
they can manage. Finally, as with many other such gatherings,
what they remember best and cherish most is being or becoming
friends while working together and of retaining friendship long
after the Assembly has passed. This personal element then spreads
far and wide and, like the adhesiveness of the Spirit, helps to
hold the Federation together and to activate its tasks with a
subtle "plus".

The first Assembly - Lund, Sweden, (June 30-July 6, 1947) -
set the pattern. The rallying theme, "The Lutheran Church in
the World Today," accentuated the new beginning and the contemporary
character of the LWF. High points included not only adopting a
constitution, but also reconciling old enmities, framing policies

and firming programs for postwar reconstruction, resettlement, and
many forms of interchurch aid. The struggle for human rights and
against racism won strong support, particularly in light of
reshuffled international relations and the demands of power.
Knowledge of the Jewish holocaust at nazi hands reinforced the
realities of guilt and the need of forgiveness. Five commissions
were authorized: (1) missions, (2) displaced persons and refugees,
(3) relief, (4) youth, (5) social welfare. None in theology? To
Anders Nygren, first LWF president (then still professor in Lund,
after 1949 bishop) a Lutheran assembly is itself a theological
event - applying faith to life.

Master-minding the Assembly was the tireless general
secretary, Sylvester C. Michelfelder (USA and Geneva). He was the
innovative leader of a functioning LWF from its formative days in
mid-1945 to the time of his sudden death in September 1951. His
five-year plan for the Federation presupposed close liaison with
the WCC and with the Commission of the Churches on International
Affairs (CCIA). Sound faith, theological competence, practical
service, and the cultivation of friendship - elements he cherished -
called for communication. News bulletins, a quarterly journal
(*Lutheran World Review*, 1948-51, and its German edition preceded
the *Lutherische Rundschau*, 1951- and *Lutheran World*, 1954-),
and a fellowship of correspondence were what he and others promoted
complementary to the main task of LWF service. And all of it
advanced with a minimum staff.

The Second Assembly - Hanover, Germany (July 25-August 3,
1952) - began to reap what Lund had sown. Work initiated well
before 1947 was beginning to take shape. The theme, "The Living
Word in a Responsible Church", attested to this sense of progress.
No less than 15 commissions were set up, most of them study
commissions without full-time staff. The other commissions, over-
seeing departments and staff, operated in the key fields of theology,
world mission and world service. This plan, incidentally, anticipated structural changes adopted for LWF program units by the 1970
Assembly.

President Anders Nygren was in his element and so were
hundreds of others as this world gathering helped restore confidence,
especially among churches in a divided Germany,that Christians
were trying to hold together. A Johannine rather than Pauline
note prevailed in Bible study. Songs of praise, with the *Te Deum*
like a daily refrain, set the tone. The variety of public events
made the Assembly at times like a Kirchentag - that rising expression
of laity alive in the church. Among the keynoters, Eivind Berggrav,

Bishop of Oslo and nazi resister, spelled out church-state relations
in cogent terms, urging Christians to practice "inventive love"
toward their fellows even when the state would seem to do everything.
An *Encyclopedia of the Lutheran Church* was authorized (out in
1965 in three volumes, and edited by Julius Bodensieck, dean of
postwar USA Lutherans serving in Europe). Despite the death of
Michelfelder less than a year before the Assembly, the new general
secretary, Carl E. Lund-Quist - aided by many others - carried on
ably. Hanns Lilje, Bishop of Hanover since 1947 (1936-46 the
first and only executive secretary of the LW Convention) became
the LWF's new president. With Lund-Quist he sought to keep the
Federation from overreaching itself while he seemingly traveled
everywhere.

The Third Assembly - Minneapolis, (August 15-25, 1957) -
was the first world gathering of Lutherans in North America. Its
theme, "Christ Frees and Unites," brought reports on the expanding
concerns of the LWF into focus. The set of 51 theses on the theme,
produced and adopted by the Assembly, were to prove helpful in
guiding the Federation and its Member Churches. International
tensions, Cold War between East and West, plus the on-going rise
and role of new nations challenged the world confessional family.
Reports by innovative all-regional Lutheran conferences in Latin
America, Asia and Africa gave encouraging signs of partnership
among widely scattered churches. A world conference on Christian
social responsibility preceding the Assembly reaffirmed Lutheran
concerns and programs for the needy and oppressed.

Assembly decisions opened the way to new ventures: Evangelism by radio in Africa and Asia (Radio Voice of the Gospel
(RVOG) in Addis Ababa, Ethiopia, began its programs February 23,
1963); Interconfessional research and dialogue with Roman Catholics
and others anticipated Vatican II. This Assembly was like a
version of "Hanover" in Minnesota. Opened by a mass worship
(10,000) and concluded with a huge rally (105,000), it marked a
high point of commitment to the concerns of the LWF and set the
stage for later growth. Federation president, Hanns Lilje, was
succeeded by Franklin Clark Fry (head of the United Lutheran
Church in America and chairman of the WCC Central Committee). Under
the mounting burdens of office, Carl Lund-Quist later retired and
was succeeded as General Secretary by Kurt Schmidt-Clausen in 1961.

The Fourth Assembly - Helsinki, Finland (July 30-August 11,
1963) - drew the biggest number of delegates thus far. They met
in the University and worshipped in the Cathedral. The theme,
"Christ Today," placed the confessing of the faith in a global

setting. Federation President Fry keynoted the wholeness of the
church and noted that the basic statements drafted by Luther and
his associates continue valid not as "partisan documents but as
ecumenical confessions." The ecclesiological concern (elaborated
by E. Clifford Nelson, USA) urged that local preoccupations in
congregations be balanced by worldwide perspectives, and that full
fellowship be achieved among all Lutheran churches - a thrust at
reluctant conservatives especially in North America. Pursuant to
Minneapolis initiative, the Assembly authorized the formal undertaking of interconfessional study; the Institute for Ecumenical
Research, Strasbourg, France (opened in January 1965) was the
result. Its subsequent work, in the wake of Vatican II, helped
to set dialogue among the communions into broader context and
fresh approaches to unity.

Theologically the focus at Helsinki was on the doctrine
of justification. Efforts were intense but results not definitive
beyond an already basic agreement. Those were disappointed who
had hoped Lutherans would produce a statement enabling a clearer
confessing of Christ today. The Federation's service to people in
need continues unabated; in 1963 the 100,000th person had been
resettled by LWF service to refugees. Aid programs were, meanwhile,
continuing among Chinese in Hong Kong, among Arabs in the Middle
East, and were presently emerging among refugees from Mozambique
to Tanzania and elsewhere. At Helsinki one out of five delegates
was from churches in Asia, Africa, or Latin America, and their
input was important. Another American, Fredrik Axel Schiotz
(president of the American Lutheran Church), and experienced
champion of churches in the non-Western world, was elected LWF
president. Schmidt-Clausen continued as general secretary until
1965, being succeeded by France's André Appel.

The Fifth Assembly - Evian-les-Bains, France (July 14-24,
1970) - became, by its abrupt relocation from Porto Alegre, Brazil,
a parable of the times. First choice for a site had been Weimar,
German Democratic Republic. This proved unfeasible. The invitation
to meet in Brazil as guest of the Evangelical Church of the Lutheran
Confession was a welcome alternative. But reports of torture and
other infractions on human rights, condoned by the government,
raised mounting protests against meeting in Brazil. The switch of
site, decided by the officers, under urging from the Geneva staff,
occured less than six weeks prior to the Assembly's opening.
Unintentionally, this switch made ecumenical history, apparently
being the first of its kind. The relocation was dared as a means
of protest against deliberate violations of human rights and practices

of oppression. The theme, "Sent into the World," was thus fired with passion for justice.

While Helsinki had gone heavy on theology, Evian accented ethics and thereby struck a note in Lutheran assemblies that had not been heard so strongly since Lund in 1947. The Evian "Resolution on Human Rights" - with an accompanying statement against racism - ranged worldwide, yet with target areas in Brazil, southern Africa, the USA and elsewhere - including an attempt to include the USSR. While some delegates cautioned against a swing from prior theological reflections to accelerated political action, Evian also offered a high point in the expression of Christian unity. The Lutheran-Roman Catholic pitch, first made at Minneapolis and then activated at Helsinki, made history at Evian. Paired lectures by Kent S. Knutson (American Lutheran Church) and Jan Cardinal Willebrands (Sectretariat for Promoting Christian Unity, Rome) spelled out the nature and implications of inter-confessional dialogue, especially when seen in relation to the Church, as People of God, being "sent into the world" to proclaim and to help. The fact that one out of three delegates at Evian was from Asia, Africa or Latin America, and that for the first time young people were delegates, gave the Assembly excitement and tone different from earlier ones.

To help it meet rapid changes in the world more readily and to consolidate its resources and energies, a restructuring of the Federation's program units - already authorized at Helsinki in 1963 - was voted at Evian. As Federation president, Fredrik Schiotz was succeeded by Mikko Juva of Finland. Professor of theology, and soon also rector of the University, Juva had served as director of the 1963 Assembly in Helsinki. A churchman and scholar, he was also politically active. His election reflected a new climate in the Federation. In the post of general secretary, André Appel - representing the needs of minority churches - was to continue in office until 1974, when elected to the presidency of the Church of the Augsburg Confession in Alsace and Lorraine, France. That year the Executive Committee elected Carl H. Mau to succeed Appel. The story of the LWF in light of its Assemblies - at this time of writing (April 1976) in anticipation of the Sixth Assembly in 1977 - thus turns, in conclusion, to the work of the Federation as carried out by its program units.

The Federation's Patterns of Service

The function of the Federation as operative in its several program units deserves far fuller treatment than can here be accorded it.

Between Assemblies, as already noted in describing the constitution, the business of the Federation is conducted by the Executive Committee (Art. VIII). The LWF president is its chairman, and the general secretary (IX) its full-time executive officer. The Executive Committee maintains contact with the Member Churches; through National Committees (X), where these exist. The influence of National Committees can be considerable. The Executive Committee is also in close touch with the Commissions, for whose functioning it has set up Terms of Reference. Since the restructuring - drawn up by the Executive Committee at Copenhagen/Vedbaek in 1969 and approved by the 1970 Assembly - the Commissions/Departments have been consolidated into three: Church Cooperation (formerly World Missions); Studies (formerly Theology, plus the study commissions on Stewardship and Evangelism, Worship and Spiritual Life, and Education); and World Service - including its complementary unit, Community Development Services (CDS). In a sense, these three major units were anticipated already in 1952 (see above, Second Assembly).

Closely related to these three is the General Secretariat. Alongside the General Secretary's office is that of the Associate General Secretary, plus the Finance Office and (as of January 1, 1976) the Office of Communication. The latter includes Broadcasting Services (the RVOG enterprise, etc.), Information Bureau, Publication Office, and Regional Development. The Institute for Ecumenical Research Strasbourg is functioning under the Lutheran Foundation for Interconfessional Research, Bishop H. Dietzfelbinger being President of its Board since 1963.

Each Commission is limited in size to nine members. It plans and develops its own program. The total effect is intended to be complementary, with emphasis on an avoidance of duplication. Yet in an agency like the LWF this has not always been possible or desirable.

Church Cooperation roots in the USA-based Commission on Younger Churches and Orphaned Missions (CYCOM), created after World War II and relocated to Geneva in 1952, being then renamed the Commission on World Missions. Church Cooperation's set-up includes a director, and area secretaries for Africa, Asia, Latin America, and Europe's Minority Churches. It sponsors projects facilitating

the missionary and related tasks of the churches in those areas.
It holds regional and also specialized conferences; among the
latter, a consultation in Africa and Madagascar for Lutheran
churches using French as a second language a tongue usually left
out when church gatherings use English or German.   In line with
its far-flung tasks, Church Cooperation has held its annual
Commission meetings in various parts of the world: Tokyo (1971),
Kecskemét, Hungary (1972), Santiago, Chile (1973), Lund, Sweden
(1974), Adelaide, Australia (1975), Saskatoon, Canada (1976).
Its total expenditures (1976) account for about 25 percent of the
Federation's inclusive budget.

          Studies, having the largest Geneva staff, comprises four
so-called Project Areas.   Area I, on "The Life of the Church Faced
with New Challenges" includes (1) worship, (2) church structures,
women in the church, church economy and stewardship, and church
law; (3) theological education, international scholarships and
personnel exchange, Christian education; (4) communication research.

          Area II is on "Interconfessional Dialogue." Its concerns
relate closely to those of the Institute for Ecumenical Research,
Strasbourg.   Most of its activities concern the involvement of
the Federation and its member churches in bilateral and other
interconfessional dialogues.

          Area III, on "Peace, Justice and Human Rights," engages
the socio-political dimensions of the churches' mission.   It deals
with the profound issues on racism, human rights, peace and justice,
which surfaced at the Evian Assembly in 1970.

          Area IV, on "The Encounter of the Church with Religions
and Ideologies," likewise follows up issues raised and actions taken
at Evian.   Its three main emphases include: (1) the encounter of
the church with Marxism in various cultural contexts; (2) implications of the new China for Christian mission in the world; and
(3) the encounter with other faiths.

          Work in all four areas is advanced by a great variety of
projects.   Still the Studies Department's total budget accounts for
less than 10 percent of the LWF's overall total for 1976.

          World Service, a Commission/Department since 1952, is
actually the oldest operation of the Federation.   It played a major
role in the rise of the LWF after 1945.   Relief, inter-church aid,
refugees, and in recent years community development have made up
the many-sided work of WS.   By 1976 its total outlay in assistance
through services and projects totaled nearly $350 million.   Its
complementary unit, Community Development Services, has in progress

or completed, as of 1976, over 600 projects in various parts of
Asia, Africa and Latin America - all on request of member churches
in those areas.

Its care of refugees has changed from an initial European
clientele to one aiding mainly non-Europeans. A noteworthy
example: Tanganyika Christian Refugee Service (TCRS). This
venture, involving the LWF, the UN/HCR, and the Tanzanian government is ecumenical; exercised also on behalf of the World Council
of Churches. For example, the LWF/WS aided settlement of over
50,000 refugees from neighboring Burundi in Ulyankulu, western
Tanzania, making it the fifth largest concentration of population
in that country and fast becoming self-supporting. The WS total
budget accounts for nearly 47 percent of the overall budget of
the Federation.

As to staff, the LWF Geneva headquarters employs nearly
100 persons in many types of tasks. Of these, 38 are in the
category of executive staff - specialist in their respective fields.
Seven of them are non-Westerners. Besides, the large majority
of the LWF World Service field staff in Asia and Africa are nationals.
Working with them are European and American specialists in agriculture and other lines.

Finally, finances (XII). Support for the LWF comes from
its Member Churches and also from a variety of donor agencies,
mainly German and Nordic. The total annual budget of the Federation,
including amounts requested - and thus far usually received - was
US $12,500,000 in 1973. Then when inflation set in and currencies
were floated in the international money market, the dollar lost in
value over against the German Mark and the Swiss Franc. This helps
account for the upswing in the Federation's budget to US $17,300,000
in 1976. Where it was initially the major donor in terms of overall contributions, the USA Lutheran constituency is now in third
place, after the Federal Republic of Germany and Sweden.

Behind this attempt to describe the function of the LWF
looms a much larger story. This story deserves telling. The role
of the Lutheran Family is an important part of the life of the
Church Universal in a century of mingled brutality and hope. This
is part of the perennial hope - as expressed in the motto chosen
for the Sixth Assembly in 1977 - "In Christ - a New Community."

EPILOG

       In concluding we would like to turn to the readers of this
book, who have taken the trouble to study this self-presentation
of the Lutheran church and who may then reflect on the problems
presented. Many of our readers have certainly asked questions, the
answers to which they have not found in this book. We would ask
for their understanding. This attempt to portray our church and
theology was only possible to a limited extent. The extensive
bibliography should give the reader material for further study.
Nevertheless it may be possible that one finds something missing in
this book which he thinks should belong to a description of Lutheran
identity. Others may like to see things presented in a different
way. Therefore it would be of interest, not only for our Institute's
study mentioned in the introduction, but also for the search for
the identity of the church at large, if a continuation of the
discussion of these problems could be encouraged by readers' reactions.
       For us the most important reactions would be those of
theologians who observe the Lutheran church from the outside or who
are participating in dialogues with her. An important role is
assigned to listening to our brothers of other confessions in the
search for our own identity. Further, if this book could encourage
some churches in the ecumenical movement to discover their own
identity, then the ecumenical aim of our task would have succeeded:
the diverse profiles of confessional charismata could be included
in the unity of the church and the ecumenical discussion could be
enriched by dialogue between different charismata. For the conviction of the Lutheran church is, and will remain, that the manifestation
of the one Church of Jesus Christ in the world can only take place
if she can describe and witness a clear profile of Christian
confession.

Strasbourg (France)
Institute for Ecumenical Research

                              The Editor

APPENDIX

SELECTED BIBLIOGRAPHY

This bibliography has been compiled on the basis
of suggestions from the authors of the essays in
this book with the kind help of Mr. Lowell Albee,
Librarian at the Lutheran School of Theology in
Chicago, Prof. Robert H. Fischer and the Rev. John
Helmke.

General

Bachmann, E. Th., (ed.), "Lutheran Churches of the World," in:
    Lutheran World No. 2, 1977. Minneapolis: Augsburg, 1977

Die Bekenntnisschriften der Evangelisch-lutherischen Kirche. 5.
    ed., Göttingen: Vandenhoeck & Ruprecht, 1963

Bente, F. (ed.), *Concordia Triglotta.* St. Louis: Concordia,
    1921

Bodensieck, J. (ed.), *Encyclopedia of the Lutheran Church.* 3
    vols. Minneapolis: Augsburg, 1965

*Doctrinal Declarations. A Collection of Official Statements on
    the Doctrinal Position of Various Lutheran Bodies in
    America.* St. Louis: Concordia, 1957

Ehrenström, N., Gassmann, G., *Confessions in Dialogue. A Survey
    of Bilateral Conversations among World Confessional
    Families 1959-1974.* 3rd ed. Geneva: World Council of
    Churches, 1975

Empie, P.C., McCord, J.I. (ed.), *Marburg Revisited. A Reexamination
    of Lutheran and Reformed Traditions.* Minneapolis: Augsburg,
    1966

Empie, P.C. and Murphy, T.A., *Lutherans and Catholics in Dialogue,*
    vols. I-V. Washington/New York: US Catholic Conference/
    USA National Committee of LWF, 1970-74

Gassmann, G., et al., *Um Amt und Herrenmahl. Dokumente zum evangelisch/römisch-katholischen Gespräch. Ökumenische Dokumentation* vol. I. Frankfurt: Verlag Otto Lembeck, Verlag Josef Knecht, 1974

Gassmann, G., et al., *Vom Dialog zur Gemeinschaft. Dokumente zum anglikanisch-lutherischen und anglikanisch-katholischen Gespräch. Ökumenische Dokumentation* vol. 2. Frankfurt: Verlag Otto Lembeck, Verlag Josef Knecht, 1975

Grosc, L.K. (ed.), *Sent Into the World. The Proceedings of the Fifth Assembly of the Lutheran World Federation*. Minneapolis: Augsburg, 1971

Grundmann, S., *Der Lutherische Weltbund. Gründung. Herkunft. Aufbau*. Köln/Graz: Böhlau, 1957

Jørgensen, A. Th., Fleisch, F. & Wentz, A.R. (ed.), *The Lutheran Churches of the World*. Minneapolis: Augsburg, 1929

Lienhard, M., *Lutherisch-reformierte Kirchengemeinschaft heute*. 2. Aufl. Ökumenische Perspektiven Bd. 2. Frankfurt: Verlag Otto Lembeck, Verlag Josef Knecht, 1973

Lueker, E. (ed.), *Lutheran Cyclopedia*. St. Louis: Concordia, 1954: revised ed. 1975

Lund-Quist, C.E. (ed.), *Proceedings of the Second Assembly of the Lutheran World Federation: Hannover, Germany, July 25 - August 3, 1952*. Gunzenhausen, Bavaria: Riedel, 1952

Lund-Quist, C.E. (ed.), *Lutheran Churches of the World*. Minneapolis: Augsburg, 1957

Lund-Quist, C.E. (ed.), *Proceedings of the Third Assembly of the Lutheran World Federation. Minneapolis, Minnesota, USA, August 15-25, 1957*. Geneva: LWF, 1958. Minneapolis: Augsburg, 1958

Luther, Martin *Werke. Kritische Gesamtausgabe*. Weimer: Böhlau, 1883ff.

Luther, Martin *Briefwechsel*. Weimar: Böhlau, 1906ff.

Luther, Martin *Die deutsche Bibel*. Weimar: Böhlau, 1906ff.

Luther, Martin *Tischreden*. Weimar: Böhlau, 1912ff.

Luther, Martin *Luther's Works*, Ed. by Jaroslav Pelikan (vol. 1-30) and Helmut T. Lehmann - (vol. 31-55). Philadelphia/St. Louis: Fortress/Concordia, 1955ff.

Lutheran Directory. Part I: Lutheran Churches of the World. Part II: Lutheran World Federation. Berlin: Lutherisches Verlagshaus, 1963

Lutheran Directory Supplement. Geneva: LWF, Information Bureau, 1975

Lutheran Episcopal Dialogue. A Progress Report. St. Louis: 1972

Lutheran World. (Quarterly) Publication of the Lutheran World Federation. Geneva, 1954ff.

Lutheran World Almanac and Annual Encyclopedia. 8 vols. Issued by the Lutheran Publicity Bureau, New York, 1920-37

Meyer, H., *Luthertum und Katholizismus im Gespräch* (Ökumenische Perspektiven vol. 3). Frankfurt: Verlag Otto Lembeck, Verlag Josef Knecht, 1973

Meyer, H. (ed.), *Evangelium - Welt - Kirche. Schlussbericht und Referate der römisch-katholisch/evangelisch-lutherischen Studienkommission* "Das Evangelium und die Kirche", 1967-1971. Frankfurt: Verlag Otto Lembeck, Verlag Josef Knecht, 1975

Michelfelder, S.C. (ed.), *Proceedings of the Lutheran World Federation Assembly Lund, Sweden, June 30 - July 6, 1947.* Philadelphia: United Lutheran Publication House, 1948

Quanbeck, W.A. *Search for Understanding. Lutheran Conversations with Reformed, Anglican and Roman Catholic Churches.* Minneapolis: Augsburg, 1972

Schmid, H. *The Doctrinal Theology of the Evangelical Lutheran Church.* Translated by C.A. Hay & H.E. Jacobs. Philadelphia: Lutheran Board of Publication, 1889; 3rd ed. revised, reprinted by Minneapolis: Augsburg, 1961

Schmidt-Clausen, K. (ed.), *Proceedings of the Fourth Assembly of the Lutheran World Federation. Helsinki, July 30 - August 11, 1963.* Berlin/Hamburg: Lutherisches Verlagshaus, 1965

Solberg, R.W. *As Between Brothers. The Story of Lutheran Response to World Need.* Minneapolis: Augsburg, 1957

Tappert, Th. G. (ed.), *The Book of Concord. The Confessions of the Evangelical Lutheran Church.* Philadelphia: Fortress, 1959

Wadensjö, B. *Toward a World Lutheran Communion.* Uppsala: Verbum/ Kyrkliga Centralförlaget, 1970 (Studia historico-ecclesiastica Upsaliensia, 18)

Wentz, A.R. (ed.), *The Lutheran Churches of the World.* Geneva: Lutheran World Federation, 1952

Wolf, R.C. *Documents of Lutheran Unity in America.* Philadelphia: Fortress, 1966

History

Aagard, J., *Mission, Konfession, Kirche* (vols. 1-2). Lund: Gleerups - Clemenstrykkeriet, 1967

Andersen, N.K., "The Reformation in Scandinavia and the Baltic," in: *The New Cambridge Modern History,* vol. 2, 1958, p. 134-160. ed. G.R. Elton, Cambridge: University Press

Antsirabé: *The Second All Africa Lutheran Conference, Sept. 8-18, 1960, Antsirabé, Madagascar.* Philadelphia: Muhlenberg, 1961

Bachmann, E. Th., *Epic of Faith. The Background of the Second Assembly of the LWF, 1952.* New York: National Lutheran Council, 1952

Bainton, R.H., *Here I Stand. A Life of Martin Luther.* New York: Abingdon, 1950

Bergrich, M., "Die Geschichte des sudamerikanischen Protestantismus," in: *Die Kirche in ihrer Geschichte* IV/S (Hrg. K.D. Schmidt, E. Wolf). Göttingen: Vandenhoeck & Ruprecht, 1963

Bergendoff, C., *Olavus Petri and the Ecclesiastical Transformation in Sweden, 1521 - 1552. At Study in the Swedish Reformation.* 2 ed. Philadelphia: Fortress, 1965

Bergendoff, C., *The Church of the Lutheran Reformation. A Historical Survey of Lutheranism.* St. Louis: Concordia, 1967

Bornkamm, H., *Das Jahrhundert der Reformation, Gestalten und Kräfte.* 2. Aufl. Göttingen: Vandenhoeck & Ruprecht, 1966

Brunner, P., *Das lutherische Bekenntnis in der Union.* Gütersloh: C. Bertelsmann, 1952

Bucsay, M., *Geschichte des Protestantismus in Ungarn.* Stuttgart: Evangelisches Verlagswerk, 1959

Burgess, A.S. (ed.), *Lutheran Churches of the Third World.* Minneapolis: Augsburg, 1970

Christian Faith and the Chinese Experience. Papers and Reports from an Ecumenical Colloquium held in Louvain, Belgium, from September 9-14, 1974. Geneva and Brussels: Lutheran World Federation/Pro Mundi Vita, 1974

Concept of the Church in an African Setting, The. Arusha, Tanzania, September 11-16, 1973. Geneva: LWF-DCC, n.d.

Dantine, W., *Strukturen der Diaspora. Situation auf dem Hintergrund des österreichischen Protestantismus.* In: *Evang. Diaspora,* 38, S. 37-56, 1967

Drummond, A.L., *German Protestantism since Luther.* London: Epworth, 1951

Dussell, E.D., *Historia de la Iglesia en América Latina.* Barcelona, 1972

Elton, G.R., *Reformation Europe 1517 - 1559.* London: Collins, 1963

Fife, R.H., *The Revolt of Martin Luther. A Biography covering the Years until the Diet of Worms.* New York: Columbia University Press, 1957

Gensichen, H.W., "Missionsgeschichte der neueren Zeit." Bd. IV T, in: *Die Kirche in ihrer Geschichte* (ed. by K.D. Schmidt and E. Wolf). Göttingen: Vandenhoeck & Ruprecht, 1961

Hartling, P. (ed.), *The Danish Church*. Copenhagen: Det Danske Selskab, 1964

Hoffmann, P.E., - Meyer, H., (ed.), *Church in Fellowship, Pulpit and Altar Fellowship among Lutheran Minority and Younger Churches*. (Church in Fellowship, vol. 2). Minneapolis: Augsburg, 1969

Hunter, L.S. (ed.), *Scandinavian Churches*. London: Faber & Faber. Minneapolis: Augsburg, 1965

Identity of the Church and Its Service to the Whole Human Being, the Report of the First International Consultation, Addis Ababa, 1974, and of the Second International Consultation, Bossey, Switzerland, 1975. Geneva: LWF Department of Studies.

Kantzenbach, F.W., *Martin Luther und die Anfänge der Reformation*. Gütersloh: G. Mohn, 1965

Kantzenbach, F.W., *Die Reformation in Deutschland und Europa*. Gütersloh: G. Mohn, 1965

Kirchner, H., *Luther and the Peasants' War*. Trans. by Darell Jodock (Facet Books, Historical Series, No. 22). Philadelphia: Fortress, 1972

Koenig, R.E., "What's Behind the Showdown in the Lutheran Church - Missouri Synod?" in: *Lutheran Forum*, November 1972, February and May 1973

Lehmann, A., (ed.), *Handbook of Lutheran World Missions*.

Lueking, F.D., *Mission in the Making. The Missionary Enterprise among Missouri Synod Lutherans, 1846 - 1963*. St. Louis: Concordia, 1964

Leskó, B., "Many tongues - One Church." in: *Lutheran World*, vol. X, No. 2. Minneapolis: Augsburg, 1963

Marangu. *A Record of the All-Africa Lutheran Conference, Nov. 12-22, 1955*, Marangu, Tanzania. Geneva: LWF, 1956

Murray, R., *The Church of Sweden. Its History and Organisation*. Stockholm: Verbum, 1970

Myklebust, O.G., *Misjonskunnskap*. Oslo: Egede Institutet, 1976

Myklebust, O.G., *Et troens fellesskap*. Oslo: Land og Kirke, 1970

Nelson, E.C., *Lutheranism in North America 1914 - 1970*. Minneapolis: Augsburg, 1972

Nelson, E.C. - Fevold, E.L., *The Lutheran Church among Norwegian-Americans. A History of the Evangelical Lutheran Church*. 2 vol. Minneapolis: Augsburg, 1960

Nelson, E.C. (ed.), *The Lutherans in North America*. Philadelphia: Fortress, 1975

Prehistory of the LWF. List of Material in Archives in Europe
and the USA. Part I. Geneva: LWF, 1968 (mimeographed)

Ranchi. *A Record of the Asia Lutheran Conference 1964.* Ranchi,
India, October 8-18, 1964. Ranchi: GELC Press, 1965

Reich, H. et al. (ed.), *Das Lutherische Hannover.* Detmold:
Verlag Glaube und Kultur, 1952

Sentzke, G., *Finland. Its Church and its People.* Helsinki:
Kirjapaino oy Lause, 1963

Stupperich, R. (ed.), *Kirche im Osten,* vols. 1ff. Stuttgart-
Göttingen: Vandenhoeck & Ruprecht, 1958ff.

Sundkler, B., *Nathan Söderblom, His Life and Work.* Lund: Gleerup,
1968

Tappert, Th. G., (ed.), *Lutheran Confessional Theology in America,
1840-1880.* New York: Oxford University Press, 1972.
(Library of Protestant Theology)

Theological Implications of the New China. Papers presented at
the Ecumenical Seminar held in Båstad, Sweden, from
January 29 - February 2, 1974. Geneva and Brussels:
Lutheran World Federation/Pro Mundi Vita, 1974

Tjernagel, N.S., *Henry VIII and the Lutherans. A Study in Anglo-
Lutheran relations from 1521 to 1547.* Saint Louis:
Concordia, 1965

Vajta, V. (ed.), *Church in Fellowship. Lutheran Interchurch
Agreements and Practices.* Vol. 1. Minneapolis: Augsburg,
1963

Vajta, V. - Weissgerber, H. (ed.), *The Church and the Confessions.
The Role of the Confessions in the Life and Doctrine of
the Lutheran Churches.* Philadelphia: Fortress, 1963

Wantula, A., *Die Evangelisch-Augsburgische Kirche in Polen.*
Warszawa, 1965

Weigandt, E., (ed.), *El llamado de Cristo y nuestra respuesta.*
V. Congreso Luterano Latinoamericano. Buenos Aires:
El Escudo, 1972

Wentz, A.R., *Basic History of Lutheranism in America.* Philadelphia:
Fortress, 4th ed. 1964

Wentz, F.K., *Lutherans in Concert. The Story of the National
Lutheran Council, 1918 - 1966.* Minneapolis: Augsburg,
1968

Theology

Allbeck, W.D., *Studies in the Lutheran Confessions.* Philadelphia:
Muhlenberg, 1952; revised ed. Philadelphia: Fortress, 1968

Althaus, P., *The Ethics of Martin Luther.* Trans. by Robert C.
Schultz. Philadelphia: Fortress, 1972

Althaus, P., *The Theology of Martin Luther*. Trans. by Robert C.
     Schultz. Philadelphia: Fortress, 1966

Archbishop of Uppsala, (ed.), *Gemensamt Nattvardsfirande* (Common
     Eucharistic Celebration). Uppsala: Fyris-Tryck AB, 1975

Asheim, I. (ed.), *Christ and Humanity*. Philadelphia: Fortress,
     1970

Asheim, I. - Gold, V.R. (ed.), *Episcopacy in the Lutheran Church?
     Studies in the Development and Definition of the Office
     of Church Leadership*. Philadelphia: Fortress, 1970

Aulén, G., *Church, Law and Society*. New York: Scribners, Fortress,
     1948

*Basic Principles for the Ordering of the Main Worship Service in
     the Evangelical-Lutheran Church*. Geneva: Lutheran World
     Federation, 1958

Bergendoff, C., *The Doctrine of the Church in American Lutheranism*.
     Philadelphia: Muhlenberg, 1956

Bohlmann, R.A., *Principles of Biblical Interpretation in the
     Lutheran Confessions*. St. Louis: Concordia, 1968

Bornkamm, H., *Luther's Doctrine of the Two Kingdoms in the Context
     of his Theology*. Trans. by Karl H. Hertz (Facet Books,
     Social Ethic Series, no. 14). Philadelphia: Fortress,
     1966

Brilioth, Y., *Eucharistic Faith and Practice*. London: SPCK, 1930

Brosseder, J., *Luthers Stellung zu den Juden im Spiegel seiner
     Interpreten*. München: M. Hueber, 1972

Brunotte, W., *Das geistliche Amt bei Luther*. Berlin: Lutherisches
     Verlagshaus, 1959

Duchrow, U., *Christenheit und Weltverantwortung: Traditions-
     geschichte und systematische Struktur der Zweireichelehre*.
     Stuttgart: E. Klett, 1970

Duchrow, U. - Huber, W. (ed.), *Umdeutungen der Zweireichelehre
     Luthers im 19. Jahrhundert*. Texte zur Kirchen- und
     Theologiegeschichte 21. Gütersloh: G. Mohn, 1975

Duchrow, U. - Huber, W. (ed.), *Die Ambivalenz der Zweireichelehre
     in lutherischen Kirchen des 20. Jahrhunderts*. Texte zur
     Theologie- und Kirchengeschichte 22, Gütersloh: G. Mohn,
     1976

Ebeling, G., *Luther. An Introduction to his Thought*. Engl. trans.
     by R.A. Wilson. Philadelphia: Fortress, 1970

Elert, W., *Morphologie des Luthertums*, 2 vols. München: Beck,
     1931-32. Engl. trans. of Vol. 1 by Walter A. Hansen: *The
     Structure of Lutheranism*. St. Louis: Concordia, 1962

Fagerberg, H., Engl. trans. by Gene J. Lund, *A New Look at the
     Lutheran Confessions, 1529 - 1537*. St. Louis: Concordia,
     1972

Fischer, R.H., "Another Look at Luther's Doctrine of the Ministry," in: *The Lutheran Quarterly* 18, No. 3, 1966

Freytag, W., *Reden und Aufsätze*, vols. I - II, München: Chr. Kaiser, 1961

Gensichen, H.W., *Glaube für die Welt*. Gütersloh: G. Mohn, 1971

Green, L., "Change in Luther's Doctrine of the Ministry," in: *The Lutheran Quarterly* 18, No. 2, 1966

Heinecken, M., *Christ Frees and Unites*. Philadelphia: Muhlenberg, 1957

Hertz, K.H. (ed.), *Two Kingdoms and One World: A Sourcebook in Lutheran Social Ethics*. Minneapolis: Augsburg, 1976

Hoekendijk, J.C., *Kirche und Volk in der deutschen Missionswissenschaft*. München: C. Kaiser, 1967

Holl, K., *The Cultural Significance of the Reformation*. Trans. by Karl and Barbara Hertz and John H. Lichtblau. New York: Meridian, 1959

The Identity of the Church and its Service to the Whole Human Being. Reports and documents from an international consultation Addis Ababa, 1974. Geneva: LWF Dept. of Studies, 1974

The Identity of the Church and its Service to the Whole Human Being. Report and documents from the Second International Consultation, Bossey, 1975. Geneva: LWF Dept. of Studies, 1975

Jenson, R.W. & Gritsch, E.W., *Lutheranism. The Theological Movement and Its Confessional Writings*. Philadelphia: Fortress, 1976

Kantzenbach, F.W., *Das Ringen um die Einheit der Kirche im Jahrhundert der Reformation*. Stuttgart: Evangelisches Verlagswerk, 1957

Letts, H.C. (ed.), *Christian Social Responsibility*. 3 vols. Philadelphia: Muhlenberg, 1957

Lieberg, H., *Amt und Ordination bei Luther und Melanchthon*. Göttingen: Vandenhoeck & Ruprecht, 1962

Löhe, W., *Gesammelte Werke*. Vols. V, 1 - 2. ed. K. Ganzert, Reprint Neuendettelsau: Freimund-Verlag, 1954-56.

Meyer, H., "Christianity without Reformation," in: *Lutheran World*, 1967/4, pp. 376-384.

Miguez Bonino, J., *Theology in a Revolutionary Situation*. Philadelphia: Fortress, 1976

The Ministry of the Church: A Lutheran Understanding. New York: Lutheran Council in the USA, Studies, 1974

Pelikan, J., *Spirit Versus Structure. Luther and the Institutions of the Church*. New York: Harper & Row, 1968

Prayer in the Life of the Congregation (Document No. 9, Fourth Assembly of the LWF 1963). Geneva: LWF, 1963

Prenter, R., *Spiritus Creator. Luther's Concept of the Holy Spirit*. Trans. by John M. Jensen. Philadelphia: Muhlenberg, 1953

Preus, J.A.O., *Statement of Scriptural and Confessional Principles*. 2. ed. St. Louis: Concordia, 1973

Preus, R.D., *Theology of Post-Reformation Lutheranism*, 2 vols. St. Louis: Concordia, 1970-72

Reed, L.D., *The Lutheran Liturgy*. Philadelphia: Muhlenberg, rev. 1959

Reumann, J. - Lazareth, W., *Righteousness and Society. Ecumenical Dialog in a Revolutionary Age*. Philadelphia: Fortress, 1967

Scherer, J.A., *Mission and Unity in Lutheranism. A Study in Confession and Ecumenicity*. Philadelphia: Fortress, 1969

Schlink, E., *Theology of the Lutheran Confessions*. Trans. by P.F. Koehneke & H.J.A. Bouman. Philadelphia: Muhlenberg, 1961

Sundkler, B., *The World of Mission*. Trans. by E.J. Sharpe. Grand Rapids: Eerdmans, 1966

Thielicke, H., *Theological Ethics*. Ed. by Williams H. Lazareth. 2 vols. Philadelphia: Fortress, 1966, 1969. Abridgement & translation of *Theologische Ethik*, Tübingen: J.C.B. Mohr, 1951-64

Troeltsch, E., *Protestantism and Progress*. Trans. by W. Montgomery. London: Williams & Norgate, 1912. Reprint, Boston: Beacon, 1958

Vajta, V. (ed.), *The Unity of the Church. Papers presented to the Commissions on Theology and Liturgy of the LWF. Rock Island, Ill.*: Augustana, 1957

Vajta, V., *Die Theologie des Gottesdienstes bei Luther*. Stockholm: Svenska kyrkans diakonistyrelses Bokförlag, 1952. Condensed Engl. trans. by U.S. Leupold, *Luther on Worship*. Philadelphia: Muhlenberg, 1958

Vajta, V. (ed.), *The Gospel and Unity* (The Gospel Encounters History, vol. 1). Minneapolis: Augsburg, 1971

Vajta, V. (ed.), *The Gospel and Human Destiny* (The Gospel Encounters History, vol. 2). Minneapolis: Augsburg, 1972

Vajta, V. (ed.), *The Gospel and the Ambiguity of the Church* (The Gospel Encounters History, vol. 3). Philadelphia: Fortress, 1973

Vajta, V. (ed.), *The Gospel as History* (The Gospel Encounters History, vol. 4). Philadelphia: Fortress, 1974

Warneck, G., *Evangelische Missionslehre*. Gotha: F.A. Perthes, 1892

Wentz, A.R., "Lutheran Churches and the Modern Ecumenical
    Movement," in: *World Lutheranism of Today. A Tribute
    to Anders Nygren*. Rock Island: Augustana, 1950, p. 391ff.

Wicks, J., *Man Yearning for Grace. Luther's Early Spiritual
    Teaching*. Washington: Corpus Books, 1968

Wingren, G., *Luther on Vocation*. Trans. by C.C. Rasmussen.
    Philadelphia: Muhlenberg, 1957

Wolf, E., *Barmen - Kirche zwischen Versuchung und Gnade*. 2 ed.
    München: C. Kaiser, 1970

AUTHORS

Johannes Aagaard, Th.D., professor of missiology and ecumenical
theology at the Theological Faculty in Aarhus, Denmark.
Aarhus University, Institut for Missionsteologi, DK-8000
Arhus C., Denmark.

Andreas Aarflot, bishop, Th.D., former professor of church history
at the Free Theological Faculty in Oslo, Norway.
Det Teologiske Menighetsfakultet, Oslo 3, Gydas Vei 4,
Norway.

Carl-Gustaf Andrén, Th.D., professor of practical theology at
the University of Lund, Sweden.
Teologiska Institutionerna, Theologicum, S - 223
50 Lund, Sweden.

E. Theodore Bachmann, editor of *Lutheran World*, publication of
the LWF, Geneva. Former professor of church history in
the USA.
The Lutheran World Federation, Publications Office,
CH - 1211 Geneva 20, Route de Ferney 150, Switzerland.

Wilhelm Dantine, D.Dr., professor of systematic theology at the
Protestant Theological Faculty at the University of
Vienna, Austria.

Robert H. Fischer, Th.D., professor of church history at the
Lutheran School of Theology, Chicago, Illinois, USA.
The Lutheran School of Theology, 1100 East 55th Street,
Chicago, Illinois, 60615, USA.

382

Günther Gassman, Th.D., president of the Lutherisches Kirchenamt
in Germany, former research professor at the Institute
for Ecumenical Research, Strasbourg, France.
VELKD, Lutherisches Kirchenamt, D-3000 Hannover,
Richard-Wagner-Strasse 26, Postfach 1860.

F.W. Kantzenbach, Th.D., professor of church history at Augustana
Hochschule, Neuendettelsau.
Augustana Hochschule, D - 8806 Neuendettelsau,
Postfach 20.

Günter Krusche, pastor, lecturer on practical theology at the
Sprachenkonvikt, Berlin, GDR.
DDR-1253 Rüdersdorf, Friedensstrasse 6a.

Bela Leskó, D.D., professor at Instituto Superior Evangélico de
Estudios Teológicos (ISEDET), Gaspar Campos 1651,
Jose C. Paz, F.C.S.M., Argentina.

Bernhard Lohse, Th.D., professor of church history at the
Theological Faculty of the University of Hamburg.
Universität Hamburg, Kirchen- und Dogmengeschichtliches
Seminar, D - 2 Hamburg 13, Sedanstrasse 19.

Inge Lønning, Th.D., professor of systematic theology at the
Theological Faculty at the University of Oslo, Norway.
Universitetet I Oslo, Institutt for systematisk Teologi,
Niels Treschows Hus, Post Boks 1023, Oslo 3, Norway.

Harding Meyer, Th.D., research professor at the Institute for
Ecumenical Research, Strasbourg.
Institute for Ecumenical Research, F - 67000 Strasbourg,
8 rue Gustave Klotz, France.

James A. Scherer, Th.D., professor of missiology at the Lutheran
School of Theology, Chicago, Illinois, USA.
The Lutheran School of Theology, 1100 East 55th Street,
Chicago, Illinois, 60615, USA.

Franklin Sherman, Th.D., professor of social ethics at the
Lutheran School of Theology at Chicago, Illinois, USA.
The Lutheran School of Theology, 1100 East 55th Street,
Chicago, Illinois, 60615 USA.

Vilmos Vajta, Th.D., research professor at the Institute for
        Ecumenical Research, Strasbourg, France.
        The Institute for Ecumenical Research, F - 67000
        Strasbourg, 8 rue Gustave Klotz, France.

Hans Weissgerber, Th.D., Commissioner for Information of the
        Evangelical Church in Hessen and Nassau.
        Evangelische Kirche in Hessen und Nassau, D-61 Darmstadt,
        Kiesstrasse 18.

Helmut Zeddies, Oberkirchenrat and Executive Secretary of the
        LWF National Committee in the German Democratic Republic.
        National Committee of the Lutheran World Federation
        in the GDR, DDR- 104 Berlin, Auguststrasse 80.

TRANSLATORS

Mrs. Donata Coleman

7 Mortimer Road
Bristol BS8 4EX
England

Miss Vanessa Dolbé

The Institute for Ecumenical
Research
F - 67000 Strasbourg
8 rue Gustave Klotz
France

Mr. Donald Dutton

First Presbyterian Church
229 East Main Street
Nanticoke, Penn. 18634
U S A

Pastor John Hinderlie

Evangelisches Pfarramt der
Reuschkirche
Oetingerstrasse 19
D - 7320 Göppingen
West Germany

Miss Margaret A. Pater

CH - 1298 Céligny/GE
Chateau de Bossey
Switzerland

Mr. William C. Weinrich

Concordia Theological
Seminary
Concordia Court
Springfield, Illinois 62702
U S A

STATISTICS

reproduced from LWF Information 20th December 1976

WORLD LUTHERAN MEMBERSHIP FIGURES 1976

General Summary   1976

LWF member churches and membership (94)	53,483,049
LWF recognized congregations and membership (16)	15,655
Lutheran constituency outside LWF	17,009,623
Total	70,508,327

Continental Lutheran membership of all Lutherans	LWF Membership
	1976	1976
Europe	54,597,983	41,519,130
U.S.A. and Canada	8,930,581	5,607,194
Asia (and adjacent islands)	2,743,967	2,658,665
Africa	2,683,982	2,621,401
Latin America	974,237	676,659
Australasia	577,577	400,000

AFRICA	1976 Membership – National Total
Cameroon	43,031
Chad	9,139
Central African Republic	15,000
Ethiopia	296,657
Ghana	208
Kenya	15,000
Liberia	27,450
Madagascar	463,072
Nigeria	66,248
Rhodesia	29,000
South Africa	585,438
South West Africa (Namibia)	371,105
Tanzania	757,789
Zambia	4,845

ASIA	
Bangladesh	6,372
China (People's Republic)	53,000
China (Republic)	11,670
Hong Kong	32,475
India	902,664
Indonesia	1,682,724
Iraq	29
Israel	---
Japan	24,856
Jordan	1,200
Korea	1,245
Lebanon	---
Malaysia	15,519
Philippines	12,213
Sri Lanka (Ceylon)	---

AUSTRALASIA	
Australia	114,064
New Zealand	3,013
Papua-New Guinea	460,500

EUROPE	1976 Membership – National Total
Austria	396,180
Belgium	2,400
Czechoslovakia	458,800
Denmark	4,700,174
Finland	4,653,495
France	311,200
Germany, Federal Republic	13,202,354
Germany, Democratic Republic	4,813,000
Great Britain	24,050
Hungary	430,000
Iceland	197,436
Ireland	120
Italy	7,000
Liechtenstein	125
Netherlands	18,706
Norway	3,519,300
Poland	79,500
Rumania	202,000
Sweden	7,754,985
Switzerland	12,000
USSR	620,000
Yugoslavia	72,358
Churches in exile	158,000

LATIN AMERICA	
Argentina	93,178
Belize (British Honduras)	---
Bolivia	4,498
Brazil	812,500
Chile	24,100
Columbia	3,220
Costa Rica	630
Ecuador	445
El Salvador	800
Guatemala	1,600
Guyana	12,659

LATIN AMERICA (continued)	1975 Membership - National Total
Honduras	181
Mexico	9,102
Nicaragua	---
Panama	32
Panama Canal Zone	200
Paraguay	---
Peru	2,980
Puerto Rico and Virgin Islands	---
Surinam	4,500
Trinidad	40
Uruguay	200
Venezuela	3,372

UNITED STATES AND CANADA

Canada	302,040
United States	8,628,541

ADDRESSES

The Lutheran World Federation
General Secretariat
150 route de Ferney
P.O. Box 66
CH - 1211 Geneva 20, Switzerland

Telephone: 022/33 34 00
Cable: LUTHERWORLD GENEVA
Telex: 23 423

The Institute for Ecumenical Research
8 rue Gustave Klotz
f - 6700 Strasbourg
France

Radio Voice of the Gospel (RVOG) Station ETLF
P.O. Box 654
Addis Ababa, Ethiopia

Telephone: 44 81 90
Cable: LUTHERWORLD ADDISABABA:
Telex: 21195

Lutheran Council in the USA
315 Park Avenue South
New York, New York 10010.

Telephone: (212) 677-3950
Cable: LUCOUSA NEWYORK

National Committee of the Lutheran World Federation
    in the USA
315 Park Avenue South
New York, New York 10010

Telephone: (212) 677-3950
Cable: LUCOUSA NEWYORK

Lutheran Council in Canada
500-365 Hargrave Street
Winnipeg
Manitoba   R3B 2K3

Telephone: (204) 942-0096

A full list of addresses of all the Lutheran churches,
church offices and officers throughout the world can be
found in the Lutheran Directory Supplement 1975, which
can be acquired from the LWF office indicated above.

$9.50

Contributors

Bernhard Lohse—*The Call for the Reformation of the Church*

Friedrich Wilhelm Kantzenbach—*The Reformation's Power to Organize the Church and Confessional Lutheranism from 1530 to 1648*

Carl-Gustaf Andren—*The Reformation in the Scandinavian Countries*

Wilhelm Dantine—*The History and Self-Understanding of the Lutheran Minority Churches of Eastern Europe*

Inge Lønning—*The Holy Scriptures*

Helmut Zeddies—*The Confession of the Church*

Vilmos Vajta—*Worship and Sacramental Life*

Andreas Aarflot—*Patterns of Lutheran Piety*

Günther Gassmann—*The Ordained Ministry and Church Order*

Franklin Sherman—*Secular Calling and Social Ethics*

Johannes Aagaard—*Missionary Theology*

Harding Meyer—*Lutheranism in the Ecumenical Movement*

Hans Weissgerber—*The Changing "Volkskirche" in Central and Northern Europe*

Günter Krusche—*The Re-Definition of the Relationship to State and Society (in Socialist Countries)*

Robert H. Fischer—*Recent Lutheranism in North America*

Béla Leskó—*The Discovery of Identity in a New Culture and Society: in South America*

James Scherer—*Growth Toward Selfhood and Maturity: in Africa, Asia and Australasia*

E. Theodore Bachmann—*The Function of the Lutheran World Federation*

AUGSBURG PUBLISHING HOUSE
Minneapolis, Minnesota 55415

10-4160

063